COLLECTED WORKS OF
Elizabeth & Robert
BROWNING

GREYSTONE PRESS
New York

PRINTED IN THE UNITED STATES
BY GEORGE McKIBBIN & SON; BROOKLYN, NEW YORK

CONTENTS

POEMS OF ELIZABETH BARRETT BROWNING

	PAGE
DEDICATION	3
PASSAGES FROM AURORA LEIGH	5
RHYME OF THE DUCHESS MAY	26
THE CRY OF THE CHILDREN	40
AN ISLAND	44
THE SOUL'S TRAVELLING	50
MAN AND NATURE	55
TO FLUSH, MY DOG	56
THE DESERTED GARDEN	60
SONNETS:	
Grief	63
The Two Sayings	63
The Look	63
The Meaning of the Look	64
Adequacy	64
A CHILD'S THOUGHT OF GOD	65
THE SLEEP	65
LESSONS FROM THE GORSE	67
THE LADY'S YES	68
A WOMAN'S SHORTCOMINGS	69
A MAN'S REQUIREMENTS	70
INSUFFICIENCY	71
SONNETS FROM THE PORTUGUESE	72
CASA GUIDI WINDOWS	87

PAGE

POEMS BEFORE CONGRESS:

Christmas Gifts 99
Italy and the World 101
A Curse for a Nation 105

LAST POEMS:

A Song for the Ragged-Schools of London 108
May's Love 112
Amy's Cruelty 113
My Heart and I 115
The Best Thing in the World 116
A Musical Instrument 116
First News from Villafranca 118
Summing Up in Italy 119
"Died . . ." 121
The Forced Recruit 122
Mother and Poet 124

POEMS OF ROBERT BROWNING

DRAMATIC LYRICS:

Cavalier Tunes.
  I. Marching Along 131
  II. Give a Rouse 132
  III. Boot and Saddle 132
The Lost Leader 133
"How They Brought the Good News from Ghent to Aix" . 134
Through the Metidja to Abd-el-Kadr 136
Nationality in Drinks 137
Garden Fancies.
  I. The Flower's Name 138
  II. Sibrandus Schafnaburgensis 139
Soliloquy of the Spanish Cloister 141
The Laboratory 144
The Confessional 145

CONTENTS

PAGE

Cristina 148
The Lost Mistress 149
Earth's Immortalities 150
Meeting at Night 151
Parting at Morning 151
Song: Nay but You, Who Do Not Love Her 151
A Woman's Last Word 152
Evelyn Hope 153
Love among the Ruins 155
A Lovers' Quarrel 157
Up at a Villa—Down in the City 161
A Toccata of Galuppi's 163
Old Pictures in Florence 165
"De Gustibus—" 173
Home-Thoughts, from Abroad 174
Home-Thoughts, from the Sea 175
Saul 175
My Star 183
By the Fireside 184
Any Wife to Any Husband 191
Two in the Campagna 195
Misconceptions 197
A Serenade at the Villa 197
One Way of Love 199
Another Way of Love 200
A Pretty Woman 201
Respectability 203
Love in a Life 204
Life in a Love 204
In Three Days 205
In a Year 206
Women and Roses 208
Before 209
After 211

PAGE

The Guardian-Angel 211
Memorabilia 213
Popularity 214
Master Hugues of Saxe-Gotha 216

DRAMATIC ROMANCES:

Incident of the French Camp 220
The Patriot 221
My Last Duchess 222
Count Gismond 224
The Boy and the Angel 227
Instans Tyrannus 230
Mesmerism 232
The Glove 236
Time's Revenges 241
The Italian in England 242
The Englishman in Italy 246
In a Gondola 252
Waring 259
The Twins 265
A Light Woman 266
The Last Ride Together 268
The Pied Piper of Hamelin 271
A Grammarian's Funeral 278
The Heretic's Tragedy 282
Holy-Cross Day 285
Protus 288
The Statue and the Bust 290
Porphyria's Lover 297
"Childe Roland to the Dark Tower Came" 298

CHRISTMAS-EVE 304

MEN AND WOMEN

How It Strikes a Contemporary 335
Fra Lippo Lippi 338
Andrea Del Sarto 346

                                                        PAGE
The Bishop Orders His Tomb at Saint Praxed's Church   . 352
Bishop Blougram's Apology 355
DRAMATIS PERSONÆ
    Abt Vogler, after He Has Been Extemporizing upon the
        Musical Instrument of His Invention 378
    Rabbi Ben Ezra 381
    Caliban upon Setebos; or, Natural Theology in the Island . 387
    Confessions 394
    Prospice 395
    Youth and Art 396
    A Face 398
    A Likeness 398
    Mr. Sludge, "the Medium" 400
    Apparent Failure 435
    Epilogue 437
AT THE "MERMAID" 440
HOUSE 444
SHOP 446
PISGAH-SIGHTS I 449
PISGAH-SIGHTS II 450
FEARS AND SCRUPLES 451
HERVÉ RIEL 453
A FORGIVENESS 457
CENCIAJA 467
FILIPPO BALDINUCCI ON THE PRIVILEGE OF BURIAL 474
PIPPA PASSES, song 486
ASOLANDO, epilogue 487

POEMS
OF
ELIZABETH BARRETT BROWNING

DEDICATION

To My Father

When your eyes fall upon this page of dedication, and you start to see to whom it is inscribed, your first thought will be of the time, far off, when I was a child, and wrote verses, and when I dedicated them to you, who were my public and my critic. Of all that such a recollection implies of saddest and sweetest to both of us, it would become neither of us to speak before the world; nor would it be possible for us to speak of it to one another with voices that did not falter. Enough, that what is in my heart when I write thus will be fully known to yours.

And my desire is, that you, who are a witness how, if this art of poetry had been a less earnest object to me, it must have fallen from exhausted hands before this day,—that you, who have shared with me in things bitter and sweet, softening or enhancing them, every day,—that you, who hold with me, over all sense of loss and transiency, one hope by one name,—may accept from me the inscription of these volumes, the exponents of a few years of an existence which has been sustained and comforted by you, as well as given. Somewhat more faint-hearted than I used to be, it is my fancy thus to seem to return to a visible personal dependence on you, as if indeed I were a child again; to conjure your beloved image between myself and the public, so as to be sure of one smile; and to satisfy my heart, while I sanctify my ambition, by associating with the great pursuit of my life its tenderest and holiest affection.

Your
E. B. B.

London, 50 Wimpole Street, 1844.

3

POEMS
OF
ELIZABETH BARRETT BROWNING

PASSAGES FROM AURORA LEIGH

Dedication to John Kenyon, Esq.

THE words "cousin" and "friend" are constantly recurring in this poem, the last pages of which have been finished under the hospitality of your roof, my own dearest cousin and friend,—cousin and friend in a sense of less equality and greater disinterestedness than "Romney's."

Ending, therefore, and preparing once more to quit England, I venture to leave in your hands this book, the most mature of my works, and the one into which my highest convictions upon life and art have entered; that as, through my various efforts in literature, and steps in life, you have believed in me, borne with me, and been generous to me, far beyond the common uses of mere relationship or sympathy of mind, so you may kindly accept in sight of the public this poor sign of esteem, gratitude, and affection from

Your unforgetting

E. B. B.

39 DEVONSHIRE PLACE,
  Oct. 17, 1856.

> OF WRITING many books there is no end;
> And I, who have written much in prose and verse
> For others' uses, will write now for mine,—
> Will write my story for my better self,
> As when you paint your portrait for a friend,
> Who keeps it in a drawer, and looks at it
> Long after he has ceased to love you, just
> To hold together what he was and is. . . .

. . . . . .

On English ground

> You understand the letter,—ere the fall
> How Adam lived in a garden. All the fields
> Are tied up fast with hedges, nosegay-like;
> The hills are crumpled plains, the plains parterres;
> The trees round, woolly, ready to be clipped;
> And if you seek for any wilderness,

5

You find at best a park. A nature tamed,
And grown domestic like a barn-door fowl,
Which does not awe you with its claws and beak,
Nor tempt you to an eyry too high up,
But which in cackling sets you thinking of
Your eggs to-morrow at breakfast, in the pause
Of finer meditation.
                            Rather say,
A sweet familiar nature, stealing in
As a dog might, or child, to touch your hand,
Or pluck your gown, and humbly mind you so
Of presence and affection, excellent
For inner uses, from the things without.

I could not be unthankful, I who was
Entreated thus, and holpen. In the room
I speak of, ere the house was well awake,
And also after it was well asleep,
I sate alone, and drew the blessing in
Of all that nature. With a gradual step,
A stir among the leaves, a breath, a ray,
It came in softly, while the angels made
A place for it beside me. The moon came,
And swept my chamber clean of foolish thoughts.
The sun came, saying, "Shall I lift this light
Against the lime-tree, and you will not look?
I make the birds sing: listen!—but, for you,
God never hears your voice, excepting when
You lie upon the bed at nights, and weep."

Then something moved me. Then I wakened up,
More slowly than I verily write now;
But wholly, at last, I wakened, opened wide
The window and my soul, and let the airs
And outdoor sights sweep gradual gospels in,
Regenerating what I was. O Life!
How oft we throw it off, and think, "Enough,
Enough of life in so much!—here's a cause
For rupture; herein we must break with Life,
Or be ourselves unworthy; here we are wronged,
Maimed, spoiled for aspiration: farewell, Life!"
And so, as froward babes, we hide our eyes
And think all ended. Then Life calls to us
In some transformed, apocalyptic voice,
Above us, or below us, or around:
Perhaps we name it Nature's voice, or Love's,

Tricking ourselves, because we are more ashamed
To own our compensations than our griefs:
Still Life's voice; still we make our peace with Life.

And I, so young then, was not sullen. Soon
I used to get up early just to sit
And watch the morning quicken in the gray,
And hear the silence open like a flower,
Leaf after leaf, and stroke with listless hand
The woodbine through the window, till at last
I came to do it with a sort of love,
At foolish unaware: whereat I smiled,
A melancholy smile, to catch myself
Smiling for joy.
                    Capacity for joy
Admits temptation. It seemed, next, worth while
To dodge the sharp sword set against my life,
To slip down stairs through all the sleepy house,
As mute as any dream there, and escape,
As a soul from the body, out of doors,
Glide through the shrubberies, drop into the lane,
And wander on the hills an hour or two,
Then back again, before the house should stir.

Or else I sate on in my chamber green,
And lived my life, and thought my thoughts, and prayed
My prayers without the vicar; read my books,
Without considering whether they were fit
To do me good. Mark there. We get no good
By being ungenerous, even to a book,
And calculating profits,—so much help
By so much reading. It is rather when
We gloriously forget ourselves, and plunge
Soul-forward, headlong, into a book's profound,
Impassioned for its beauty and salt of truth,—
'Tis then we get the right good from a book.

· · · · ·

                                        For me, I wrote
False poems, like the rest, and thought them true
Because myself was true in writing them
I, peradventure, have writ true ones since
With less complacence.
                        But I could not hide
My quickening inner life from those at watch.
They saw a light at a window now and then

They had not set there: who had set it there?
My father's sister started when she caught
My soul agaze in my eyes. She could not say
I had no business with a sort of soul;
But plainly she objected, and demurred
That souls were dangerous things to carry straight
Through all the spilt saltpetre of the world.
She said sometimes, "Aurora, have you done
Your task this morning? have you read that book?
And are you ready for the crochet here?"—
As if she said, "I know there's something wrong;
I know I have not ground you down enough
To flatten and bake you to a wholesome crust,
For household uses and proprieties,
Before the rain has got into my barn,
And set the grains a-sprouting. What, you're green
With outdoor impudence? you almost grow?"
To which I answered, "Would she hear my task,
And verify my abstract of the book?
Or should I sit down to the crochet-work?
Was such her pleasure?" Then I sate and teased
The patient needle till it spilt the thread,
Which oozed off from it in meandering lace
From hour to hour. I was not therefore sad;
My soul was singing at a work apart,
Behind the wall of sense, as safe from harm
As sings the lark when sucked up out of sight
In vortices of glory and blue air. . . .

.   .   .   .   .

I learnt to love that England. Very oft,
Before the day was born, or otherwise
Through secret windings of the afternoons,
I threw my hunters off, and plunged myself
Among the deep hills, as a hunted stag
Will take the waters, shivering with the fear
And passion of the course. And when at last
Escaped, so many a green slope built on slope
Betwixt me and the enemy's house behind,
I dared to rest, or wander in a rest
Made sweeter for the step upon the grass,
And view the ground's most gentle dimplement
(As if God's finger touched, but did not press,
In making England); such an up-and-down
Of verdure, nothing too much up or down,

A ripple of land; such little hills the sky
Can stoop to tenderly, and the wheatfields climb;
Such nooks of valleys lined with orchises,
Fed full of noises by invisible streams;
And open pastures where you scarcely tell
White daisies from white dew; at intervals
The mythic oaks and elm-trees standing out
Self-poised upon their prodigy of shade,—
I thought my father's land was worthy too
Of being my Shakspeare's. . . .

     .   .   .   .   .

                                Ofter we walked only two,
If cousin Romney pleased to walk with me.
We read, or talked, or quarrelled, as it chanced.
We were not lovers, nor even friends well matched:
Say, rather, scholars upon different tracks,
And thinkers disagreed,—he, overfull
Of what is, and I, haply, overbold
For what might be.
                 But then the thrushes sang,
And shook my pulses and the elm's new leaves;
At which I turned, and held my finger up,
And bade him mark, that howsoe'er the world
Went ill, as he related, certainly
The thrushes still sang in it. At the word
His brow would soften; and he bore with me
In melancholy patience, not unkind,
While, breaking into voluble ecstasy,
I flattered all the beauteous country round,
As poets use,—the skies, the clouds, the fields,
The happy violets hiding from the roads
The primroses run down to, carrying gold;
The tangled hedgerows, where the cows push out
Impatient horns and tolerant churning mouths
'Twixt dripping ash-boughs; hedgerows all alive
With birds and gnats, and large white butterflies
Which look as if the Mayflower had caught life,
And palpitated forth upon the wind;
Hills, vales, woods, netted in a silver mist;
Farms, granges, doubled up among the hills;
And cattle grazing in the watered vales;
And cottage-chimneys smoking from the woods;
And cottage-gardens smelling everywhere,
Confused with smell of orchards. "See!" I said,

"And see! is not God with us on the earth?
And shall we put him down by aught we do?
Who says there's nothing for the poor and vile
Save poverty and wickedness? Behold!"
And ankle-deep in English grass I leaped,
And clapped my hands, and called all very fair.

In the beginning, when God called all good,
Even then, was evil near us, it is writ;
But we indeed who call things good and fair,
The evil is upon us while we speak:
Deliver us from evil, let us pray . . .

    .   .   .   .   .

"Aurora, let's be serious, and throw by
This game of head and heart. Life means, be sure,
Both heart and head,—both active, both complete,
And both in earnest. Men and women make
The world, as head and heart make human life.
Work, man, work, woman, since there's work to do
In this beleaguered earth for head and heart;
And thought can never do the work of love:
But work for ends, I mean for uses, not
For such sleek fringes (do you call them ends,
Still less God's glory?) as we sew ourselves
Upon the velvet of those baldaquins
Held 'twixt us and the sun. That book of yours
I have not read a page of; but I toss
A rose up—it falls calyx down, you see!
The chances are, that being a woman, young
And pure, with such a pair of large, calm eyes,
You write as well . . . and ill . . . upon the whole,
As other women. If as well, what then?
If even a little better . . . still, what then?
We want the best in art now, or no art.
The time is done for facile settings-up
Of minnow-gods, nymphs here, and tritons there:
The polytheists have gone out in God,
That unity of bests. No best, no God!
And so with art, we say. Give art's divine,
Direct, indubitable, real as grief,
Or, leave us to the grief, we grow ourselves
Divine by overcoming with mere hope
And most prosaic patience. You, you are young
As Eve with nature's daybreak on her face:

But this same world you are come to, dearest coz,
Has done with keeping birthdays, saves her wreaths
To hang upon her ruins, and forgets
To rhyme the cry with which she still beats back
Those savage, hungry dogs that hunt her down
To the empty grave of Christ. The world's hard pressed:
The sweat of labor in the early curse
Has (turning acrid in six thousand years)
Become the sweat of torture. Who has time,
An hour's time . . . think!—to sit upon a bank,
And hear the cymbal tinkle in white hands?
When Egypt's slain, I say, let Miriam sing!—
Before—where's Moses?"
                                        "Ah, exactly that.
Where's Moses? Is a Moses to be found?
You'll seek him vainly in the bulrushes,
While I in vain touch cymbals. Yet concede,
Such sounding brass has done some actual good
(The application in a woman's hand,
If that were credible, being scarcely spoilt),
In colonizing beehives."
                                        "There it is!
You play beside a death-bed like a child,
Yet measure to yourself a prophet's place
To teach the living. None of all these things
Can women understand. You generalize,
Oh, nothing,—not even grief! Your quick-breathed hearts,
So sympathetic to the personal pang,
Close on each separate knife-stroke, yielding up
A whole life at each wound, incapable
Of deepening, widening a large lap of life
To hold the world-full woe. The human race
To you means such a child, or such a man,
You saw one morning waiting in the cold
Beside that gate, perhaps. You gather up
A few such cases, and when strong sometimes
Will write of factories and of slaves, as if
Your father were a negro, and your son
A spinner in the mills. All's yours and you,
All colored with your blood, or otherwise
Just nothing to you. Why, I call you hard
To general suffering. Here's the world half-blind
With intellectual light, half-brutalized
With civilization, having caught the plague
In silks from Tarsus, shrieking east and west
Along a thousand railroads, mad with pain

And sin too! . . . does one woman of you all
(You who weep easily) grow pale to see
This tiger shake his cage? Does one of you
Stand still from dancing, stop from stringing pearls,
And pine and die, because of the great sum
Of universal anguish? Show me a tear
Wet as Cordelia's in eyes bright as yours,
Because the world is mad. You cannot count
That you should weep for this account, not you!
You weep for what you know. A redhaired child
Sick in a fever, if you touch him once,
Though but so little as with a fingertip,
Will set you weeping; but a million sick . . .
You could as soon weep for the rule of three
Or compound fractions. Therefore this same world
Uncomprehended by you, must remain
Uninfluenced by you. Women as you are,
Mere women, personal and passionate,
You give us doating mothers, and perfect wives,
Sublime Madonnas, and enduring saints:
We get no Christ from you, and verily
We shall not get a poet, in my mind."

"With which conclusion you conclude" . . .
                                   "But this:
That you, Aurora, with the large live brow
And steady eyelids, cannot condescend
To play at art, as children play at swords,
To show a pretty spirit, chiefly admired
Because true action is impossible.
You never can be satisfied with praise
Which men give women when they judge a book
Not as mere work, but as mere woman's work,
Expressing the comparative respect,
Which means the absolute scorn. 'Oh, excellent!
What grace, what facile turns, what fluent sweeps,
What delicate discernment . . . almost thought!
The book does honor to the sex, we hold.
Among our female authors we make room
For this fair writer, and congratulate
The country that produces in these times
Such women, competent to' . . . spell.'"
                                   "Stop there,"
I answered, burning through his thread of talk
With a quick flame of emotion,—"you have read
My soul, if not my book, and argue well

I would not condescend . . . we will not say
To such a kind of praise (a worthless end
Is praise of all kinds), but to such a use
Of holy art and golden life. I am young,
And peradventure weak—you tell me so—
Through being a woman. And for all the rest,
Take thanks for justice. I would rather dance
At fairs on tight-rope, till the babies dropped
Their gingerbread for joy, than shift the types
For tolerable verse, intolerable
To men who act and suffer. Better far
Pursue a frivolous trade by serious means,
Than a sublime art frivolously."

       "You
Choose nobler work than either, O moist eyes,
And hurrying lips, and heaving heart! We are young,
Aurora, you and I. The world,—look round,—
The world we're come to late is swollen hard
With perished generations and their sins:
The civilizer's spade grinds horribly
On dead men's bones, and cannot turn up soil
That's otherwise than fetid. All success
Proves partial failure; all advance implies
What's left behind; all triumph, something crushed
At the chariot-wheels; all government, some wrong;
And rich men make the poor, who curse the rich,
Who agonize together, rich and poor,
Under and over, in the social spasm
And crisis of the ages. Here's an age
That makes its own vocation; here we have stepped
Across the bounds of time; here's nought to see,
But just the rich man and just Lazarus,
And both in torments with a mediate gulf,
Though not a hint of Abraham's bosom. Who,
Being man, Aurora, can stand calmly by
And view these things, and never tease his soul
For some great cure? No physic for this grief,
In all the earth and heavens too?"

       "You believe
In God, for your part?—ay? that He who makes
Can make good things from ill things, best from worst,
As men plant tulips upon dunghills when
They wish them finest?"

      "True. A death-heat is
The same as life-heat, to be accurate;
And in all nature is no death at all,

As men account of death, so long as God
Stands witnessing for life perpetually,
By being just God. That's abstract truth, I know,
Philosophy, or sympathy with God;
But I, I sympathize with man, not God,
(I think I was a man for chiefly this,)
And, when I stand beside a dying bed,
'Tis death to me. Observe: it had not much
Consoled the race of mastodons to know,
Before they went to fossil, that anon
Their place would quicken with the elephant:
They were not elephants, but mastodons;
And I, a man, as men are now, and not
As men may be hereafter, feel with men
In the agonizing present."
                              "Is it so,"
I said, "my cousin? Is the world so bad,
While I hear nothing of it through the trees?
The world was always evil,—but so bad?"

"So bad, Aurora. Dear, my soul is gray
With poring over the long sum of ill;
So much for vice, so much for discontent,
So much for the necessities of power,
So much for the connivances of fear,
Coherent in statistical despairs
With such a total of distracted life . . .
To see it down in figures on a page,
Plain, silent, clear, as God sees through the earth
The sense of all the graves,—that's terrible
For one who is not God, and cannot right
The wrong he looks on. May I choose indeed
But vow away my years, my means, my aims,
Among the helpers, if there's any help
In such a social strait? The common blood
That swings along my veins is strong enough
To draw me to this duty."

.   .   .   .   .

My talk, meanwhile, is arid to you, ay,
Since all my talk can only set you where
You look down coldly on the arena-heaps
Of headless bodies, shapeless, indistinct. . . ."

.   .   .   .   .

With quiet indignation I broke in,
"You misconceive the question like a man,
Who sees a woman as the complement
Of his sex merely. You forget too much
That every creature, female as the male,
Stands single in responsible act and thought
As also in birth and death. Whoever says
To a loyal woman, 'Love and work with me,'
Will get fair answers, if the work and love,
Being good themselves, are good for her,—the best
She was born for. Women of a softer mood,
Surprised by men when scarcely awake to life,
Will sometimes only hear the first word, love,
And catch up with it any kind of work,
Indifferent, so that dear love go with it.
I do not blame such women, though for love
They pick much oakum: earth's fanatics make
Too frequently heaven's saints. But *me* your work
Is not the best for, nor your love the best,
Nor able to commend the kind of work
For love's sake merely. Ah! you force me, sir,
To be over-bold in speaking of myself:
I, too, have my vocation,—work to do,
The heavens and earth have set me since I changed
My father's face for theirs, and, though your world
Were twice as wretched as you represent,
Most serious work, most necessary work
As any of the economists'. Reform,
Make trade a Christian possibility,
And individual right no general wrong,
Wipe out earth's furrows of the thine and mine,
And leave one green for men to play at bowls,
With innings for them all! . . . what then, indeed,
If mortals are not greater by the head
Than any of their prosperities? what then,
Unless the artist keep up open roads
Betwixt the seen and unseen, bursting through
The best of your conventions with his best,
The speakable, imaginable best
God bids him speak, to prove what lies beyond
Both speech and imagination? A starved man
Exceeds a fat beast: we'll not barter, sir,
The beautiful for barley. And, even so,
I hold you will not compass your poor ends
Of barley-feeding and material ease
Without a poet's individualism

To work your universal. It takes a soul
To move a body: it takes a high-souled man
To move the masses even to a cleaner sty:
It takes the ideal to blow a hair's-breadth off
The dust of the actual. Ah! your Fouriers failed,
Because not poets enough to understand
That life develops from within. For me,
Perhaps I am not worthy, as you say,
Of work like this: perhaps a woman's soul
Aspires, and not creates: yet we aspire,
And yet I'll try out your perhapses, sir,
And if I fail . . . why, burn me up my straw
Like other false works. I'll not ask for grace:
Your scorn is better, cousin Romney. I
Who love my art would never wish it lower
To suit my stature. I may love my art.
You'll grant that even a woman may love art,
Seeing that to waste true love on any thing
Is womanly, past question."
                                        I retain
The very last word which I said that day. . . .

.   .   .   .   .

When Romney Leigh and I had parted thus,
I took a chamber up three flights of stairs
Not far from being as steep as some larks climb,
And there, in a certain house in Kensington,
Three years I lived and worked. Get leave to work
In this world—'tis the best you get at all;
For God, in cursing, gives us better gifts
Than men in benediction. God says, "Sweat
For foreheads:" men say, "Crowns." And so we are crowned,
Ay, gashed by some tormenting circle of steel
Which snaps with a secret spring. Get work, get work!
Be sure 'tis better than what you work to get.

Serene, and unafraid of solitude,
I worked the short days out, and watched the sun
On lurid morns or monstrous afternoons
(Like some Druidic idol's fiery brass,
With fixed unflickering outline of dead heat,
From which the blood of wretches pent inside
Seems oozing forth to incarnadine the air)
Push out through fog with his dilated disk,
And startle the slant roofs and chimney-pots

With splashes of fierce color. Or I saw
Fog only—the great tawny weltering fog—
Involve the passive city, strangle it
Alive, and draw it off into the void,—
Spires, bridges, streets, and squares,—as if a sponge
Had wiped out London, or as noon and night
Had clapped together, and utterly struck out
The intermediate time, undoing themselves
In the act. Your city poets see such things
Not despicable. Mountains of the south,
When, drunk and mad with elemental wines
They rend the seamless mist, and stand up bare,
Make fewer singers, haply. No one sings,
Descending Sinai: on Parnassus-mount
You take a mule to climb, and not a muse,
Except in fable and figure: forests chant
Their anthems to themselves, and leave you dumb.
But sit in London at the day's decline,
And view the city perish in the mist
Like Pharaoh's armaments in the deep Red Sea,
The chariots, horsemen, footmen, all the host,
Sucked down and choked to silence—then, surprised
By a sudden sense of vision and of tune,
You feel as conquerors, though you did not fight;
And you and Israel's other singing girls,
Ay, Miriam with them, sing the song you choose.

I worked with patience, which means almost power.
I did some excellent things indifferently,
Some bad things excellently. Both were praised,
The latter loudest. And by such a time
That I myself had set them down as sins
Scarce worth the price of sackcloth, week by week
Arrived some letter through the sedulous post,
Like these I've read, and yet dissimilar,
With pretty maiden seals,—initials twined
Of lilies, or a heart marked *Emily*,
(Convicting Emily of being all heart;)
Or rarer tokens from young bachelors,
Who wrote from college with the same goosequill,
Suppose, they had just been plucked of, and a snatch
From Horace, "Collegisse juvat," set
Upon the first page. Many a letter, signed
Or unsigned, showing the writers at eighteen
Had lived too long, although a muse should help
Their dawn by holding candles,—compliments

To smile or sigh at. Such could pass with me
No more than coins from Moscow circulate
At Paris: would ten roubles buy a tag
Of ribbon on the boulevard, worth a sou?
I smiled that all this youth should love me, sighed
That such a love could scarcely raise them up
To love what was more worthy than myself;
Then sighed again, again, less generously,
To think the very love they lavished so
Proved me inferior. The strong loved me not,
And he . . . my cousin Romney . . . did not write.
I felt the silent finger of his scorn
Prick every bubble of my frivolous fame
As my breath blew it, and resolve it back
To the air it came from. Oh, I justified
The measure he had taken of my height:
The thing was plain—he was not wrong a line;
I played at art, made thrusts with a toy-sword,
Amused the lads and maidens.
                               Came a sigh
Deep, hoarse with resolution,—I would work
To better ends, or play in earnest. "Heavens,
I think I should be almost popular
If this went on!"—I ripped my verses up,
And found no blood upon the rapier's point;
The heart in them was just an embryo's heart,
Which never yet had beat, that it should die;
Just gasps of make-believe galvanic life;
Mere tones, inorganized to any tune.

And yet I felt it in me where it burnt,
Like those hot fire-seeds of creation held
In Jove's clenched palm before the worlds were sown;
But I—I was not Juno even! my hand
Was shut in weak convulsion, woman's ill;
And when I yearned to loose a finger—lo,
The nerve revolted. . . .

                .   .   .   .   .

                               I worked on, on.
Through all the bristling fence of nights and days
Which hedges time in from the eternities
I struggled, never stopped to note the stakes
Which hurt me in my course. The midnight oil
Would stink sometimes; there came some vulgar needs:
I had to live that therefore I might work,

And, being but poor, I was constrained, for life,
To work with one hand for the booksellers
While working with the other for myself
And art: you swim with feet, as well as hands,
Or make small way. I apprehended this.
In England no one lives by verse that lives;
And, apprehending, I resolved by prose
To make a space to sphere my living verse.
I wrote for cyclopædias, magazines,
And weekly papers, holding up my name
To keep it from the mud. I learnt the use
Of the editorial "we" in a review,
As courtly ladies the fine trick of trains,
And swept it grandly through the open doors,
As if one could not pass through doors at all,
Save so encumbered. I wrote tales beside,
Carved many an article on cherry-stones
To suit light readers,—something in the lines
Revealing, it was said, the mallet-hand;
But that I'll never vouch for. What you do
For bread will taste of common grain, not grapes,
Although you have a vineyard in Champagne,
Much less in Nephelococcygia,
As mine was, peradventure.
                                    Having bread
For just so many days, just breathing-room
For body and verse, I stood up straight, and worked
My veritable work. And as the soul
Which grows within a child makes the child grow,
Or as the fiery sap, the touch from God,
Careering through a tree, dilates the bark,
And roughs with scale and knob, before it strikes
The summer-foliage out in a green flame,
So life, in deepening with me, deepened all
The course I took, the work I did. Indeed,
The academic law convinced of sin:
The critics cried out on the falling off,
Regretting the first manner. But I felt
My heart's life throbbing in my verse to show
It lived, it also—certes incomplete,
Disordered with all Adam in the blood,
But even its very tumors, warts, and wens
Still organized by and implying life.

A lady called upon me on such a day.
She had the low voice of your English dames,—

Unused, it seems, to need rise half a note
To catch attention,—and their quiet mood,
As if they lived too high above the earth
For that to put them out in any thing:
So gentle, because verily so proud;
So wary and afraid of hurting you,
By no means that you are not really vile,
But that they would not touch you with their foot
To push you to your place; so self-possessed,
Yet gracious and conciliating, it takes
An effort in their presence to speak truth:
You know the sort of woman,—brilliant stuff,
And out of nature. "Lady Waldemar."
She said her name quite simply, as if it meant
Not much, indeed, but something; took my hands,
And smiled as if her smile could help my case,
And dropped her eyes on me, and let them melt.
"Is this," she said, "the muse?"
                                "No sibyl, even,"
I answered, "since she fails to guess the cause
Which taxed you with this visit, madam."
                                        "Good,"
She said.

            .   .   .   .   .

                        Distrust that word.
"There is none good save God," said Jesus Christ
If he once, in the first creation-week,
Called creatures good, forever afterward,
The Devil only has done it, and his heirs,
The knaves who win so, and the fools who lose:
The word's grown dangerous. In the middle age
I think they called malignant fays and imps
Good people. A good neighbor, even in this,
Is fatal sometimes, cuts your morning up
To mince-meat of the very smallest talk,
Then helps to sugar her bohea at night
With your reputation. I have known good wives,
As chaste, or nearly so, as Potiphar's;
And good, good mothers, who would use a child
To better an intrigue; good friends, beside,
(Very good) who hung succinctly round your neck
And sucked your breath, as cats are fabled to do
By sleeping infants. And we all have known
Good critics who have stamped out poet's hope,
Good statesmen who pulled ruin on the state,

Good patriots who for a theory risked a cause,
Good kings who disembowelled for a tax,
Good popes who brought all good to jeopardy,
Good Christians who sate still in easy-chairs
And damned the general world for standing up.
Now may the good God pardon all good men!

.   .   .   .   .

                                   "My dear friend,"
Lord Howe began . . .
"A happy life means prudent compromise;
The tare runs through the farmer's garnered sheaves,
And, though the gleaner's apron holds pure wheat
We count her poorer. Tare with wheat, we cry,
And good with drawbacks. You, you love your art,
And, certain of vocation, set your soul
On utterance. Only, in this world we have made,
(They say God made it first, but if he did
'Twas so long since, and, since, we have spoiled it so,
He scarce would know it, if he looked this way,
From hells we preach of, with the flames blown out,)
—In this bad, twisted, topsy-turvy world,
Where all the heaviest wrongs get uppermost,—
In this uneven, unfostering England here,
Where ledger-strokes and sword-strokes count indeed,
But soul-strokes merely tell upon the flesh
They strike from,—it is hard to stand for art,
Unless some golden tripod from the sea
Be fished up, by Apollo's divine chance,
To throne such feet as yours, my prophetess,
At Delphi. . . ."

.   .   .   .   .

I answered slow,—as some wayfaring man,
Who feels himself at night too far from home,
Makes steadfast face against the bitter wind,—
"Is art so less a thing than virtue is,
That artists first must cater for their ease,
Or ever they make issue past themselves
To generous use? Alas! and is it so,
That we who would be somewhat clean must sweep
Our ways, as well as walk them, no friend
Confirm us nobly,—'Leave results to God,
But you, be clean!' What! 'prudent compromise
Makes acceptable life,' you say instead,—
You, you, Lord Howe?—in things indifferent, well.

For instance, compromise the wheaten bread
For rye, the meat for lentils, silk for serge,
And sleep on down, if needs, for sleep on straw;
But there end compromise. I will not bate
One artist-dream on straw or down, my lord,
Nor pinch my liberal soul, though I be poor,
Nor cease to love high, though I live thus low."

.   .   .   .   .

The book, too—pass it. "A good book," says he,
"And you a woman." I had laughed at that
But long since. I'm a woman, it is true;
Alas, and woe to us, when we feel it most!
Then least care have we for the crowns and goals
And compliments on writing our good books.

The book has some truth in it, I believe;
And truth outlives pain, as the soul does life.
I know we talk our Phædons to the end,
Through all the dismal faces that we make,
O'er-wrinkled with dishonoring agony
From decomposing drugs. I have written truth,
And I a woman,—feebly, partially,
Inaptly in presentation, Romney'll add,
Because a woman. For the truth itself,
That's neither man's nor woman's, but just God's;
None else has reason to be proud of truth:
Himself will see it sifted, disinthralled,
And kept upon the height and in the light,
As far as and no farther than 'tis truth;
For now he has left off calling firmaments
And strata, flowers and creatures, very good,
He says it still of truth, which is his own.

Truth, so far, in my book,—the truth which draws
Through all things upwards,—that a twofold world
Must go to a perfect cosmos. Natural things
And spiritual,—who separates those two
In art, in morals, or the social drift,
Tears up the bond of nature, and brings death,
Paints futile pictures, writes unreal verse,
Leads vulgar days, deals ignorantly with men,
Is wrong, in short, at all points. We divide
This apple of life, and cut it through the pips:
The perfect round which fitted Venus' hand

Has perished as utterly as if we ate
Both halves. Without the spiritual, observe,
The natural's impossible, no form,
No motion: without sensuous, spiritual
Is inappreciable, no beauty or power.
And in this twofold sphere the twofold man
(For still the artist is intensely a man)
Holds firmly by the natural to reach
The spiritual beyond it, fixes still
The type with mortal vision to pierce through,
With eyes immortal to the antetype
Some call the ideal, better called the real,
And certain to be called so presently,
When things shall have their names.

.   .   .   .   .

                                   "There's nothing great
Nor small," has said a poet of our day,
Whose voice will ring beyond the curfew of eve,
And not be thrown out by the matin's bell:
And truly, I reiterate, Nothing's small!
No lily-muffled hum of a summer-bee,
But finds some coupling with the spinning stars;
No pebble at your foot, but proves a sphere;
No chaffinch, but implies the cherubim;
And (glancing on my own thin, veinèd wrist)
In such a little tremor of the blood
The whole strong clamor of a vehement soul
Doth utter itself distinct. Earth's crammed with heaven,
And every common bush afire with God;
But only he who sees takes off his shoes,
The rest sit round it and pluck blackberries,
And daub their natural faces unaware
More and more from the first similitude.

Truth, so far, in my book!—a truth which draws
From all things upward. I, Aurora, still
Have felt it hound me through the wastes of life
As Jove did Io; and until that hand
Shall overtake me wholly, and on my head
Lay down its large unfluctuating peace,
The feverish gad-fly pricks me up and down.
It must be. Art's the witness of what is
Behind this show. If this world's show were all,
Then imitation would be all in art.

There Jove's hand gripes us! for we stand here, we,
If genuine artists, witnessing for God's
Complete, consummate, undivided work;
—That every natural flower which grows on earth
Implies a flower upon the spiritual side,
Substantial, archetypal, all aglow
With blossoming causes,—not so far away,
But we whose spirit-sense is somewhat cleared
May catch at something of the bloom and breath,—
Too vaguely apprehended, though, indeed,
Still apprehended, consciously or not,
And still transferred to picture, music, verse,
For thrilling audient and beholding souls
By signs and touches which are known to souls.
How known, they know not; why, they cannot find:
So straight call out on genius, say, "A man
Produced this," when much rather they should say,
" 'Tis insight, and he saw this."
                              Thus is art
Self-magnified in magnifying a truth
Which, fully recognized, would change the world,
And shift its morals. If a man could feel,
Not one day, in the artist's ecstasy,
But every day,—feast, fast, or working day,—
The spiritual significance burn through
The hieroglyphic of material shows,
Henceforward he would paint the globe with wings,
And reverence fish and fowl, the bull, the tree,
And even his very body as a man;
Which now he counts so vile, that all the towns
Make offal of their daughters for its use
On summer-nights, when God is sad in heaven
To think what goes on in his recreant world
He made quite other; while that moon he made
To shine there, at the first love's covenant,
Shines still, convictive as a marriage-ring
Before adulterous eyes.
                              How sure it is,
That, if we say a true word, instantly
We feel 'tis God's, not ours, and pass it on,
Like bread at sacrament we taste and pass,
Nor handle for a moment, as indeed
We dared to set up any claim to such!
And I—my poem—let my readers talk.
I'm closer to it, I can speak as well:
I'll say with Romney, that the book is weak,

The range uneven, the points of sight obscure,
The music interrupted.
Let us go.
The end of woman (or of man, I think)
Is not a book. Alas, the best of books
Is but a word in art, which soon grows cramped,
Stiff, dubious-statured, with the weight of years, . . .

.   .   .   .   .

"Speak wisely, cousin Leigh."
"Yes, wisely, dear Aurora, though too late,
But then, not wisely. I was heavy then,
And stupid, and distracted with the cries
Of tortured prisoners in the polished brass
Of that Phalarian bull, society,
Which seems to bellow bravely like ten bulls,
But, if you listen, moans and cries instead
Despairingly, like victims tossed and gored
And trampled by their hoofs. I heard the cries
Too close: I could not hear the angels lift
A fold of rustling air, nor what they said
To help my pity. I beheld the world
As one great famishing carnivorous mouth,—
A huge, deserted, callow, blind bird thing,
With piteous open beak that hurt my heart,
Till down upon the filthy ground I dropped,
And tore the violets up to get the worms.
Worms, worms, was all my cry: an open mouth,
A gross want, bread to fill it to the lips,
No more. That poor men narrowed their demands
To such an end was virtue, I supposed,
Adjudicating that to see it so
Was reason. Oh, I did not push the case
Up higher, and ponder how it answers when
The rich take up the same cry for themselves,
Professing equally,—'An open mouth
A gross need, food to fill us, and no more.'
Why, that's so far from virtue, only vice
Can find excuse for't! that makes libertines,
And slurs our cruel streets from end to end
With eighty thousand women in one smile,
Who only smile at night beneath the gas. . . .

.   .   .   .   .

"The world waits
For help. Beloved, let us love so well,

Our work shall still be better for our love,
And still our love be sweeter for our work,
And both commended, for the sake of each,
By all true workers and true lovers born.
Now press the clarion on thy woman's lip,
(Love's holy kiss shall still keep consecrate)
And breathe thy fine keen breath along the brass,
And blow all class-walls level as Jericho's
Past Jordan, crying from the top of souls,
To souls, that here assembled on earth's flats,
They get them to some purer eminence
Than any hitherto beheld for clouds!
What height we know not, but the way we know,
And how, by mounting ever, we attain,
And so climb on. It is the hour for souls,
That bodies, leavened by the will and love,
Be lightened to redemption. The world's old;
But the old world waits the time to be renewed,
Toward which new hearts in individual growth
Must quicken, and increase to multitude
In new dynasties of the race of men,
Developed whence shall grow spontaneously
New churches, new economies, new laws
Admitting freedom, new societies
Excluding falsehood: HE shall make all new."

RHYME OF THE DUCHESS MAY

I.

To THE BELFRY, one by one, went the ringers from the sun,
              (*Toll slowly*)
And the oldest ringer said, "Ours is music for the dead
  When the rebecs are all done."

II.

Six abeles i' the churchyard grow on the north side in a row,
              (*Toll slowly*)
And the shadows of their tops rock across the little slopes
  Of the grassy graves below.

III.

On the south side and the west a small river runs in haste,
              (*Toll slowly*)
And, between the river flowing and the fair green trees a-growing,
  Do the dead lie at their rest.

IV.

On the east I sate that day, up against a willow gray,
   (*Toll slowly*)
Through the rain of willow-branches I could see the low hill-ranges,
   And the river on its way.

V.

There I sate beneath the tree, and the bell tolled solemnly,
   (*Toll slowly*)
While the trees' and river's voices flowed between the solemn noises,—
   Yet death seemed more loud to me.

VI.

There I read this ancient rhyme while the bell did all the time
   (*Toll slowly*)
And the solemn knell fell in with the tale of life and sin,
   Like a rhythmic fate sublime.

THE RHYME.

I.

Broad the forests stood (I read) on the hills of Linteged;
   (*Toll slowly*)
And three hundred years had stood mute adown each hoary wood,
   Like a full heart having prayed.

II.

And the little birds sang east, and the little birds sang west;
   (*Toll slowly*)
And but little thought was theirs of the silent antique years,
   In the building of their nest.

III.

Down the sun dropt large and red on the towers of Linteged,—
   (*Toll slowly*)
Lance and spear upon the height, bristling strange in fiery light,
   While the castle stood in shade.

IV.

There the castle stood up black with the red sun at its back,
   (*Toll slowly*)
Like a sullen, smouldering pyre with a top that flickers fire
   When the wind is on its track.

V.

And five hundred archers tall did besiege the castle wall,
   (*Toll slowly*)
And the castle seethed in blood, fourteen days and nights had stood
   And to-night was near its fall.

VI.

Yet thereunto, blind to doom, three months since, a bride did come,
          (*Toll slowly*)
One who proudly trod the floors, and softly whispered in the doors,
    "May good angels bless our home."

VII.

Oh, a bride of queenly eyes, with a front of constancies,
          (*Toll slowly*)
Oh, a bride of cordial mouth where the untired smile of youth
    Did light outward its own sighs!

VIII.

'Twas a duke's fair orphan-girl, and her uncle's ward—the earl,
          (*Toll slowly*)
Who betrothed her twelve years old, for the sake of dowry gold,
    To his son Lord Leigh the churl.

IX.

But what time she had made good all her years of womanhood,
          (*Toll slowly*)
Unto both these lords of Leigh spake she out right sovranly,
    "My will runneth as my blood.

X.

"And while this same blood makes red this same right hand's veins," she said,
          (*Toll slowly*)
" 'Tis my will as lady free, not to wed a lord of Leigh,
    But Sir Guy of Linteged."

XI.

The old earl he smilèd smooth, then he sighed for wilful youth,—
          (*Toll slowly*)
"Good my niece, that hand withal looketh somewhat soft and small
    For so large a will in sooth."

XII.

She, too, smiled by that same sign; but her smile was cold and fine.
          (*Toll slowly*)
"Little hand clasps muckle gold, or it were not worth the hold
    Of thy son, good uncle mine."

XIII.

Then the young lord jerked his breath, and sware thickly in his teeth,—
          (*Toll slowly*)
"He would wed his own betrothed, an she loved him an she loathed,
    Let the life come, or the death."

XIV.

Up she rose with scornful eyes, as her father's child might rise,—
(*Toll slowly*)
"Thy hound's blood, my Lord of Leigh, stains thy knightly heel," quoth she,
"And he moans not where he lies;

XV.

"But a woman's will dies hard, in the hall or on the sward—
(*Toll slowly*)
"By that grave, my lords, which made me orphaned girl and dowered lady,
I deny you wife and ward!"

XVI.

Unto each she bowed her head, and swept past with lofty tread.
(*Toll slowly*)
Ere the midnight-bell had ceased, in the chapel had the priest
Blessed her, bride of Linteged.

XVII.

Fast and fain the bridal train along the night-storm rode amain:
(*Toll slowly*)
Hard the steeds of lord and serf struck their hoofs out on the turf,
In the pauses of the rain.

XVIII.

Fast and fain the kinsmen's train along the storm pursued amain,
(*Toll slowly*)
Steed on steed-track, dashing off,—thickening, doubling, hoof on hoof,
In the pauses of the rain.

XIX.

And the bridegroom led the flight on his red-roan steed of might,
(*Toll slowly*)
And the bride lay on his arm, still, as if she feared no harm,
Smiling out into the night.

XX.

"Dost thou fear?" he said at last. "Nay," she answered him in haste,—
(*Toll slowly*)
"Not such death as we could find: only life with one behind.
Ride on fast as fear, ride fast!"

XXI.

Up the mountain wheeled the steed, girth to ground, and fetlocks spread,
(*Toll slowly*)
Headlong bounds, and rocking flanks,—down he staggered, down the banks,
To the towers of Linteged.

XXII.

High and low the serfs looked out, red the flambeaus tossed about,
  (*Toll slowly*)
In the courtyard rose the cry, "Live the duchess and Sir Guy!"
  But she never heard them shout.

XXIII.

On the steed she dropped her cheek, kissed his mane, and kissed his neck,—
  (*Toll slowly*)
"I had happier died by thee than lived on a Lady Leigh,"
  Were the first words she did speak.

XXIV.

But a three-months' joyaunce lay 'twixt that moment and to-day,
  (*Toll slowly*)
When five hundred archers tall stand beside the castle-wall
  To recapture Duchess May.

XXV.

And the castle standeth black, with the red sun at its back;
  (*Toll slowly*)
And a fortnight's siege is done; and, except the duchess, none
  Can misdoubt the coming wrack.

XXVI.

Then the captain, young Lord Leigh, with his eyes so gray of blee,
  (*Toll slowly*)
And thin lips that scarcely sheath the cold white gnashing of his teeth,
  Gnashed in smiling, absently,

XXVII.

Cried aloud, "So goes the day, bridegroom fair of Duchess May!"
  (*Toll slowly*)
"Look thy last upon that sun! if thou seest to-morrow's one
  'Twill be through a foot of clay.

XXVIII.

"Ha, fair bride! dost hear no sound, save that moaning of the hound?"
  (*Toll slowly*)
"Thou and I have parted troth; yet I keep my vengeance-oath,
  And the other may come round.

XXIX.

"Ha! thy will is brave to dare, and thy new love past compare;"
  (*Toll slowly*)
"Yet thine old love's falchion brave is as strong a thing to have
  As the will of lady fair.

XXX.

"Peck on blindly, netted dove! If a wife's name thee behove,"
      (Toll slowly)
"Thou shalt wear the same to-morrow, ere the grave has hid the sorrow
  Of thy last ill-mated love.

XXXI.

"O'er his fixed and silent mouth thou and I will call back troth;"
      (Toll slowly)
"He shall altar be and priest; and he will not cry at least,
  'I forbid you, I am loath!'

XXXII.

"I will wring thy fingers pale in the gauntlet of my mail:"
      (Toll slowly)
" 'Little hand and muckle gold' close shall lie within my hold,
  As the sword did to prevail."

XXXIII.

Oh, the little birds sang east, and the little birds sang west,
      (Toll slowly)
Oh, and laughed the Duchess May, and her soul did put away
  All his boasting, for a jest.

XXXIV.

In her chamber did she sit, laughing low to think of it,—
      (Toll slowly)
"Tower is strong, and will is free: thou canst boast, my Lord of Leigh;
  But thou boastest little wit."

XXXV.

In her tire-glass gazèd she, and she blushed right womanly:
      (Toll slowly)
She blushed half from her disdain, half her beauty was so plain;
  "Oath for oath, my Lord of Leigh!"

XXXVI.

Straight she called her maidens in,—"Since ye gave me blame herein,"
      (Toll slowly)
"That a bridal such as mine should lack gauds to make it fine,
  Come and shrive me from that sin.

XXXVII.

"It is three months gone to-day since I gave mine hand away:"
      (Toll slowly)
"Bring the gold, and bring the gem, we will keep bride-state in them,
  While we keep the foe at bay.

XXXVIII.

"On your arms I loose mine hair; comb it smooth, and crown it fair:"
            (Toll slowly)
"I would look in purple pall from this lattice down the wall,
  And throw scorn to one that's there!"

XXXIX.

Oh, the little birds sang east, and the little birds sang west:
            (Toll slowly)
On the tower the castle's lord leant in silence on his sword,
  With an anguish in his breast.

XL.

With a spirit-laden weight did he lean down passionate:
            (Toll slowly)
They have almost sapped the wall,—they will enter therewithal
  With no knocking at the gate.

XLI.

Then the sword he leant upon shivered, snapped upon the stone:
            (Toll slowly)
"Sword," he thought with inward laugh, "ill thou servest for a staff
  When thy nobler use is done!

XLII.

"Sword, thy nobler use is done! tower is lost, and shame begun."
            (Toll slowly)
"If we met them in the breach, hilt to hilt, or speech to speech,
  We should die there, each for one.

XLIII.

"If we met them at the wall, we should singly, vainly fall;"
            (Toll slowly)
"But if *I* die here alone,—then I die who am but one,
  And die nobly for them all.

XLIV.

"Five true friends lie, for my sake, in the moat and in the brake;"
            (Toll slowly)
"Thirteen warriors lie at rest, with a black wound in the breast:
  And not one of these will wake.

XLV.

"So, no more of this shall be. Heartblood weighs too heavily;"
            (Toll slowly)
"And I could not sleep in grave, with the faithful and the brave
  Heaped around and over me.

XLVI.

"Since young Clare a mother hath, and young Ralph a plighted faith;"
(Toll slowly)
"Since my pale young sister's cheeks blush like rose when Ronald speaks,
Albeit never a word she saith,—

XLVII.

"These shall never die for me: lifeblood falls too heavily."
(Toll slowly)
"And if *I* die here apart, o'er my dead and silent heart
They shall pass out safe and free.

XLVIII.

"When the foe hath heard it said, 'Death holds Guy of Linteged,' "
(Toll slowly)
"That new corse new peace shall bring, and a blessèd, blessèd thing
Shall the stone be at its head.

XLIX.

"Then my friends shall pass out free, and shall bear my memory;"
(Toll slowly)
"Then my foes shall sleek their pride, soothing fair my widowed bride,
Whose sole sin was love of me.

L.

"With their words all smooth and sweet, they will front her, and entreat,"
(Toll slowly)
"And their purple pall will spread underneath her fainting head
While her tears drop over it.

LI.

"She will weep her woman's tears, she will pray her woman's prayers;"
(Toll slowly)
"But her heart is young in pain, and her hopes will spring again
By the suntime of her years.

LII.

"Ah, sweet May! ah, sweetest grief! once I vowed thee my belief"
(Toll slowly)
"That thy name expressed thy sweetness,—May of poets in completeness!
Now my May-day seemeth brief."

LIII.

All these silent thoughts did swim o'er his eyes grown strange and dim,
(Toll slowly)
Till his true men in the place wished they stood there face to face
With the foe, instead of him.

LIV.

"One last oath, my friends that wear faithful hearts to do and dare!"
(*Toll slowly*)
"Tower must fall, and bride be lost: swear me service worth the cost!"
Bold they stood around to swear.

LV.

"Each man clasp my hand, and swear, by the deed we failed in there,"
(*Toll slowly*)
"Not for vengeance, not for right, will ye strike one blow to-night!"
Pale they stood around to swear.

LVI.

"One last boon, young Ralph and Clare! faithful hearts to do and dare!"
(*Toll slowly*)
"Bring that steed up from his stall, which she kissed before you all,
Guide him up the turret-stair.

LVII.

"Ye shall harness him aright, and lead upward to this height;"
(*Toll slowly*)
"Once in love, and twice in war, hath he borne me strong and far:
He shall bear me far to-night."

LVIII.

Then his men looked to and fro when they heard him speaking so,
(*Toll slowly*)
"'Las! the noble heart," they thought: "he, in sooth, is grief-distraught:
Would we stood here with the foe!"

LIX.

But a fire flashed from his eye 'twixt their thought and their reply,—
(*Toll slowly*)
"Have ye so much time to waste? We who ride here must ride fast
As we wish our foes to fly."

LX.

They have fetched the steed with care, in the harness he did wear,
(*Toll slowly*)
Past the court, and through the doors, across the rushes of the floors;
But they goad him up the stair.

LXI.

Then, from out her bower chambère, did the Duchess May repair:
(*Toll slowly*)
"Tell me now what is your need," said the lady, "of this steed,
That ye goad him up the stair?"

LXII.

Calm she stood; unbodkined through fell her dark hair to her shoe;
(Toll slowly)
And the smile upon her face, ere she left the tiring-glass,
Had not time enough to go.

LXIII.

"Get thee back, sweet Duchess May! hope is gone like yesterday:"
(Toll slowly)
"One half-hour completes the breach; and thy lord grows wild of speech—
Get thee in, sweet lady, and pray!

LXIV.

"In the east tower, high'st of all, loud he cries for steed from stall:"
(Toll slowly)
"He would ride as far," quoth he, "as for love and victory,
Though he rides the castle-wall."

LXV.

"And we fetch the steed from stall, up where never a hoof did fall"—
(Toll slowly)
"Wifely prayer meets deathly need: may the sweet heavens hear thee plead
If he rides the castle-wall!"

LXVI.

Low she dropt her head, and lower, till her hair coiled on the floor,
(Toll slowly)
And tear after tear you heard fall distinct as any word
Which you might be listening for.

LXVII.

"Get thee in, thou soft ladye! here is never a place for thee!"
(Toll slowly)
"Braid thine hair, and clasp thy gown, that thy beauty in its moan
May find grace with Leigh of Leigh."

LXVIII.

She stood up in bitter case, with a pale yet steady face,
(Toll slowly)
Like a statue thunderstruck, which, though quivering, seems to look
Right against the thunder-place.

LXIX.

And her foot trod in with pride her own tears i' the stone beside:
(Toll slowly)
"Go to, faithful friends, go to! judge no more what ladies do,
No, nor how their lords may ride!"

LXX.

Then the good steed's rein she took, and his neck did kiss and stroke:
(Toll slowly)
Soft he neighed to answer her, and then followed up the stair
  For the love of her sweet look.

LXXI.

Oh, and steeply, steeply wound up the narrow stair around,
(Toll slowly)
Oh, and closely, closely speeding, step by step beside her treading,
  Did he follow, meek as hound.

LXXII.

On the east tower, high'st of all,—there, where never a hoof did fall,—
(Toll slowly)
Out they swept, a vision steady, noble steed and lovely lady,
  Calm as if in bower or stall.

LXXIII.

Down she knelt at her lord's knee, and she looked up silently,
(Toll slowly)
And he kissed her twice and thrice, for that look within her eyes
  Which he could not bear to see.

LXXIV.

Quoth he, "Get thee from this strife, and the sweet saints bless thy life!"
(Toll slowly)
"In this hour I stand in need of my noble red-roan steed,
  But no more of my noble wife."

LXXV.

Quoth she, "Meekly have I done all thy biddings under sun;"
(Toll slowly)
"But by all my womanhood, which is proved so, true and good,
  I will never do this one.

LXXVI.

"Now by womanhood's degree and by wifehood's verity,"
(Toll slowly)
"In this hour, if thou hast need of thy noble red-roan steed,
  Thou hast also need of *me*.

LXXVII.

"By this golden ring ye see on this lifted hand pardiè,"
(Toll slowly)
"If this hour, on castle-wall can be room for steed from stall,
  Shall be also room for *me*.

LXXVIII.

"So the sweet saints with me be!" (did she utter solemnly)
   (*Toll slowly*)
"If a man, this eventide, on this castle-wall will ride,
   He shall ride the same with *me*."

LXXIX.

Oh, he sprang up in the selle, and he laughed out bitter-well,—
   (*Toll slowly*)
"Wouldst thou ride among the leaves, as we used on other eves,
   To hear chime a vesper-bell?"

LXXX.

She clung closer to his knee—"Ay, beneath the cypress-tree!"
   (*Toll slowly*)
"Mock me not; for otherwhere than along the greenwood fair
   Have I ridden fast with thee.

LXXXI.

"Fast I rode with new-made vows from my angry kinsman's house:"
   (*Toll slowly*)
"What! and would you men should reck that I dared more for love's sake
   As a bride than as a spouse?

LXXXII.

"What! and would you it should fall, as a proverb, before all,"
   (*Toll slowly*)
"That a bride may keep your side while through castle-gate you ride,
   Yet eschew the castle-wall?"

LXXXIII.

Ho! the breach yawns into ruin, and roars up against her suing,
   (*Toll slowly*)
With the inarticulate din, and the dreadful falling-in—
   Shrieks of doing and undoing!

LXXXIV.

Twice he wrung her hands in twain; but the small hands closed again.
   (*Toll slowly*)
Back he reined the steed—back, back! but she trailed along his track
   With a frantic clasp and strain.

LXXXV.

Evermore the foemen pour through the crash of window and door,
   (*Toll slowly*)
And the shouts of Leigh and Leigh, and the shrieks of "Kill!" and "Flee!"
   Strike up clear amid the roar.

LXXXVI.

Thrice he wrung her hands in twain; but they closed and clung again,
      (*Toll slowly*)
While she clung, as one, withstood, clasps a Christ upon the rood,
  In a spasm of deathly pain.

LXXXVII.

She clung wild, and she clung mute, with her shuddering lips half-shut;
      (*Toll slowly*)
Her head fallen as half in swound, hair and knee swept on the ground,
  She clung wild to stirrup and foot.

LXXXVIII.

Back he reined his steed back-thrown on the slippery coping-stone;
      (*Toll slowly*)
Back the iron hoofs did grind on the battlement behind,
  Whence a hundred feet went down;

LXXXIX.

And his heel did press and goad on the quivering flank bestrode,—
      (*Toll slowly*)
"Friends and brothers, save my wife! Pardon, sweet, in change for life;
  But I ride alone to God."

XC.

Straight, as if the holy name had upbreathed her like a flame,
      (*Toll slowly*)
She upsprang, she rose upright, in his selle she sate in sight.
  By her love she overcame.

XCI.

And her head was on his breast, where she smiled as one at rest,—
      (*Toll slowly*)
"Ring," she cried, "O vesper-bell, in the beechwood's old chapelle,
  But the passing-bell rings best!"

XCII.

They have caught out at the rein which Sir Guy threw loose, in vain;
      (*Toll slowly*)
For the horse, in stark despair, with his front hoofs poised in air,
  On the last verge rears amain.

XCIII.

Now he hangs, he rocks between, and his nostrils curdle in;
      (*Toll slowly*)
Now he shivers head and hoof, and the flakes of foam fall off,
  And his face grows fierce and thin;

XCIV.

And a look of human woe from his staring eyes did go;
(*Toll slowly*)
And a sharp cry uttered he, in a foretold agony
Of the headlong death below;

XCV.

And, "Ring, ring, thou passing-bell," still she cried, "i' the old chapelle!"
(*Toll slowly*)
Then back-toppling, crashing back, a dead weight flung out to wrack,
Horse and riders overfell.

———————

I.

Oh, the little birds sang east, and the little birds sang west,
(*Toll slowly*)
And I read this ancient Rhyme in the churchyard, while the chime
Slowly tolled for one at rest.

II.

The abeles moved in the sun, and the river smooth did run,
(*Toll slowly*)
And the ancient Rhyme rang strange, with its passion and its change,
Here, where all done lay undone.

III.

And beneath a willow-tree I a little grave did see,
(*Toll slowly*)
Where was graved, "HERE UNDEFILED, LIETH MAUD, A THREE-YEAR CHILD,
EIGHTEEN HUNDRED, FORTY-THREE."

IV.

Then, O spirits, did I say, ye who rode so fast that day,
(*Toll slowly*)
Did star-wheels and angel-wings, with their holy winnowings,
Keep beside you all the way?

V.

Though in passion ye would dash with a blind and heavy crash,
(*Toll slowly*)
Up against the thick-bossed shield of God's judgment in the field,—
Though your heart and brain were rash,—

VI.

Now your will is all unwilled, now your pulses are all stilled,
(*Toll slowly*)
Now ye lie as meek and mild (whereso laid) as Maud, the child
Whose small grave was lately filled.

VII.

Beating heart and burning brow, ye are very patient now,
          (*Toll slowly*)
And the children might be bold to pluck the kingcups from your mould,
   Ere a month had let them grow.

VIII.

And you let the goldfinch sing, in the alder near in spring,—
          (*Toll slowly*)
Let her build her nest, and sit all the three weeks out on it,
   Murmuring not at any thing.

IX.

In your patience ye are strong; cold and heat ye take not wrong:
          (*Toll slowly*)
When the trumpet of the angel blows eternity's evangel,
   Time will seem to you not long.

X.

Oh, the little birds sang east, and the little birds sang west,
          (*Toll slowly*)
And I said in under-breath, "All our life is mixed with death,
   And who knoweth which is best?"

XI.

Oh, the little birds sang east, and the little birds sang west,
          (*Toll slowly*)
And I smiled to think God's greatness flowed around our incompleteness,—
   Round our restlessness, his rest.

THE CRY OF THE CHILDREN

"Φεῦ, φεῦ, τι προσδερκεσθε μ' ομμασιν, τεκνα;"—MEDEA.

I.

Do YE HEAR the children weeping, O my brothers,
   Ere the sorrow comes with years?
They are leaning their young heads against their mothers,
   And *that* cannot stop their tears.
The young lambs are bleating in the meadows;
   The young birds are chirping in the nest;
The young fawns are playing with the shadows;
   The young flowers are blowing toward the west:
But the young, young children, O my brothers!
   They are weeping bitterly.
They are weeping in the playtime of the others,
   In the country of the free.

II.

Do you question the young children in the sorrow,
    Why their tears are falling so?
The old man may weep for his tomorrow
    Which is lost in long ago;
The old tree is leafless in the forest;
    The old year is ending in the frost;
The old wound, if stricken, is the sorest;
    The old hope is hardest to be lost:
But the young, young children, O my brothers!
    Do you ask them why they stand
Weeping sore before the bosoms of their mothers,
    In our happy fatherland?

III.

They look up with their pale and sunken faces;
    And their looks are sad to see,
For the man's hoary anguish draws and presses
    Down the cheeks of infancy.
"Your old earth," they say, "is very dreary;
    Our young feet," they say, "are very weak;
Few paces have we taken, yet are weary;
    Our grave-rest is very far to seek.
Ask the aged why they weep, and not the children;
    For the outside earth is cold,
And we young ones stand without in our bewildering,
    And the graves are for the old."

IV.

"True," say the children, "it may happen
    That we die before our time:
Little Alice died last year; her grave is shapen
    Like a snowball in the rime.
We looked into the pit prepared to take her:
    Was no room for any work in the close clay:
From the sleep wherein she lieth, none will wake her,
    Crying, 'Get up, little Alice! it is day.'
If you listen by that grave, in sun and shower,
    With your ear down, little Alice never cries.
Could we see her face, be sure we should not know her,
    For the smile has time for growing in her eyes;
And merry go her moments, lulled and stilled in
    The shroud by the kirk-chime.
It is good when it happens," say the children,
    "That we die before our time."

v.

Alas, alas, the children! They are seeking
    Death in life, as best to have.
They are binding up their hearts away from breaking,
    With a cerement from the grave.
Go out, children, from the mine and from the city;
    Sing out, children, as the little thrushes do;
Pluck your handfuls of the meadow-cowslips pretty;
    Laugh aloud, to feel your fingers let them through.
But they answer, "Are your cowslips of the meadows
    Like our weeds anear the mine?
Leave us quiet in the dark of the coal-shadows,
    From your pleasures fair and fine.

vi.

"For oh!" say the children, "we are weary,
    And we cannot run or leap:
If we cared for any meadows, it were merely
    To drop down in them, and sleep.
Our knees tremble sorely in the stooping;
    We fall upon our faces, trying to go;
And, underneath our heavy eyelids drooping,
    The reddest flower would look as pale as snow;
For all day we drag our burden tiring
    Through the coal-dark, underground;
Or all day we drive the wheels of iron
    In the factories, round and round.

vii.

"For all day the wheels are droning, turning;
    Their wind comes in our faces,
Till our hearts turn, our heads with pulses burning,
    And the walls turn in their places.
Turns the sky in the high window blank and reeling,
    Turns the long light that drops adown the wall,
Turn the black flies that crawl along the ceiling,—
    All are turning, all the day, and we with all.
And all day the iron wheels are droning,
    And sometimes we could pray,
'O ye wheels' (breaking out in a mad moaning),
    'Stop! be silent for to-day!' "

viii.

Ay, be silent! Let them hear each other breathing
    For a moment, mouth to mouth;
Let them touch each other's hands, in a fresh wreathing
    Of their tender human youth;

Let them feel that this cold metallic motion
    Is not all the life God fashions or reveals;
Let them prove their living souls against the notion
    That they live in you, or under you, O wheels!
Still, all day, the iron wheels go onward,
    Grinding life down from its mark;
And the children's souls, which God is calling sunward,
    Spin on blindly in the dark.

IX.

Now tell the poor young children, O my brothers,
    To look up to Him, and pray;
So the blessed One who blesseth all the others
    Will bless them another day.
They answer, "Who is God, that he should hear us
    While the rushing of the iron wheels is stirred?
When we sob aloud, the human creatures near us
    Pass by, hearing not, or answer not a word;
And *we* hear not (for the wheels in their resounding)
    Strangers speaking at the door.
Is it likely God, with angels singing round him,
    Hears our weeping any more?

X.

"Two words, indeed, of praying we remember;
    And at midnight's hour of harm,
'Our Father,' looking upward in the chamber,
    We say softly for a charm.[1]
We know no other words except 'Our Father;'
    And we think, that, in some pause of angels' song,
God may pluck them with the silence sweet to gather,
    And hold both within his right hand, which is strong
'Our Father!' If he heard us, he would surely
    (For they call him good and mild)
Answer, smiling down the steep world very purely,
    'Come and rest with me, my child.'

XI.

"But, no!" say the children, weeping faster,
    "He is speechless as a stone;
And they tell us, of his image is the master
    Who commands us to work on.

[1] A fact rendered pathetically historical by Mr. Horne's report of his commission. The name of the poet of "Orion" and "Cosmo de' Medici" has, however, a change of associations, and comes in time to remind me that we have some noble poetic heat of literature still, however open to the reproach of being somewhat gelid in our humanity.—1844.

Go to!" say the children,—"up in heaven,
  Dark, wheel-like, turning clouds are all we find.
Do not mock us: grief has made us unbelieving:
  We look up for God; but tears have made us blind."
Do you hear the children weeping and disproving,
  O my brothers, what ye preach?
For God's possible is taught by his world's loving—
  And the children doubt of each.

XII.

And well may the children weep before you!
  They are weary ere they run;
They have never seen the sunshine, nor the glory
  Which is brighter than the sun.
They know the grief of man, without its wisdom;
  They sink in man's despair, without its calm;
Are slaves, without the liberty in Christdom;
  Are martyrs, by the pang without the palm:
Are worn as if with age, yet unretrievingly
  The harvest of its memories cannot reap;
Are orphans of the earthly love and heavenly—
  Let them weep! let them weep!

XIII.

They look up with their pale and sunken faces,
  And their look is dread to see.
For they mind you of their angels in high places,
  With eyes turned on Deity.
"How long," they say, "how long, O cruel nation,
  Will you stand, to move the world on a child's heart,—
Stifle down with a mailed heel its palpitation,
  And tread onward to your throne amid the mart?
Our blood splashes upward, O gold-heaper,
  And your purple shows your path!
But the child's sob in the silence curses deeper
  Than the strong man in his wrath."

AN ISLAND

"All goeth but Goddis will."—OLD POET.

I.

MY DREAM is of an island place,
  Which distant seas keep lonely,—
A little island on whose face
  The stars are watchers only:
Those bright, still stars! they need not seem
Brighter or stiller in my dream.

II.

An island full of hills and dells,
　　All rumpled and uneven
With green recesses, sudden swells,
　　And odorous valleys driven
So deep and straight, that always there
The wind is cradled to soft air.

III.

Hills running up to heaven for light
　　Through woods that half-way ran,
As if the wild earth mimicked right
　　The wilder heart of man:
Only it shall be greener far,
And gladder, than hearts ever are.

IV.

More like, perhaps, that mountain piece
　　Of Dante's paradise,
Disrupt to an hundred hills like these,
　　In falling from the skies;
Bringing within it all the roots
Of heavenly trees and flowers and fruits:

V.

For, saving where the gray rocks strike
　　Their javelins up the azure,
Or where deep fissures, miser-like,
　　Hoard up some fountain treasure,
(And e'en in them, stoop down and hear
Leaf sounds with water in your ear),

VI.

The place is all awave with trees,—
　　Limes, myrtles purple-beaded,
Acacias having drunk the lees
　　Of the night-dew, faint-headed,
And wan gray olive-woods, which seem
The fittest foliage for a dream.

VII.

Trees, trees, on all sides! They combine
　　Their plumy shades to throw,
Through whose clear fruit and blossom fine
　　Whene'er the sun may go,
The ground beneath he deeply stains,
As passing through cathedral panes.

VIII.

But little needs this earth of ours
  That shining from above her,
When many pleiades of flowers
  (Not one lost) star her over;
The rays of their unnumbered hues
Being all refracted by the dews.

IX.

Wide-petalled plants that boldly drink
  The Amreeta of the sky,
Shut bells that dull with rapture sink,
  And lolling buds, half shy:
I cannot count them, but between
Is room for grass and mosses green,

X.

And brooks, that glass in different strengths
  All colors in disorder,
Or, gathering up their silver lengths
  Beside their winding border,
Sleep, haunted through the slumber hidden,
By lilies white as dreams in Eden.

XI.

Nor think each archèd tree with each
  Too closely interlaces
To admit of vistas out of reach,
  And broad moon-lighted places,
Upon whose sward the antlered deer
May view their double image clear.

XII.

For all this island's creature-full
  (Kept happy not by halves),
Mild cows, that at the vine-wreaths pull,
  Then low back at their calves
With tender lowings, to approve
The warm mouths milking them for love.

XIII.

Free, gamesome horses, antelopes,
  And harmless leaping leopards,
And buffaloes upon the slopes,
  And sheep unruled by shepherds;
Hares, lizards, hedgehogs, badgers, mice,
Snakes, squirrels, frogs, and butterflies.

XIV.

And birds that live there in a crowd,
   Horned owls, rapt nightingales,
Larks bold with heaven, and peacocks proud,
   Self-sphered in those grand tails;
All creatures glad and safe, I deem:
No guns nor springes in my dream!

XV.

The island's edges are a-wing
   With trees that overbranch
The sea with song-birds welcoming
   The curlews to green change;
And doves from half-closed lids espy
The red and purple fish go by.

XVI.

One dove is answering in trust
   The water every minute,
Thinking so soft a murmur must
   Have her mate's cooing in it:
So softly doth earth's beauty round
Infuse itself in ocean's sound.

XVII.

My sanguine soul bounds forwarder
   To meet the bounding waves;
Beside them straightway I repair,
   To live within the caves:
And near me two or three may dwell,
Whom dreams fantastic please as well.

XVIII.

Long winding caverns, glittering far
   Into a crystal distance!
Through clefts of which, shall many a star
   Shine clear without resistance!
And carry down its rays the smell
Of flowers above invisible.

XIX.

I said that two or three might choose
   Their dwelling near mine own,—
Those who would change man's voice and use,
   For Nature's way and tone;
Man's veering heart and careless eyes,
For Nature's steadfast sympathies.

XX.

Ourselves, to meet her faithfulness,
 Shall play a faithful part;
Her beautiful shall ne'er address
 The monstrous at our heart:
Her musical shall ever touch
Something within us also such.

XXI.

Yet shall she not our mistress live,
 As doth the moon of ocean,
Though gently as the moon she give
 Our thoughts a light and motion:
More like a harp of many lays,
Moving its master while he plays.

XXII.

No sod in all that island doth
 Yawn open for the dead;
No wind hath borne a traitor's oath;
 No earth, a mourner's tread:
We cannot say by stream or shade,
"I suffered *here,* was *here* betrayed."

XXIII.

Our only "farewell" we shall laugh
 To shifting cloud or hour,
And use our only epitaph
 To some bud turned a flower:
Our only tears shall serve to prove
Excess in pleasure or in love.

XXIV.

Our fancies shall their plumage catch
 From fairest island-birds,
Whose eggs let young ones out at hatch,
 Born singing! then our words
Unconsciously shall take the dyes
Of those prodigious fantasies.

XXV.

Yea, soon, no consonant unsmooth
 Our smile-tuned lips shall reach;
Sounds sweet as Hellas spake in youth
 Shall glide into our speech:
(What music, certes, can you find
As soft as voices which are kind?)

XXVI.

And often, by the joy without
  And in us overcome,
We, through our musing, shall let float
  Such poems—sitting dumb—
As Pindar might have writ if he
Had tended sheep in Arcady;

XXVII.

Or Æschylus—the pleasant fields
  He died in, longer knowing;
Or Homer, had men's sins and shields
  Been lost in Meles flowing;
Or poet Plato, had the undim
Unsetting Godlight broke on him.

XXVIII.

Choose me the cave most worthy choice,
  To make a place for prayer,
And I will choose a praying voice
  To pour our spirits there:
How silverly the echoes run!
Thy will be done,—thy will be done.

XXIX.

Gently yet strangely uttered words!
  They lift me from my dream;
The island fadeth with its swards
  That did no more than seem:
The streams are dry, no sun could find—
The fruits are fallen without wind.

XXX.

So oft the doing of God's will
  Our foolish wills undoeth!
And yet what idle dream breaks ill,
  Which morning-light subdueth?
And who would murmur and misdoubt,
When God's great sunrise finds him out?

THE SOUL'S TRAVELLING

Ηδη νοερους
Πετασαι ταρσους.
SYNESIUS.

I.

I DWELL amid the city ever.
The great humanity which beats
Its life along the stony streets,
Like a strong and unsunned river
In a self-made course,
I sit and hearken while it rolls.
Very sad and very hoarse
Certes is the flow of souls;
Infinitest tendencies:
By the finite prest and pent,
In the finite, turbulent:
How we tremble in surprise
When sometimes, with an awful sound,
God's great plummet strikes the ground!

II.

The champ of the steeds on the silver bit
As they whirl the rich man's carriage by;
The beggar's whine as he looks at it—
But it goes too fast for charity;
The trail on the street of the poor man's broom,
That the lady who walks to her palace-home,
On her silken skirt may catch no dust;
The tread of the business-men who must
Count their per-cents by the paces they take;
The cry of the babe unheard of its mother
Though it lie on her breast, while she thinks of the other
Laid yesterday where it will not wake;
The flower-girl's prayer to buy roses and pinks,
Held out in the smoke, like stars by day;
The gin-door's oath that hollowly chinks
Guilt upon grief, and wrong upon hate;
The cabman's cry to get out of the way;
The dustman's call down the area-grate;
The young maid's jest, and the old wife's scold,
The haggling talk of the boys at a stall,
The fight in the street which is backed for gold,
The plea of the lawyers in Westminster Hall;

The drop on the stones of the blind man's staff
As he trades in his own grief's sacredness;
The brothel shriek, and the Newgate laugh;
The hum upon 'Change, and the organ's grinding;
(The grinder's face being nevertheless
Dry and vacant of even woe
While the children's hearts are leaping so
At the merry music's winding);
The black-plumed funeral's creeping train
Long and slow (and yet they will go
As fast as life, though it hurry and strain!)
Creeping the populous houses through,
And nodding their plumes at either side,—
At many a house where an infant, new
To the sunshiny world, has just struggled and cried,—
At many a house where sitteth a bride
Trying to-morrow's coronals
With a scarlet blush to-day:
　　Slowly creep the funerals,
As none should hear the noise, and say,
"The living, the living, must go away
　　　To multiply the dead."
　　Hark! an upward shout is sent:
In grave, strong joy from tower to steeple
　　　The bells ring out,
The trumpets sound, the people shout,
The young queen goes to her parliament;
She turneth round her large blue eyes,
More bright with childish memories
Than royal hope, upon the people;
On either side she bows her head
　　Lowly, with a queenly grace,
And smile most trusting-innocent,
As if she smiled upon her mother;
The thousands press before each other
　　　To bless her to her face;
And booms the deep majestic voice
Through trump and drum, "May the queen rejoice
　　　In the people's liberties."

III.

　　I dwell amid the city,
　　And hear the flow of souls in act and speech,
For pomp or trade, for merrymake or folly:
I hear the confluence and sum of each,
　　And that is melancholy!

Thy voice is a complaint, O crownèd city,
The blue sky covering thee like God's great pity.

IV.

O blue sky! it mindeth me
Of places where I used to see
Its vast unbroken circle thrown
From the far pale-peakèd hill
Out to the last verge of ocean,
As by God's arm it were done
Then for the first time, with the emotion
Of that first impulse on it still.
Oh we spirits fly at will
Faster than the wingèd steed
Whereof in old book we read,
With the sunlight foaming back
From his flanks to a misty wrack,
And his nostril reddening proud
As he breasteth the steep thundercloud,—
Smoother than Sabrina's chair,
Gliding up from wave to air,
While she smileth debonair
Yet holy, coldly and yet brightly,
Like her own mooned waters nightly,
Through her dripping hair.

V.

Very fast and smooth we fly,
Spirits, though the flesh be by:
All looks feed not from the eye,
Nor all hearings from the ear:
We can hearken and espy
Without either, we can journey
Bold and gay as knight to tourney;
And, though we wear no visor down
To dark our countenance, the foe
Shall never chafe us as we go.

VI.

I am gone from peopled town!
It passeth its street-thunder round
My body which yet hears no sound;
For now another sound, another
Vision, my soul's senses have—
O'er a hundred valleys deep
Where the hills' green shadows sleep,

Scarce known because the valley-trees
Cross those upland images,
O'er a hundred hills each other,
Watching to the western wave,
I have travelled,—I have found
The silent, lone, remembered ground.

VII.

I have found a grassy niche
Hollowed in a seaside-hill,
As if the ocean-grandeur, which
Is aspectable from the place,
Had struck the hill as with a mace,
Sudden and cleaving. You might fill
That little nook with the little cloud
Which sometimes lieth by the moon
To beautify a night of June,—
A cavelike nook, which, opening all
To the wide sea, is disallowed
From its own earth's sweet pastoral;
Cavelike, but roofless overhead,
And made of verdant banks instead
Of any rocks, with flowerets spread
Instead of spar and stalactite,
Cowslips and daisies gold and white:
Such pretty flowers on such green sward,
You think the sea they look toward
Doth serve them for another sky,
As warm and blue as that on high.

VIII.

And in this hollow is a seat,
And when you shall have crept to it,
Slipping down the banks too steep
To be o'erbrowsèd by the sheep,
Do not think—though at your feet
The cliff's disrupt—you shall behold
The line where earth and ocean meet:
You sit too much above to view
The solemn confluence of the two:
You can hear them as they greet,
You can hear that evermore
Distance-softened noise more old
Than Nereid's singing, the tide spent
Joining soft issues with the shore
In harmony of discontent;

And when you hearken to the grave
Lamenting of the underwave,
You must believe in earth's communion,
Albeit you witness not the union.

IX.

Except that sound, the place is full
Of silences, which, when you cull
By any word, it thrills you so,
That presently you let them grow
To meditation's fullest length
Across your soul, with a soul's strength:
And, as they touch your soul, they borrow
Both of its grandeur and its sorrow,
That deathly odor which the clay
Leaves on its deathlessness alway.

X.

Alway! alway? must this be?
Rapid Soul from city gone,
Dost thou carry inwardly
What doth make the city's moan?
Must this deep sigh of thine own
Haunt thee with humanity?
Green visioned banks that are too steep
To be o'erbrowsèd by the sheep,
May all sad thoughts adown you creep
Without a shepherd? Mighty sea,
Can we dwarf thy magnitude
And fit it to our straitest mood?
O fair, fair Nature, are we thus
Impotent and querulous
Among thy workings glorious,
Wealth and sanctities, that still
Leave us vacant and defiled,
And wailing like a soft-kissed child,
Kissed soft against his will?

XI.

God, God!
With a child's voice I cry,
Weak, sad, confidingly—
God, God!
Thou knowest, eyelids raised not always up
Unto thy love (as none of ours are) droop
As ours o'er many a tear;

Thou knowest, though thy universe is broad,
Two little tears suffice to cover all;
Thou knowest, thou who art so prodigal
Of beauty, we are oft but stricken deer
Expiring in the woods, that care for none
Of those delightsome flowers they die upon.

XII.

O blissful Mouth which breathed the mournful breath
We name our souls, self-spoilt! by that strong passion
Which paled thee once with sighs, by that strong death
Which made thee once unbreathing, from the wrack
Themselves have called around them, called them back,—
Back to thee in continuous aspiration!
    For here, O Lord,
For here they travel vainly, vainly pass
From city-pavement to untrodden sward
Where the lark finds her deep nest in the grass
Cold with the earth's last dew. Yea, very vain
The greatest speed of all these souls of men
Unless they travel upward to the throne
Where sittest Thou the satisfying One,
With help for sins and holy perfectings
For all requirements; while the archangel, raising
Unto thy face his full ecstatic gazing,
Forgets the rush and rapture of his wings.

MAN AND NATURE

A sad man on a summer day
Did look upon the earth, and say,—
"Purple cloud the hilltop binding;
Folded hills, the valleys wind in;
Valleys, with fresh streams among you;
Streams, with bosky trees along you;
Trees, with many birds and blossoms;
Birds, with music-trembling bosoms;
Blossoms, dropping dews that wreathe you
To your fellow-flowers beneath you;
Flowers, that constellate on earth;
Earth, that shakest to the mirth
Of the merry Titan ocean,
All his shining hair in motion!—
Why am I thus the only one
Who can be dark beneath the sun?"

But, when the summer day was past,
He looked to heaven, and smiled at last,
Self-answered so,—
                "Because, O cloud,
Pressing with thy crumpled shroud
Heavily on mountain-top;
Hills, that almost seem to drop,
Stricken with a misty death,
To the valleys underneath;
Valleys, sighing with the torrent;
Waters, streaked with branches horrent;
Branchless trees, that shake your head
Wildly o'er your blossoms spread
Where the common flowers are found;
Flowers, with foreheads to the ground;
Ground, that shriekest while the sea
With his iron smiteth thee,—
I am, besides, the only one
Who can be bright *without* the sun."

TO FLUSH, MY DOG

I.

LOVING FRIEND, the gift of one
Who her own true faith has run
    Through thy lower nature,[1]
Be my benediction said
With my hand upon thy head,
    Gentle fellow-creature!

II.

Like a lady's ringlets brown,
Flow thy silken ears adown
    Either side demurely
Of thy silver-suited breast,
Shining out from all the rest
    Of thy body purely.

III.

Darkly brown thy body is,
Till the sunshine striking this
    Alchemize its dulness,

[1] This dog was the gift of my dear and admired friend, Miss Mitford, and belongs to the beautiful race she has rendered celebrated among English and American readers. The Flushes have their laurels as well as the Cæsars, the chief

When the sleek curls manifold
Flash all over into gold
  With a burnished fulness.

IV.

Underneath my stroking hand,
Startled eyes of hazel bland
  Kindling, growing larger,
Up thou leapest with a spring,
Full of prank and curvetting,
  Leaping like a charger.

V.

Leap! thy broad tail waves a light,
Leap! thy slender feet are bright,
  Canopied in fringes;
Leap! those tasselled ears of thine
Flicker strangely, fair and fine
  Down their golden inches.

VI.

Yet, my pretty sportive friend,
Little is't to such an end
  That I praise thy rareness:
Other dogs may be thy peers
Haply in these drooping ears
  And this glossy fairness.

VII.

But of *thee* it shall be said,
This dog watched beside a bed
  Day and night unweary,—
Watched within a curtained room
Where no sunbeam brake the gloom,
  Round the sick and dreary.

VIII.

Roses, gathered for a vase,
In that chamber died apace,
  Beam and breeze resigning:
This dog only waited on,
Knowing, that, when light is gone,
  Love remains for shining.

difference (at least the very head and front of it) consisting, perhaps, in the bald head of the latter under the crown.—1844.

IX.

Other dogs in thymy dew
Tracked the hares, and followed through
    Sunny moor or meadow:
This dog only crept and crept
Next a languid cheek that slept,
    Sharing in the shadow.

X.

Other dogs of loyal cheer
Bounded at the whistle clear,
    Up the woodside hieing:
This dog only watched in reach
Of a faintly uttered speech,
    Or a louder sighing.

XI.

And if one or two quick tears
Dropped upon his glossy ears,
    Or a sigh came double,
Up he sprang in eager haste,
Fawning, fondling, breathing fast,
    In a tender trouble.

XII.

And this dog was satisfied
If a pale, thin hand would glide
    Down his dewlaps sloping,—
Which he pushed his nose within,
After,—platforming his chin
    On the palm left open.

XIII.

This dog, if a friendly voice
Call him now to blither choice
    Than such chamber-keeping,
"Come out!" praying from the door,
Presseth backward as before,
    Up against me leaping.

XIV.

Therefore to this dog will I,
Tenderly not scornfully,
    Render praise and favor:
With my hand upon his head,
Is my benediction said
    Therefore and forever.

xv.

And because he loves me so,
Better than his kind will do
  Often man or woman,
Give I back more love again
Than dogs often take of men,
  Leaning from my human.

xvi.

Blessings on thee, dog of mine,
Pretty collars make thee fine,
  Sugared milk make fat thee!
Pleasures wag on in thy tail,
Hands of gentle motion fail
  Nevermore to pat thee!

xvii.

Downy pillow take thy head,
Silken coverlet bestead,
  Sunshine help thy sleeping!
No fly's buzzing wake thee up,
No man break thy purple cup
  Set for drinking deep in!

xviii.

Whiskered cats aroynted flee,
Sturdy stoppers keep from thee
  Cologne distillations;
Nuts lie in thy path for stones,
And thy feast-day macaroons
  Turn to daily rations!

xix.

Mock I thee, in wishing weal?
Tears are in my eyes to feel
  Thou art made so straitly:
Blessings need must straiten too,—
Little canst thou joy or do,
  Thou who lovest *greatly*.

xx.

Yet be blessèd to the height
Of all good and all delight
  Pervious to thy nature;
Only *loved* beyond that line,
With a love that answers thine,
  Loving fellow-creature!

THE DESERTED GARDEN

I MIND ME, in the days departed,
How often underneath the sun
With childish bounds I used to run
 To a garden long deserted.

The beds and walks were vanished quite;
And whereso'er had struck the spade,
The greenest grasses Nature laid
 To sanctify her right.

I called the place my wilderness,
For no one entered there but I:
The sheep looked in the grass to espy,
 And passed it ne'ertheless.

The trees were interwoven wild,
And spread their boughs enough about
To keep both sheep and shepherd out,
 But not a happy child.

Adventurous joy it was for me!
I crept beneath the boughs, and found
A circle smooth of mossy ground
 Beneath a poplar-tree.

Old garden rose-trees hedged it in,
Bedropt with roses waxen-white
Well satisfied with dew and light,
 And careless to be seen.

Long years ago, it might befall,
When all the garden-flowers were trim,
The grave old gardener prided him
 On these the most of all.

Some lady, stately overmuch,
Here moving with a silken noise,
Has blushed beside them at the voice
 That likened her to such.

And these, to make a diadem,
She often may have plucked and twined,
Half-smiling as it came to mind
 That few would look at *them*.

Oh, little thought that lady proud,
A child would watch her fair white rose,
When buried lay her whiter brows,
    And silk was changed for shroud!

Nor thought that gardener (full of scorns
For men unlearned and simple phrase),
A child would bring it all its praise
    By creeping through the thorns.

To me upon my low moss seat,
Though never a dream the roses sent
Of science or love's compliment,
    I ween they smelt as sweet.

It did not move my grief to see
The trace of human step departed:
Because the garden was deserted,
    The blither place for me.

Friends, blame me not! a narrow ken
Has childhood 'twixt the sun and sward:
We draw the moral afterward,
    We feel the gladness then.

And gladdest hours for me did glide
In silence at the rose-tree wall:
A thrush made gladness musical
    Upon the other side.

Nor he nor I did e'er incline
To peck or pluck the blossoms white:
How should I know but roses might
    Lead lives as glad as mine?

To make my hermit-home complete,
I brought clear water from the spring
Praised in its own low murmuring,
    And cresses glossy wet.

And so, I thought, my likeness grew
(Without the melancholy tale)
To "gentle hermit of the dale,"
    And Angelina too.

For oft I read within my nook
Such minstrel stories, till the breeze

Made sounds poetic in the trees,
And then I shut the book.

If I shut this wherein I write,
I hear no more the wind athwart
Those trees, nor feel that childish heart
Delighting in delight.

My childhood from my life is parted,
My footstep from the moss which drew
Its fairy circle round: anew
The garden is deserted.

Another thrush may there rehearse
The madrigals which sweetest are:
No more for me! myself afar
Do sing a sadder verse.

Ah me, ah me! when erst I lay
In that child's-nest so greenly wrought,
I laughed unto myself, and thought
"The time will pass away."

And still I laughed, and did not fear
But that, whene'er was passed away
The childish time, some happier play
My womanhood would cheer.

I knew the time would pass away,
And yet, beside the rose-tree wall,
Dear God, how seldom, if at all,
Did I look up to pray!

The time is past; and now that grows
The cypress high among the trees,
And I behold white sepulchres,
As well as the white rose,—

When graver, meeker thoughts are given,
And I have learnt to lift my face,
Reminded how earth's greenest place
The color draws from heaven,—

It something saith for earthly pain,
But more for heavenly promise free,
That I who was, would shrink to be
That happy child again.

SONNETS

☆

GRIEF

I TELL YOU hopeless grief is passionless;
That only men incredulous of despair,
Half-taught in anguish, through the midnight air
Beat upward to God's throne in loud access
Of shrieking and reproach. Full desertness,
In souls as countries, lieth silent-bare
Under the blanching, vertical eye-glare
Of the absolute heavens. Deep-hearted man, express
Grief for thy dead in silence like to death—
Most like a monumental statue set
In everlasting watch and moveless woe
Till itself crumble to the dust beneath.
Touch it; the marble eyelids are not wet:
If it could weep, it could arise and go.

THE TWO SAYINGS

Two SAYINGS of the Holy Scriptures beat
Like pulses in the church's brow and breast;
And by them we find rest in our unrest,
And, heart-deep in salt tears, do yet entreat,
God's fellowship as if on heavenly seat.
The first is, JESUS WEPT, whereon is prest
Full many a sobbing face that drops its best
And sweetest waters on the record sweet:
And one is where the Christ, denied and scorned,
LOOKED UPON PETER. Oh, to render plain,
By help of having loved a little, and mourned,
That look of sovran love and sovran pain
Which HE, who could not sin yet suffered, turned
On him who could reject, but not sustain!

THE LOOK

THE Saviour looked on Peter. Ay, no word,
No gesture of reproach: the heavens serene,
Though heavy with armed justice, did not lean
Their thunders that way: the forsaken Lord
Looked only on the traitor. None record

What that look was, none guess; for those who have seen
Wronged lovers loving through a death-pang keen,
Or pale-cheeked martyrs smiling to a sword,
Have missed Jehovah at the judgment-call.
And Peter, from the height of blasphemy,—
"I never knew this man"—did quail and fall
As knowing straight THAT GOD, and turnèd free
And went out speechless from the face of all,
And filled the silence, weeping bitterly.

THE MEANING OF THE LOOK

I THINK that look of Christ might seem to say,
"Thou Peter! art thou, then, a common stone
Which I at last must break my heart upon,
For all God's charge to his high angels may
Guard my foot better? Did I yesterday
Wash *thy* feet, my beloved, that they should run
Quick to deny me 'neath the morning sun?
And do thy kisses, like the rest, betray?
The cock crows coldly.—Go, and manifest
A late contrition, but no bootless fear;
For, when thy final need is dreariest,
Thou shalt not be denied, as I am here:
My voice to God and angels shall attest,
Because I KNOW *this man, let him be clear.*"

ADEQUACY

Now, by the verdure on thy thousand hills,
Belovèd England, doth the earth appear
Quite good enough for men to overbear
The will of God in, with rebellious wills!
We cannot say the morning-sun fulfils
Ingloriously its course, nor that the clear,
Strong stars without significance insphere
Our habitation: we, meantime, our ills
Heap up against this good, and lift a cry
Against this work-day world, this ill-spread feast,
As if ourselves were better certainly
Than what we come to. Maker and High Priest,
I ask thee not my joys to multiply,
Only to make me worthier of the least.

A CHILD'S THOUGHT OF GOD

I.

THEY say that God lives very high;
  But, if you look above the pines,
You cannot see our God; and why?

II.

And, if you dig down in the mines,
  You never see him in the gold;
Though from him all that's glory shines.

. III.

God is so good he wears a fold
  Of heaven and earth across his face,
Like secrets kept for love, untold.

IV.

But still I feel that his embrace
  Slides down by thrills through all
    things made,—
Through sight and sound of every place.

V.

As if my tender mother laid
  On my shut lips her kisses' pressure,
Half waking me at night, and said
  "Who kissed you through the dark,
    dear guesser?"

THE SLEEP

"He giveth His belovèd sleep."—Ps. cxxvii. 2

I.

OF ALL the thoughts of God that are
Borne inward into souls afar
Along the Psalmist's music deep,
Now tell me if that any is,
For gift or grace, surpassing this,—
"He giveth His belovèd sleep."

II.

What would we give to our beloved?
The hero's heart to be unmoved,
The poet's star-tuned harp to sweep,
The patriot's voice to teach and rouse,
The monarch's crown to light the brows?—
He giveth His belovèd sleep.

III.

What do we give to our beloved?
A little faith all undisproved,
A little dust to overweep,
And bitter memories to make
The whole earth blasted for our sake:
He giveth His belovèd sleep.

IV.

"Sleep soft, beloved!" we sometimes say,
Who have no tune to charm away
Sad dreams that through the eyelids creep;
But never doleful dream again
Shall break the happy slumber when
He giveth His belovèd sleep.

V.

O earth, so full of dreary noises!
O men with wailing in your voices!
O delvèd gold the wailers heap!
O strife, O curse, that o'er it fall!
God strikes a silence through you all,
And giveth His belovèd sleep.

VI.

His dews drop mutely on the hill,
His cloud above it saileth still,
Though on its slope men sow and reap:
More softly than the dew is shed,
Or cloud is floated overhead,
He giveth His belovèd sleep.

VII.

Ay, men may wonder while they scan
A living, thinking, feeling man
Confirmed in such a rest to keep;
But angels say, and through the word
I think their happy smile is *heard*,
"He giveth His belovèd sleep."

VIII.

For me, my heart that erst did go
Most like a tired child at a show,
That sees through tears the mummers leap,
Would now its wearied vision close,
Would childlike on His love repose
Who giveth His belovèd sleep.

IX.

And friends, dear friends, when it shall be
That this low breath is gone from me,
And round my bier ye come to weep,
Let one most loving of you all,
Say, "Not a tear must o'er her fall!
He giveth His belovèd sleep."

LESSONS FROM THE GORSE

"To win the secret of a weed's plain heart."—LOWELL.

I.

MOUNTAIN gorses, ever golden,
Cankered not the whole year long,
Do ye teach us to be strong,
Howsoever pricked and holden,
Like your thorny blooms, and so
Trodden on by rain and snow,
Up the hillside of this life, as bleak as where ye grow?

II.

Mountain blossoms, shining blossoms,
Do ye teach us to be glad
When no summer can be had,
Blooming in our inward bosoms?—
Ye whom God preserveth still,
Set as lights upon a hill,
Tokens to the wintry earth that beauty liveth still.

III.

Mountain gorses, do ye teach us
From that academic chair
Canopied with azure air,
That the wisest word man reaches
Is the humblest he can speak?—
Ye who live on mountain peak,
Yet live low along the ground, beside the grasses meek.

IV.

Mountain gorses, since Linnæus
Knelt beside you on the sod,
For your beauty thanking God,
For your teaching, ye should see us
Bowing in prostration new!
Whence arisen, if one or two
Drops be on our cheeks, O world, they are not tears, but dew.

THE LADY'S YES

I.

"Yes," I answered you last night;
"No," this morning, sir, I say:
Colors seen by candle-light
Will not look the same by day.

II.

When the viols played their best,
Lamps above, and laughs below,
Love me sounded like a jest,
Fit for *yes*, or fit for *no*.

III.

Call me false, or call me free,
Vow, whatever light may shine,
No man on your face shall see
Any grief for change on mine.

IV.

Yet the sin is on us both;
Time to dance is not to woo:
Wooing light makes fickle troth,
Scorn of *me* recoils on *you*.

V.

Learn to win a lady's faith
Nobly, as the thing is high,
Bravely, as for life and death,
With a loyal gravity.

VI.

Lead her from the festive boards,
Point her to the starry skies;
Guard her by your truthful words
Pure from courtship's flatteries.

VII.

By your truth she shall be true,
   Ever true, as wives of yore;
And her *yes* once said to you
   SHALL be yes forevermore.

A WOMAN'S SHORTCOMINGS

I.

SHE HAS LAUGHED as softly as if she sighed,
   She has counted six and over,
Of a purse well filled, and a heart well tried—
   Oh each a worthy lover!
They "give her time;" for her soul must slip
   Where the world has set the grooving:
She will lie to none with her fair red lip—
   But love seeks truer loving.

II.

She trembles her fan in a sweetness dumb,
   As her thoughts were beyond recalling,
With a glance for *one*, and a glance for *some*,
   From her eyelids rising and falling;
Speaks common words with a blushful air,
   Hears bold words, unreproving;
But her silence says—what she never will swear—
   And love seeks better loving.

III.

Go, lady, lean to the night-guitar,
   And drop a smile to the bringer,
Then smile as sweetly, when he is far,
   At the voice of an indoor singer.
Bask tenderly beneath tender eyes;
   Glance lightly on their removing;
And join new vows to old perjuries—
   But dare not call it loving.

IV.

Unless you can think, when the song is done,
   No other is soft in the rhythm;
Unless you can feel, when left by one,
   That all men else go with him;
Unless you can know, when unpraised by his breath,
   That your beauty itself wants proving;
Unless you can swear, "For life, for death!"—
   Oh fear to call it loving!

v.

Unless you can muse in a crowd all day,
  On the absent face that fixed you;
Unless you can love, as the angels may,
  With the breadth of heaven betwixt you;
Unless you can dream that his faith is fast,
  Through behoving and unbehoving;
Unless you can *die* when the dream is past—
  Oh never call it loving!

A MAN'S REQUIREMENTS

I.

Love me, sweet, with all thou art,
  Feeling, thinking, seeing;
Love me in the lightest part,
  Love me in full being.

II.

Love me with thine open youth
  In its frank surrender,
With the vowing of thy mouth,
  With its silence tender.

III.

Love me with thine azure eyes,
  Made for earnest granting;
Taking color from the skies,
  Can heaven's truth be wanting?

IV.

Love me with their lids, that fall
  Snow-like at first meeting;
Love me with thine heart, that all
  Neighbors then see beating.

V.

Love me with thine hand stretched out
  Freely, open minded;
Love me with thy loitering foot,
  Hearing one behind it.

VI.

Love me with thy voice, that turns
  Sudden faint above me;
Love me with thy blush, that burns
  When I murmur, *Love me!*

VII.

Love me with thy thinking soul,
  Break it to love-sighing;
Love me with thy thoughts that roll
  On through living—dying.

VIII.

Love me in thy gorgeous airs,
  When the world has crowned thee;
Love me, kneeling at thy prayers,
  With the angels round thee.

IX.

Love me pure, as musers do,
  Up the woodlands shady;
Love me gayly, fast, and true,
  As a winsome lady.

X.

Through all hopes that keep us brave,
  Farther off or nigher;
Love me for the house and grave—
  And for something higher.

XI.

Thus, if thou wilt prove me, dear,
  Woman's love no fable,
I will love *thee*—half a year—
  As a man is able.

INSUFFICIENCY

I.

THERE is no one beside thee, and no one above thee;
  Thou standest alone, as the nightingale sings!
And my words that would praise thee are impotent things,
For none can express thee, though all should approve thee.
  I love thee so, dear, that I only can love thee.

II.

Say, what can I do for thee? Weary thee, grieve thee?
  Lean on thy shoulder, new burdens to add?
  Weep my tears over thee, making thee sad?
Oh, hold me not, love me not! let me retrieve thee.
  I love thee so, dear, that I only can leave thee.

SONNETS FROM THE PORTUGUESE

I.

I THOUGHT once how Theocritus had sung
Of the sweet years, the dear and wished-for years,
Who each one in a gracious hand appears
To bear a gift for mortals, old or young;
And, as I mused it in his antique tongue,
I saw in gradual vision, through my tears,
The sweet, sad years, the melancholy years,
Those of my own life, who by turns had flung
A shadow across me. Straightway I was 'ware,
So weeping, how a mystic shape did move
Behind me, and drew me backward by the hair;
And a voice said in mastery, while I strove,
"Guess now who holds thee?"—"Death," I said. But there
The silver answer rang, "Not Death, but Love."

II.

But only three in all God's universe
Have heard this word thou hast said,—Himself, beside
Thee speaking, and me listening! and replied
One of us . . . *that* was God . . . and laid the curse
So darkly on my eyelids as to amerce
My sight from seeing thee,—that if I had died,
The death-weights placed there would have signified
Less absolute exclusion. "Nay," is worse
From God than from all others, O my friend!
Men could not part us with their worldly jars,
Nor the seas change us, nor the tempests bend;
Our hands would touch for all the mountain-bars:
And, heaven being rolled between us at the end,
We should but vow the faster for the stars.

III.

Unlike are we, unlike, O princely Heart!
Unlike our uses and our destinies.
Our ministering two angels look surprise
On one another as they strike athwart
Their wings in passing. Thou, bethink thee, art
A guest for queens to social pageantries,
With gages from a hundred brighter eyes
Than tears even can make mine, to play thy part
Of chief musician. What hast *thou* to do
With looking from the lattice-lights at me,
A poor, tired, wandering singer, singing through

The dark, and leaning up a cypress-tree?
The chrism is on thine head; on mine the dew:
And Death must dig the level where these agree.

IV.

Thou hast thy calling to some palace-floor,
Most gracious singer of high poems, where
The dancers will break footing, from the care
Of watching up thy pregnant lips for more.
And dost thou lift this house's latch too poor
For hand of thine? and canst thou think, and bear
To let thy music drop here unaware
In folds of golden fulness at my door?
Look up, and see the casement broken in,
The bats and owlets builders in the roof!
My cricket chirps against thy mandolin.
Hush, call no echo up in further proof
Of desolation! there's a voice within
That weeps . . . as thou must sing . . . alone, aloof.

V.

I lift my heavy heart up solemnly,
As once Electra her sepulchral urn,
And, looking in thine eyes, I overturn
The ashes at thy feet. Behold and see
What a great heap of grief lay hid in me,
And how the red wild sparkles dimly burn
Through the ashen grayness. If thy foot in scorn
Could tread them out to darkness utterly,
It might be well, perhaps. But if, instead,
Thou wait beside me for the wind to blow
The gray dust up . . . those laurels on thine head,
O my belovèd, will not shield thee so,
That none of all the fires shall scorch and shred
The hair beneath. Stand farther off, then! Go.

VI.

Go from me. Yet I feel that I shall stand
Henceforward in thy shadow. Nevermore
Alone upon the threshold of my door
Of individual life, I shall command
The uses of my soul, nor lift my hand
Serenely in the sunshine as before,
Without the sense of that which I forbore,—
Thy touch upon the palm. The widest land
Doom takes to part us leaves thy heart in mine
With pulses that beat double. What I do

And what I dream include thee, as the wine
Must taste of its own grapes. And, when I sue
God for myself, he hears that name of thine,
And sees within my eyes the tears of two.

VII.

The face of all the world is changed, ᴵ think,
Since first I heard the footsteps of thy soul
Move still, oh, still, beside me as they stole
Betwixt me and the dreadful outer brink
Of obvious death, where I, who thought to sink,
Was caught up into love, and taught the whole
Of life in a new rhythm. The cup of dole
God gave for baptism, I am fain to drink,
And praise its sweetness, sweet, with thee anear
The names of country, heaven, are changed away
For where thou art or shalt be, there or here;
And this . . . this lute and song . . . loved yesterday,
(The singing angels know) are only dear
Because thy name moves right in what they say.

VIII.

What can I give thee back, O liberal
And princely giver, who hast brought the gold
And purple of thine heart, unstained, untold,
And laid them on the outside of the wall
For such as I do take or leave withal,
In unexpected largesse? Am I cold,
Ungrateful, that, for these most manifold
High gifts, I render nothing back at all?
Not so; not cold, but very poor instead.
Ask God, who knows. For frequent tears have run
The colors from my life, and left so dead
And pale a stuff, it were not fitly done
To give the same as pillow to thy head.
Go farther! let it serve to trample on.

IX.

Can it be right to give what I can give?
To let thee sit beneath the fall of tears
As salt as mine, and hear the sighing years
Re-sighing on my lips renunciative
Through those infrequent smiles which fail to live
For all thy adjurations? Oh, my fears,
That this can scarce be right! We are not peers,
So to be lovers, and I own and grieve
That givers of such gifts as mine are must

Be counted with the ungenerous. Out, alas!
I will not soil thy purple with my dust,
Nor breathe my poison on thy Venice-glass,
Nor give thee any love—which were unjust.
Beloved, I only love thee! let it pass.

x.

Yet love, mere love, is beautiful indeed,
And worthy of acceptation. Fire is bright,
Let temple burn, or flax: an equal light
Leaps in the flame from cedar-plank or weed:
And love is fire. And when I say at need
I love thee . . . mark! . . . *I love thee*—in thy sight
I stand transfigured, glorified aright,
With conscience of the new rays that proceed
Out of my face toward thine. There's nothing low
In love, when love the lowest: meanest creatures
Who love God, God accepts while loving so.
And what I *feel*, across the inferior features
Of what I *am*, doth flash itself, and show
How that great work of love enhances Nature's.

xi.

And therefore, if to love can be desert,
I am not all unworthy. Cheeks as pale
As these you see, and trembling knees that fail
To bear the burden of a heavy heart;
This weary minstrel-life that once was girt
To climb Aornus, and can scarce avail
To pipe now 'gainst the valley nightingale
A melancholy music,—why advert
To these things? O belovèd, it is plain
I am not of thy worth, nor for thy place!
And yet, because I love thee, I obtain
From that same love this vindicating grace,
To live on still in love, and yet in vain,—
To bless thee, yet renounce thee to thy face.

xii.

Indeed, this very love which is my boast,
And which, when rising up from breast to brow,
Doth crown me with a ruby large enow
To draw men's eyes, and prove the inner cost,—
This love even, all my worth, to the uttermost,
I should not love withal, unless that thou
Hadst set me an example, shown me how,
When first thine earnest eyes with mine were crosst,

And love called love. And thus I cannot speak
Of love even, as a good thing of my own;
Thy soul hath snatched up mine all faint and weak,
And placed it by thee on a golden throne,—
And that I love (O soul! we must be meek)
Is by thee only, whom I love alone.

XIII.

And wilt thou have me fashion into speech
The love I bear thee, finding words enough,
And hold the torch out, while the winds are rough,
Between our faces, to cast light on each?
I drop it at thy feet. I cannot teach
My hand to hold my spirit so far off
From myself—me—that I should bring thee proof
In words of love hid in me out of reach.
Nay, let the silence of my womanhood
Commend my woman-love to thy belief,
Seeing that I stand unwon, however wooed,
And rend the garment of my life, in brief,
By a most dauntless, voiceless fortitude,
Lest one touch of this heart convey its grief.

XIV.

If thou must love me, let it be for nought
Except for love's sake only. Do not say
"I love her for her smile, her look, her way
Of speaking gently, for a trick of thought
That falls in well with mine, and certes brought
A sense of pleasant ease on such a day;"
For these things in themselves, belovèd, may
Be changed, or change for thee: and love so wrought
May be unwrought so. Neither love me for
Thine own dear pity's wiping my cheeks dry:
A creature might forget to weep, who bore
Thy comfort long, and lose thy love thereby.
But love me for love's sake, that evermore
Thou mayst love on through love's eternity.

XV.

Accuse me not, beseech thee, that I wear
Too calm and sad a face in front of thine;
For we two look two ways, and cannot shine
With the same sunlight on our brow and hair.
On me thou lookest with no doubting care,
As on a bee shut in a crystalline;
Since sorrow hath shut me safe in love's divine,

And to spread wing, and fly in the outer air,
Were most impossible failure, if I strove
To fail so. But I look on thee, on thee,
Beholding, besides love, the end of love,
Hearing oblivion beyond memory;
As one who sits and gazes from above,
Over the rivers to the bitter sea.

XVI.

And yet, because thou overcomest so,
Because thou art more noble, and like a king,
Thou canst prevail against my fears, and fling
Thy purple round me, till my heart shall grow
Too close against thine heart henceforth to know
How it shook when alone. Why, conquering
May prove as lordly and complete a thing
In lifting upward as in crushing low!
And, as a vanquished soldier yields his sword
To one who lifts him from the bloody earth,
Even so, belovèd, I at last record,
Here ends my strife. If *thou* invite me forth,
I rise above abasement at the word.
Make thy love larger to enlarge my worth.

XVII.

My poet, thou canst touch on all the notes
God set between his After and Before,
And strike up and strike off the general roar
Of the rushing worlds a melody that floats
In a serene air purely. Antidotes
Of medicated music, answering for
Mankind's forlornest uses, thou canst pour
From thence into their ears. God's will devotes
Thine to such ends, and mine to wait on thine.
How, dearest, wilt thou have me for most use?—
A hope to sing by gladly, or a fine
Sad memory, with thy songs to interfuse?
A shade, in which to sing, of palm or pine?
A grave, on which to rest from singing? Choose.

XVIII.

I never gave a lock of hair away
To a man, dearest, except this to thee,
Which now upon my fingers thoughtfully
I ring out to the full brown length, and say
"Take it." My day of youth went yesterday.
My hair no longer bounds to my foot's glee,

Nor plant I it from rose or myrtle-tree,
As girls do, any more: it only may
Now shade on two pale cheeks the mark of tears,
Taught drooping from the head that hangs aside
Through sorrow's trick. I thought the funeral-shears
Would take this first; but love is justified,—
Take it thou, finding pure, from all those years,
The kiss my mother left here when she died.

XIX.

The soul's Rialto hath its merchandise:
I barter curl for curl upon that mart,
And from my poet's forehead to my heart
Receive this lock, which outweighs argosies,—
As purply black as erst to Pindar's eyes
The dim purpureal tresses gloomed athwart
The nine white Muse-brows. For this counterpart, . . .
The bay-crown's shade, belovèd, I surmise,
Still lingers on thy curl, it is so black.
Thus, with a fillet of smooth-kissing breath,
I tie the shadows safe from gliding back,
And lay the gift where nothing hindereth;
Here on my heart, as on thy brow, to lack
No natural heat till mine grows cold in death.

XX.

Belovèd, my belovèd, when I think
That thou wast in the world a year ago,
What time I sate alone here in the snow,
And saw no footprint, heard the silence sink
No moment at thy voice, but, link by link,
Went counting all my chains as if that so
They never could fall off at any blow
Struck by thy possible hand,—why, thus I drink
Of life's great cup of wonder! Wonderful,
Never to feel thee thrill the day or night
With personal act or speech, nor ever cull
Some prescience of thee with the blossoms white
Thou sawest growing! Atheists are as dull,
Who cannot guess God's presence out of sight.

XXI.

Say over again, and yet once over again,
That thou dost love me. Though the word repeated
Should seem a "cuckoo-song," as thou dost treat it,
Remember, never to the hill or plain,
Valley and wood, without her cuckoo-strain

Comes the fresh Spring in all her green completed.
Belovèd, I, amid the darkness greeted
By a doubtful spirit-voice, in that doubt's pain
Cry, "Speak once more--thou lovest!" Who can fear
Too many stars, though each in heaven shall roll,
Too many flowers, though each shall crown the year?
Say thou dost love me, love me, love me; toll
The silver iterance, only minding, dear,
To love me also in silence with thy soul.

XXII.

When our two souls stand up erect and strong,
Face to face, silent, drawing nigh and nigher,
Until the lengthening wings break into fire
At either curvèd point, what bitter wrong
Can the earth do to us, that we should not long
Be here contented? Think. In mounting higher,
The angels would press on us, and aspire
To drop some golden orb of perfect song
Into our deep, dear silence. Let us stay
Rather on earth, belovèd, where the unfit
Contrarious moods of men recoil away,
And isolate pure spirits, and permit
A place to stand and love in for a day,
With darkness and the death-hour rounding it.

XXIII.

Is it indeed so? If I lay here dead,
Wouldst thou miss any life in losing mine?
And would the sun for thee more coldly shine,
Because of grave-damps falling round my head?
I marvelled, my belovèd, when I read
Thy thought so in the letter. I am thine—
But . . . *so* much to thee? Can I pour thy wine
While my hands tremble? Then my soul, instead
Of dreams of death, resumes life's lower range.
Then love me, Love! look on me, breathe on me!
As brighter ladies do not count it strange,
For love, to give up acres and degree,
I yield the grave for thy sake, and exchange
My near sweet view of heaven, for earth with thee!

XXIV.

Let the world's sharpness, like a clasping knife,
Shut in upon itself, and do no harm
In this close hand of love, now soft and warm;
And let us hear no sound of human strife

After the click of the shutting. Life to life—
I lean upon thee, dear, without alarm,
And feel as safe as guarded by a charm
Against the stab of worldlings, who, if rife,
Are weak to injure. Very whitely still
The lilies of our lives may re-assure
Their blossoms from their roots, accessible
Alone to heavenly dews that drop not fewer;
Growing straight, out of man's reach, on the hill.
God only, who made us rich, can make us poor.

xxv.

A heavy heart, belovèd, have I borne
From year to year, until I saw thy face,
And sorrow after sorrow took the place
Of all those natural joys as lightly worn
As the stringed pearls, each lifted in its turn
By a beating heart at dance-time. Hopes apace
Were changed to long despairs, till God's own grace
Could scarcely lift above the world forlorn
My heavy heart. Then *thou* didst bid me bring
And let it drop adown thy calmly great
Deep being. Fast it sinketh, as a thing
Which its own nature doth precipitate,
While thine doth close above it, mediating
Betwixt the stars and the unaccomplished fate.

xxvi.

I lived with visions for my company,
Instead of men and women, years ago,
And found them gentle mates, nor thought to know
A sweeter music than they played to me.
But soon their trailing purple was not free
Of this world's dust, their lutes did silent grow,
And I myself grew faint and blind below
Their vanishing eyes. Then THOU didst come—to be,
Belovèd, what they seemed. Their shining fronts,
Their songs, their splendors (better, yet the same,
As river-water hallowed into fonts,)
Met in thee, and from out thee overcame
My soul with satisfaction of all wants,
Because God's gifts put man's best dreams to shame.

xxvii.

My own belovèd, who hast lifted me
From this drear flat of earth where I was thrown,
And, in betwixt the languid ringlets, blown

A life-breath, till the forehead hopefully
Shines out again, as all the angels see,
Before thy saving kiss! My own, my own,
Who camest to me when the world was gone,
And I, who looked for only God, found *thee!*
I find thee; I am safe and strong and glad.
As one who stands in dewless asphodel
Looks backward on the tedious time he had
In the upper-life, so I, with bosom-swell,
Make witness here, between the good and bad,
That love, as strong as death, retrieves as well.

XXVIII.

My letters! all dead paper, mute and white!
And yet they seem alive, and quivering
Against my tremulous hands which loose the string,
And let them drop down on my knee to-night.
This said, he wished to have me in his sight
Once, as a friend; this fixed a day in spring
To come and touch my hand . . . a simple thing,
Yet I wept for it; this . . . the paper's light . . .
Said, *Dear, I love thee;* and I sank and quailed
As if God's future thundered on my past.
This said, *I am thine,* and so its ink has paled
With lying at my heart that beat too fast;
And this . . . O love, thy words have ill availed
If what this said I dared repeat at last!

XXIX.

I think of thee!—my thoughts do twine and bud
About thee, as wild vines about a tree
Put out broad leaves, and soon there's nought to see
Except the straggling green which hides the wood.
Yet, O my palm-tree! be it understood
I will not have my thoughts instead of thee
Who art dearer, better. Rather, instantly
Renew thy presence: as a strong tree should,
Rustle thy boughs and set thy trunk all bare,
And let these bands of greenery which ensphere thee
Drop heavily down, burst, shattered, everywhere!
Because, in this deep joy to see and hear thee,
And breathe within thy shadow a new air,
I do not think of thee—I am too near thee.

XXX.

I see thine image through my tears to-night,
And yet to-day I saw thee smiling. How

Refer the cause? Belovèd, is it thou
Or I who makes me sad? The acolyte,
Amid the chanted joy and thankful rite,
May so fall flat, with pale insensate brow,
On the altar-stair. I hear thy voice and vow,
Perplexed, uncertain, since thou art out of sight,
As he, in his swooning ears, the choir's amen.
Belovèd, dost thou love? or did I see all
The glory as I dreamed, and fainted when
Too vehement light dilated my ideal,
For my soul's eyes? Will that light come again,
As now these tears come falling hot and real?

XXXI.

Thou comest! all is said without a word.
I sit beneath thy looks, as children do
In the noon sun, with souls that tremble through
Their happy eyelids from an unaverred
Yet prodigal inward joy. Behold, I erred
In that last doubt! and yet I cannot rue
The sin most, but the occasion,—that we two
Should for a moment stand unministered
By a mutual presence. Ah, keep near and close,
Thou dove-like help! and, when my fears would rise,
With thy broad heart serenely interpose:
Brood down with thy divine sufficiencies
These thoughts which tremble when bereft of those,
Like callow birds left desert to the skies.

XXXII.

The first time that the sun rose on thine oath
To love me, I looked forward to the moon
To slacken all those bonds which seemed too soon
And quickly tied to make a lasting troth.
Quick-loving hearts, I thought, may quickly loathe;
And, looking on myself, I seemed not one
For such man's love!—more like an out-of-tune
Worn viol a good singer would be wroth
To spoil his song with, and which, snatched in haste,
Is laid down at the first ill-sounding note.
I did not wrong myself so; but I placed
A wrong on *thee*. For perfect strains may float
'Neath master-hands, from instruments defaced,
And great souls at one stroke may do and dote.

XXXIII.

Yes, call me by my pet name! let me hear
The name I used to run at, when a child,
From innocent play, and leave the cowslips piled,
To glance up in some face that proved me dear
With the look of its eyes. I miss the clear
Fond voices, which, being drawn and reconciled
Into the music of heaven's undefiled,
Call me no longer. Silence on the bier,
While I call God—call God! So let thy mouth
Be heir to those who are now exanimate.
Gather the north flowers to complete the south,
And catch the early love up in the late.
Yes, call me by that name, and I, in truth,
With the same heart, will answer, and not wait.

XXXIV.

With the same heart, I said, I'll answer thee
As those, when thou shalt call me by my name.
Lo, the vain promise! is the same, the same,
Perplexed and ruffled by life's strategy?
When called before, I told how hastily
I dropped my flowers, or brake off from a game,
To run and answer with the smile that came
At play last moment, and went on with me
Through my obedience. When I answer now,
I drop a grave thought, break from solitude;
Yet still my heart goes to thee; ponder how,—
Not as to a single good, but all my good!
Lay thy hand on it, best one, and allow
That no child's foot could run fast as this blood.

XXXV.

If I leave all for thee, wilt thou exchange,
And be all to me? Shall I never miss
Home-talk and blessing, and the common kiss
That comes to each in turn, nor count it strange,
When I lock up, to drop on a new range
Of walls and floors,—another home than this?
Nay, wilt thou fill that place by me which is
Filled by dead eyes too tender to know change?
That's hardest. If to conquer love has tried,
To conquer grief tries more, as all things prove;
For grief, indeed, is love and grief beside.
Alas! I have grieved so, I am hard to love.
Yet love me, wilt thou? Open thine heart wide,
And fold within the wet wings of thy dove.

XXXVI.

When we met first and loved, I did not build
Upon the event with marble. Could it mean
To last,—a love set pendulous between
Sorrow and sorrow? Nay, I rather thrilled,
Distrusting every light that seemed to gild
The onward path, and feared to overlean
A finger even. And, though I have grown serene
And strong since then, I think that God has willed
A still renewable fear . . . O love, O troth . . .
Lest these enclaspèd hands should never hold,
This mutual kiss drop down between us both
As an unowned thing, once the lips being cold.
And Love, be false! if *he*, to keep one oath,
Must lose one joy, by his life's star foretold.

XXXVII.

Pardon, oh, pardon, that my soul should make,
Of all that strong divineness which I know
For thine and thee, an image only so
Formed of the sand, and fit to shift and break.
It is that distant years which did not take
Thy sovranty, recoiling with a blow,
Have forced my swimming brain to undergo
Their doubt and dread, and blindly to forsake
Thy purity of likeness, and distort
Thy worthiest love to a worthless counterfeit:
As if a shipwrecked Pagan, safe in port,
His guardian sea-god to commemorate,
Should set a sculptured porpoise, gills a-snort
And vibrant tail, within the temple-gate.

XXXVIII.

First time he kissed me, he but only kissed
The fingers of this hand wherewith I write;
And ever since, it grew more clean and white,
Slow to world-greetings, quick with its "Oh list!"
When the angels speak. A ring of amethyst
I could not wear here plainer to my sight
Than that first kiss. The second passed in height
The first, and sought the forehead, and half missed,
Half falling on the hair. Oh beyond meed!
That was the chrism of love, which love's own crown
With sanctifying sweetness did precede.
The third upon my lips was folded down
In perfect purple state; since when, indeed,
I have been proud and said, "My love, my own."

XXXIX.

Because thou hast the power, and own'st the grace,
To look through and behind this mask of me,
(Against which years have beat thus blanchingly
With their rains), and behold my soul's true face,
The dim and weary witness of life's race;
Because thou hast the faith and love to see,
Through that same soul's distracting lethargy,
The patient angel waiting for a place
In the new heavens; because nor sin nor woe,
Nor God's infliction, nor death's neighborhood,
Nor all which others, viewing, turn to go,
Nor all which makes me tired of all, self-viewed,—
Nothing repels thee, . . . dearest, teach me so
To pour out gratitude, as thou dost, good!

XL.

Oh yes! they love through all this world of ours!
I will not gainsay love, called love, forsooth.
I have heard love talked in my early youth,
And since, not so long back but that the flowers
Then gathered smell still. Mussulmans and Giaours
Throw kerchiefs at a smile, and have no ruth
For any weeping. Polypheme's white tooth
Slips on the nut, if, after frequent showers,
The shell is over-smooth; and not so much
Will turn the thing called love aside to hate,
Or else to oblivion. But thou art not such
A lover, my belovèd! thou canst wait
Through sorrow and sickness, to bring souls to touch,
And think it soon when others cry, "Too late!"

XLI.

I thank all who have loved me in their hearts,
With thanks and love from mine. Deep thanks to all
Who paused a little near the prison-wall
To hear my music in its louder parts,
Ere they went onward, each one to the mart's
Or temple's occupation, beyond call.
But thou, who, in my voice's sink and fall
When the sob took it, thy divinest art's
Own instrument didst drop down at thy foot
To hearken what I said between my tears, . . .
Instruct me how to thank thee! Oh, to shoot
My soul's full meaning into future years,
That *they* should lend it utterance, and salute
Love that endures, from Life that disappears!

XLII.

"My future will not copy fair my past:"
I wrote that once: and thinking at my side
My ministering life-angel justified
The word by his appealing look upcast
To the white throne of God, I turned at last,
And there, instead, saw thee, not unallied
To angels in thy soul. Then I, long tried
By natural ills, received the comfort fast;
While budding, at thy sight, my pilgrim's staff
Gave out green leaves with morning dews impearled.
I seek no copy now of life's first half:
Leave here the pages with long musing curled,
And write me new my future's epigraph,—
New angel mine, unhoped for in the world!

XLIII.

How do I love thee? Let me count the ways.
I love thee to the depth and breadth and height
My soul can reach, when feeling out of sight
For the ends of being and ideal grace.
I love thee to the level of every day's
Most quiet need, by sun and candlelight.
I love thee freely, as men strive for right.
I love thee purely, as they turn from praise.
I love thee with the passion put to use
In my old griefs, and with my childhood's faith.
I love thee with a love I seemed to lose
With my lost saints. I love thee with the breath,
Smiles, tears, of all my life; and, if God choose,
I shall but love thee better after death.

XLIV.

Belovèd, thou hast brought me many flowers
Plucked in the garden all the summer through
And winter; and it seemed as if they grew
In this close room, nor missed the sun and showers.
So, in the like name of that love of ours,
Take back these thoughts which here unfolded too,
And which on warm and cold days I withdrew
From my heart's ground. Indeed, those beds and bowers
Be overgrown with bitter weeds and rue,
And wait thy wedding; yet here's eglantine,
Here's ivy! Take them, as I used to do
Thy flowers, and keep them where they shall not pine.
Instruct thine eyes to keep their colors true,
And tell thy soul their roots are left in mine.

CASA GUIDI WINDOWS

A Poem,
in Two Parts

This poem contains the impressions of the writer upon events in Tuscany of which she was a witness. "From a window," the critic may demur. She bows to the objection in the very title of her work. No continuous narrative nor exposition of political philosophy is attempted by her. It is a simple story of personal impressions, whose only value is in the intensity with which they were received, as proving her warm affection for a beautiful and unfortunate country, and the sincerity with which they are related, as indicating her own good faith, and freedom from partisanship.

Of the two parts of this poem, the first was written nearly three years ago; while the second resumes the actual situation of 1851. The discrepancy between the two parts is a sufficient guaranty to the public of the truthfulness of the writer, who, though she certainly escaped the epidemic "falling sickness" of enthusiasm for Pio Nono, takes shame upon herself that she believed, like a woman, some royal oaths, and lost sight of the probable consequences of some obvious popular defects. If the discrepancy should be painful to the reader, let him understand that to the writer it has been more so. But such discrepancies we are called upon to accept at every hour by the conditions of our nature, implying the interval between aspiration and performance, between faith and disillusion, between hope and fact.

> "O trusted broken prophecy,
> O richest fortune sourly crosst,
> Born for the future, to the future lost!"

Nay, not lost to the future in this case. The future of Italy shall not be disinherited.

Florence, 1851.

Part i.

I heard last night a little child go singing
    'Neath Casa Guidi windows, by the church,
"O bella libertà, O bella!" stringing
    The same words still on notes, he went in search
So high for, you concluded the upspringing
    Of such a nimble bird to sky from perch
Must leave the whole bush in a tremble green,
    And that the heart of Italy must beat,
While such a voice had leave to rise serene
    'Twixt church and palace of a Florence street:

A little child, too, who not long had been
  By mother's finger steadied on his feet,
And still "*O bella libertà*" he sang.
Then I thought, musing, of the innumerous
  Sweet songs which still for Italy outrang
From older singers' lips, who sang not thus
  Exultingly and purely, yet, with pang
Fast sheathed in music, touched the heart of us
  So finely, that the pity scarcely pained.
I thought how Filicaja led on others,
  Bewailers for their Italy enchained,
And how they call her childless among mothers,
  Widow of empires, ay, and scarce refrained
Cursing her beauty to her face, as brothers
  Might a shamed sister's,—"Had she been less fair,
She were less wretched,"—how, evoking so
  From congregated wrong and heaped despair
Of men and women writhing under blow,
  Harrowed and hideous in a filthy lair,
Some personating image wherein woe
  Was wrapt in beauty from offending much,
They called it Cybele, or Niobe,
  Or laid it corpse-like on a bier for such,
Where all the world might drop for Italy
  Those cadenced tears which burn not where they touch,—
"Juliet of nations, canst thou die as we?
  And was the violet crown that crowned thy head
So over-large, though new buds made it rough,
  It slipped down, and across thine eyelids dead,
O sweet, fair Juliet?" Of such songs enough,
  Too many of such complaints! Behold, instead,
Void at Verona, Juliet's marble trough:[1]
  As void as that is, are all images
Men set between themselves and actual wrong
  To catch the weight of pity, meet the stress
Of conscience; since 'tis easier to gaze long
  On mournful masks and sad effigies
Than on real, live, weak creatures crushed by strong.

  For me, who stand in Italy to-day
Where worthier poets stood and sang before,
  I kiss their footsteps, yet their words gainsay.
I can but muse in hope upon this shore
  Of golden Arno as it shoots away

[1] They show at Verona, as the tomb of Juliet, an empty trough of stone.

Through Florence' heart beneath her bridges four,—
  Bent bridges seeming to strain off like bows,
And tremble while the arrowy undertide
  Shoots on, and cleaves the marble as it goes,
And strikes up palace-walls on either side,
  And froths the cornice out in glittering rows,
With doors and windows quaintly multiplied,
  And terrace-sweeps, and gazers upon all,
By whom if flower or kerchief were thrown out
  From any lattice there, the same would fall
Into the river underneath, no doubt,
  It runs so close and fast 'twixt wall and wall.
How beautiful! The mountains from without
  In silence listen for the word said next. . . .

         •   •   •   •

"Less wretched if less fair." Perhaps a truth
Is so far plain in this, that Italy,
  Long trammelled with the purple of her youth
Against her age's ripe activity,
  Sits still upon her tombs, without death's ruth,
But also without life's brave energy.
  "Now tell us what is Italy?" men ask;
And others answer, "Virgil, Cicero,
  Catullus, Cæsar." What beside, to task
The memory closer?—"Why, Boccaccio,
  Dante, Petrarca,"—and if still the flask
Appears to yield its wine by drops too slow,—
  "Angelo, Raffael, Pergolese,"—all
Whose strong hearts beat through stone, or charged again
  The paints with fire of souls electrical,
Or broke up heaven for music. What more then?
  Why, then, no more. The chaplet's last beads fall
In naming the last saintship within ken,
  And, after that, none prayeth in the land.
Alas! this Italy has too long swept
  Heroic ashes up for hour-glass sand;
Of her own past, impassioned nympholept!
  Consenting to be nailed here by the hand
To the very bay-tree under which she stept
  A queen of old, and plucked a leafy branch;
And, licensing the world too long indeed
  To use her broad phylacteries to stanch
And stop her bloody lips, she takes no heed
  How one clear word would draw an avalanche

Of living sons around her to succeed
  The vanished generations. Can she count
These oil-eaters with large, live, mobile mouths
  Agape for macaroni, in the amount
Of consecrated heroes of her south's
  Bright rosary? The pitcher at the fount,
The gift of gods, being broken, she much loathes
  To let the ground-leaves of the place confer
A natural bowl. So henceforth she would seem
  No nation, but the poet's pensioner,
With alms from every land of song and dream,
  While aye her pipers sadly pipe of her
Until their proper breaths, in that extreme
  Of sighing, split the reed on which they played;
Of which, no more. But never say "No more"
  To Italy's life! Her memories undismayed
Still argue "evermore;" her graves implore
  Her future to be strong, and not afraid;
Her very statues send their looks before.

We do not serve the dead: the past is past.
God lives, and lifts his glorious mornings up
  Before the eyes of men awake at last,
Who put away the meats they used to sup,
  And down upon the dust of earth outcast
The dregs remaining of the ancient cup,
  Then turned to wakeful prayer and worthy act.
The dead, upon their awful 'vantage ground,
  The sun not in their faces, shall abstract
No more our strength: we will not be discrowned
  As guardians of their crowns, nor deign transact
A barter of the present, for a sound
  Of good so counted in the foregone days. . . .

.   .   .   .   .

So rise up henceforth with a cheerful smile,
And, having strewn the violets, reap the corn,
  And, having reaped and garnered, bring the plough
And draw new furrows 'neath the healthy morn,
  And plant the great Hereafter in this Now. . . .

.   .   .   .   .

How we gazed
From Casa Guidi windows, while, in trains
Of orderly procession—banners raised,
  And intermittent bursts of martial strains

Which died upon the shout, as if amazed
  By gladness beyond music—they passed on!
The Magistracy, with insignia, passed,
  And all the people shouted in the sun,
And all the thousand windows which had cast
  A ripple of silks in blue and scarlet down,
(As if the houses overflowed at last,)
  Seemed growing larger with fair heads and eyes.
The Lawyers passed, and still arose the shout,
  And hands broke from the windows to surprise
Those grave, calm brows with bay-tree leaves thrown out.
  The Priesthood passed, the friars with worldly-wise
Keen, sidelong glances from their beards about
  The street to see who shouted; many a monk
Who takes a long rope in the waist was there:
  Whereat the popular exultation drunk
With indrawn "vivas" the whole sunny air,
  While through the murmuring windows rose and sunk
A cloud of kerchiefed hands,—"The Church makes fair
  Her welcome in the new Pope's name." Ensued
The black sign of the "Martyrs"—(name no name,
  But count the graves in silence.) Next were viewed
The Artists; next the Trades; and after came
  The People,—flag and sign, and rights as good,—
And very loud the shout was for that same
  Motto, "Il popolo." IL POPOLO,—
The word means dukedom, empire, majesty,
  And kings in such an hour might read it so. . . .

             .   .   .   .   .

        Yet the heavens forbid
  That we should call on passion to confront
The brutal with the brutal, and, amid
  This ripening world, suggest a lion-hunt
And lion's vengeance for the wrongs men did
  And do now, though the spears are getting blunt.
We only call, because the sight and proof
  Of lion-strength hurts nothing; and to show
A lion-heart, and measure paw with hoof,
  Helps something, even, and will instruct a foe,
As well as the onslaught, how to stand aloof:
  Or else the world gets past the mere brute blow,
Or given or taken. Children use the fist
  Until they are of age to use the brain;
And so we needed Cæsars to assist
  Man's justice, and Napoleons to explain

God's counsel, when a point was nearly missed,
  Until our generations should attain
Christ's stature nearer. Not that we, alas!
  Attain already; but a single inch
Will raise to look down on the swordsman's pass,
  As knightly Roland on the coward's flinch:
And, after chloroform and ether-gas,
  We find out slowly what the bee and finch
Have ready found, through Nature's lamp in each,—
  How to our races we may justify
Our individual claims, and, as we reach
  Our own grapes, bend the top vines to supply
The children's uses,—how to fill a breach
  With olive-branches,—how to quench a lie
With truth, and smite a foe upon the cheek
  With Christ's most conquering kiss. Why, these are things
Worth a great nation's finding, to prove weak
  The "glorious arms" of military kings.
And so, with wide embrace, my England, seek
  To stifle the bad heat and flickerings
Of this world's false and nearly expended fire.
  Draw palpitating arrows to the wood,
And twang abroad thy high hopes and thy higher
  Resolves from that most virtuous altitude,
Till nations shall unconsciously aspire
  By looking up to thee, and learn that good
And glory are not different. Announce law
  By freedom; exalt chivalry by peace;
Instruct how clear, calm eyes can overawe,
  And how pure hands, stretched simply to release
A bond-slave, will not need a sword to draw
  To be held dreadful. O my England, crease
Thy purple with no alien agonies,
  No struggles toward encroachment, no vile war!
Disband thy captains, change thy victories;
  Be henceforth prosperous, as the angels are,
Helping, not humbling.

                Drums and battle-cries
  Go out in music of the morning-star;
And soon we shall have thinkers in the place
  Of fighters, each found able as a man
To strike electric influence through a race,
  Unstayed by city-wall and barbican.
The poet shall look grander in the face
  Than even of old (when he of Greece began

To sing "that Achillean wrath which slew
  So many heroes"), seeing he shall treat
The deeds of souls heroic toward the true,
  The oracles of life, previsions sweet
And awful, like divine swans gliding through
  White arms of Ledas, which will leave the heat
Of their escaping godship to endue
  The human medium with a heavenly flush.
Meanwhile, in this same Italy we want
  Not popular passion, to arise and crush,
But popular conscience, which may covenant
  For what it knows. Concede without a blush,
To grant the "civic guard" is not to grant
  The civic spirit, living and awake:
Those lappets on your shoulders, citizens,
  Your eyes strain after sideways till they ache,
(While still, in admirations and amens,
  The crowd comes up on fiesta-days to take
The great sight in), are not intelligence,
  Not courage even: alas! if not the sign
Of something very noble, they are nought;
  For every day ye dress your sallow kine
With fringes down their cheeks, though unbesought
  They loll their heavy heads, and drag the wine,
And bear the wooden yoke as they were taught
  The first day. What ye want is light; indeed
Not sunlight (ye may well look up surprised
  To those unfathomable heavens that feed
Your purple hills), but God's light organized
  In some high soul crowned capable to lead
The conscious people, conscious and advised;
  For, if we lift a people like mere clay,
It falls the same. We want thee, O unfound
  And sovran teacher! if thy beard be gray
Or black, we bid thee rise up from the ground,
  And speak the word God giveth thee to say,
Inspiring into all this people round,
  Instead of passion, thought, which pioneers
All generous passion, purifies from sin,
  And strikes the hour for. Rise up, teacher! here's
A crowd to make a nation! best begin
  By making each a man, till all be peers
Of earth's true patriots and pure martyrs in
  Knowing and daring. Best unbar the doors
Which Peter's heirs kept locked so overclose
  They only let the mice across the floors,

While every churchman dangles, as he goes,
  The great key at his girdle, and abhors
In Christ's name meekly. Open wide the house,
  Concede the entrance with Christ's liberal mind,
And set the tables with his wine and bread.
  What! "Commune in both kinds?" In every kind—
Wine, wafer, love, hope, truth, unlimited,
  Nothing kept back. For, when a man is blind
To starlight, will he see the rose is red?
  A bondsman shivering at a Jesuit's foot—
"Væ! meâ culpâ!"—is not like to stand
  A freedman at a despot's, and dispute
His titles by the balance in his hand,
  Weighing them "suo jure." Tend the root,
If careful of the branches, and expand
  The inner souls of men before you strive
For civic heroes. . . .

.   .   .   .   .

      Therefore let us all
Refreshed in England or in other land,
  By visions, with their fountain rise and fall,
Of this earth's darling,—we, who understand
  A little how the Tuscan musical
Vowels do round themselves as if they planned
  Eternities of separate sweetness,—we,
Who loved Sorrento vines in picture-book,
  Or ere in winecup we pledged faith or glee,—
Who loved Rome's wolf with demigods at suck,
  Or ere we loved truth's own divinity,—
Who loved, in brief, the classic hill and brook,
  And Ovid's dreaming tales and Petrarch's song,
Or e'er we loved Love's self even,—let us give
  The blessing of our souls (and wish them strong
To bear it to the height where prayers arrive,
  When faithful spirits pray against a wrong,)
To this great cause of southern men who strive
  In God's name for man's rights, and shall not fail!

Behold they shall not fail. The shouts ascend
  Above the shrieks, in Naples, and prevail.
Rows of shot corpses, waiting for the end
  Of burial, seem to smile up straight and pale
Into the azure air, and apprehend
  That final gun-flash from Palermo's coast

Which lightens their apocalypse of death.
  So let them die! The world shows nothing lost;
Therefore not blood. Above or underneath,
  What matter, brothers, if ye keep your post
On duty's side? As sword returns to sheath,
  So dust to grave; but souls find place in heaven.
Heroic daring is the true success,
  The eucharistic bread requires no leaven;
And, though your ends were hopeless, we should bless
  Your cause as holy. Strive—and, having striven,
Take for God's recompense that righteousness!

Part II.

I wrote a meditation and a dream,
  Hearing a little child sing in the street:
I leant upon his music as a theme,
  Till it gave way beneath my heart's full beat
Which tried at an exultant prophecy,
  But dropped before the measure was complete—
Alas for songs and hearts! O Tuscany,
  O Dante's Florence, is the type too plain?
Didst thou, too, only sing of liberty,
  As little children take up a high strain
With unintentioned voices, and break off
  To sleep upon their mothers' knees again?

· · · · ·

O holy knowledge, holy liberty!
O holy rights of nations! If I speak
  These bitter things against the jugglery
Of days that in your names proved blind and weak,
  It is that tears are bitter. When we see
The brown skulls grin at death in churchyards bleak,
  We do not cry, "This Yorick is too light,"
For death grows deathlier with that mouth he makes.
  So with my mocking. Bitter things I write
Because my soul is bitter for your sakes,
  O freedom! O my Florence!

· · · · ·

Behold, the people waits,
Like God: as he, in his serene of might,
  So they, in their endurance of long straits.

Ye stamp no nation out, though day and night
   Ye tread them with that absolute heel which grates
And grinds them flat from all attempted height.
   You kill worms sooner with a garden spade
Than you kill peoples: peoples will not die;
   The tail curls stronger when you lop the head:
They writhe at every wound, and multiply
   And shudder into a heap of life that's made
Thus vital from God's own vitality.
   'Tis hard to shrivel back a day of God's
Once fixed for judgment; 'tis as hard to change
   The peoples when they rise beneath their loads,
And heave them from their backs with violent wrench
   To crush the oppressor: for that judgment-rod's
The measure of this popular revenge. . . .

     ·   ·   ·   ·   ·

A cry is up in England, which doth ring
   The hollow world through, that for ends of trade
And virtue, and God's better worshiping,
   We henceforth should exalt the name of Peace,
And leave those rusty wars that eat the soul,—
   Besides their clippings at our golden fleece.
I, too, have loved peace, and from bole to bole
   Of immemorial undeciduous trees
Would write, as lovers use upon a scroll,
   The holy name of Peace, and set it high
Where none could pluck it down. On trees, I say,
   Not upon gibbets!—With the greenery
Of dewy branches and the flowery May,
   Sweet mediation betwixt earth and sky
Providing, for the shepherd's holiday.
   Not upon gibbets! though the vulture leaves
The bones to quiet, which he first picked bare.
Not upon dungeons! though the wretch who grieves
   And groans within, less stirs the outer air
Than any little field-mouse stirs the sheaves.
Not upon chain-bolts! though the slave's despair
   Has dulled his helpless miserable brain,
And left him blank beneath the freeman's whip
   To sing and laugh out idiocies of pain.
Nor yet on starving homes! where many a lip
   Has sobbed itself asleep through curses vain.
I love no peace which is not fellowship,
   And which includes not mercy. I would have

Rather the raking of the guns across
  The world, and shrieks against heaven's architrave;
Rather the struggle in the slippery fosse
  Of dying men and horses, and the wave
Blood-bubbling. . . . Enough said!—by Christ's own cross,
  And by this faint heart of my womanhood,
Such things are better than a Peace that sits
  Beside a hearth in self-commended mood,
And takes no thought how wind and rain by fits
  Are howling out of doors against the good
Of the poor wanderer. What! your peace admits
  Of outside anguish while it keeps at home?
I loathe to take its name upon my tongue.
  'Tis nowise peace: 'tis treason, stiff with doom;
'Tis gagged despair, and inarticulate wrong,
  Annihilated Poland, stifled Rome,
Dazed Naples, Hungary fainting 'neath the thong,
  And Austria wearing a smooth olive-leaf
On her brute forehead, while her hoofs outpress
  The life from these Italian souls in brief.
O Lord of peace, who art Lord of righteousness,
  Constrain the anguished worlds from sin and grief,
Pierce them with conscience, purge them with redress,
  And give us peace which is no counterfeit!

·   ·   ·   ·

But now, the world is busy: it has grown
  A Fair-going world. Imperial England draws
The flowing ends of the earth from Fez, Canton,
  Delhi, and Stockholm, Athens and Madrid,
The Russias and the vast Americas,
  As if a queen drew in her robes amid
Her golden cincture,—isles, peninsulas,
  Capes, continents, far inland countries hid
By jasper-sands and hills of chrysopras,
  All trailing in their splendors through the door
Of the gorgeous Crystal Palace. Every nation,
  To every other nation strange of yore,
Gives face to face the civic salutation,
  And holds up in a proud right hand before
That congress the best work which she can fashion
  By her best means. "These corals, will you please
To match against your oaks? They grow as fast
  Within my wilderness of purple seas."—
"This diamond stared upon me as I passed

(As a live god's eye from a marble frieze)
Along a dark of diamonds. Is it classed?"—
"I wove these stuffs so subtly that the gold
Swims to the surface of the silk like cream
    And curdles to fair patterns. Ye behold!"—
"These delicatest muslins rather seem
    Than be, you think? Nay, touch them and be bold,
Though such veiled Chakhi's face in Hafiz' dream."—
    "These carpets—you walk slow on them like kings,
Inaudible like spirits, while your foot
    Dips deep in velvet roses and such things."—
"Even Apollonius might commend this flute:[2]
    The music, winding through the stops, upsprings
To make the player very rich: compute!"
    "Here's goblet-glass, to take in with your wine
The very sun its grapes were ripened under:
    Drink light and juice together, and each fine."—
"This model of a steam-ship moves your wonder?
    You should behold it crushing down the brine
Like a blind Jove, who feels his way with thunder."—
    "Here's sculpture! Ah, *we* live too! why not throw
Our life into our marbles? Art has place
    For other artists after Angelo."—
"I tried to paint out here a natural face;
    For nature includes Raffael, as we know,
Not Raffael nature. Will it help my case?"—
    "Methinks you will not match this steel of ours!"—
"Nor you this porcelain! One might dream the clay
    Retained in it the larvæ of the flowers,
They bud so round the cup, the old spring-way."—
    "Nor you these carven woods, where birds in bowers
With twisting snakes and climbing cupids play."

O Magi of the east and of the west,
    Your incense, gold, and myrrh are excellent!—
What gifts for Christ, then, bring ye with the rest?
Your hands have worked well: is your courage spent
    In handwork only? Have you nothing best,
Which generous souls may perfect and present,
    And He shall thank the givers for? no light
Of teaching, liberal nations, for the poor
    Who sit in darkness when it is not night?

---

[2]Philostratus relates of Apollonius, how he objected to the musical instrument of Linus the Rhodian, that it could not enrich or beautify. The history of music in our day would satisfy the philosopher on one point at least.

No cure for wicked children? Christ—no cure!
  No help for women sobbing out of sight
Because men made the laws? no brothel-lure
  Burnt out by popular lightnings? Hast thou found
No remedy, my England, for such woes?
  No outlet, Austria, for the scourged and bound,
No entrance for the exiled? no repose,
  Russia, for knouted Poles worked underground,
And gentle ladies bleached among the snows?
  No mercy for the slave, America?
No hope for Rome, free France, chivalric France?
  Alas, great nations have great shames, I say.
No pity, O world, no tender utterance
  Of benediction, and prayers stretched this way
For poor Italia, baffled by mischance?
  O gracious nations, give some ear to me!
You all go to your Fair, and I am one
  Who at the roadside of humanity
Beseech your alms,—God's justice to be done.
  So, prosper!
        In the name of Italy,
Meantime her patriot dead have benison. . . .

POEMS BEFORE CONGRESS

☆

CHRISTMAS GIFTS

ὡς βασιλει, ὡς θεῷ ὡς νεκρῷ.

GREGORY NAZIANZEN.

I.

THE POPE on Christmas Day
  Sits in St. Peter's chair;
But the peoples murmur, and say,
  "Our souls are sick and forlorn,
And who will show us where
  Is the stable where Christ was born?"

II.

The star is lost in the dark;
  The manger is lost in the straw:
The Christ cries faintly . . . hark!—
  Through bands that swaddle and strangle—
But the Pope in the chair of awe
  Looks down the great quadrangle.

III.

The magi kneel at his foot,
  Kings of the east and west;
But, instead of the angels (mute
  Is the "Peace on earth" of their song),
The peoples, perplexed and opprest,
  Are sighing, "How long! how long!"

IV.

And, instead of the kine, bewilder in
  Shadow of aisle and dome,
The bear who tore up the children,
  The fox who burnt up the corn,
And the wolf who suckled at Rome
  Brothers to slay and to scorn.

V.

Cardinals left and right of him,
  Worshippers round and beneath,
The silver trumpets at sight of him,
  Thrill with a musical blast:
But the people say through their teeth,
  "Trumpets? we wait for the Last!"

VI.

He sits in the place of the Lord,
  And asks for the gifts of the time,—
Gold, for the haft of a sword,
  To win back Romagna averse,
Incense to sweeten a crime,
  And myrrh to imbitter a curse.

VII.

Then a king of the west said, "Good!
  I bring thee the gifts of the time,—
Red, for the patriot's blood;
  Green, for the martyr's crown;
White for the dew and the rime,
  When the morning of God comes down."

VIII.

—O mystic tricolor bright!
  The Pope's heart quailed like a man's:
The cardinals froze at the sight,
  Bowing their tonsures hoary;
And the eyes in the peacock-fans
  Winked at the alien glory.

IX.

But the peoples exclaimed in hope,
  "Now blessed be he who has brought
These gifts of the time to the Pope,
  When our souls were sick and forlorn;
—And *here* is the star we sought,
  To show us where Christ was born!"

ITALY AND THE WORLD

I.

FLORENCE, Bologna, Parma, Modena,
  When you named them a year ago,
So many graves reserved by God, in a
  Day of Judgment, you seemed to know,
To open and let out the resurrection.

II.

And meantime (you made your reflection,
  If you were English) was nought to be done
But sorting sables, in predilection
  For all those martyrs dead and gone,
Till the new earth and heaven made ready.

III.

And if your politics were not heady,
  Violent . . . "Good," you added, "good
In all things! mourn on sure and steady.
  Churchyard thistles are wholesome food
For our European wandering asses.

IV.

"The date of the resurrection passes
  Human foreknowledge: men unborn
Will gain by it (even in the lower classes);
  But none of these. It is not the morn
Because the cock of France is crowing.

V.

"Cocks crow at midnight, seldom knowing
  Starlight from dawn-light. 'Tis a mad
Poor creature." Here you paused, and growing
  Scornful, suddenly, let us add,
The trumpet sounded, the graves were open.

VI.

Life and life and life! agrope in
   The dusk of death, warm hands stretched out
For swords, proved more life still to hope in,
   Beyond and behind. Arise with a shout,
Nation of Italy, slain and buried!

VII.

Hill to hill, and turret to turret,
   Flashing the tricolor,—newly created
Beautiful Italy, calm, unhurried,
   Rise heroic and renovated,
Rise to the final restitution.

VIII.

Rise; prefigure the grand solution
   Of earth's municipal, insular schisms,
Statesmen draping self-love's conclusion
   In cheap vernacular patriotisms,
Unable to give up Judæa for Jesus.

IX.

Bring us the higher example; release us
   Into the larger coming time;
And into Christ's broad garment piece us
   Rags of virtue as poor as crime,
National selfishness, civic vaunting.

X.

No more Jew nor Greek then, taunting
   Nor taunted; no more England nor France!
But one confederate brotherhood planting
   One flag only to mark the advance,
Onward and upward, of all humanity

XI.

For civilization perfected
   Is fully developed Christianity.
"Measure the frontier," shall it be said,
   "Count the ships," in national vanity?
—Count the nation's heart-beats sooner.

XII.

For, though behind by a cannon or schooner,
   That nation still is predominant,
Whose pulse beats quickest in zeal to oppugn or
   Succor another, in wrong or want,
Passing the frontier in love and abhorrence.

XIII.

Modena, Parma, Bologna, Florence,
  Open us out the wider way!
Dwarf in that chapel of old St. Lawrence
  Your Michel Angelo's giant Day,
With the grandeur of this Day breaking o'er us!

XIV.

Ye who, restrained as an ancient chorus,
  Mute while the coryphæus spake,
Hush your separate voices before us,
  Sink your separate lives for the sake
Of one sole Italy's living forever!

XV.

Givers of coat and cloak too,—never
  Grudging that purple of yours at the best,—
By your heroic will and endeavor
  Each sublimely dispossest,
That all may inherit what each surrenders!

XVI.

Earth shall bless you, O noble emenders
  On egotist nations! Ye shall lead
The plough of the world, and sow new splendors
  Into the furrow of things for seed,
Ever the richer for what ye have given.

XVII.

Lead us and teach us, till earth and heaven
  Grow larger around us, and higher above.
Our sacrament bread has a bitter leaven;
  We bait our traps with the name of love,
Till hate itself has a kinder meaning.

XVIII.

Oh, this world: this cheating, and screening
  Of cheats! this conscience for candle-wicks,
Not beacon-fires! this over-weening
  Of underhand diplomatical tricks,
Dared for the country while scorned for the counter!

XIX.

Oh, this envy of those who mount here,
  And oh, this malice to make them trip!
Rather quenching the fire there, drying the fount here,
  To frozen body and thirsty lip,
Than leave to a neighbor their ministration.

XX.

I cry aloud in my poet-passion,
　　Viewing my England o'er Alp and sea.
I loved her more in her ancient fashion:
　　She carries her rifles too thick for me,
Who spares them so in the cause of a brother.

XXI.

Suspicion, panic? end this pother.
　　The sword kept sheathless at peace time rusts.
None fears for himself while he feels for another:
　　The brave man either fights or trusts,
And wears no mail in his private chamber.

XXII.

Beautiful Italy! golden amber
　　Warm with the kisses of lover and traitor!
Thou who hast drawn us on to remember,
　　Draw us to hope now: let us be greater
By this new future than that old story,

XXIII.

Till truer glory replaces all glory,
　　As the torch grows blind at the dawn of day;
And the nations, rising up, their sorry
　　And foolish sins shall put away,
As children their toys when the teacher enters.

XXIV.

Till Love's one centre devour these centres
　　Of many self-loves; and the patriot's trick
To better his land by egotist ventures,
　　Defamed from a virtue. shall make men sick,
As the scalp at the belt of some red hero.

XXV.

For certain virtues have dropped to zero,
　　Left by the sun on the mountain's dewy side;
Churchman's charities, tender as Nero,
　　Indian suttee, heathen suicide,
Service to rights divine proved hollow:

XXVI.

And Heptarchy patriotisms must follow.
　　—National voices, distinct yet dependent,
Ensphering each other, as swallow does swallow,
　　With circles still widening and ever ascendent,
In multiform life to united progression,—

XXVII.

These shall remain. And when in the session
   Of nations, the separate language is heard,
Each shall aspire, in sublime indiscretion,
   To help with a thought or exalt with a word
Less her own than her rival's honor.

XXVIII.

Each Christian nation shall take upon her
   The law of the Christian man in vast:
The crown of the getter shall fall to the donor,
   And last shall be first while first shall be last,
And to love best shall still be to reign unsurpassed.

A CURSE FOR A NATION

PROLOGUE

I HEARD an angel speak last night,
      And he said, "Write!—
Write a nation's curse for me,
And send it over the Western Sea."

I faltered, taking up the word:
      "Not so, my lord!
If curses must be, choose another
To send thy curse against my brother.

"For I am bound by gratitude,
      By love and blood,
To brothers of mine across the sea,
Who stretch out kindly hands to me."

"Therefore," the voice said, "shalt thou write
      My curse to-night.
From the summits of love a curse is driven,
As lightning is from the tops of heaven."

"Not so," I answered. "Evermore
      My heart is sore
For my own land's sins: for little feet
Of children bleeding along the street:

"For parked-up honors that gainsay
      The right of way:
For almsgiving through a door that is
Not open enough for two friends to kiss:

"For love of freedom which abates
    Beyond the Straits:
For patriot virtue starved to vice on
Self-praise, self-interest, and suspicion:

"For an oligarchic parliament,
    And bribes well-meant.
What curse to another land assign,
When heavy-souled for the sins of mine?"

"Therefore," the voice said, "shalt thou write
    My curse to-night.
Because thou hast strength to see and hate
A foul thing done *within* thy gate."

"Not so," I answered once again.
    "To curse choose men.
For I, a woman, have only known
How the heart melts, and the tears run down."

"Therefore," the voice said, "shalt thou write
    My curse to-night.
Some women weep and curse, I say,
(And no one marvels) night and day.

"And thou shalt take their part to-night,
    Weep and write.
A curse from the depths of womanhood
Is very salt, and bitter, and good."

So thus I wrote, and mourned indeed,
    What all may read.
And thus as was enjoined on me,
I send it over the Western Sea.

The Curse

I.

BECAUSE ye have broken your own chain
    With the strain
Of brave men climbing a nation's height,
Yet thence bear down with brand and thong
On souls of others,—for this wrong
    This is the curse. Write.

Because yourselves are standing straight
    In the state
Of Freedom's foremost acolyte,
Yet keep calm footing all the time
On writhing bond-slaves,—for this crime
    This is the curse. Write.

Because ye prosper in God's name,
    With a claim
To honor in the old world's sight,
Yet do the fiend's work perfectly
In strangling martyrs,—for this lie
    This is the curse. Write.

II.

Ye shall watch while kings conspire
Round the people's smouldering fire,
    And, warm for your part,
Shall never dare—O shame!
To utter the thought into flame
    Which burns at your heart.
    This is the curse. Write.

Ye shall watch while nations strive
With the bloodhounds, die or survive,
    Drop faint from their jaws,
Or throttle them backward to death;
And only under your breath
    Shall favor the cause.
    This is the curse. Write.

Ye shall watch while strong men draw
The nets of feudal law
    To strangle the weak;
And, counting the sin for a sin,
Your soul shall be sadder within
    Than the word ye shall speak.
    This is the curse. Write.

When good men are praying erect
That Christ may avenge his elect,
    And deliver the earth,
The prayer in your ears, said low,
Shall sound like the tramp of a foe
    That's driving you forth.
    This is the curse. Write.

When wise men give you their praise,
They shall pause in the heat of the phrase,
  As if carried too far.
When ye boast your own charters kept true,
Ye shall blush; for the thing which ye do
  Derides what ye are.
      This is the curse. Write.

When fools cast taunts at your gate,
Your scorn ye shall somewhat abate
  As ye look o'er the wall:
For your conscience, tradition, and name
Explode with a deadlier blame
  Than the worst of them all.
      This is the curse. Write.

Go, wherever ill deeds shall be done,
Go, plant your flag in the sun
  Beside the ill-doers!
And recoil from clenching the curse
Of God's witnessing Universe
  With a curse of yours.
      THIS is the curse. Write.

LAST POEMS

A SONG FOR THE RAGGED-SCHOOLS OF LONDON

WRITTEN IN ROME

I.

I AM listening here in Rome.
  "England's strong," say many speakers:
"If she winks, the Czar must come,
  Prow and topsail to the breakers."

II.

"England's rich in coal and oak,"
  Adds a Roman, getting moody:
"If she shakes a travelling-cloak,
  Down our Appian roll the scudi."

III.

"England's righteous," they rejoin:
  "Who shall grudge her exaltations,
When her wealth of golden coin
  Works the welfare of the nations?"

IV.

I am listening here in Rome.
  Over Alps a voice is sweeping,—
"England's cruel, save us some
  Of these victims in her keeping!"

V.

As the cry beneath the wheel
  Of an old triumphal Roman
Cleft the people's shouts like steel,
  While the show was spoilt for no man,

VI.

Comes that voice. Let others shout,
  Other poets praise my land here:
I am sadly sitting out,
  Praying, "God forgive her grandeur."

VII.

Shall we boast of empire, where
  Time with ruin sits commissioned?
In God's liberal blue air
  Peter's dome itself looks wizened;

VIII.

And the mountains, in disdain,
  Gather back their lights of opal
From the dumb despondent plain,
  Heaped with jaw-bones of a people.

IX.

Lordly English think it o'er,
  Cæsar's doing is all undone!
You have cannons on your shore,
  And free Parliaments in London,

X.

Princes' parks, and merchants' homes,
  Tents for soldiers, ships for seamen,—
Ay, but ruins worse than Rome's
  In your pauper men and women.

XI.

Women leering through the gas,
  (Just such bosoms used to nurse you,)
Men, turned wolves by famine,—pass!
  Those can speak themselves, and curse you.

XII.

But these others—children small,
  Spilt like blots about the city,
Quay and street, and palace-wall—
  Take them up into your pity!

XIII.

Ragged children with bare feet,
  Whom the angels in white raiment
Know the names of, to repeat
  When they come on you for payment.

XIV.

Ragged children, hungry-eyed,
  Huddled up out of the coldness
On your doorsteps, side by side,
  Till your footman damns their boldness.

XV.

In the alleys, in the squares,
  Begging, lying little rebels;
In the noisy thoroughfares,
  Struggling on with piteous trebles.

XVI.

Patient children—think what pain
  Makes a young child patient—ponder!
Wronged too commonly to strain
  After right, or wish, or wonder.

XVII.

Wicked children, with peaked chins,
  And old foreheads! there are many
With no pleasures except sins,
  Gambling with a stolen penny.

XVIII.

Sickly children, that whine low
  To themselves, and not their mothers,
From mere habit,—never so
  Hoping help or care from others.

XIX.

Healthy children, with those blue
  English eyes, fresh from their Maker,
Fierce and ravenous, staring through
  At the brown loaves of the baker.

xx.

I am listening here in Rome,
  And the Romans are confessing,
"English children pass in bloom
  All the prettiest made for blessing.

xxi.

"*Angli angeli!*" (resumed
  From the mediæval story)
"Such rose angelhoods, emplumed
  In such ringlets of pure glory!"

xxii.

Can we smooth down the bright hair,
  O my sisters! calm, unthrilled in
Our heart's pulses? Can we bear
  The sweet looks of our own children,

xxiii.

While those others, lean and small,
  Scurf and mildew of the city,
Spot our streets, convict us all
  Till we take them into pity?

xxiv.

"Is it our fault?" you reply,
  "When, throughout civilization,
Every nation's empery
  Is asserted by starvation?

xxv.

"All these mouths we cannot feed,
  And we cannot clothe these bodies."
Well, if man's so hard indeed,
  Let them learn, at least, what God is!

xxvi.

Little outcasts from life's fold,
  The grave's hope they may be joined in,
By Christ's covenant consoled
  For our social contract's grinding.

xxvii.

If no better can be done,
  Let us do but this,—endeavor
That the sun behind the sun
  Shine upon them while they shiver!

XXVIII.

On the dismal London flags,
　Through the cruel social juggle,
Put a thought beneath their rags
　To ennoble the heart's struggle.

XXIX.

O my sisters! not so much
　Are we asked for,—not a blossom
From our children's nosegay, such
　As we gave it from our bosom,

XXX.

Not the milk left in their cup,
　Not the lamp while they are sleeping,
Not the little cloak hung up
　While the coat's in daily keeping,

XXXI.

But a place in Ragged-Schools,
　Where the outcasts may to-morrow
Learn by gentle words and rules
　Just the uses of their sorrow.

XXXII.

O my sisters! children small,
　Blue-eyed, wailing through the city,
Our own babes cry in them all:
　Let us take them into pity.

MAY'S LOVE

I.

You love all, you say,—
　Round, beneath, above, me:
Find me, then, some way
　Better than to love me,
Me, too, dearest May!

II.

O world-kissing eyes
　Which the blue heavens melt to;
I, sad, overwise,
　Loathe the sweet looks dealt to
All things—men and flies.

III.

You love all, you say:
    Therefore, dear, abate me
Just your love, I pray!
    Shut your eyes and hate me—
Only *me*, fair May!

AMY'S CRUELTY

I.

FAIR Amy of the terraced house,
    Assist me to discover
Why you, who would not hurt a mouse,
    Can torture so your lover.

II.

You give your coffee to the cat,
    You stroke the dog for coming,
And all your face grows kinder at
    The little brown bee's humming.

III.

But when *he* haunts your door . . . the town
    Marks coming, and marks going . . .
You seem to have stitched your eyelids down
    To that long piece of sewing!

IV.

You never give a look, not you,
    Nor drop him a "Good-morning,"
To keep his long day warm and blue,
    So fretted by your scorning.

V.

She shook her head—"The mouse and bee
    For crumb or flower will linger;
The dog is happy at my knee;
    The cat purrs at my finger.

VI.

"But *he* . . . to *him*, the least thing given
    Means great things at a distance:
He wants my world, my sun, my heaven,
    Soul, body, whole existence.

VII.

"They say love gives, as well as takes;
　But I'm a simple maiden,—
My mother's first smile when she wakes
　I still have smiled and prayed in.

VIII.

"I only know my mother's love,
　Which gives all, and asks nothing;
And this new loving sets the groove
　Too much the way of loathing.

IX.

"Unless he gives me all in change,
　I forfeit all things by him:
The risk is terrible and strange—
　I tremble, doubt . . . deny him

X.

"He's sweetest friend or hardest foe,
　Best angel or worst devil:
I either hate or . . . love him so,
　I can't be merely civil!

XI.

"You trust a woman who puts forth
　Her blossoms thick as summer's?
You think she dreams what love is worth,
　Who casts it to new-comers?

XII.

"Such love's a cowslip-ball to fling,—
　A moment's pretty pastime:
I give . . . all me, if any thing,
　The first time and the last time.

XIII.

"Dear neighbor of the trellised house,
　A man should murmur never,
Though treated worse than dog and mouse,
　Till doted on forever!"

MY HEART AND I

I.

Enough! we're tired, my heart and I.
  We sit beside the headstone thus,
  And wish that name were carved for us.
The moss reprints more tenderly
  The hard types of the mason's knife,
  As heaven's sweet life renews earth's life
With which we're tired, my heart and I.

II.

You see we're tired, my heart and I.
  We dealt with books, we trusted men,
  And in our own blood drenched the pen,
As if such colors could not fly.
  We walked too straight for fortune's end,
  We loved too true to keep a friend:
At last we're tired, my heart and I.

III.

How tired we feel, my heart and I!
  We seem of no use in the world:
  Our fancies hang gray and uncurled
About men's eyes indifferently;
  Our voice, which thrilled you so, will let
  You sleep; our tears are only wet:
What do we here, my heart and I?

IV.

So tired, so tired, my heart and I!
  It was not thus in that old time
  When Ralph sat with me 'neath the lime
To watch the sunset from the sky.
  "Dear love, you're looking tired," he said;
  I, smiling at him, shook my head:
'Tis now we're tired, my heart and I.

V.

So tired, so tired, my heart and I!
  Though now none takes me on his arm
  To fold me close, to kiss me warm
Till each quick breath end in a sigh
  Of happy languor. Now, alone,
  We lean upon this graveyard stone,
Uncheered, unkissed, my heart and I.

VI.

Tired out we are, my heart and I.
　Suppose the world brought diadems
　To tempt us, crusted with loose gems
Of powers and pleasures? Let it try.
　We scarcely care to look at even
　A pretty child, or God's blue heaven,
We feel so tired, my heart and I.

VII.

Yet who complains? My heart and I?
　In this abundant earth no doubt
　Is little room for things worn out:
Disdain them, break them, throw them by!
　And if, before the days grew rough,
　We *once* were loved, used,—well enough
I think we've fared, my heart and I.

THE BEST THING IN THE WORLD

　WHAT's the best thing in the world?
　June-rose, by May-dew impearled;
　Sweet south wind that means no rain;
　Truth, not cruel to a friend;
　Pleasure, not in haste to end;
　Beauty, not self-decked and curled
　Till its pride is over plain;
　Light, that never makes you wink;
　Memory, that gives no pain;
　Love, when, *so*, you're loved again.
　What's the best thing in the world?
　—Something out of it, I think.

A MUSICAL INSTRUMENT

I.

WHAT was he doing, the great god Pan,
　Down in the reeds by the river?
Spreading ruin, and scattering ban,
Splashing and paddling with hoofs of a goat,
And breaking the golden lilies afloat
　With the dragon-fly on the river.

II.

He tore out a reed, the great god Pan,
  From the deep, cool bed of the river.
The limpid water turbidly ran,
And the broken lilies a-dying lay,
And the dragon-fly had fled away,
  Ere he brought it out of the river.

III.

High on the shore sat the great god Pan,
  While turbidly flowed the river,
And hacked and hewed as a great god can,
With his hard bleak steel at the patient reed,
Till there was not a sign of the leaf indeed
  To prove it fresh from the river.

IV.

He cut it short, did the great god Pan,
  (How tall it stood in the river!)
Then drew the pith, like the heart of a man,
Steadily from the outside ring,
And notched the poor, dry, empty thing
  In holes as he sat by the river.

V.

"This is the way," laughed the great god Pan,
  (Laughed while he sat by the river,)
"The only way, since gods began
To make sweet music, they could succeed."
Then, dropping his mouth to a hole in the reed,
  He blew in power by the river.

VI.

Sweet, sweet, sweet, O Pan,
  Piercing sweet by the river!
Blinding sweet, O great god Pan
The sun on the hill forgot to die,
And the lilies revived, and the dragon-fly
  Came back to dream on the river.

VII.

Yet half a beast is the great god Pan,
  To laugh as he sits by the river,
Making a poet out of a man:
The true gods sigh for the cost and pain,—
For the reed which grows nevermore again
  As a reed with the reeds in the river.

FIRST NEWS FROM VILLAFRANCA

I.

PEACE, peace, peace, do you say?
    What!—with the enemy's guns in our ears?
    With the country's wrong not rendered back?
What!—while Austria stands at bay
    In Mantua, and our Venice bears
    The cursed flag of the yellow and black?

II.

Peace, peace, peace, do you say?
    And this the Mincio? Where's the fleet,
    And where's the sea? Are we all blind
Or mad with the blood shed yesterday,
    Ignoring Italy under our feet,
    And seeing things before, behind?

III.

Peace, peace, peace, do you say?
    What!—uncontested, undenied?
    Because we triumph, we succumb?
A pair of emperors stand in the way,
    (One of whom is a man, beside)
    To sign and seal our cannons dumb?

IV.

No, not Napoleon!—he who mused
    At Paris, and at Milan spake,
    And at Solferino led the fight:
Not he we trusted, honored, used
    Our hopes and hearts for . . . till they break—
    Even so, you tell us . . . in his sight.

V.

Peace, peace, is still your word?
    We say you lie then!—that is plain.
    There *is* no peace, and shall be none.
Our very dead would cry, "Absurd!"
    And clamor that they died in vain,
    And whine to come back to the sun.

VI.

Hush! more reverence for the dead!
    They've done the most for Italy

Evermore since the earth was fair.
Now would that *we* had died instead,
Still dreaming peace meant liberty,
And did not, could not, mean despair.

VII.

Peace, you say?—yes, peace, in truth!
But such a peace as the ear can achieve
'Twixt the rifle's click and the rush of the ball,
'Twixt the tiger's spring and the crunch of the tooth,
'Twixt the dying atheist's negative
And God's face—waiting, after all!

SUMMING UP IN ITALY

Inscribed to Intelligent Publics out of It

I.

Observe how it will be at last,
When our Italy stands at full stature,
A year ago tied down so fast
That the cord cut the quick of her nature!
You'll honor the deed and its scope,
Then in logical sequence upon it,
Will use up the remnants of rope
By hanging the men who have done it.

II.

The speech in the Commons, which hits you
A sketch off, how dungeons must feel;
The official despatch, which commits you
From stamping out groans with your heel;
Suggestions in journal or book for
Good efforts are praised as is meet,—
But what in this world can men look for,
Who only achieve and complete?

III.

True, you've praise for the fireman who sets his
Brave face to the axe of the flame,
Disappears in the smoke, and then fetches
A babe down, or idiot that's lame,—
For the boor even, who rescues through pity
A sheep from the brute who would kick it:
But saviors of nations!—'tis pretty,
And doubtful: they *may* be so wicked:

IV.

Azeglio, Farini, Mamiani,
   Ricasoli,—doubt by the dozen,—here's
Pepoli too, and Cipriani,
   Imperial cousins and cozeners—
Arese, Laiatico,—courtly
   Of manners, if stringent of mouth:
Garibaldi! we'll come to him shortly,
   (As soon as he *ends* in the South)

V.

Napoleon—as strong as ten armies,
   Corrupt as seven devils—a fact
You accede to, then seek where the harm is
   Drained off from the man to his act,
And find—a free nation! Suppose
   Some hell-brood in Eden's sweet greenery,
Convoked for creating—a rose!
   Would it suit the infernal machinery?

VI.

Cavour—to the despot's desire,
   Who his own thought so craftily marries—
What is he but just a thin wire
   For conducting the lightning from Paris?
Yes, write down the two as compeers,
   Confessing (you would not permit a lie)
He bore up his Piedmont ten years
   Till she suddenly smiled, and was Italy.

VII.

And the king, with that "stain on his scutcheon,"[1]
   Savoy—as the calumny runs;
(If it be not his blood,—with his clutch on
   The sword, and his face to the guns).
O first, where the battle-storm gathers,
   O loyal of heart on the throne,
Let those keep the "graves of their fathers"
   Who quail in a nerve from their own!

VIII.

For *thee*—through the dim Hades-portal
   The dream of a voice—"Blessed thou
Who hast made all thy race twice immortal!
   No need of the sepulchres now!

[1]Blue Book. Diplomatical Correspondence.

—Left to Bourbons and Hapsburgs, who fester
  Above-ground with worm-eaten souls,
While the ghost of some pale feudal jester
  Before them strews treaties in holes."

IX.

But hush!—am I dreaming a poem
  Of Hades, Heaven, Justice? Not I;
I began too far off, in my proem,
  With what men believe and deny;
And on earth, whatsoever the need is,
  (To sum up as thoughtful reviewers)
The moral of every great deed is—
  The virtue of slandering the doers.

"DIED . . ."

THE "TIMES" OBITUARY

I.

WHAT shall we add now? He is dead.
  And I who praise, and you who blame,
  With wash of words across his name,
Find suddenly declared instead—
  "*On Sunday, third of August, dead.*"

II.

Which stops the whole we talked to-day,
  I, quickened to a plausive glance
  At his large general tolerance
By common people's narrow way,
Stopped short in praising. Dead, they say.

III.

And you, who had just put in a sort
  Of cold deduction—"rather, large
  Through weakness of the continent marge,
Than greatness of the thing contained"—
Broke off. Dead!—there, you stood restrained.

IV.

As if we had talked in following one
  Up some long gallery. "Would you choose
  An air like that? The gait is loose,
Or noble." Sudden in the sun
An oubliette winks. Where *is* he? Gone.

V.

Dead. Man's "I was," by God's "I am"—
  All hero-worship comes to that.
  High heart, high thought, high fame, as flat
As a gravestone. Bring your *Jacet jam*—
The epitaph's an epigram.

VI.

Dead. There's an answer to arrest
  All carping. Dust's his natural place?
  He'll let the flies buzz round his face,
And, though you slander, not protest?
—From such an one exact the best?

VII.

Opinions gold or brass are null.
  We chuck our flattery or abuse,
  Called Cæsar's due, as Charon's dues,
I' the teeth of some dead sage or fool,
To mend the grinning of the skull.

VIII.

Be abstinent in praise and blame.
  The man's still mortal, who stands first,
  And mortal only, if last and worst.
Then slowly lift so frail a fame,
Or softly drop so poor a shame.

THE FORCED RECRUIT

Solferino, 1859

I.

In the ranks of the Austrian you found him,
  He died with his face to you all;
Yet bury him here where around him
  You honor your bravest that fall.

II.

Venetian, fair-featured and slender,
  He lies shot to death in his youth,
With a smile on his lips over-tender
  For any mere soldier's dead mouth.

III.

No stranger, and yet not a traitor,
  Though alien the cloth on his breast,
Underneath it how seldom a greater
  Young heart has a shot sent to rest!

IV.

By your enemy tortured and goaded
  To march with them, stand in their file,
His musket (see) never was loaded,
  He facing your guns with that smile!

V.

As orphans yearn on to their mothers,
  He yearned to your patriot bands;—
"Let me die for our Italy, brothers,
  If not in your ranks, by your hands!

VI.

"Aim straightly, fire steadily! spare me
  A ball in the body which may
Deliver my heart here, and tear me
  This badge of the Austrian away!"

VII.

So thought he, so died he this morning.
  What then? many others have died.
Ay, but easy for men to die scorning
  The death-stroke, who fought side by side--

VIII.

One tricolor floating above them;
  Struck down 'mid triumphant acclaims
Of an Italy rescued to love them
  And blazon the brass with their names.

IX.

But he, without witness or honor,
  Mixed, shamed in his country's regard,
With the tyrants who march in upon her,
  Died faithful and passive: 'twas hard.

X.

'Twas sublime. In a cruel restriction
  Cut off from the guerdon of sons,
With most filial obedience, conviction,
  His soul kissed the lips of her guns.

XI.

That moves you? Nay, grudge not to show it,
    While digging a grave for him here:
The others who died, says your poet,
    Have glory,—let *him* have a tear.

MOTHER AND POET

TURIN, AFTER NEWS FROM GAETA, 1861

I.

DEAD! One of them shot by the sea in the east,
    And one of them shot in the west by the sea.
Dead! both my boys! When you sit at the feast,
    And are wanting a great song for Italy free,
        Let none look at *me*.

II.

Yet I was a poetess only last year,
    And good at my art, for a woman, men said;
But *this* woman, *this*, who is agonized here,
    —The east sea and west sea rhyme on in her head
        Forever instead.

III.

What art can a woman be good at? Oh, vain!
    What art *is* she good at, but hurting her breast
With the milk-teeth of babes, and a smile at the pain?
    Ah, boys, how you hurt! you were strong as you prest,
        And I proud by that test.

IV.

What art's for a woman? To hold on her knees
    Both darlings! to feel all their arms round her throat,
Cling, strangle a little! to sew by degrees,
    And 'broider the long-clothes and neat little coat;
        To dream and to dote.

V.

To teach them. . . . It stings there! *I* made them indeed
    Speak plain the word *country*. *I* taught them, no doubt,
That a country's a thing men should die for at need.
    I prated of liberty, rights, and about
        The tyrant cast out.

VI.

And when their eyes flashed . . . O my beautiful eyes! . . .
　　I exulted; nay, let them go forth at the wheels
Of the guns, and denied not. But then the surprise
　　When one sits quite alone! Then one weeps, then one kneels.
　　　　God, how the house feels!

VII.

At first, happy news came, in gay letters moiled
　　With my kisses, of camp-life and glory, and how
They both loved me; and, soon coming home to be spoiled,
　　In return would fan off every fly from my brow
　　　　With their green laurel-bough.

VIII.

Then was triumph at Turin: "Ancona was free!"
　　And some one came out of the cheers in the street,
With a face pale as stone, to say something to me.
　　My Guido was dead! I fell down at his feet,
　　　　While they cheered in the street.

IX.

I bore it; friends soothed me; my grief looked sublime
　　As the ransom of Italy. One boy remained
To be leant on and walked with, recalling the time
　　When the first grew immortal, while both of us strained
　　　　To the height he had gained.

X.

And letters still came, shorter, sadder, more strong,
　　Writ now but in one hand. "I was not to faint,—
One loved me for two, would be with me ere long:
　　And *Viva l'Italia!—he* died for, our saint,
　　　　Who forbids our complaint."

XI.

My Nanni would add, "he was safe, and aware
　　Of a presence that turned off the balls,—was imprest
It was Guido himself, who knew what I could bear,
　　And how 'twas impossible, quite dispossest,
　　　　To live on for the rest."

XII.

On which, without pause, up the telegraph-line
　　Swept smoothly the next news from Gaeta,—*Shot.*

Tell his mother. Ah, ah! "his," "their" mother, not "mine:"
No voice says, "*My* mother," again to me. What!
   You think Guido forgot?

XIII.

Are souls straight so happy, that, dizzy with heaven,
   They drop earth's affections, conceive not of woe?
I think not. Themselves were too lately forgiven
   Through THAT Love and Sorrow which reconciled so
      The Above and Below.

XIV.

O Christ of the five wounds, who look'dst through the dark
   To the face of thy mother! consider, I pray,
How we common mothers stand desolate, mark,
   Whose sons, not being Christs, die with eyes turned away,
      And no last word to say.

XV.

Both boys dead? but that's out of nature. We all
   Have been patriots, yet each house must always keep one.
'Twere imbecile, hewing out roads to a wall;
   And, when Italy's made, for what end is it done,
      If we have not a son?

XVI.

Ah, ah, ah! when Gaeta's taken, what then?
   When the fair wicked queen sits no more at her sport
Of the fire-balls of death crashing souls out of men?
   When the guns of Cavalli with final retort
      Have cut the game short?

XVII.

When Venice and Rome keep their new jubilee;
   When your flag takes all heaven for its white, green, and red;
When *you* have your country from mountain to sea;
   When King Victor has Italy's crown on his head,
      (And *I* have my dead),—

XVIII.

What then? Do not mock me. Ah, ring your bells low,
   And burn your lights faintly! *My* country is *there*,
Above the star pricked by the last peak of snow:
   My Italy's THERE, with my brave civic pair
      To disfranchise despair!

xix.

Forgive me. Some women bear children in strength,
  And bite back the cry of their pain in self-scorn;
But the birth-pangs of nations will wring us at length
  Into wail such as this; and we sit on forlorn
    When the man-child is born.

xx.

Dead! One of them shot by the sea in the east,
  And one of them shot in the west by the sea.
Both! both my boys! If in keeping the feast
  You want a great song for your Italy free,
    Let none look at *me!*

[*This was Laura Savio of Turin, a poetess and patriot, whose sons were killed at Ancona and Gaeta.*]

POEMS OF ROBERT BROWNING

POEMS OF ROBERT BROWNING

DRAMATIC LYRICS

In a late edition were collected and redistributed the pieces first published in 1842, 1845, and 1855, respectively, under the titles of "Dramatic Lyrics," "Dramatic Romances," and "Men and Women." It is not worth while to disturb this arrangement.

Such Poems as the majority in this volume might also come properly enough, I suppose, under the head of "Dramatic Pieces;" being, though often Lyric in expression, always Dramatic in principle, and so many utterances of so many imaginary persons, not mine.

Part of the Poems were inscribed to my dear friend John Kenyon; I hope the whole may obtain the honor of an association with his memory.   R. B.

CAVALIER TUNES

I. Marching Along

I.

Kentish Sir Byng stood for his King,
Bidding the crop-headed Parliament swing:
And, pressing a troop unable to stoop
And see the rogues flourish and honest folk droop,
Marched them along, fifty-score strong,
Great-hearted gentlemen, singing this song.

II.

God for King Charles! Pym and such carles
To the Devil that prompts 'em their treasonous parles!
Cavaliers, up! Lips from the cup,
Hands from the pasty, nor bite take nor sup
Till you're—
    Chorus.—Marching along, fifty-score strong,
        Great-hearted gentlemen, singing this song.

III.

Hampden to hell, and his obsequies' knell.
Serve Hazelrig, Fiennes, and young Harry as well!
England, good cheer! Rupert is near!
Kentish and loyalists, keep we not here,
    Chorus.—Marching along, fifty-score strong,
        Great-hearted gentlemen, singing this song.

131

IV.

Then, God for King Charles! Pym and his snarls
To the Devil that pricks on such pestilent carles!
Hold by the right, you double your might;
So, onward to Nottingham, fresh for the fight,
CHORUS.—March we along, fifty-score strong,
　　　　Great-hearted gentlemen, singing this song!

II. GIVE A ROUSE

I.

KING CHARLES, and who'll do him right now?
King Charles, and who's ripe for fight now?
Give a rouse: here's, in hell's despite now,
King Charles!

II.

Who gave me the goods that went since?
Who raised me the house that sank once?
Who helped me to gold I spent since?
Who found me in wine you drank once?
CHORUS.—King Charles, and who'll do him right now?
　　　　King Charles, and who's ripe for fight now?
　　　　Give a rouse: here's, in hell's despite now,
　　　　King Charles!

III.

To whom used my boy George quaff else,
By the old fool's side that begot him?
For whom did he cheer and laugh else,
While Noll's damned troopers shot him?
CHORUS.—King Charles, and who'll do him right now?
　　　　King Charles, and who's ripe for fight now?
　　　　Give a rouse: here's, in hell's despite now,
　　　　King Charles!

III. BOOT AND SADDLE

I.

BOOT, saddle, to horse, and away!
Rescue my castle before the hot day
Brightens to blue from its silvery gray.
CHORUS.—Boot, saddle, to horse, and away!

II.

Ride past the suburbs, asleep as you'd say;
Many's the friend there, will listen and pray
"God's luck to gallants that strike up the lay—
  CHORUS.—Boot, saddle, to horse, and away!"

III.

Forty miles off, like a roebuck at bay,
Flouts Castle Brancepeth the Roundheads' array:
Who laughs, "Good fellows ere this, by my fay,
  CHORUS.—Boot, saddle, to horse, and away!"

IV.

Who? My wife Gertrude; that, honest and gay,
Laughs when you talk of surrendering, "Nay!
I've better counsellors; what counsel they?
  CHORUS.—Boot, saddle, to horse, and away!"

THE LOST LEADER

I.

JUST for a handful of silver he left us,
  Just for a riband to stick in his coat—
Found the one gift of which fortune bereft us,
  Lost all the others she lets us devote;
They, with the gold to give, doled him out silver,
  So much was theirs who so little allowed:
How all our copper had gone for his service!
  Rags—were they purple, his heart had been proud!
We that had loved him so, followed him, honored him,
  Lived in his mild and magnificent eye,
Learned his great language, caught his clear accents,
  Made him our pattern to live and to die!
Shakespeare was of us, Milton was for us,
  Burns, Shelley, were with us,—they watch from their graves!
He alone breaks from the van and the freemen,
  —He alone sinks to the rear and the slaves!

II.

We shall march prospering,—not through his presence;
  Songs may inspirit us,—not from his lyre;
Deeds will be done,—while he boasts his quiescence,
  Still bidding crouch whom the rest bade aspire:
Blot out his name, then, record one lost soul more,
  One task more declined, one more footpath untrod,

One more devils'-triumph and sorrow for angels,
  One wrong more to man, one more insult to God!
Life's night begins: let him never come back to us!
  There would be doubt, hesitation and pain,
Forced praise on our part—the glimmer of twilight,
  Never glad confident morning again!
Best fight on well, for we taught him—strike gallantly,
  Menace our heart ere we master his own;
Then let him receive the new knowledge and wait us,
  Pardoned in heaven, the first by the throne!

"HOW THEY BROUGHT THE GOOD NEWS FROM GHENT TO AIX."

[16-.]

I.

I SPRANG to the stirrup, and Joris, and he;
I galloped, Dirck galloped, we galloped all three;
"Good speed!" cried the watch, as the gate-bolts undrew;
"Speed!" echoed the wall to us galloping through;
Behind shut the postern, the lights sank to rest,
And into the midnight we galloped abreast.

II.

Not a word to each other; we kept the great pace
Neck by neck, stride by stride, never changing our place;
I turned in my saddle and made its girths tight,
Then shortened each stirrup, and set the pique right,
Rebuckled the cheek-strap, chained slacker the bit,
Nor galloped less steadily Roland a whit.

III.

'T was moonset at starting; but while we drew near
Lokeren, the cocks crew and twilight dawned clear;
At Boom, a great yellow star came out to see;
At Düffeld, 't was morning as plain as could be;
And from Mecheln church-steeple we heard the half-chime,
So, Joris broke silence with, "Yet there is time!"

IV.

At Aershot, up leaped of a sudden the sun,
And against him the cattle stood black every one,
To stare through the mist at us galloping past,

And I saw my stout galloper Roland at last,
With resolute shoulders, each butting away
The haze, as some bluff river headland its spray:

v.

And his low head and crest, just one sharp ear bent back
For my voice, and the other pricked out on his track;
And one eye's black intelligence,—ever that glance
O'er its white edge at me, his own master, askance!
And the thick heavy spume-flakes which aye and anon
His fierce lips shook upwards in galloping on.

vi.

By Hasselt, Dirck groaned; and cried Joris, "Stay spur!
Your Roos galloped bravely, the fault's not in her,
We'll remember at Aix"—for one heard the quick wheeze
Of her chest, saw the stretched neck and staggering knees,
And sunk tail, and horrible heave of the flank,
As down on her haunches she shuddered and sank.

vii.

So, we were left galloping, Joris and I,
Past Looz and past Tongres, no cloud in the sky;
The broad sun above laughed a pitiless laugh,
'Neath our feet broke the brittle bright stubble like chaff;
Till over by Dalhem a dome-spire sprang white,
And "Gallop," gasped Joris, "for Aix is in sight!"

viii.

"How they'll greet us!"—and all in a moment his roan
Rolled neck and croup over, lay dead as a stone;
And there was my Roland to bear the whole weight
Of the news which alone could save Aix from her fate,
With his nostrils like pits full of blood to the brim,
And with circles of red for his eye-sockets' rim.

ix.

Then I cast loose my buffcoat, each holster let fall,
Shook off both my jack-boots, let go belt and all,
Stood up in the stirrup, leaned, patted his ear,
Called my Roland his pet-name, my horse without peer;
Clapped my hands, laughed and sang, any noise, bad or good,
Till at length into Aix Roland galloped and stood.

x.

And all I remember is—friends flocking round
As I sat with his head 'twixt my knees on the ground;

And no voice but was praising this Roland of mine,
As I poured down his throat our last measure of wine,
Which (the burgesses voted by common consent)
Was no more than his due who brought good news from Ghent.

THROUGH THE METIDJA TO ABD-EL-KADR

1842

I.

As I RIDE, as I ride,
With a full heart for my guide,
So its tide rocks my side,
As I ride, as I ride,
That, as I were double-eyed,
He, in whom our Tribes confide,
Is descried, ways untried,
As I ride, as I ride.

II.

As I ride, as I ride
To our Chief and his Allied,
Who dares chide my heart's pride
As I ride, as I ride?
Or are witnesses denied—
Through the desert waste and wide
Do I glide unespied
As I ride, as I ride?

III.

As I ride, as I ride,
When an inner voice has cried,
The sands slide, nor abide
(As I ride, as I ride)
O'er each visioned homicide
That came vaunting (has he lied?)
To reside—where he died,
As I ride, as I ride.

IV.

As I ride, as I ride,
Ne'er has spur my swift horse plied,
Yet his hide, streaked and pied,
As I ride, as I ride,
Shows where sweat has sprung and dried,

—Zebra-footed, ostrich-thighed—
How has vied stride with stride
As I ride, as I ride!

v.

As I ride, as I ride,
Could I loose what Fate has tied,
Ere I pried, she should hide
(As I ride, as I ride)
All that's meant me—satisfied
When the Prophet and the Bride
Stop veins I'd have subside
As I ride, as I ride!

NATIONALITY IN DRINKS

I.

My HEART sank with our Claret-flask,
  Just now, beneath the heavy sedges
That serve this pond's black face for mask;
  And still at yonder broken edges
O' the hole, where up the bubbles glisten,
After my heart I look and listen.

II.

Our laughing little flask, compelled
  Through depth to depth more bleak and shady;
As when, both arms beside her held,
  Feet straightened out, some gay French lady
Is caught up from life's light and motion,
And dropped into death's silent ocean!

—Up jumped Tokay on our table,
Like a pygmy castle-warder,
Dwarfish to see, but stout and able,
Arms and accoutrements all in order;
And fierce he looked North, then, wheeling South,
Blew with his bugle a challenge to Drouth,
Cocked his flap-hat with the tosspot-feather,
Twisted his thumb in his red moustache,
Jingled his huge brass spurs together,
Tightened his waist with its Buda sash,
And then, with an impudence nought could abash,
Shrugged his hump-shoulder, to tell the beholder,
For twenty such knaves he should laugh but the bolder:

And so, with his sword-hilt gallantly jutting,
And dexter-hand on his haunch abutting,
Went the little man, Sir Ausbruch, strutting!

—Here's to Nelson's memory!
'T is the second time that I, at sea,
Right off Cape Trafalgar here,
Have drunk it deep in British Beer.
Nelson forever—any time
Am I his to command in prose or rhyme!
Give me of Nelson only a touch,
And I save it, be it little or much:
Here's one our Captain gives, and so
Down at the word, by George, shall it go!
He says that at Greenwich they point the beholder
To Nelson's coat, "still with tar on the shoulder:
For he used to lean with one shoulder digging,
Jigging, as it were, and zig-zag-zigging
Up against the mizzen-rigging!"

GARDEN FANCIES

I. The Flower's Name

I.

Here's the garden she walked across,
    Arm in my arm, such a short while since:
Hark, now I push its wicket, the moss
    Hinders the hinges and makes them wince!
She must have reached this shrub ere she turned,
    As back with that murmur the wicket swung;
For she laid the poor snail, my chance foot spurned,
    To feed and forget it the leaves among.

II.

Down this side of the gravel-walk
    She went while her robe's edge brushed the box:
And here she paused in her gracious talk
    To point me a moth on the milk-white phlox.
Roses, ranged in valiant row,
    I will never think that she passed you by!
She loves you, noble roses, I know;
    But yonder, see, where the rock-plants lie!

III.

This flower she stopped at, finger on lip,
  Stooped over, in doubt, as settling its claim;
Till she gave me, with pride to make no slip,
  Its soft meandering Spanish name:
What a name! Was it love or praise?
  Speech half-asleep or song half-awake?
I must learn Spanish, one of these days,
  Only for that slow sweet name's sake.

IV.

Roses, if I live and do well,
  I may bring her, one of these days,
To fix you fast with as fine a spell,
  Fit you each with his Spanish phrase;
But do not detain me now; for she lingers
  There, like sunshine over the ground,
And ever I see her soft white fingers
  Searching after the bud she found.

V.

Flower, you Spaniard, look that you grow not,
  Stay as you are and be loved forever!
Bud, if I kiss you 't is that you blow not,
  Mind, the shut pink mouth opens never!
For while it pouts, her fingers wrestle,
  Twinkling the audacious leaves between,
Till round they turn and down they nestle—
  Is not the dear mark still to be seen?

VI.

Where I find her not, beauties vanish;
  Whither I follow her, beauties flee;
Is there no method to tell her in Spanish
  June's twice June since she breathed it with me?
Come, bud, show me the least of her traces,
  Treasure my lady's lightest footfall!
—Ah, you may flout and turn up your faces—
  Roses, you are not so fair after all!

II. SIBRANDUS SCHAFNABURGENSIS

I.

PLAGUE take all your pedants, say I!
  He who wrote what I hold in my hand,
Centuries back was so good as to die,

Leaving this rubbish to cumber the land;
This, that was a book in its time,
   Printed on paper and bound in leather,
Last month in the white of a matin-prime,
   Just when the birds sang all together.

II.

Into the garden I brought it to read,
   And under the arbute and laurustine
Read it, so help me grace in my need,
   From title-page to closing line.
Chapter on chapter did I count,
   As a curious traveller counts Stonehenge;
Added up the mortal amount;
   And then proceeded to my revenge.

III.

Yonder's a plum-tree with a crevice
   An owl would build in, were he but sage;
For a lap of moss, like a fine pont-levis
   In a castle of the Middle Age,
Joins to a lip of gum, pure amber;
   When he'd be private, there might he spend
Hours alone in his lady's chamber:
   Into this crevice I dropped our friend.

IV.

Splash, went he, as under he ducked,
   —At the bottom, I knew, rain-drippings stagnate;
Next, a handful of blossoms I plucked
   To bury him with, my bookshelf's magnate;
Then I went in-doors, brought out a loaf,
   Half a cheese, and a bottle of Chablis;
Lay on the grass and forgot the oaf
   Over a jolly chapter of Rabelais.

V.

Now, this morning, betwixt the moss
   And gum that locked our friend in limbo,
A spider had spun his web across,
   And sat in the midst with arms akimbo:
So, I took pity, for learning's sake,
   And, *de profundis, accentibus lætis,*
Cantate! quoth I, as I got a rake;
   And up I fished his delectable treatise.

VI.

Here you have it, dry in the sun,
  With all the binding all of a blister,
And great blue spots where the ink has run,
  And reddish streaks that wink and glister
O'er the page so beautifully yellow:
  Oh, well have the droppings played their tricks!
Did he guess how toadstools grow, this fellow?
  Here's one stuck in his chapter six!

VII.

How did he like it when the live creatures
  Tickled and toused and browsed him all over,
And worm, slug, eft, with serious features,
  Came in, each one, for his right of trover?
—When the water-beetle with great blind deaf face
  Made of her eggs the stately deposit,
And the newt borrowed just so much of the preface
  As tiled in the top of his black wife's closet?

VIII.

All that life and fun and romping,
  All that frisking and twisting and coupling,
While slowly our poor friend's leaves were swamping
  And clasps were cracking and covers suppling!
As if you had carried sour John Knox
  To the play-house at Paris, Vienna or Munich,
Fastened him into a front-row box,
  And danced off the ballet with trousers and tunic.

IX.

Come, old martyr! What, torment enough is it?
  Back to my room shall you take your sweet self.
Good-bye, mother-beetle; husband-eft, *sufficit!*
  See the snug niche I have made on my shelf!
A's book shall prop you up, B's shall cover you,
  Here's C to be grave with, or D to be gay,
And with E on each side, and F right over you,
  Dry-rot at ease till the Judgment-day!

SOLILOQUY OF THE SPANISH CLOISTER

I.

Gr-r-r—there go, my heart's abhorrence!
  Water your damned flower-pots, do!
If hate killed men, Brother Lawrence,

God's blood, would not mine kill you!
What? your myrtle-bush wants trimming?
  Oh, that rose has prior claims—
Needs its leaden vase filled brimming?
  Hell dry you up with its flames!

II.

At the meal we sit together:
  Salve tibi! I must hear
Wise talk of the kind of weather,
  Sort of season, time of year:
Not a plenteous cork-crop: scarcely
  Dare we hope oak-galls, I doubt:
What's the Latin name for "parsley"?
  What's the Greek name for Swine's Snout?

III.

Whew! We'll have our platter burnished,
  Laid with care on our own shelf!
With a fire-new spoon we're furnished,
  And a goblet for ourself,
Rinsed like something sacrificial
  Ere 't is fit to touch our chaps—
Marked with L for our initial!
  (He-he! There his lily snaps!)

IV.

Saint, forsooth! While brown Dolores
  Squats outside the Convent bank
With Sanchicha, telling stories,
  Steeping tresses in the tank,
Blue-black, lustrous, thick like horsehairs,
  —Can't I see his dead eye glow,
Bright as 't were a Barbary corsair's?
  (That is, if he'd let it show!)

V.

When he finishes refection,
  Knife and fork he never lays
Cross-wise, to my recollection,
  As do I, in Jesu's praise.
I the Trinity illustrate,
  Drinking watered orange-pulp—
In three sips the Arian frustrate;
  While he drains his at one gulp.

VI.

Oh, those melons! If he's able
    We're to have a feast! so nice!
One goes to the Abbot's table,
    All of us get each a slice.
How go on your flowers? None double?
    Not one fruit-sort can you spy?
Strange!—And I, too, at such trouble
    Keep them close-nipped on the sly!

VII.

There's a great text in Galatians,
    Once you trip on it, entails
Twenty-nine distinct damnations,
    One sure, if another fails:
If I trip him just a-dying,
    Sure of heaven as sure can be,
Spin him round and send him flying
    Off to hell, a Manichee?

VIII.

Or, my scrofulous French novel
    On gray paper with blunt type!
Simply glance at it, you grovel
    Hand and foot in Belial's gripe:
If I double down its pages
    At the woful sixteenth print,
When he gathers his greengages,
    Ope a sieve and slip it in 't?

IX.

Or, there's Satan!—one might venture
    Pledge one's soul to him, yet leave
Such a flaw in the indenture
    As he'd miss till, past retrieve,
Blasted lay that rose-acacia
    We're so proud of! *Hy, Zy, Hine* . . .
'St, there's Vespers! *Plena gratiâ*,
    Ave, Virgo! Gr-r-r—you swine!

THE LABORATORY

ANCIEN RÉGIME

I.

Now that I, tying thy glass mask tightly,
May gaze through these faint smokes curling whitely,
As thou pliest thy trade in this devil's-smithy—
Which is the poison to poison her, prithee?

II.

He is with her, and they know that I know
Where they are, what they do: they believe my tears flow
While they laugh, laugh at me, at me fled to the drear
Empty church, to pray God in, for them!—I am here.

III.

Grind away, moisten and mash up thy paste,
Pound at thy powder,—I am not in haste!
Better sit thus, and observe thy strange things,
Than go where men wait me and dance at the King's.

IV.

That in the mortar—you call it a gum?
Ah, the brave tree whence such gold oozings come!
And yonder soft phial, the exquisite blue,
Sure to taste sweetly,—is that poison too?

V.

Had I but all of them, thee and thy treasures,
What a wild crowd of invisible pleasures!
To carry pure death in an earring, a casket,
A signet, a fan-mount, a filigree basket!

VI.

Soon, at the King's, a mere lozenge to give,
And Pauline should have just thirty minutes to live!
But to light a pastile, and Elise, with her head
And her breast and her arms and her hands, should drop dead!

VII.

Quick—is it finished? The color's too grim!
Why not soft like the phial's, enticing and dim?
Let it brighten her drink, let her turn it and stir,
And try it and taste, ere she fix and prefer!

VIII.

What a drop! She's not little, no minion like me!
That's why she ensnared him: this never will free
The soul from those masculine eyes,—say, "no!"
To that pulse's magnificent come-and-go.

IX.

For only last night, as they whispered, I brought
My own eyes to bear on her so, that I thought
Could I keep them one half minute fixed, she would fall
Shrivelled; she fell not; yet this does it all!

X.

Not that I bid you spare her the pain;
Let death be felt and the proof remain:
Brand, burn up, bite into its grace—
He is sure to remember her dying face!

XI.

Is it done? Take my mask off! Nay, be not morose;
It kills her, and this prevents seeing it close:
The delicate droplet, my whole fortune's fee!
If it hurts her, beside, can it ever hurt me?

XII.

Now, take all my jewels, gorge gold to your fill,
You may kiss me, old man, on my mouth if you will!
But brush this dust off me, lest horror it brings
Ere I know it—next moment I dance at the King's!

THE CONFESSIONAL

[SPAIN.]

I.

IT IS a lie—their Priests, their Pope,
Their Saints, their . . . all they fear or hope
Are lies, and lies—there! through my door
And ceiling, there! and walls and floor,
There, lies, they lie—shall still be hurled
Till spite of them I reach the world!

II.

You think Priests just and holy men!
Before they put me in this den

I was a human creature too,
With flesh and blood like one of you,
A girl that laughed in beauty's pride
Like lilies in your world outside.

III.

I had a lover—shame avaunt!
This poor wrenched body, grim and gaunt,
Was kissed all over till it burned,
By lips the truest, love e'er turned
His heart's own tint: one night they kissed
My soul out in a burning mist.

IV.

So, next day when the accustomed train
Of things grew round my sense again,
"That is a sin," I said: and slow
With downcast eyes to church I go,
And pass to the confession-chair,
And tell the old mild father there.

V.

But when I falter Beltran's name,
"Ha!" quoth the father; "much I blame
The sin; yet wherefore idly grieve?
Despair not—strenuously retrieve!
Nay, I will turn this love of thine
To lawful love, almost divine;

VI.

"For he is young, and led astray,
This Beltran, and he schemes, men say,
To change the laws of church and state;
So, thine shall be an angel's fate,
Who, ere the thunder breaks, should roll
Its cloud away and save his soul.

VII.

"For, when he lies upon thy breast,
Thou mayst demand and be possessed
Of all his plans, and next day steal
To me, and all those plans reveal,
That I and every priest, to purge
His soul, may fast and use the scourge."

VIII.

That father's beard was long and white,
With love and truth his brow seemed bright;
I went back, all on fire with joy,
And, that same evening, bade the boy
Tell me, as lovers should, heart-free,
Something to prove his love of me.

IX.

He told me what he would not tell
For hope of heaven or fear of hell;
And I lay listening in such pride!
And, soon as he had left my side,
Tripped to the church by morning-light
To save his soul in his despite.

X.

I told the father all his schemes,
Who were his comrades, what their dreams;
"And now make haste," I said, "to pray
The one spot from his soul away;
To-night he comes, but not the same
Will look!" At night he never came.

XI.

Nor next night: on the after-morn,
I went forth with a strength new-born.
The church was empty; something drew
My steps into the street; I knew
It led me to the market-place:
Where, lo, on high, the father's face!

XII.

That horrible black scaffold dressed,
That stapled block . . . God sink the rest!
That head strapped back, that blinding vest,
Those knotted hands and naked breast,
Till near one busy hangman pressed,
And, on the neck these arms caressed. . . .

XIII.

No part in aught they hope or fear!
No heaven with them, no hell!—and here,
No earth, not so much space as pens
My body in their worst of dens
But shall bear God and man my cry,
Lies—lies, again—and still, they lie!

CRISTINA

I.

She should never have looked at me
  If she meant I should not love her!
There are plenty . . . men, you call such,
  I suppose . . . she may discover
All her soul to, if she pleases,
  And yet leave much as she found them:
But I'm not so, and she knew it
  When she fixed me, glancing round them.

II.

What? To fix me thus meant nothing?
  But I can't tell (there's my weakness)
What her look said!—no vile cant, sure,
  About "need to strew the bleakness
Of some lone shore with its pearl-seed,
  That the sea feels"—no "strange yearning
That such souls have, most to lavish
  Where there's chance of least returning."

III.

Oh we're sunk enough here, God knows!
  But not quite so sunk that moments,
Sure though seldom, are denied us,
  When the spirit's true endowments
Stand out plainly from its false ones,
  And apprise it if pursuing
Or the right way or the wrong way,
  To its triumph or undoing.

IV.

There are flashes struck from midnights,
  There are fire-flames noondays kindle,
Whereby piled-up honors perish,
  Whereby swollen ambitions dwindle,
While just this or that poor impulse,
  Which for once had play unstifled,
Seems the sole work of a lifetime,
  That away the rest have trifled.

V.

Doubt you if, in some such moment,
  As she fixed me, she felt clearly,

Ages past the soul existed,
  Here an age 't is resting merely,
And hence fleets again for ages,
  While the true end, sole and single,
It stops here for is, this love-way,
  With some other soul to mingle?

VI.

Else it loses what it lived for,
  And eternally must lose it;
Better ends may be in prospect,
  Deeper blisses (if you choose it),
But this life's end and this love-bliss
  Have been lost here. Doubt you whether
This she felt as, looking at me,
  Mine and her souls rushed together?

VII.

Oh, observe! Of course, next moment,
  The world's honors, in derision,
Trampled out the light forever:
  Never fear but there's provision
Of the devil's to quench knowledge
  Lest we walk the earth in rapture!
—Making those who catch God's secret
  Just so much more prize their capture!

VIII.

Such am I: the secret's mine now!
  She has lost me, I have gained her;
Her soul's mine: and thus, grown perfect,
  I shall pass my life's remainder.
Life will just hold out the proving
  Both our powers, alone and blended:
And then, come the next life quickly!
  This world's use will have been ended.

THE LOST MISTRESS

I.

ALL'S OVER, then: does truth sound bitter
  As one at first believes?
Hark, 't is the sparrows' good-night twitter
  About your cottage eaves!

II.

And the leaf-buds on the vine are woolly,
  I noticed that, to-day;
One day more bursts them open fully
  —You know the red turns gray.

III.

To-morrow we meet the same then, dearest?
  May I take your hand in mine?
Mere friends are we,—well, friends the merest
  Keep much that I resign:

IV.

For each glance of the eye so bright and black,
  Though I keep with heart's endeavor,—
Your voice, when you wish the snowdrops back,
  Though it stay in my soul forever!—

V.

Yet I will but say what mere friends say,
  Or only a thought stronger;
I will hold your hand but as long as all may,
  Or so very little longer!

EARTH'S IMMORTALITIES

FAME

See, as the prettiest graves will do in time,
Our poet's wants the freshness of its prime;
Spite of the sexton's browsing horse, the sods
Have struggled through its binding osier rods;
Headstone and half-sunk footstone lean awry,
Wanting the brick-work promised by-and-by;
How the minute gray lichens, plate o'er plate,
Have softened down the crisp-cut name and date!

LOVE

So, the year's done with!
  (*Love me forever!*)
All March begun with,
  April's endeavor;
May-wreaths that bound me
  June needs must sever;
Now snows fall round me,
  Quenching June's fever—
  (*Love me forever!*)

MEETING AT NIGHT

I.

THE gray sea and the long black land;
And the yellow half-moon large and low;
And the startled little waves that leap
In fiery ringlets from their sleep,
As I gain the cove with pushing prow,
And quench its speed i' the slushy sand.

II.

Then a mile of warm sea-scented beach;
Three fields to cross till a farm appears;
A tap at the pane, the quick sharp scratch
And blue spurt of a lighted match,
And a voice less loud, through its joys and fears,
Than the two hearts beating each to each!

PARTING AT MORNING

ROUND the cape of a sudden came the sea,
And the sun looked over the mountain's rim:
And straight was a path of gold for him,
And the need of a world of men for me.

SONG

I.

NAY but you, who do not love her,
  Is she not pure gold, my mistress?
Holds earth aught—speak truth—above her?
  Aught like this tress, see, and this tress,
And this last fairest tress of all,
So fair, see, ere I let it fall?

II.

Because, you spend your lives in praising;
  To praise, you search the wide world over:
Then why not witness, calmly gazing,
  If earth holds aught—speak truth—above her?
Above this tress, and this, I touch
But cannot praise, I love so much!

A WOMAN'S LAST WORD

I.

LET'S CONTEND no more, Love,
　Strive nor weep:
All be as before, Love,
　—Only sleep!

II.

What so wild as words are?
　I and thou
In debate, as birds are,
　Hawk on bough!

III.

See the creature stalking
　While we speak!
Hush and hide the talking,
　Cheek on cheek!

IV.

What so false as truth is,
　False to thee?
Where the serpent's tooth is
　Shun the tree—

V.

Where the apple reddens
　Never pry—
Lest we lose our Edens,
　Eve and I.

VI.

Be a god and hold me
　With a charm!
Be a man and fold me
　With thine arm!

VII.

Teach me, only teach, Love!
　As I ought
I will speak thy speech, Love,
　Think thy thought—

VIII.

Meet, if thou require it,
 Both demands,
Laying flesh and spirit
 In thy hands.

IX.

That shall be to-morrow,
 Not to-night:
I must bury sorrow
 Out of sight:

X.

—Must a little weep, Love,
 (Foolish me!)
And so fall asleep, Love,
 Loved by thee.

EVELYN HOPE

I.

BEAUTIFUL Evelyn Hope is dead!
 Sit and watch by her side an hour.
That is her book-shelf, this her bed;
 She plucked that piece of geranium-flower,
Beginning to die too, in the glass;
 Little has yet been changed, I think:
The shutters are shut, no light may pass
 Save two long rays through the hinge's chink.

II.

Sixteen years old when she died!
 Perhaps she had scarcely heard my name;
It was not her time to love; beside,
 Her life had many a hope and aim,
Duties enough and little cares,
 And now was quiet, now astir,
Till God's hand beckoned unawares,—
 And the sweet white brow is all of her.

III.

Is it too late then, Evelyn Hope?
 What, your soul was pure and true,
The good stars met in your horoscope,
 Made you of spirit, fire and dew—

And, just because I was thrice as old
  And our paths in the world diverged so wide,
Each was nought to each, must I be told?
  We were fellow mortals, nought beside?

IV.

No, indeed! for God above
  Is great to grant, as mighty to make,
And creates the love to reward the love:
  I claim you still, for my own love's sake!
Delayed it may be for more lives yet,
  Through worlds I shall traverse, not a few:
Much is to learn, much to forget
  Ere the time be come for taking you.

V.

But the time will come,—at last it will,
  When, Evelyn Hope, what meant (I shall say)
In the lower earth, in the years long still,
  That body and soul so pure and gay?
Why your hair was amber, I shall divine,
  And your mouth of your own geranium's red—
And what you would do with me, in fine,
  In the new life come in the old one's stead.

VI.

I have lived (I shall say) so much since then,
  Given up myself so many times,
Gained me the gains of various men,
  Ransacked the ages, spoiled the climes;
Yet one thing, one, in my soul's full scope,
  Either I missed or itself missed me:
And I want and find you, Evelyn Hope!
  What is the issue? let us see!

VII.

I loved you, Evelyn, all the while!
  My heart seemed full as it could hold;
There was place and to spare for the frank young smile,
  And the red young mouth, and the hair's young gold.
So, hush,—I will give you this leaf to keep:
  See, I shut it inside the sweet cold hand!
There, that is our secret: go to sleep!
  You will wake, and remember, and understand.

LOVE AMONG THE RUINS

I.

WHERE the quiet-colored end of evening smiles
    Miles and miles
On the solitary pastures where our sheep
    Half-asleep
Tinkle homeward through the twilight, stray or stop
    As they crop—
Was the site once of a city great and gay,
    (So they say)
Of our country's very capital, its prince
    Ages since
Held his court in, gathered councils, wielding far
    Peace or war.

II.

Now,—the country does not even boast a tree,
    As you see,
To distinguish slopes of verdure, certain rills
    From the hills
Intersect and give a name to, (else they run
    Into one,)
Where the domed and daring palace shot its spires
    Up like fires
O'er the hundred-gated circuit of a wall
    Bounding all,
Made of marble, men might march on nor be pressed,
    Twelve abreast.

III.

And such plenty and perfection, see, of grass
    Never was!
Such a carpet as, this summer-time, o'erspreads
    And embeds
Every vestige of the city, guessed alone,
    Stock or stone—
Where a multitude of men breathed joy and woe
    Long ago;
Lust of glory pricked their hearts up, dread of shame
    Struck them tame;
And that glory and that shame alike, the gold
    Bought and sold.

IV.

Now,--the single little turret that remains
 On the plains,
By the caper overrooted, by the gourd
 Overscored,
While the patching houseleek's head of blossom winks
 Through the chinks--
Marks the basement whence a tower in ancient time
 Sprang sublime,
And a burning ring, all round, the chariots traced
 As they raced,
And the monarch and his minions and his dames
 Viewed the games.

V.

And I know, while thus the quiet-colored eve
 Smiles to leave
To their folding, all our many-tinkling fleece
 In such peace,
And the slopes and rills in undistinguished gray
 Melt away--
That a girl with eager eyes and yellow hair
 Waits me there
In the turret whence the charioteers caught soul
 For the goal,
When the king looked, where she looks now, breathless, **dumb**
 Till I come.

VI.

But he looked upon the city, every side,
 Far and wide,
All the mountains topped with temples, all the glades'
 Colonnades,
All the causeys, bridges, aqueducts,--and then,
 All the men!
When I do come, she will speak not, she will stand,
 Either hand
On my shoulder, give her eyes the first embrace
 Of my face,
Ere we rush, ere we extinguish sight and speech
 Each on each.

VII.

In one year they sent a million fighters forth
 South and North,
And they built their gods a brazen pillar high
 As the sky,

Yet reserved a thousand chariots in full force—
    Gold, of course.
Oh heart! oh blood that freezes, blood that burns!
    Earth's returns
For whole centuries of folly, noise and sin!
    Shut them in,
With their triumphs and their glories and the rest!
    Love is best.

A LOVERS' QUARREL

I.

Oh, what a dawn of day!
How the March sun feels like May!
    All is blue again
    After last night's rain,
And the South dries the hawthorn-spray
    Only, my Love's away!
I'd as lief that the blue were gray.

II.

Runnels, which rillets swell,
Must be dancing down the dell,
    With a foaming head
    On the beryl bed
Paven smooth as a hermit's cell;
    Each with a tale to tell,
Could my Love but attend as well.

III.

Dearest, three months ago!
When we lived blocked-up with snow,—
    When the wind would edge
    In and in his wedge,
In, as far as the point could go—
    Not to our ingle, though,
Where we loved each the other so!

IV.

Laughs with so little cause!
We devised games out of straws.
    We would try and trace
    One another's face
In the ash, as an artist draws;
    Free on each other's flaws,
How we chattered like two church daws!

v.

What's in the "Times"?—a scold
At the Emperor deep and cold;
   He has taken a bride
   To his gruesome side,
That's as fair as himself is bold:
   There they sit ermine-stoled,
And she powders her hair with gold.

vi.

Fancy the Pampas' sheen!
Miles and miles of gold and green
   Where the sunflowers blow
   In a solid glow,
And—to break now and then the screen—
   Black neck and eyeballs keen,
Up a wild horse leaps between!

vii.

Try, will our table turn?
Lay your hands there light, and yearn
   Till the yearning slips
   Through the finger-tips
In a fire which a few discern,
   And a very few feel burn,
And the rest, they may live and learn!

viii.

Then we would up and pace,
For a change, about the place,
   Each with arm o'er neck:
   'T is our quarter-deck,
We are seamen in woful case.
   Help in the ocean-space!
Or, if no help, we'll embrace.

ix.

See, how she looks now, dressed
In a sledging-cap and vest!
   'T is a huge fur cloak—
   Like a reindeer's yoke
Falls the lappet along the breast:
   Sleeves for her arms to rest,
Or to hang, as my Love likes best.

x.

Teach me to flirt a fan
As the Spanish ladies can,
    Or I tint your lip
    With a burnt stick's tip
And you turn into such a man!
    Just the two spots that span
Half the bill of the young male swan.

xi.

Dearest, three months ago
When the mesmerizer Snow
    With his hand's first sweep
    Put the earth to sleep:
'T was a time when the heart could show
    All—how was earth to know,
'Neath the mute hand's to-and-fro?

xii.

Dearest, three months ago
When we loved each other so,
    Lived and loved the same
    Till an evening came
When a shaft from the devil's bow
    Pierced to our ingle-glow,
And the friends were friend and foe!

xiii.

Not from the heart beneath—
'T was a bubble born of breath,
    Neither sneer nor vaunt,
    Nor reproach nor taunt.
See a word, how it severeth!
    Oh, power of life and death
In the tongue, as the Preacher saith!

xiv.

Woman, and will you cast
For a word, quite off at last
    Me, your own, your You,—
    Since, as truth is true,
I was You all the happy past—
    Me do you leave aghast
With the memories We amassed?

XV.

Love, if you knew the light
That your soul casts in my sight,
    How I look to you
    For the pure and true,
And the beauteous and the right,—
    Bear with a moment's spite
When a mere mote threats the white!

XVI.

What of a hasty word?
Is the fleshly heart not stirred
    By a worm's pin-prick
    Where its roots are quick?
See the eye, by a fly's-foot blurred—
    Ear, when a straw is heard
Scratch the brain's coat of curd!

XVII.

Foul be the world or fair
More or less, how can I care
    'T is the world the same
    For my praise or blame,
And endurance is easy there.
    Wrong in the one thing rare—
Oh, it is hard to bear!

XVIII.

Here's the spring back or close,
When the almond-blossom blows;
    We shall have the word
    In a minor third,
There is none but the cuckoo knows:
    Heaps of the guelder-rose!
I must bear with it, I suppose.

XIX.

Could but November come,
Were but noisy birds struck dumb
    At the warning slash
    Of his driver's-lash—
I would laugh like the valiant Thumb
    Facing the castle glum
And the giant's fee-faw-fum!

xx.

Then, were the world well stripped
Of the gear wherein equipped
    We can stand apart,
    Heart dispense with heart
In the sun, with the flowers unnipped,—
    Oh, the world's hangings ripped,
We were both in a bare-walled crypt!

xxi.

Each in the crypt would cry
"But one freezes here! and why?
    When a heart, as chill,
    At my own would thrill
Back to life, and its fires out-fly?
    Heart, shall we live or die?
The rest, . . . settle by and by!"

xxii.

So, she'd efface the score,
And forgive me as before.
    It is twelve o'clock:
    I shall hear her knock
In the worst of a storm's uproar,
    I shall pull her through the door,
I shall have her for evermore!

UP AT A VILLA—DOWN IN THE CITY

(As Distinguished by an Italian Person of Quality)

i.

Had I but plenty of money, money enough and to spare,
The house for me, no doubt, were a house in the city-square;
Ah, such a life, such a life, as one leads at the window there!

ii.

Something to see, by Bacchus, something to hear, at least!
There, the whole day long, one's life is a perfect feast;
While up at a villa one lives, I maintain it, no more than a beast.

iii.

Well now, look at our villa! stuck like the horn of a bull
Just on a mountain-edge as bare as the creature's skull,

Save a mere shag of a bush with hardly a leaf to pull!
—I scratch my own, sometimes, to see if the hair's turned wool.

IV.

But the city, oh the city—the square with the houses! Why?
They are stone-faced, white as a curd, there's something to take the eye!
Houses in four straight lines, not a single front awry;
You watch who crosses and gossips, who saunters, who hurries by;
Green blinds, as a matter of course, to draw when the sun gets high;
And the shops with fanciful signs which are painted properly.

V.

What of a villa? Though winter be over in March by rights,
'T is May perhaps ere the snow shall have withered well off the heights:
You've the brown ploughed land before, where the oxen steam and wheeze,
And the hills over-smoked behind by the faint gray olive-trees.

VI.

Is it better in May, I ask you? You've summer all at once;
In a day he leaps complete with a few strong April suns.
'Mid the sharp short emerald wheat, scarce risen three fingers well,
The wild tulip, at end of its tube, blows out its great red bell
Like a thin clear bubble of blood, for the children to pick and sell.

VII.

Is it ever hot in the square? There's a fountain to spout and splash!
In the shade it sings and springs; in the shine such foambows flash
On the horses with curling fish-tails, that prance and paddle and pash
Round the lady atop in her conch—fifty gazers do not abash,
Though all that she wears is some weeds round her waist in a sort of sash.

VIII.

All the year long at the villa, nothing to see though you linger,
Except yon cypress that points like death's lean lifted forefinger.
Some think fireflies pretty, when they mix i' the corn and mingle,
Or thrid the stinking hemp till the stalks of it seem a-tingle.
Late August or early September, the stunning cicala is shrill,
And the bees keep their tiresome whine round the resinous firs on the hill.
Enough of the seasons,—I spare you the months of the fever and chill.

IX.

Ere you open your eyes in the city, the blessed church-bells begin:
No sooner the bells leave off than the diligence rattles in:
You get the pick of the news, and it costs you never a pin.
By-and-by there's the travelling doctor gives pills, lets blood, draws teeth;

Or the Pulcinello-trumpet breaks up the market beneath.
At the post-office such a scene-picture—the new play, piping hot!
And a notice how, only this morning, three liberal thieves were shot.
Above it, behold the Archbishop's most fatherly of rebukes,
And beneath, with his crown and his lion, some little new law of the Duke's!
Or a sonnet with flowery marge, to the Reverend Don So-and-so
Who is Dante, Boccaccio, Petrarca, Saint Jerome, and Cicero,
"And moreover," (the sonnet goes rhyming,) "the skirts of Saint Paul has
    reached,
Having preached us those six Lent-lectures more unctuous than ever he
    preached."
Noon strikes,—here sweeps the procession! our Lady borne smiling and smart
With a pink gauze gown all spangles, and seven swords stuck in her heart!
Bang-whang-whang goes the drum, *tootle-te-tootle* the fife;
No keeping one's haunches still: it's the greatest pleasure in life.

x.

But bless you, it's dear—it's dear! fowls, wine, at double the rate.
They have clapped a new tax upon salt, and what oil pays passing the gate
It's a horror to think of. And so, the villa for me, not the city!
Beggars can scarcely be choosers: but still—ah, the pity, the pity!
Look, two and two go the priests, then the monks with cowls and sandals,
And the penitents dressed in white shirts, a-holding the yellow candles;
One, he carries a flag up straight, and another a cross with handles,
And the Duke's guard brings up the rear, for the better prevention of
    scandals:
Bang-whang-whang goes the drum, *tootle-te-tootle* the fife.
Oh, a day in the city-square, there is no such pleasure in life!

A TOCCATA OF GALUPPI'S

I.

OH GALUPPI, Baldassaro, this is very sad to find!
I can hardly misconceive you; it would prove me deaf and blind;
But although I take your meaning, 'tis with such a heavy mind!

II.

Here you come with your old music, and here's all the good it brings.
What, they lived once thus at Venice where the merchants were the kings,
Where St. Mark's is, where the Doges used to wed the sea with rings?

III.

Ay, because the sea's the street there; and 'tis arched by . . . what you call
. . . Shylock's bridge with houses on it, where they kept the carnival:
I was never out of England—it's as if I saw it all.

IV.

Did young people take their pleasure when the sea was warm in May?
Balls and masks begun at midnight, burning ever to mid-day,
When they made up fresh adventures for the morrow, do you say?

V.

Was a lady such a lady, cheeks so round and lips so red,—
On her neck the small face buoyant, like a bell-flower on its bed,
O'er the breast's superb abundance where a man might base his head?

VI.

Well, and it was graceful of them—they'd break talk off and afford
—She, to bite her mask's black velvet—he, to finger on his sword,
While you sat and played Toccatas, stately at the clavichord?

VII.

What? Those lesser thirds so plaintive, sixths diminished, sigh on sigh,
Told them something? Those suspensions, those solutions—"Must we die?"
Those commiserating sevenths—"Life might last! we can but try!"

VIII.

"Were you happy?"—"Yes."—"And are you still as happy?"—"Yes. And
    you?"
—"Then, more kisses!"—"Did *I* stop them, when a million seemed so few?"
Hark, the dominant's persistence till it must be answered to!

IX.

So, an octave struck the answer. Oh, they praised you, I dare say!
"Brave Galuppi! that was music! good alike at grave and gay!
I can always leave off talking when I hear a master play!"

X.

Then they left you for their pleasure: till in due time, one by one,
Some with lives that came to nothing, some with deeds as well undone,
Death stepped tacitly and took them where they never see the sun.

XI.

But when I sit down to reason, think to take my stand nor swerve,
While I triumph o'er a secret wrung from nature's close reserve,
In you come with your cold music till I creep through every nerve.

XII.

Yes, you, like a ghostly cricket, creaking where a house was burned:
"Dust and ashes, dead and done with, Venice spent what Venice earned.
The soul, doubtless, is immortal—where a soul can be discerned.

XIII.

"Yours for instance: you know physics, something of geology,
Mathematics are your pastime; souls shall rise in their degree;
Butterflies may dread extinction,—you'll not die, it cannot be!

XIV.

"As for Venice and her people, merely born to bloom and drop,
Here on earth they bore their fruitage, mirth and folly were the crop:
What of soul was left, I wonder, when the kissing had to stop?

XV.

"Dust and ashes!" So you creak it, and I want the heart to scold.
Dear dead women, with such hair, too—what's become of all the gold
Used to hang and brush their bosoms? I feel chilly and grown old.

OLD PICTURES IN FLORENCE

I.

THE MORN when first it thunders in March,
  The eel in the pond gives a leap, they say:
As I leaned and looked over the aloed arch
  Of the villa-gate this warm March day,
No flash snapped, no dumb thunder rolled
  In the valley beneath where, white and wide
And washed by the morning water-gold,
  Florence lay out on the mountain-side.

II.

River and bridge and street and square
  Lay mine, as much at my beck and call,
Through the live translucent bath of air,
  As the sights in a magic crystal ball.
And of all I saw and of all I praised,
  The most to praise and the best to see,
Was the startling bell-tower Giotto raised:
  But why did it more than startle me?

III.

Giotto, how, with that soul of yours,
  Could you play me false who loved you so?
Some slights if a certain heart endures
  Yet it feels, I would have your fellows know!
I' faith, I perceive not why I should care
  To break a silence that suits them best,
But the thing grows somewhat hard to bear
  When I find a Giotto join the rest.

IV.

On the arch where olives overhead
  Print the blue sky with twig and leaf,
(That sharp-curled leaf which they never shed)
  'Twixt the aloes, I used to lean in chief,
And mark through the winter afternoons,
  By a gift God grants me now and then,
In the mild decline of those suns like moons,
  Who walked in Florence, besides her men.

V.

They might chirp and chaffer, come and go
  For pleasure or profit, her men alive—
My business was hardly with them, I trow,
  But with empty cells of the human hive;
—With the chapter-room, the cloister-porch,
  The church's apsis, aisle or nave,
Its crypt, one fingers along with a torch,
  Its face set full for the sun to shave.

VI.

Wherever a fresco peels and drops,
  Wherever an outline weakens and wanes
Till the latest life in the painting stops,
  Stands One whom each fainter pulse-tick pains:
One, wishful each scrap should clutch the brick,
  Each tinge not wholly escape the plaster,
—A lion who dies of an ass's kick,
  The wronged great soul of an ancient Master.

VII.

For oh, this world and the wrong it does!
  They are safe in heaven with their backs to it,
The Michaels and Rafaels, you hum and buzz
  Round the works of, you of the little wit!
Do their eyes contract to the earth's old scope,
  Now that they see God face to face,
And have all attained to be poets, I hope?
  'Tis their holiday now, in any case.

VIII.

Much they reck of your praise and you!
  But the wronged great souls—can they be quit
Of a world where their work is all to do,
  Where you style them, you of the little wit,

Old Master This and Early the Other,
  Not dreaming that Old and New are fellows:
A younger succeeds to an elder brother,
  Da Vincis derive in good time from Dellos.

IX.

And here where your praise might yield returns,
  And a handsome word or two give help,
Here, after your kind, the mastiff girns
  And the puppy pack of poodles yelp.
What, not a word for Stefano there,
  Of brow once prominent and starry,
Called Nature's Ape, and the world's despair
  For his peerless painting? (see Vasari.)

X.

There stands the Master. Study, my friends,
  What a man's work comes to! So he plans it,
Performs it, perfects it, makes amends
  For the toiling and moiling, and then, *sic transit!*
Happier the thrifty blind-folk labor,
  With upturned eye while the hand is busy,
Not sidling a glance at the coin of their neighbor!
  'Tis looking downward that makes one dizzy.

XI.

"If you knew their work you would deal your dole."
  May I take upon me to instruct you?
When Greek Art ran and reached the goal,
  Thus much had the world to boast *in fructu*—
The Truth of Man, as by God first spoken,
  Which the actual generations garble,
Was re-uttered, and Soul (which Limbs betoken)
  And Limbs (Soul informs) made new in marble.

XII.

So, you saw yourself as you wished you were,
  As you might have been, as you cannot be;
Earth here, rebuked by Olympus there:
  And grew content in your poor degree
With your little power, by those statues' godhead,
  And your little scope, by their eyes' full sway,
And your little grace, by their grace embodied,
  And your little date, by their forms that stay.

XIII.

You would fain be kinglier, say, than I am?
   Even so, you will not sit like Theseus.
You would prove a model? The Son of Priam
   Has yet the advantage in arms' and knees' use.
You're wroth—can you slay your snake like Apollo?
   You're grieved—still Niobe's the grander!
You live—there's the Racers' frieze to follow:
   You die—there's the dying Alexander.

XIV.

So, testing your weakness by their strength,
   Your meagre charms by their rounded beauty,
Measured by Art in your breadth and length,
   You learned—to submit is a mortal's duty.
—When I say "you" 'tis the common soul,
   The collective, I mean: the race of Man
That receives life in parts to live in a whole,
   And grow here according to God's clear plan.

XV.

Growth came when, looking your last on them all,
   You turned your eyes inwardly one fine day
And cried with a start—What if we so small
   Be greater and grander the while than they?
Are they perfect of lineament, perfect of stature?
   In both, of such lower types are we
Precisely because of our wider nature;
   For time, theirs—ours, for eternity.

XVI.

To-day's brief passion limits their range;
   It seethes with the morrow for us and more.
They are perfect—how else? they shall never change:
   We are faulty—why not? we have time in store.
The Artificer's hand is not arrested
   With us; we are rough-hewn, nowise polished:
They stand for our copy, and, once invested
   With all they can teach, we shall see them abolished.

XVII.

'Tis a life-long toil till our lump be leaven—
   The better! What's come to perfection perishes.
Things learned on earth, we shall practise in heaven:
   Works done least rapidly, Art most cherishes.

Thyself shalt afford the example, Giotto!
  Thy one work, not to decrease or diminish,
Done at a stroke, was just (was it not?) "O!"
  Thy great Campanile is still to finish.

XVIII.

Is it true that we are now, and shall be hereafter,
  But what and where depend on life's minute?
Hails heavenly cheer or infernal laughter
  Our first step out of the gulf or in it?
Shall Man, such step within his endeavor,
  Man's face, have no more play and action
Than joy which is crystallized forever,
  Or grief, an eternal petrifaction?

XIX.

On which I conclude, that the early painters,
  To cries of "Greek Art and what more wish you?"—
Replied, "To become now self-acquainters,
  And paint man, man, whatever the issue!
Make new hopes shine through the flesh they fray,
  New fears aggrandize the rags and tatters:
To bring the invisible full into play!
  Let the visible go to the dogs—what matters?"

XX.

Give these, I exhort you, their guerdon and glory
  For daring so much, before they well did it.
The first of the new, in our race's story,
  Beats the last of the old; 'tis no idle quiddit.
The worthies began a revolution,
  Which if on earth you intend to acknowledge,
Why, honor them now! (ends my allocution)
  Nor confer your degree when the folk leave college.

XXI.

There's a fancy some lean to and others hate—
  That, when this life is ended, begins
New work for the soul in another state,
  Where it strives and gets weary, loses and wins:
Where the strong and the weak, this world's congeries,
  Repeat in large what they practised in small,
Through life after life in unlimited series;
  Only the scale's to be changed, that's all.

XXII.

Yet I hardly know. When a soul has seen
   By the means of Evil that Good is best,
And, through earth and its noise, what is heaven's serene,—
   When our faith in the same has stood the test—
Why, the child grown man, you burn the rod,
   The uses of labor are surely done;
There remaineth a rest for the people of God:
   And I have had troubles enough, for one.

XXIII.

But at any rate I have loved the season
   Of Art's spring-birth so dim and dewy;
My sculptor is Nicolo the Pisan,
   My painter—who but Cimabue?
Nor ever was man of them all indeed,
   From these to Ghiberti and Ghirlandajo,
Could say that he missed my critic-meed.
   So, now to my special grievance—heigh-ho!

XXIV.

Their ghosts still stand, as I said before,
   Watching each fresco flaked and rasped,
Blocked up, knocked out, or whitewashed o'er:
   —No getting again what the church has grasped!
The works on the wall must take their chance;
   "Works never conceded to England's thick clime!"
(I hope they prefer their inheritance
   Of a bucketful of Italian quick-lime.)

XXV.

When they go at length, with such a shaking
   Of heads o'er the old delusion, sadly
Each master his way through the black streets taking,
   Where many a lost work breathes though badly—
Why don't they bethink them of who has merited?
   Why not reveal, while their pictures dree
Such doom, how a captive might be out-ferreted?
   Why is it they never remember me?

XXVI.

Not that I expect the great Bigordi,
   Nor Sandro to hear me, chivalric, bellicose;
Nor the wronged Lippino; and not a word I
   Say of a scrap of Fra Angelico's:

But are you too fine, Taddeo Gaddi,
   To grant me a taste of your intonaco,
Some Jerome that seeks the heaven with a sad eye?
   Not a churlish saint, Lorenzo Monaco?

XXVII.

Could not the ghost with the close red cap,
   My Pollajolo, the twice a craftsman,
Save me a sample, give me the hap
   Of a muscular Christ that shows the draughtsman?
No Virgin by him the somewhat petty,
   Of finical touch and tempera crumbly—
Could not Alesso Baldovinetti
   Contribute so much, I ask him humbly?

XXVIII.

Margheritone of Arezzo,
   With the grave-clothes garb and swaddling barret,
(Why purse up mouth and beak in a pet so,
   You bald old saturnine poll-clawed parrot?)
Not a poor glimmering Crucifixion,
   Where in the foreground kneels the donor?
If such remain, as is my conviction,
   The hoarding it does you but little honor.

XXIX.

They pass; for them the panels may thrill,
   The tempera grow alive and tinglish;
Their pictures are left to the mercies still
   Of dealers and stealers, Jews and the English,
Who, seeing mere money's worth in their prize,
   Will sell it to somebody calm as Zeno
At naked High Art, and in ecstasies
   Before some clay-cold vile Carlino!

XXX.

No matter for these! But Giotto, you,
   Have you allowed, as the town-tongues babble it,—
Oh, never! it shall not be counted true—
   That a certain precious little tablet
Which Buonarroti eyed like a lover—
   Was buried so long in oblivion's womb
And, left for another than I to discover,
   Turns up at last! and to whom?—to whom?

XXXI.

I, that have haunted the dim San Spirito,
   (Or was it rather the Ognissanti?)
Patient on altar-step planting a weary toe!
   Nay, I shall have it yet! *Detur amanti!*
My Koh-i-noor—or (if that's a platitude)
   Jewel of Giamschid, the Persian Sofi's eye;
So, in anticipative gratitude,
   What if I take up my hope and prophesy?

XXXII.

When the hour grows ripe, and a certain dotard
   Is pitched, no parcel that needs invoicing,
To the worse side of the Mont St. Gothard,
   We shall begin by way of rejoicing;
None of that shooting the sky (blank cartridge),
   Nor a civic guard, all plumes and lacquer,
Hunting Radetzky's soul like a partridge
   Over Morello with squib and cracker.

XXXIII.

This time we'll shoot better game and bag 'em hot—
   No mere display at the stone of Dante,
But a kind of sober Witanagemot
   (Ex: "Casa Guidi," *quod videas ante*)
Shall ponder, once Freedom restored to Florence,
   How Art may return that departed with her.
Go, hated house, go each trace of the Loraine's,
   And bring us the days of Orgagna hither!

XXXIV.

How we shall prologuize, how we shall perorate,
   Utter fit things upon art and history,
Feel truth at blood-heat and falsehood at zero rate,
   Make of the want of the age no mystery;
Contrast the fructuous and sterile eras,
   Show—monarchy ever its uncouth cub licks
Out of the bear's shape into Chimæra's,
   While Pure Art's birth is still the republic's.

XXXV.

Then one shall propose in a speech (curt Tuscan,
   Expurgate and sober, with scarcely an *"issimo,"*)
To end now our half-told tale of Cambuscan,
   And turn the bell-tower's *alt* to *altissimo:*

And fine as the beak of a young beccaccia
  The Campanile, the Duomo's fit ally,
Shall soar up in gold full fifty braccia,
  Completing Florence, as Florence, Italy.

XXXVI.

Shall I be alive that morning the scaffold
  Is broken away, and the long-pent fire,
Like the golden hope of the world, unbaffled
  Springs from its sleep, and up goes the spire
While "God and the People" plain for its motto,
  Thence the new tricolor flaps at the sky?
At least to foresee that glory of Giotto
  And Florence together, the first am I!

"DE GUSTIBUS—"

I.

YOUR ghost will walk, you lover of trees,
      (If our loves remain)
      In an English lane,
By a cornfield-side a-flutter with poppies.
Hark, those two in the hazel coppice—
A boy and a girl, if the good fates please,
      Making love, say,—
      The happier they!
Draw yourself up from the light of the moon,
And let them pass, as they will too soon,
      With the beanflowers' boon,
      And the blackbird's tune,
      And May, and June!

II.

What I love best in all the world
Is a castle, precipice-encurled,
In a gash of the wind-grieved Apennine.
Or look for me, old fellow of mine,
(If I get my head from out the mouth
O' the grave, and loose my spirit's bands,
And come again to the land of lands)—
In a sea-side house to the farther South,
Where the baked cicala dies of drouth,
And one sharp tree—'tis a cypress—stands,
By the many hundred years red-rusted,
Rough iron-spiked, ripe fruit-o'ercrusted,

My sentinel to guard the sands
To the water's edge. For, what expands
Before the house, but the great opaque
Blue breadth of sea without a break?
While, in the house, forever crumbles
Some fragment of the frescoed walls,
From blisters where a scorpion sprawls.
A girl bare-footed brings, and tumbles
Down on the pavement, green-flesh melons,
And says there's news to-day—the king
Was shot at, touched in the liver-wing,
Goes with his Bourbon arm in a sling:
—She hopes they have not caught the felons.
Italy, my Italy!
Queen Mary's saying serves for me—
   (When fortune's malice
   Lost her, Calais)
Open my heart and you will see
Graved inside of it, "Italy."
Such lovers old are I and she:
So it always was, so shall ever be!

HOME-THOUGHTS, FROM ABROAD

I.

OH, TO BE in England
Now that April's there,
And whoever wakes in England
Sees, some morning, unaware,
That the lowest boughs and the brush-wood sheaf
Round the elm-tree bole are in tiny leaf,
While the chaffinch sings on the orchard bough
In England—now!

II.

And after April, when May follows,
And the whitethroat builds, and all the swallows!
Hark, where my blossomed pear-tree in the hedge
Leans to the field and scatters on the clover
Blossoms and dewdrops—at the bent spray's edge—
That's the wise thrush; he sings each song twice over,
Lest you should think he never could recapture
The first fine careless rapture!
And though the fields look rough with hoary dew,

All will be gay when noontide wakes anew
The buttercups, the little children's dower
—Far brighter than this gaudy melon-flower!

HOME-THOUGHTS, FROM THE SEA

NOBLY, nobly Cape Saint Vincent to the North-West died away;
Sunset ran, one glorious blood-red, reeking into Cadiz Bay;
Bluish 'mid the burning water, full in face Trafalgar lay;
In the dimmest North-East distance dawned Gibraltar grand and gray;
"Here and here did England help me: how can I help England?"—say,
Whoso turns as I, this evening, turn to God to praise and pray,
While Jove's planet rises yonder, silent over Africa.

SAUL

I.

SAID Abner, "At last thou art come! Ere I tell, ere thou speak,
Kiss my cheek, wish me well!" Then I wished it, and did kiss his cheek.
And he: "Since the King, O my friend, for thy countenance sent,
Neither drunken nor eaten have we; nor until from his tent
Thou return with the joyful assurance the King liveth yet,
Shall our lip with the honey be bright, with the water be wet.
For out of the black mid-tent's silence, a space of three days,
Not a sound hath escaped to thy servants, of prayer nor of praise,
To betoken that Saul and the Spirit have ended their strife,
And that, faint in his triumph, the monarch sinks back upon life.

II.

"Yet now my heart leaps, O beloved! God's child with his dew
On thy gracious gold hair, and those lilies still living and blue
Just broken to twine round thy harp-strings, as if no wild heat
Were now raging to torture the desert!"

III.

Then I, as was meet,
Knelt down to the God of my fathers, and rose on my feet,
And ran o'er the sand burnt to powder. The tent was unlooped;
I pulled up the spear that obstructed, and under I stooped;
Hands and knees on the slippery grass-patch, all withered and gone,
That extends to the second enclosure, I groped my way on
Till I felt where the foldskirts fly open. Then once more I prayed,
And opened the foldskirts and entered, and was not afraid
But spoke, "Here is David, thy servant!" And no voice replied.

At the first I saw nought but the blackness; but soon I descried
A something more black than the blackness—the vast, the upright
Main prop which sustains the pavilion: and slow into sight
Grew a figure against it, gigantic and blackest of all.
Then a sunbeam, that burst through the tent-roof, showed Saul.

IV.

He stood as erect as that tent-prop, both arms stretched out wide
On the great cross-support in the centre, that goes to each side;
He relaxed not a muscle, but hung there as, caught in his pangs
And waiting his change, the king-serpent all heavily hangs,
Far away from his kind, in the pine, till deliverance come
With the spring-time,—so agonized Saul, drear and stark, blind and dumb.

V.

Then I tuned my harp,—took off the lilies we twine round its chords
Lest they snap 'neath the stress of the noontide—those sunbeams like swords!
And I first played the tune all our sheep know, as, one after one,
So docile they come to the pen-door till folding be done.
They are white and untorn by the bushes, for lo, they have fed
Where the long grasses stifle the water within the stream's bed;
And now one after one seeks its lodging, as star follows star
Into eve and the blue far above us,—so blue and so far!

VI.

—Then the tune, for which quails on the cornland will each leave his mate
To fly after the player; then, what makes the crickets elate
Till for boldness they fight one another: and then, what has weight
To set the quick jerboa a-musing outside his sand house—
There are none such as he for a wonder, half bird and half mouse!
God made all the creatures and gave them our love and our fear,
To give sign, we and they are his children, one family here.

VII.

Then I played the help-tune of our reapers, their wine-song, when hand
Grasps at hand, eye lights eye in good friendship, and great hearts expand
And grow one in the sense of this world's life.—And then, the last song
When the dead man is praised on his journey—"Bear, bear him along,
With his few faults shut up like dead flowerets! Are balm seeds not here
To console us? The land has none left such as he on the bier.
Oh, would we might keep thee, my brother!"—And then, the glad chaunt
Of the marriage,—first go the young maidens, next, she whom we vaunt
As the beauty, the pride of our dwelling.—And then, the great march
Wherein man runs to man to assist him and buttress an arch
Nought can break; who shall harm them, our friends? Then, the chorus in-
     toned

As the levites go up to the altar in glory enthroned.
But I stopped here: for here in the darkness Saul groaned.

VIII.

And I paused, held my breath in such silence, and listened apart;
And the tent shook, for mighty Saul shuddered: and sparkles 'gan dart
From the jewels that woke in his turban, at once with a start,
All its lordly male-sapphires, and rubies courageous at heart.
So the head: but the body still moved not, still hung there erect.
And I bent once again to my playing, pursued it unchecked,
As I sang:—

IX.

       "Oh, our manhood's prime vigor! No spirit feels waste,
Not a muscle is stopped in its playing nor sinew unbraced.
Oh, the wild joys of living! the leaping from rock up to rock,
The strong rending of boughs from the fir-tree, the cool silver shock
Of the plunge in a pool's living water, the hunt of the bear,
And the sultriness showing the lion is couched in his lair.
And the meal, the rich dates yellowed over with gold dust divine,
And the locust-flesh steeped in the pitcher, the full draught of wine,
And the sleep in the dried river-channel where bulrushes tell
That the water was wont to go warbling so softly and well.
How good is man's life, the mere living! how fit to employ
All the heart and the soul and the senses forever in joy!
Hast thou loved the white locks of thy father, whose sword thou didst guard
When he trusted thee forth with the armies, for glorious reward?
Didst thou see the thin hands of thy mother, held up as men sung
The low song of the nearly-departed, and hear her faint tongue
Joining in while it could to the witness, 'Let one more attest,
I have lived, seen God's hand through a lifetime, and all was for best?'
Then they sung through their tears in strong triumph, not much, but the rest.
And thy brothers, the help and the contest, the working whence grew
Such result as, from seething grape-bundles, the spirit strained true:
And the friends of thy boyhood—that boyhood of wonder and hope,
Present promise and wealth of the future beyond the eye's scope,—
Till lo, thou art grown to a monarch; a people is thine;
And all gifts, which the world offers singly, on one head combine!
On one head, all the beauty and strength, love and rage (like the throe
That, a-work in the rock, helps its labor and lets the gold go)
High ambition and deeds which surpass it, fame crowning them,—all
Brought to blaze on the head of one creature—King Saul!"

X.

And lo, with that leap of my spirit,—heart, hand, harp and voice,
Each lifting Saul's name out of sorrow, each bidding rejoice
Saul's fame in the light it was made for—as when, dare I say,

The Lord's army, in rapture of service, strains through its array,
And upsoareth the cherubim-chariot—"Saul!" cried I, and stopped,
And waited the thing that should follow. Then Saul, who hung propped
By the tent's cross-support in the centre, was struck by his name.
Have ye seen when Spring's arrowy summons goes right to the aim,
And some mountain, the last to withstand her, that held (he alone,
While the vale laughed in freedom and flowers) on a broad bust of stone
A year's snow bound about for a breastplate,—leaves grasp of the sheet?
Fold on fold all at once it crowds thunderously down to his feet,
And there fronts you, stark, black, but alive yet, your mountain of old,
With his rents, the successive bequeathings of ages untold—
Yea, each harm got in fighting your battles, each furrow and scar
Of his head thrust 'twixt you and the tempest—all hail, there they are!
—Now again to be softened with verdure, again hold the nest
Of the dove, tempt the goat and its young to the green on his crest
For their food in the ardors of summer. One long shudder thrilled
All the tent till the very air tingled, then sank and was stilled
At the King's self left standing before me, released and aware.
What was gone, what remained? All to traverse 'twixt hope and despair,
Death was past, life not come: so he waited. Awhile his right hand
Held the brow, helped the eyes left too vacant forthwith to remand
To their place what new objects should enter: 'twas Saul as before.
I looked up and dared gaze at those eyes, nor was hurt any more
Than by slow pallid sunsets in autumn, ye watch from the shore,
At their sad level gaze o'er the ocean—a sun's slow decline
Over hills which, resolved in stern silence, o'erlap and entwine
Base with base to knit strength more intensely: so, arm folded arm
O'er the chest whose slow heavings subsided.

XI.

                                    What spell or what charm,
(For, awhile there was trouble within me,) what next should I urge
To sustain him where song had restored him?—Song filled to the verge
His cup with the wine of this life, pressing all that it yields
Of mere fruitage, the strength and the beauty: beyond, on what fields,
Glean a vintage more potent and perfect to brighten the eye
And bring blood to the lip, and commend them the cup they put by?
He saith, "It is good;" still he drinks not: he lets me praise life,
Gives assent, yet would die for his own part.

XII.

                                    Then fancies grew rife
Which had come long ago on the pasture, when round me the sheep
Fed in silence—above, the one eagle wheeled slow as in sleep;
And I lay in my hollow and mused on the world that might lie
'Neath his ken, though I saw but the strip 'twixt the hill and the sky:

And I laughed—"Since my days are ordained to be passed with my flocks,
Let me people at least, with my fancies, the plains and the rocks,
Dream the life I am never to mix with, and image the show
Of mankind as they live in those fashions I hardly shall know!
Schemes of life, its best rules and right uses, the courage that gains,
And the prudence that keeps what men strive for." And now these old trains
Of vague thought came again; I grew surer; so, once more the string
Of my harp made response to my spirit, as thus—

XIII.

                                                "Yea, my King,"
I began—"thou dost well in rejecting mere comforts that spring
From the mere mortal life held in common by man and by brute:
In our flesh grows the branch of this life, in our soul it bears fruit.
Thou hast marked the slow rise of the tree,—how its stem trembled first
Till it passed the kid's lip, the stag's antler; then safely outburst
The fan-branches all round; and thou mindest when these too, in turn,
Broke a-bloom and the palm-tree seemed perfect: yet more was to learn,
E'en the good that comes in with the palm-fruit. Our dates shall we slight,
When their juice brings a cure for all sorrow? or care for the plight
Of the palm's self whose slow growth produced them? Not so! stem and
    branch
Shall decay, nor be known in their place, while the palm-wine shall stanch
Every wound of man's spirit in winter. I pour thee such wine.
Leave the flesh to the fate it was fit for! the spirit be thine!
By the spirit, when age shall o'ercome thee, thou still shalt enjoy
More indeed, than at first when inconscious, the life of a boy.
Crush that life, and behold its wine running! Each deed thou hast done
Dies, revives, goes to work in the world; until e'en as the sun
Looking down on the earth, though clouds spoil him, though tempests efface,
Can find nothing his own deed produced not, must everywhere trace
The results of his past summer-prime,—so, each ray of thy will,
Every flash of thy passion and prowess, long over, shall thrill
Thy whole people, the countless, with ardor, till they too give forth
A like cheer to their sons, who in turn, fill the South and the North
With the radiance thy deed was the germ of. Carouse in the past!
But the license of age has its limit; thou diest at last:
As the lion when age dims his eyeball, the rose at her height,
So with man—so his power and his beauty forever take flight.
No! Again a long draught of my soul-wine! Look forth o'er the years!
Thou hast done now with eyes for the actual; begin with the seer's!
Is Saul dead? In the depth of the vale make his tomb—bid arise
A gray mountain of marble heaped four-square, till, built to the skies,
Let it mark where the great First King slumbers: whose fame would ye
    know?
Up above see the rock's naked face, where the record shall go

In great characters cut by the scribe,—Such was Saul, so he did;
With the sages directing the work, by the populace chid,—
For not half, they'll affirm, is comprised there! Which fault to amend,
In the grove with his kind grows the cedar, whereon they shall spend
(See, in tablets 't is level before them) their praise, and record
With the gold of the graver, Saul's story,—the statesman's great word
Side by side with the poet's sweet comment. The river's a-wave
With smooth paper-reeds grazing each other when prophet-winds rave:
So the pen gives unborn generations their due and their part
In thy being! Then, first of the mighty, thank God that thou art!"

XIV.

And behold while I sang . . . but O Thou who didst grant me that day.
And before it not seldom hast granted thy help to essay,
Carry on and complete an adventure,—my shield and my sword
In that act where my soul was thy servant, thy word was my word,—
Still be with me, who then at the summit of human endeavor
And scaling the highest, man's thought could, gazed hopeless as ever
On the new stretch of heaven above me—till, mighty to save,
Just one lift of thy hand cleared that distance—God's throne from man's
    grave!
Let me tell out my tale to its ending—my voice to my heart
Which can scarce dare believe in what marvels last night I took part,
As this morning I gather the fragments, alone with my sheep,
And still fear lest the terrible glory evanish like sleep!
For I wake in the gray dewy covert, while Hebron upheaves
The dawn struggling with night on his shoulder, and Kidron retrieves
Slow the damage of yesterday's sunshine.

XV.

                                  I say then,—my song
While I sang thus, assuring the monarch, and ever more strong
Made a proffer of good to console him—he slowly resumed
His old motions and habitudes kingly. The right hand replumed
His black locks to their wonted composure, adjusted the swathes
Of his turban, and see—the huge sweat that his countenance bathes,
He wipes off with the robe; and he girds now his loins as of yore,
And feels slow for the armlets of price, with the clasp set before.
He is Saul, ye remember in glory,—ere error had bent
The broad brow from the daily communion; and still, though much spent
Be the life and the bearing that front you, the same, God did choose.
To receive what a man may waste, desecrate, never quite lose.
So sank he along by the tent-prop till, stayed by the pile
Of his armor and war-cloak and garments, he leaned there awhile,
And sat out my singing,—one arm round the tent-prop, to raise
His bent head, and the other hung slack—till I touched on the praise

I foresaw from all men in all time, to the man patient there;
And thus ended, the harp falling forward. Then first I was 'ware
That he sat, as I say, with my head just above his vast knees
Which were thrust out on each side around me, like oak roots which please
To encircle a lamb when it slumbers. I looked up to know
If the best I could do had brought solace: he spoke not, but slow
Lifted up the hand slack at his side, till he laid it with care
Soft and grave, but in mild settled will, on my brow: through my hair
The large fingers were pushed, and he bent back my head, with kind power—
All my face back, intent to peruse it, as men do a flower.
Thus held he me there with his great eyes that scrutinized mine—
And oh, all my heart how it loved him! but where was the sign?
I yearned—"Could I help thee, my father, inventing a bliss,
I would add, to that life of the past, both the future and this;
I would give thee new life altogether, as good, ages hence,
As this moment,—had love but the warrant, love's heart to dispense!"

XVI.

Then the truth came upon me. No harp more—no song more! out-broke—

XVII.

"I have gone the whole round of creation: I saw and I spoke:
I, a work of God's hand for that purpose, received in my brain
And pronounced on the rest of his handwork—returned him again
His creation's approval or censure: I spoke as I saw:
I report, as a man may of God's work—all's love, yet all's law.
Now I lay down the judgeship he lent me. Each faculty tasked
To perceive him, has gained an abyss, where a dewdrop was asked.
Have I knowledge? confounded it shrivels at Wisdom laid bare.
Have I forethought? how purblind, how blank, to the Infinite Care!
Do I task any faculty highest, to image success?
I but open my eyes,—and perfection, no more and no less,
In the kind I imagined, full-fronts me, and God is seen God
In the star, in the stone, in the flesh, in the soul and the clod.
And thus looking within and around me, I ever renew
(With that stoop of the soul which in bending upraises it too)
The submission of man's nothing-perfect to God's all-complete,
As by each new obeisance in spirit, I climb to his feet.
Yet with all this abounding experience, this deity known,
I shall dare to discover some province, some gift of my own.
There's a faculty pleasant to exercise, hard to hoodwink,
I am fain to keep still in abeyance, (I laugh as I think)
Lest, insisting to claim and parade in it, wot ye, I worst
E'en the Giver in one gift.—Behold, I could love if I durst!
But I sink the pretension as fearing a man may o'ertake
God's own speed in the one way of love: I abstain for love's sake.

—What, my soul? see thus far and no farther? when doors great and small,
Nine-and-ninety flew ope at our touch, should the hundredth appall?
In the least things have faith, yet distrust in the greatest of all?
Do I find love so full in my nature, God's ultimate gift,
That I doubt his own love can compete with it? Here, the parts shift?
Here, the creature surpass the Creator,—the end, what Began?
Would I fain in my impotent yearning do all for this man,
And dare doubt he alone shall not help him, who yet alone can?
Would it ever have entered my mind, the bare will, much less power,
To bestow on this Saul what I sang of, the marvellous dower
Of the life he was gifted and filled with? to make such a soul,
Such a body, and then such an earth for insphering the whole?
And doth it not enter my mind (as my warm tears attest)
These good things being given, to go on, and give one more, the best?
Ay, to save and redeem and restore him, maintain at the height
This perfection,—succeed with life's dayspring, death's minute of night?
Interpose at the difficult minute, snatch Saul the mistake,
Saul the failure, the ruin he seems now,—and bid him awake
From the dream, the probation, the prelude, to find himself set
Clear and safe in new light and new life,—a new harmony yet
To be run, and continued, and ended—who knows?—or endure!
The man taught enough by life's dream, of the rest to make sure;
By the pain-throb, triumphantly winning intensified bliss,
And the next world's reward and repose, by the struggles in this.

XVIII.

"I believe it! 'T is thou, God, that givest, 't is I who receive:
In the first is the last, in thy will is my power to believe.
All's one gift: thou canst grant it moreover, as prompt to my prayer
As I breathe out this breath, as I open these arms to the air.
From thy will, stream the worlds, life and nature, thy dread Sabaoth:
I will?—the mere atoms despise me! Why am I not loth
To look that, even that in the face too? Why is it I dare
Think but lightly of such impuissance? What stops my despair?
This;—'t is not what man Does which exalts him, but what man Would do!
See the King—I would help him but cannot, the wishes fall through.
Could I wrestle to raise him from sorrow, grow poor to enrich,
To fill up his life, starve my own out, I would—knowing which,
I know that my service is perfect. Oh, speak through me now!
Would I suffer for him that I love? So wouldst thou—so wilt thou!
So shall crown thee the topmost, ineffablest, uttermost crown—
And thy love fill infinitude wholly, nor leave up nor down
One spot for the creature to stand in! It is by no breath,
Turn of eye, wave of hand, that salvation joins issue with death!
As thy Love is discovered almighty, almighty be proved
Thy power, that exists with and for it, of being Beloved!

He who did most, shall bear most; the strongest shall stand the most weak.
'T is the weakness in strength, that I cry for! my flesh, that I seek
In the Godhead! I seek and I find it. O Saul, it shall be
A Face like my face that receives thee; a Man like to me,
Thou shalt love and be loved by, forever: a Hand like this hand
Shall throw open the gates of new life to thee! See the Christ stand!"

XIX.

I know not too well how I found my way home in the night.
There were witnesses, cohorts about me, to left and to right,
Angels, powers, the unuttered, unseen, the alive, the aware:
I repressed, I got through them as hardly, as strugglingly there,
As a runner beset by the populace famished for news—
Life or death. The whole earth was awakened, hell loosed with her crews;
And the stars of night beat with emotion, and tingled and shot
Out in fire the strong pain of pent knowledge: but I fainted not,
For the Hand still impelled me at once and supported, suppressed
All the tumult, and quenched it with quiet, and holy behest,
Till the rapture was shut in itself, and the earth sank to rest.
Anon at the dawn, all that trouble had withered from earth—
Not so much, but I saw it die out in the day's tender birth;
In the gathered intensity brought to the gray of the hills;
In the shuddering forests' held breath; in the sudden wind-thrills;
In the startled wild beasts that bore oft, each with eye sidling still
Though averted with wonder and dread; in the birds stiff and chill
That rose heavily, as I approached them, made stupid with awe:
E'en the serpent that slid away silent,—he felt the new law.
The same stared in the white humid faces upturned by the flowers;
The same worked in the heart of the cedar and moved the vinebowers:
And the little brooks witnessing murmured, persistent and low,
With their obstinate, all but hushed voices—"E'en so, it is so!"

MY STAR

ALL that I know
  Of a certain star
Is, it can throw
  (Like the angled spar)
Now a dart of red,
  Now a dart of blue;
Till my friends have said
  They would fain see, too,
My star that dartles the red and the blue!
Then it stops like a bird; like a flower, hangs furled:
  They must solace themselves with the Saturn above it.
What matter to me if their star is a world?
  Mine has opened its soul to me; therefore I love it.

BY THE FIRESIDE

I.

How well I know what I mean to do
  When the long dark autumn evenings come;
And where, my soul, is thy pleasant hue?
  With the music of all thy voices, dumb
In life's November too!

II.

I shall be found by the fire, suppose,
  O'er a great wise book as beseemeth age,
While the shutters flap as the cross-wind blows,
  And I turn the page, and I turn the page,
Not verse now, only prose!

III.

Till the young ones whisper, finger on lip,
  "There he is at it, deep in Greek:
Now then, or never, out we slip
  To cut from the hazels by the creek
A mainmast for our ship!"

IV.

I shall be at it indeed, my friends!
  Greek puts already on either side
Such a branch-work forth as soon extends
  To a vista opening far and wide,
And I pass out where it ends.

V.

The outside-frame, like your hazel-trees—
  But the inside-archway widens fast,
And a rarer sort succeeds to these,
  And we slope to Italy at last
And youth, by green degrees.

VI.

I follow wherever I am led,
  Knowing so well the leader's hand:
Oh woman-country, wooed not wed,
  Loved all the more by earth's male-lands,
Laid to their hearts instead!

VII.

Look at the ruined chapel again
   Half-way up in the Alpine gorge!
Is that a tower, I point you plain,
   Or is it a mill, or an iron forge
Breaks solitude in vain?

VIII.

A turn, and we stand in the heart of things;
   The woods are round us, heaped and dim;
From slab to slab how it slips and springs,
   The thread of water single and slim,
Through the ravage some torrent brings!

IX.

Does it feed the little lake below?
   That speck of white just on its marge
Is Pella; see, in the evening-glow,
   How sharp the silver spear-heads charge
When Alp meets heaven in snow!

X.

On our other side is the straight-up rock;
   And a path is kept 'twixt the gorge and it
By boulder-stones where lichens mock
   The marks on a moth, and small ferns fit
Their teeth to the polished block.

XI.

Oh the sense of the yellow mountain-flowers,
   And thorny balls, each three in one,
The chestnuts throw on our path in showers!
   For the drop of the woodland fruit's begun,
These early November hours,

XII.

That crimson the creeper's leaf across
   Like a splash of blood, intense, abrupt,
O'er a shield else gold from rim to boss,
   And lay it for show on the fairy-cupped
Elf-needled mat of moss,

XIII.

By the rose-flesh mushrooms, undivulged
   Last evening—nay, in to-day's first dew
Yon sudden coral nipple bulged,
   Where a freaked fawn-colored flaky crew
Of toad-stools peep indulged.

XIV.

And yonder, at foot of the fronting ridge
   That takes the turn to a range beyond,
Is the chapel reached by the one-arched bridge
   Where the water is stopped in a stagnant pond
Danced over by the midge.

XV.

The chapel and bridge are of stone alike,
   Blackish-gray and mostly wet;
Cut hemp-stalks steep in the narrow dyke.
   See here again, how the lichens fret
And the roots of the ivy strike!

XVI.

Poor little place, where its one priest comes
   On a festa-day, if he comes at all,
To the dozen folk from their scattered homes,
   Gathered within that precinct small
By the dozen ways one roams—

XVII.

To drop from the charcoal-burners' huts,
   Or climb from the hemp-dressers' low shed,
Leave the grange where the woodman stores his nuts,
   Or the wattled cote where the fowlers spread
Their gear on the rock's bare juts.

XVIII.

It has some pretension too, this front,
   With its bit of fresco half-moon-wise
Set over the porch, Art's early wont:
   'T is John in the Desert, I surmise,
But has borne the weather's brunt—

XIX.

Not from the fault of the builder, though,
   For a pent-house properly projects
Where three carved beams make a certain show,
   Dating—good thought of our architect's—
'Five, six, nine, he lets you know.

XX.

And all day long a bird sings there,
   And a stray sheep drinks at the pond at times;
The place is silent and aware;
   It has had its scenes, its joys and crimes,
But that is its own affair.

XXI.

My perfect wife, my Leonor,
  Oh heart, my own, oh eyes, mine too,
Whom else could I dare look backward for,
  With whom beside should I dare pursue
The path gray heads abhor?

XXII.

For it leads to a crag's sheer edge with them;
  Youth, flowery all the way, there stops—
Not they; age threatens and they contemn,
  Till they reach the gulf wherein youth drops,
One inch from life's safe hem!

XXIII.

With me, youth led . . . I will speak now,
  No longer watch you as you sit
Reading by fire-light, that great brow
  And the spirit-small hand propping it,
Mutely, my heart knows how—

XXIV.

When, if I think but deep enough,
  You are wont to answer, prompt as rhyme;
And you, too, find without rebuff
  Response your soul seeks many a time
Piercing its fine flesh-stuff.

XXV.

My own, confirm me! If I tread
  This path back, is it not in pride
To think how little I dreamed it led
  To an age so blest that, by its side,
Youth seems the waste instead?

XXVI.

My own, see where the years conduct!
  At first, 't was something our two souls
Should mix as mists do; each is sucked
  In each now: on, the new stream rolls,
Whatever rocks obstruct.

XXVII.

Think, when our one soul understands
  The great Word which makes all things new,
When earth breaks up and heaven expands,
  How will the change strike me and you
In the house not made with hands?

XXVIII.

Oh I must feel your brain prompt mine,
  Your heart anticipate my heart,
You must be just before, in fine,
  See and make me see, for your part,
New depths of the divine!

XXIX.

But who could have expected this
  When we two drew together first
Just for the obvious human bliss,
  To satisfy life's daily thirst
With a thing men seldom miss?

XXX.

Come back with me to the first of all,
  Let us lean and love it over again,
Let us now forget and now recall,
  Break the rosary in a pearly rain
And gather what we let fall!

XXXI.

What did I say?—that a small bird sings
  All day long, save when a brown pair
Of hawks from the wood float with wide wings
  Strained to a bell: 'gainst noon-day glare
You count the streaks and rings.

XXXII.

But at afternoon or almost eve
  'T is better; then the silence grows
To that degree, you half believe
  It must get rid of what it knows,
Its bosom does so heave.

XXXIII.

Hither we walked then, side by side,
  Arm in arm and cheek to cheek,
And still I questioned or replied,
  While my heart, convulsed to really speak,
Lay choking in its pride.

XXXIV.

Silent the crumbling bridge we cross,
  And pity and praise the chapel sweet,
And care about the fresco's loss,
  And wish for our souls a like retreat,
And wonder at the moss.

XXXV.

Stoop and kneel on the settle under,
  Look through the window's grated square:
Nothing to see! For fear of plunder,
  The cross is down and the altar bare,
As if thieves don't fear thunder.

XXXVI.

We stoop and look in through the grate,
  See the little porch and rustic door,
Read duly the dead builder's date;
  Then cross the bridge that we crossed before,
Take the path again—but wait!

XXXVII.

Oh moment, one and infinite!
  The water slips o'er stock and stone;
The West is tender, hardly bright:
  How gray at once is the evening grown—
One star, its chrysolite!

XXXVIII.

We two stood there with never a third,
  But each by each, as each knew well:
The sights we saw and the sounds we heard,
  The lights and the shades made up a spell
Till the trouble grew and stirred.

XXXIX.

Oh, the little more, and how much it is!
  And the little less, and what worlds away!
How a sound shall quicken content to bliss,
  Or a breath suspend the blood's best play,
And life be a proof of this!

XL.

Had she willed it, still had stood the screen
  So slight, so sure, 'twixt my love and her:
I could fix her face with a guard between,
  And find her soul as when friends confer,
Friends—lovers that might have been.

XLI.

For my heart had a touch of the woodland-time,
  Wanting to sleep now over its best.
Shake the whole tree in the summer-prime,
  But bring to the last leaf no such test!
"Hold the last fast!" runs the rhyme.

XLII.

For a chance to make your little much,
  To gain a lover and lose a friend,
Venture the tree and a myriad such,
  When nothing you mar but the year can mend:
But a last leaf—fear to touch!

XLIII.

Yet should it unfasten itself and fall
  Eddying down till it find your face
At some slight wind—best chance of all!
  Be your heart henceforth its dwelling-place
You trembled to forestall!

XLIV.

Worth how well, those dark gray eyes,
  That hair so dark and dear, how worth
That a man should strive and agonize,
  And taste a veriest hell on earth
For the hope of such a prize!

XLV.

You might have turned and tried a man,
  Set him a space to weary and wear,
And prove which suited more your plan,
  His best of hope or his worst despair,
Yet end as he began.

XLVI.

But you spared me this, like the heart you are,
  And filled my empty heart at a word.
If two lives join, there is oft a scar,
  They are one and one, with a shadowy third;
One near one is too far.

XLVII.

A moment after, and hands unseen
  Were hanging the night around us fast;
But we knew that a bar was broken between
  Life and life: we were mixed at last
In spite of the mortal screen.

XLVIII.

The forests had done it; there they stood;
  We caught for a moment the powers at play:
They had mingled us so, for once and good,
  Their work was done —we might go or stay,
They relapsed to their ancient mood.

XLIX.

How the world is made for each of us!
　How all we perceive and know in it
Tends to some moment's product thus,
　When a soul declares itself—to wit,
By its fruit, the thing it does!

L.

Be hate that fruit or love that fruit,
　It forwards the general deed of man,
And each of the Many helps to recruit
　The life of the race by a general plan;
Each living his own, to boot.

LI.

I am named and known by that moment's feat;
　There took my station and degree;
So grew my own small life complete,
　As nature obtained her best of me—
One born to love you, sweet!

LII.

And to watch you sink by the fireside now
　Back again, as you mutely sit
Musing by fire-light, that great brow
　And the spirit-small hand propping it,
Yonder, my heart knows how!

LIII.

So, earth has gained by one man the more,
　And the gain of earth must be heaven's gain too,
And the whole is well worth thinking o'er
　When autumn comes: which I mean to do
One day, as I said before.

ANY WIFE TO ANY HUSBAND

I.

My love, this is the bitterest, that thou—
Who art all truth, and who dost love me now
　As thine eyes say, as thy voice breaks to say—
Shouldst love so truly, and couldst love me still
A whole long life through, had but love its will,
　Would death that leads me from thee brook delay.

II.

I have but to be by thee, and thy hand
Will never let mine go, nor heart withstand
  The beating of my heart to reach its place.
When shall I look for thee and feel thee gone?
When cry for the old comfort and find none?
  Never, I know! Thy soul is in thy face.

III.

Oh, I should fade—'t is willed so! Might I save,
Gladly I would, whatever beauty gave
  Joy to thy sense, for that was precious too.
It is not to be granted. But the soul
Whence the love comes, all ravage leaves that whole;
  Vainly the flesh fades; soul makes all things new.

IV.

It would not be because my eye grew dim
Thou couldst not find the love there, thanks to Him
  Who never is dishonored in the spark
He gave us from his fire of fires, and bade
Remember whence it sprang, nor be afraid
  While that burns on, though all the rest grow dark.

V.

So, how thou wouldst be perfect, white and clean
Outside as inside, soul and soul's demesne
  Alike, this body given to show it by!
Oh, three-parts through the worst of life's abyss,
What plaudits from the next world after this,
  Couldst thou repeat a stroke and gain the sky!

VI.

And is it not the bitterer to think
That disengage our hands and thou wilt sink
  Although thy love was love in very deed?
I know that nature! Pass a festive day,
Thou dost not throw its relic-flower away
  Nor bid its music's loitering echo speed.

VII.

Thou let'st the stranger's glove lie where it fell;
If old things remain old things all is well,
  For thou art grateful as becomes man best:
And hadst thou only heard me play one tune,
Or viewed me from a window, not so soon
  With thee would such things fade as with the rest.

VIII.

I seem to see! We meet and part; 't is brief;
The book I opened keeps a folded leaf,
  The very chair I sat on, breaks the rank;
That is a portrait of me on the wall—
Three lines, my face comes at so slight a call:
  And for all this, one little hour to thank!

IX.

But now, because the hour through years was fixed,
Because our inmost beings met and mixed,
  Because thou once hast loved me—wilt thou dare
Say to thy soul and Who may list beside,
"Therefore she is immortally my bride;
  Chance cannot change my love, nor time impair.

X.

"So, what if in the dusk of life that's left,
I, a tired traveller of my sun bereft,
  Look from my path when, mimicking the same,
The fire-fly glimpses past me, come and gone?
—Where was it till the sunset? where anon
  It will be at the sunrise! What's to blame?"

XI.

Is it so helpful to thee? Canst thou take
The mimic up, nor, for the true thing's sake,
  Put gently by such efforts at a beam?
Is the remainder of the way so long,
Thou need'st the little solace, thou the strong?
  Watch out thy watch, let weak ones doze and dream!

XII.

—Ah, but the fresher faces! "Is it true,"
Thou'lt ask, "some eyes are beautiful and new?
  Some hair,—how can one choose but grasp such wealth?
And if a man would press his lips to lips
Fresh as the wilding hedge-rose-cup there slips
  The dewdrop out of, must it be by stealth?

XIII.

"It cannot change the love still kept for Her,
More than if such a picture I prefer
  Passing a day with, to a room's bare side:
The painted form takes nothing she possessed,
Yet, while the Titian's Venus lies at rest,
  A man looks. Once more, what is there to chide?"

xiv.

So must I see, from where I sit and watch,
My own self sell myself, my hand attach
    Its warrant to the very thefts from me—
Thy singleness of soul that made me proud,
Thy purity of heart I loved aloud,
    Thy man's-truth I was bold to bid God see!

xv.

Love so, then, if thou wilt! Give all thou canst
Away to the new faces—disentranced,
    (Say it and think it) obdurate no more:
Re-issue looks and words from the old mint,
Pass them afresh, no matter whose the print
    Image and superscription once they bore!

xvi.

Re-coin thyself and give it them to spend,—
It all comes to the same thing at the end,
    Since mine thou wast, mine art and mine shalt be
Faithful or faithless, sealing up the sum
Or lavish of my treasure, thou must come
    Back to the heart's place here I keep for thee!

xvii.

Only, why should it be with stain at all?
Why must I, 'twixt the leaves of coronal,
    Put any kiss of pardon on thy brow?
Why need the other women know so much,
And talk together, "Such the look and such
    The smile he used to love with, then as now!"

xviii.

Might I die last and show thee! Should I find
Such hardship in the few years left behind,
    If free to take and light my lamp, and go
Into thy tomb, and shut the door and sit,
Seeing thy face on those four sides of it
    The better that they are so blank, I know!

xix.

Why, time was what I wanted, to turn o'er
Within my mind each look, get more and more
    By heart each word, too much to learn at first;
And join thee all the fitter for the pause
'Neath the low doorway's lintel. That were cause
    For lingering, though thou calledst, if I durst!

XX.

And yet thou art the nobler of us two:
What dare I dream of, that thou canst not do,
  Outstripping my ten small steps with one stride?
I'll say then, here's a trial and a task—
Is it to bear?—if easy, I'll not ask:
  Though love fail, I can trust on in thy pride.

XXI.

Pride?—when those eyes forestall the life behind
The death I have to go through!—when I find,
  Now that I want thy help most, all of thee!
What did I fear? Thy love shall hold me fast
Until the little minute's sleep is past
  And I wake saved.—And yet it will not be!

TWO IN THE CAMPAGNA

I.

I WONDER do you feel to-day
  As I have felt since, hand in hand,
We sat down on the grass, to stray
  In spirit better through the land,
This morn of Rome and May?

II.

For me, I touched a thought, I know,
  Has tantalized me many times,
(Like turns of thread the spiders throw
  Mocking across our path) for rhymes
To catch at and let go.

III.

Help me to hold it! First it left
  The yellowing fennel, run to seed
There, branching from the brickwork's cleft,
  Some old tomb's ruin: yonder weed
Took up the floating weft,

IV.

Where one small orange cup amassed
  Five beetles,—blind and green they grope
Among the honey-meal: and last,
  Everywhere on the grassy slope
I traced it. Hold it fast!

v.

The champaign with its endless fleece
   Of feathery grasses everywhere!
Silence and passion, joy and peace,
   An everlasting wash of air—
Rome's ghost since her decease.

vi.

Such life here, through such lengths of hours,
   Such miracles performed in play,
Such primal naked forms of flowers,
   Such letting nature have her way
While heaven looks from its towers!

vii.

How say you? Let us, O my dove,
   Let us be unashamed of soul,
As earth lies bare to heaven above!
   How is it under our control
To love or not to love?

viii.

I would that you were all to me,
   You that are just so much, no more.
Nor yours nor mine, nor slave nor free!
   Where does the fault lie? What the core
O' the wound, since wound must be?

ix.

I would I could adopt your will,
   See with your eyes, and set my heart
Beating by yours, and drink my fill
   At your soul's springs,—your part my part
In life, for good and ill.

x.

No. I yearn upward, touch you close,
   Then stand away. I kiss your cheek,
Catch your soul's warmtn,—I pluck the rose
   And love it more than tongue can speak—
Then the good minute goes.

xi.

Already how am I so far
   Out of that minute? Must I go
Still like the thistle-ball, no bar,
   Onward, whenever light winds blow,
Fixed by no friendly star?

XII.

Just when I seemed about to learn!
  Where is the thread now? Off again!
The old trick! Only I discern—
  Infinite passion, and the pain
Of finite hearts that yearn.

MISCONCEPTIONS

I.

THIS is a spray the Bird clung to,
  Making it blossom with pleasure,
Ere the high tree-top she sprung to,
  Fit for her nest and her treasure.
  Oh, what a hope beyond measure
Was the poor spray's, which the flying feet hung to,—
So to be singled out, built in, and sung to!

II.

This is a heart the Queen leant on.
  Thrilled in a minute erratic,
Ere the true bosom she bent on,
  Meet for love's regal dalmatic.
  Oh, what a fancy ecstatic
Was the poor heart's, ere the wanderer went on—
Love to be saved for it, proffered to, spent on!

A SERENADE AT THE VILLA

I.

THAT was I, you heard last night
  When there rose no moon at all,
Nor, to pierce the strained and tight
  Tent of heaven, a planet small:
Life was dead and so was light.

II.

Not a twinkle from the fly,
  Not a glimmer from the worm;
When the crickets stopped their cry,
  When the owls forbore a term,
You heard music; that was I.

III.

Earth turned in her sleep with pain,
  Sultrily suspired for proof:
In at heaven and out again,
  Lightning!—where it broke the roof,
Bloodlike, some few drops of rain.

IV.

What they could my words expressed,
  O my love, my all, my one!
Singing helped the verses best,
  And when singing's best was done,
To my lute I left the rest.

V.

So wore night; the East was gray,
  White the broad-faced hemlock-flowers:
There would be another day;
  Ere its first of heavy hours
Found me, I had passed away.

VI.

What became of all the hopes,
  Words and song and lute as well?
Say, this struck you—"When life gropes
  Feebly for the path where fell
Light last on the evening slopes,

VII.

"One friend in that path shall be,
  To secure my step from wrong;
One to count night day for me,
  Patient through the watches long,
Serving most with none to see."

VIII.

Never say—as something bodes—
  "So, the worst has yet a worse!
When life halts 'neath double loads,
  Better the task-master's curse
Than such music on the roads!

IX.

"When no moon succeeds the sun,
  Nor can pierce the midnight's tent
Any star, the smallest one,
  While some drops, where lightning rent,
Show the final storm begun—

X.

"When the fire-fly hides its spot,
    When the garden-voices fail
In the darkness thick and hot,—
    Shall another voice avail,
That shape be where these are not?

XI.

"Has some plague a longer lease,
    Proffering its help uncouth?
Can't one even die in peace?
    As one shuts one's eyes on youth,
Is that face the last one sees?"

XII.

Oh how dark your villa was,
    Windows fast and obdurate!
How the garden grudged me grass
    Where I stood—the iron gate
Ground its teeth to let me pass!

ONE WAY OF LOVE

I.

ALL June I bound the rose in sheaves.
Now, rose by rose, I strip the leaves
And strew them where Pauline may pass.
She will not turn aside? Alas!
Let them lie. Suppose they die?
The chance was they might take her eye.

II.

How many a month I strove to suit
These stubborn fingers to the lute!
To-day I venture all I know.
She will not hear my music? So!
Break the string; fold music's wing:
Suppose Pauline had bade me sing!

III.

My whole life long I learned to love.
This hour my utmost art I prove
And speak my passion—heaven or hell?
She will not give me heaven? 'T is well!
Lose who may—I still can say,
Those who win heaven, blest are they!

ANOTHER WAY OF LOVE

I.

June was not over
  Though past the full,
And the best of her roses
  Had yet to blow,
  When a man I know
(But shall not discover,
  Since ears are dull,
And time discloses)
Turned him and said with a man's true air,
Half sighing a smile in a yawn, as 't were,—
"If I tire of your June, will she greatly care?"

II.

Well, dear, in-doors with you!
  True! serene deadness
Tries a man's temper.
  What's in the blossom
  June wears on her bosom?
Can it clear scores with you?
  Sweetness and redness,
  Eadem semper!
Go, let me care for it greatly or slightly!
If June mend her bower now, your hand left unsightly
By plucking the roses,—my June will do rightly.

III.

And after, for pastime,
  If June be refulgent
With flowers in completeness,
  All petals, no prickles,
  Delicious as trickles
Of wine poured at mass-time,—
  And choose One indulgent
  To redness and sweetness:
Or if, with experience of man and of spider,
June use my June-lightning, the strong insect-ridder,
And stop the fresh film-work,—why, June will consider.

A PRETTY WOMAN

I.

THAT fawn-skin-dappled hair of hers,
    And the blue eye
    Dear and dewy,
And that infantine fresh air of hers!

II.

To think men cannot take you, Sweet,
    And enfold you,
    Ay, and hold you,
And so keep you what they make you, Sweet!

III.

You like us for a glance, you know—
    For a word's sake
    Or a sword's sake,
All's the same, whate'er the chance, you know.

IV.

And in turn we make you ours, we say—
    You and youth too,
    Eyes and mouth too,
All the face composed of flowers, we say.

V.

All's our own, to make the most of, Sweet—
    Sing and say for,
    Watch and pray for,
Keep a secret or go boast of, Sweet!

VI.

But for loving, why, you would not, Sweet,
    Though we prayed you,
    Paid you, brayed you
In a mortar—for you could not, Sweet!

VII.

So, we leave the sweet face fondly there:
    Be its beauty
    Its sole duty!
Let all hope of grace beyond, lie there!

VIII.

And while the face lies quiet there,
 Who shall wonder
 That I ponder
A conclusion? I will try it there.

IX.

As,—why must one, for the love foregone,
 Scout mere liking?
 Thunder-striking
Earth,—the heaven, we looked above for, gone!

X.

Why, with beauty, needs there money be,
 Love with liking?
 Crush the fly-king
In his gauze, because no honey-bee?

XI.

May not liking be so simple-sweet,
 If love grew there
 'T would undo there
All that breaks the cheek to dimples sweet?

XII.

Is the creature too imperfect, say?
 Would you mend it
 And so end it?
Since not all addition perfects aye!

XIII.

Or is it of its kind, perhaps,
 Just perfection—
 Whence, rejection
Of a grace not to its mind, perhaps?

XIV.

Shall we burn up, tread that face at once
 Into tinder,
 And so hinder
Sparks from kindling all the place at once?

XV.

Or else kiss away one's soul on her?
 Your love-fancies!
 —A sick man sees
Truer, when his hot eyes roll on her!

XVI.

Thus the craftsman thinks to grace the rose,—
　　Plucks a mould-flower
　　For his gold flower,
Uses fine things that efface the rose:

XVII.

Rosy rubies make its cup more rose,
　　Precious metals
　　Ape the petals,—
Last, some old king locks it up, morose!

XVIII.

Then how grace a rose? I know a way!
　　Leave it, rather.
　　Must you gather?
Smell, kiss, wear it—at last, throw away!

RESPECTABILITY

I.

DEAR, had the world in its caprice
　　Deigned to proclaim "I know you both,
　　Have recognized your plighted troth,
Am sponsor for you: live in peace!"—
How many precious months and years
　　Of youth had passed, that speed so fast,
　　Before we found it out at last,
The world, and what it fears!

II.

How much of priceless life were spent
　　With men that every virtue decks,
　　And women models of their sex,
Society's true ornament,—
Ere we dared wander, nights like this,
　　Through wind and rain, and watch the Seine,
　　And feel the Boulevard break again
To warmth and light and bliss!

III.

I know! the world proscribes not love;
　　Allows my finger to caress
　　Your lips' contour and downiness,
Provided it supply a glove.

The world's good word!—the Institute!
  Guizot receives Montalembert!
  Eh? Down the court three lampions flare:
Put forward your best foot!

LOVE IN A LIFE

I.

ROOM after room,
I hunt the house through
We inhabit together.
Heart, fear nothing, for, heart, thou shalt find her—
Next time, herself!—not the trouble behind her
Left in the curtain, the couch's perfume!
As she brushed it, the cornice-wreath blossomed anew:
Yon looking-glass gleamed at the wave of her feather.

II.

Yet the day wears,
And door succeeds door;
I try the fresh fortune—
Range the wide house from the wing to the centre.
Still the same chance! she goes out as I enter.
Spend my whole day in the quest,—who cares?
But 't is twilight, you see,—with such suites to explore,
Such closets to search, such alcoves to importune!

LIFE IN A LOVE

ESCAPE me?
Never—
Beloved!
While I am I, and you are you,
  So long as the world contains us both,
  Me the loving and you the loth,
While the one eludes, must the other pursue.
My life is a fault at last, I fear:
  It seems too much like a fate, indeed!
  Though I do my best I shall scarce succeed.
But what if I fail of my purpose here?
It is but to keep the nerves at strain,
  To dry one's eyes and laugh at a fall,
And baffled, get up and begin again,—
  So the chase takes up one's life, that's all.
While, look but once from your farthest bound

At me so deep in the dust and dark,
No sooner the old hope goes to ground
   Than a new one, straight to the selfsame mark,
I shape me—
Ever
Removed!

IN THREE DAYS

I.

So, I shall see her in three days
And just one night, but nights are short,
Then two long hours, and that is morn.
See how I come, unchanged, unworn!
Feel, where my life broke off from thine,
How fresh the splinters keep and fine,—
Only a touch and we combine!

II.

Too long, this time of year, the days!
But nights, at least the nights are short.
As night shows where her one moon is,
A hand's-breadth of pure light and bliss,
So life's night gives my lady birth
And my eyes hold her! What is worth
The rest of heaven, the rest of earth?

III.

O loaded curls, release your store
Of warmth and scent, as once before
The tingling hair did, lights and darks
Outbreaking into fairy sparks,
When under curl and curl I pried
After the warmth and scent inside,
Through lights and darks how manifold—
The dark inspired, the light controlled!
As early Art embrowns the gold.

IV.

What great fear, should one say, "Three days
That change the world might change as well
Your fortune; and if joy delays,
Be happy that no worse befell!"
What small fear, if another says,
"Three days and one short night beside

May throw no shadow on your ways;
But years must teem with change untried,
With chance not easily defied,
With an end somewhere undescried."
No fear!—or if a fear be born
This minute, it dies out in scorn.
Fear? I shall see her in three days
And one night, now the nights are short,
Then just two hours, and that is morn.

IN A YEAR

I.

NEVER any more,
  While I live,
Need I hope to see his face
  As before.
Once his love grown chill,
  Mine may strive:
Bitterly we re-embrace,
  Single still.

II.

Was it something said,
  Something done,
Vexed him? was it touch of hand,
  Turn of head?
Strange! that very way
  Love begun:
I as little understand
  Love's decay.

III.

When I sewed or drew,
  I recall
How he looked as if I sung,
  —Sweetly too.
If I spoke a word,
  First of all
Up his cheek the color sprung,
  Then he heard.

IV.

Sitting by my side,
  At my feet,
So he breathed but air I breathed,
  Satisfied!

I, too, at love's brim
   Touched the sweet:
I would die if death bequeathed
   Sweet to him.

V.

"Speak, I love thee best!"
   He exclaimed:
"Let thy love my own foretell!"
   I confessed:
"Clasp my heart on thine
   Now unblamed,
Since upon thy soul as well
   Hangeth mine!"

VI.

Was it wrong to own,
   Being truth?
Why should all the giving prove
   His alone?
I had wealth and ease,
   Beauty, youth:
Since my lover gave me love,
   I gave these.

VII.

That was all I meant,
   —To be just,
And the passion I had raised,
   To content.
Since he chose to change
   Gold for dust,
If I gave him what he praised
   Was it strange?

VIII.

Would he loved me yet,
   On and on,
While I found some way undreamed
   —Paid my debt!
Gave more life and more,
   Till, all gone,
He should smile "She never seemed
   Mine before.

IX.

"What, she felt the while,
  Must I think?
Love's so different with us men!"
  He should smile:
"Dying for my sake—
  White and pink!
Can't we touch these bubbles then
  But they break?"

X.

Dear, the pang is brief,
  Do thy part,
Have thy pleasure! How perplexed
  Grows belief!
Well, this cold clay clod
  Was man's heart:
Crumble it, and what comes next?
  Is it God?

WOMEN AND ROSES

I.

I DREAM of a red-rose tree.
And which of its roses three
Is the dearest rose to me?

II.

Round and round, like a dance of snow
In a dazzling drift, as its guardians, go
Floating the women faded for ages,
Sculptured in stone, on the poet's pages.
Then follow women fresh and gay,
Living and loving and loved to-day,
Last, in the rear, flee the multitude of maidens,
Beauties yet unborn. And all, to one cadence,
They circle their rose on my rose tree.

III.

Dear rose, thy term is reached,
Thy leaf hangs loose and bleached:
Bees pass it unimpeached.

IV.

Stay then, stoop, since I cannot climb,
You, great shapes of the antique time!

How shall I fix you, fire you, freeze you,
Break my heart at your feet to please you?
Oh, to possess and be possessed!
Hearts that beat 'neath each pallid breast!
Once but of love, the poesy, the passion,
Drink but once and die!—In vain, the same fashion,
They circle their rose on my rose tree.

v.

Dear rose, thy joy's undimmed,
Thy cup is ruby-rimmed,
Thy cup's heart nectar-brimmed.

vi.

Deep, as drops from a statue's plinth
The bee sucked in by the hyacinth,
So will I bury me while burning,
Quench like him at a plunge my yearning,
Eyes in your eyes, lips on your lips!
Fold me fast where the cincture slips,
Prison all my soul in eternities of pleasure,
Girdle me for once! But no—the old measure,
They circle their rose on my rose tree.

vii.

Dear rose without a thorn,
Thy bud's the babe unborn:
First streak of a new morn.

viii.

Wings, lend wings for the cold, the clear!
What is far conquers what is near.
Roses will bloom nor want beholders,
Sprung from the dust where our flesh moulders.
What shall arrive with the cycle's change?
A novel grace and a beauty strange.
I will make an Eve, be the artist that began her,
Shaped her to his mind!—Alas! in like manner
They circle their rose on my rose tree.

BEFORE

i.

Let them fight it out, friend! things have gone too far.
God must judge the couple: leave them as they are
—Whichever one's the guiltless, to his glory,
And whichever one the guilt's with, to my story!

II.

Why, you would not bid men, sunk in such a slough,
Strike no arm out further, stick and stink as now,
Leaving right and wrong to settle the embroilment,
Heaven with snaky hell, in torture and entoilment?

III.

Who's the culprit of them? How must he conceive
God—the queen he caps to, laughing in his sleeve,
" 'T is but decent to profess oneself beneath her:
Still, one must not be too much in earnest, either!"

IV.

Better sin the whole sin, sure that God observes;
Then go live his life out! Life will try his nerves,
When the sky, which noticed all, makes no disclosure,
And the earth keeps up her terrible composure.

V.

Let him pace at pleasure, past the walls of rose,
Pluck their fruits when grape-trees graze him as he goes!
For he 'gins to guess the purpose of the garden,
With the sly mute thing, beside there, for a warden.

VI.

What's the leopard-dog-thing, constant at his side,
A leer and lie in every eye of its obsequious hide?
When will come an end to all the mock obeisance,
And the price appear that pays for the misfeasance?

VII.

So much for the culprit. Who's the martyred man?
Let him bear one stroke more, for be sure he can!
He that strove thus evil's lump with good to leaven,
Let him give his blood at last and get his heaven!

VIII.

All or nothing, stake it! Trusts he God or no?
Thus far and no farther? farther? be it so!
Now, enough of your chicane of prudent pauses,
Sage provisos, sub-intents and saving-clauses!

IX.

Ah, "forgive" you bid him? While God's champion lives,
Wrong shall be resisted: dead, why, he forgives.
But you must not end my friend ere you begin him;
Evil stands not crowned on earth, while breath is in him.

x.

Once more—Will the wronger, at this last of all,
Dare to say, "I did wrong," rising in his fall?
No?—Let go, then! Both the fighters to their places!
While I count three, step you back as many paces!

AFTER

Take the cloak from his face, and at first
    Let the corpse do its worst!

How he lies in his rights of a man!
    Death has done all death can.
And, absorbed in the new life he leads,
    He recks not, he heeds
Nor his wrong nor my vengeance; both strike
    On his senses alike,
And are lost in the solemn and strange
    Surprise of the change.

Ha, what avails death to erase
    His offence, my disgrace?
I would we were boys as of old
    In the field, by the fold:
His outrage, God's patience, man's scorn
    Were so easily borne!

I stand here now, he lies in his place:
    Cover the face!

THE GUARDIAN-ANGEL

A Picture at Fano

I.

Dear and great Angel, wouldst thou only leave
    That child, when thou hast done with him, for me!
Let me sit all the day here, that when eve
    Shall find performed thy special ministry,
And time come for departure, thou, suspending
Thy flight, may'st see another child for tending,
    Another still, to quiet and retrieve.

II.

Then I shall feel thee step one step, no more,
    From where thou standest now, to where I gaze,
—And suddenly my head is covered o'er
    With those wings, white above the child who prays
Now on that tomb—and I shall feel thee guarding
Me, out of all the world; for me, discarding
    Yon heaven thy home, that waits and opes its door.

III.

I would not look up thither past thy head
    Because the door opes, like that child, I know,
For I should have thy gracious face instead,
    Thou bird of God! And wilt thou bend me low
Like him, and lay, like his, my hands together,
And lift them up to pray, and gently tether
    Me, as thy lamb there, with thy garment's spread?

IV.

If this was ever granted, I would rest
    My head beneath thine, while thy healing hands
Close-covered both my eyes beside thy breast,
    Pressing the brain, which too much thought expands,
Back to its proper size again, and smoothing
Distortion down till every nerve had soothing,
    And all lay quiet, happy and suppressed.

V.

How soon all worldly wrong would be repaired!
    I think how I should view the earth and skies
And sea, when once again my brow was bared
    After thy healing, with such different eyes.
O world, as God has made it! All is beauty:
And knowing this, is love, and love is duty.
    What further may be sought for or declared?

VI.

Guercino drew this angel I saw teach
    (Alfred, dear friend!)—that little child to pray,
Holding the little hands up, each to each
    Pressed gently,—with his own head turned away
Over the earth where so much lay before him
Of work to do, though heaven was opening o'er him,
    And he was left at Fano by the beach.

VII.

We were at Fano, and three times we went
  To sit and see him in his chapel there,
And drink his beauty to our soul's content
  —My angel with me too: and since I care
For dear Guercino's fame (to which in power
And glory comes this picture for a dower,
  Fraught with a pathos so magnificent)—

VIII.

And since he did not work thus earnestly
  At all times, and has else endured some wrong—
I took one thought his picture struck from me,
  And spread it out, translating it to song.
My love is here. Where are you, dear old friend?
How rolls the Wairoa at your world's far end?
  This is Ancona, yonder is the sea.

MEMORABILIA

I.

Ah, did you once see Shelley plain,
  And did he stop and speak to you,
And did you speak to him again?
  How strange it seems and new!

II.

But you were living before that,
  And also you are living after;
And the memory I started at—
  My starting moves your laughter!

III.

I crossed a moor, with a name of its own
  And a certain use in the world no doubt,
Yet a hand's-breadth of it shines alone
  'Mid the blank miles round about:

IV.

For there I picked up on the heather,
  And there I put inside my breast
A moulted feather, an eagle-feather!
  Well, I forgot the rest.

POPULARITY

I.

STAND still, true poet that you are!
    I know you; let me try and draw you.
Some night you'll fail us: when afar
    You rise, remember one man saw you,
Knew you, and named a star!

II.

My star, God's glow-worm! Why extend
    That loving hand of his which leads you,
Yet locks you safe from end to end
    Of this dark world, unless he needs you,
Just saves your light to spend?

III.

His clenched hand shall unclose at last,
    I know, and let out all the beauty:
My poet holds the future fast,
    Accepts the coming ages' duty,
Their present for this past.

IV.

That day, the earth's feast-master's brow
    Shall clear, to God the chalice raising;
"Others give best at first, but thou
    Forever set'st our table praising,
Keep'st the good wine till now!"

V.

Meantime, I'll draw you as you stand,
    With few or none to watch and wonder:
I'll say—a fisher, on the sand
    By Tyre the old, with ocean-plunder,
A netful, brought to land.

VI.

Who has not heard how Tyrian shells
    Enclosed the blue, that dye of dyes
Whereof one drop worked miracles,
    And colored like Astarte's eyes
Raw silk the merchant sells?

VII.

And each bystander of them all
    Could criticise, and quote tradition

How depths of blue sublimed some pall
  —To get which, pricked a king's ambition;
Worth sceptre, crown and ball.

VIII.

Yet there's the dye, in that rough mesh,
  The sea has only just o'er-whispered!
Live whelks, each lip's beard dripping fresh,
  As if they still the water's lisp heard
Through foam the rock-weeds thresh.

IX.

Enough to furnish Solomon
  Such hangings for his cedar-house,
That, when gold-robed he took the throne
  In that abyss of blue, the Spouse
Might swear his presence shone

X.

Most like the centre-spike of gold
  Which burns deep in the bluebell's womb
What time, with ardors manifold,
  The bee goes singing to her groom,
Drunken and overbold.

XI.

Mere conchs! not fit for warp or woof!
  Till cunning come to pound and squeeze
And clarify,—refine to proof
  The liquor filtered by degrees,
While the world stands aloof.

XII.

And there's the extract, flasked and fine,
  And priced and salable at last!
And Hobbs, Nobbs, Stokes and Nokes combine
  To paint the future from the past,
Put blue into their line.

XIII.

Hobbs hints blue,—straight he turtle eats:
  Nobbs prints blue,—claret crowns his cup:
Nokes outdares Stokes in azure feats,—
  Both gorge. Who fished the murex up?
What porridge had John Keats?

MASTER HUGUES OF SAXE–GOTHA

I.

Hist, but a word, fair and soft!
Forth and be judged, Master Hugues!
Answer the question I've put you so oft:
    What do you mean by your mountainous fugues?
See, we're alone in the loft,—

II.

I, the poor organist here,
    Hugues, the composer of note,
Dead though, and done with, this many a year:
    Let's have a colloquy, something to quote,
Make the world prick up its ear!

III.

See, the church empties apace:
    Fast they extinguish the lights.
Hallo there, sacristan! Five minutes' grace!
    Here's a crank pedal wants setting to rights,
Balks one of holding the base.

IV.

See, our huge house of the sounds,
    Hushing its hundreds at once,
Bids the last loiterer back to his bounds!
    —O you may challenge them, not a response
Get the church-saints on their rounds!

V.

(Saints go their rounds, who shall doubt?
    —March, with the moon to admire,
Up nave, down chancel, turn transept about,
    Supervise all betwixt pavement and spire,
Put rats and mice to the rout—

VI.

Aloys and Jurien and Just—
    Order things back to their place,
Have a sharp eye lest the candlesticks rust,
    Rub the church-plate, darn the sacrament-lace,
Clear the desk-velvet of dust.)

VII.

Here's your book, younger folks shelve!
    Played I not off-hand and runningly,

Just now, your masterpiece, hard number twelve?
   Here's what should strike, could one handle it cunningly:
Help the axe, give it a helve!

VIII.

Page after page as I played,
   Every bar's rest, where one wipes
Sweat from one's brow, I looked up and surveyed,
   O'er my three claviers, yon forest of pipes
Whence you still peeped in the shade.

IX.

Sure you were wishful to speak?
   You, with brow ruled like a score,
Yes, and eyes buried in pits on each cheek,
   Like two great breves, as they wrote them of yore,
Each side that bar, your straight beak!

X.

Sure you said—"Good, the mere notes!
   Still, couldst thou take my intent,
Know what procured me our Company's votes—
   A master were lauded and sciolists shent,
Parted the sheep from the goats!"

XI.

Well then, speak up, never flinch!
   Quick, ere my candle's a snuff
—Burnt, do you see? to its uttermost inch—
   I believe in you, but that's not enough:
Give my conviction a clinch!

XII.

First you deliver your phrase
   —Nothing propound, that I see,
Fit in itself for much blame or much praise—
   Answered no less, where no answer needs be;
Off start the Two on their ways.

XIII.

Straight must a Third interpose,
   Volunteer needlessly help;
In strikes a Fourth, a Fifth thrusts in his nose,
   So the cry's open, the kennel's a-yelp,
Argument's hot to the close.

XIV.

One dissertates, he is candid;
  Two must discept,—has distinguished;
Three helps the couple, if ever yet man did;
  Four protests; Five makes a dart at the thing wished:
Back to One, goes the case bandied.

XV.

One says his say with a difference;
  More of expounding, explaining!
All now is wrangle, abuse and vociferance;
  Now there's a truce, all's subdued, self-restraining:
Five, though, stands out all the stiffer hence.

XVI.

One is incisive, corrosive;
  Two retorts, nettled, curt, crepitant;
Three makes rejoinder, expansive, explosive;
  Four overbears them all, strident and strepitant:
Five . . . O Danaides, O Sieve!

XVII.

Now, they ply axes and crowbars;
  Now, they prick pins at a tissue
Fine as a skein of the casuist Escobar's
  Worked on the bone of a lie. To what issue?
Where is our gain at the Two-bars?

XVIII.

Est fuga, volvitur rota.
  On we drift: where looms the dim port?
One, Two, Three, Four, Five, contribute their quota;
  Something is gained, if one caught but the import—
Show it us, Hugues of Saxe-Gotha!

XIX.

What with affirming, denying,
  Holding, risposting, subjoining,
All's like . . . it's like . . . for an instance I'm trying . . .
  There! See our roof, its gilt moulding and groining
Under those spider-webs lying!

XX.

So your fugue broadens and thickens,
  Greatens and deepens and lengthens,

Till we exclaim—"But where's music, the dickens?
  Blot ye the gold, while your spider-web strengthens
—Blacked to the stoutest of tickens?"

XXI.

I for man's effort am zealous:
  Prove me such censure unfounded!
Seems it surprising a lover grows jealous—
  Hopes 't was for something, his organ-pipes sounded,
Tiring three boys at the bellows?

XXII.

Is it your moral of Life?
  Such a web, simple and subtle,
Weave we on earth here in impotent strife,
  Backward and forward each throwing his shuttle,
Death ending all with a knife?

XXIII.

Over our heads truth and nature—
  Still our life's zigzags and dodges,
Ins and outs, weaving a new legislature—
  God's gold just shining its last where that lodges,
Palled beneath man's usurpature.

XXIV.

So we o'ershroud stars and roses,
  Cherub and trophy and garland;
Nothings grow something which quietly closes
  Heaven's earnest eye: not a glimpse of the far land
Gets through our comments and glozes.

XXV.

Ah but traditions, inventions,
  (Say we and make up a visage)
So many men with such various intentions,
  Down the past ages, must know more than this age!
Leave we the web its dimensions!

XXVI.

Who thinks Hugues wrote for the deaf,
  Proved a mere mountain in labor?
Better submit; try again; what's the clef?
  'Faith, 'tis no trifle for pipe and for tabor—
Four flats, the minor in F.

XXVII.

Friend, your fugue taxes the finger:
   Learning it once, who would lose it?
Yet all the while a misgiving will linger,
   Truth's golden o'er us although we refuse it—
Nature, through cobwebs we string her.

XXVIII.

Hugues! I advise *meâ pœnâ*
   (Counterpoint glares like a Gorgon)
Bid One, Two, Three, Four, Five, clear the arena!
   Say the word, straight I unstop the full-organ,
Blare out the *mode Palestrina*.

XXIX.

While in the roof, if I'm right there,
   . . . Lo you, the wick in the socket!
Hallo, you sacristan, show us a light there!
   Down it dips, gone like a rocket.
What, you want, do you, to come unawares,
Sweeping the church up for first morning-prayers,
And find a poor devil has ended his cares
At the foot of your rotten-runged rat-riddled stairs?
   Do I carry the moon in my pocket?

DRAMATIC ROMANCES

☆

INCIDENT OF THE FRENCH CAMP

I.

You know, we French stormed Ratisbon:
   A mile or so away,
On a little mound, Napoleon
   Stood on our storming-day;
With neck out-thrust, you fancy how,
   Legs wide, arms locked behind,
As if to balance the prone brow
   Oppressive with its mind.

II.

Just as perhaps he mused "My plans
   That soar, to earth may fall,
Let once my army-leader Lannes
   Waver at yonder wall,"—

Out 'twixt the battery-smokes there flew
  A rider, bound on bound
Full-galloping; nor bridle drew
  Until he reached the mound.

III.

Then off there flung in smiling joy,
  And held himself erect
By just his horse's mane, a boy:
  You hardly could suspect—
(So tight he kept his lips compressed,
  Scarce any blood came through)
You looked twice ere you saw his breast
  Was all but shot in two.

IV.

"Well," cried he, "Emperor, by God's grace
  We've got you Ratisbon!
The Marshal's in the market-place,
  And you'll be there anon
To see your flag-bird flap his vans
  Where I, to heart's desire,
Perched him!" The chief's eye flashed; his plans
  Soared up again like fire.

V.

The chief's eye flashed; but presently
  Softened itself, as sheathes
A film the mother-eagle's eye
  When her bruised eaglet breathes;
"You're wounded!" "Nay," the soldier's pride
  Touched to the quick, he said:
"I'm killed, Sire!" And his chief beside,
  Smiling the boy fell dead.

THE PATRIOT

AN OLD STORY

I.

IT WAS roses, roses, all the way,
  With myrtle mixed in my path like mad:
The house-roofs seemed to heave and sway,
  The church-spires flamed, such flags they had,
A year ago on this very day.

II.

The air broke into a mist with bells,
  The old walls rocked with the crowd and cries.
Had I said, "Good folk, mere noise repels—
  But give me your sun from yonder skies!"
They had answered, "And afterward, what else?"

III.

Alack, it was I who leaped at the sun
  To give it my loving friends to keep!
Nought man could do, have I left undone:
  And you see my harvest, what I reap
This very day, now a year is run.

IV.

There's nobody on the house-tops now—
  Just a palsied few at the windows set;
For the best of the sight is, all allow,
  At the Shambles' Gate—or, better yet,
By the very scaffold's foot, I trow.

V.

I go in the rain, and, more than needs,
  A rope cuts both my wrists behind;
And I think, by the feel, my forehead bleeds,
  For they fling, whoever has a mind,
Stones at me for my year's misdeeds.

VI.

Thus I entered, and thus I go!
  In triumphs, people have dropped down dead.
"Paid by the world, what dost thou owe
  Me?"—God might question; now instead,
'Tis God shall repay: I am safer so.

MY LAST DUCHESS

Ferrara

That's my last Duchess painted on the wall,
Looking as if she were alive. I call
That piece a wonder, now: Frà Pandolf's hands
Worked busily a day, and there she stands.
Will 't please you sit and look at her? I said
"Frà Pandolf" by design, for never read

Strangers like you that pictured countenance,
The depth and passion of its earnest glance,
But to myself they turned (since none puts by
The curtain I have drawn for you, but I)
And seemed as they would ask me, if they durst,
How such a glance came there; so, not the first
Are you to turn and ask thus. Sir, 'twas not
Her husband's presence only, called that spot
Of joy into the Duchess' cheek: perhaps
Frà Pandolf chanced to say "Her mantle laps
Over my lady's wrist too much," or "Paint
Must never hope to reproduce the faint
Half-flush that dies along her throat:" such stuff
Was courtesy, she thought, and cause enough
For calling up that spot of joy. She had
A heart—how shall I say?—too soon made glad,
Too easily impressed; she liked whate'er
She looked on, and her looks went everywhere.
Sir, 'twas all one! My favor at her breast,
The dropping of the daylight in the West,
The bough of cherries some officious fool
Broke in the orchard for her, the white mule
She rode with round the terrace—all and each
Would draw from her alike the approving speech,
Or blush, at least. She thanked men,—good! but thanked
Somehow—I know not how—as if she ranked
My gift of a nine-hundred-years-old name
With anybody's gift. Who'd stoop to blame
This sort of trifling? Even had you skill
In speech—(which I have not)—to make your will
Quite clear to such an one, and say, "Just this
Or that in you disgusts me; here you miss,
Or there exceed the mark"—and if she let
Herself be lessoned so, nor plainly set
Her wits to yours, forsooth, and made excuse,
—E'en then would be some stooping; and I choose
Never to stoop. Oh sir, she smiled, no doubt,
Whene'er I passed her; but who passed without
Much the same smile? This grew; I gave commands;
Then all smiles stopped together. There she stands
As if alive. Will 't please you rise? We'll meet
The company below, then. I repeat,
The Count your master's known munificence
Is ample warrant that no just pretence
Of mine for dowry will be disallowed;
Though his fair daughter's self, as I avowed

At starting, is my object. Nay, we'll go
Together down, sir. Notice Neptune, though,
Taming a sea-horse, thought a rarity,
Which Claus of Innsbruck cast in bronze for me!

COUNT GISMOND

AIX IN PROVENCE

I.

CHRIST GOD who savest man, save most
    Of men Count Gismond who saved me!
Count Gauthier, when he chose his post,
    Chose time and place and company
To suit it; when he struck at length
My honor, 'twas with all his strength.

II.

And doubtlessly ere he could draw
    All points to one, he must have schemed!
That miserable morning saw
    Few half so happy as I seemed,
While being dressed in queen's array
To give our tourney prize away.

III.

I thought they loved me, did me grace
    To please themselves; 'twas all their deed;
God makes, or fair or foul, our face;
    If showing mine so caused to bleed
My cousins' hearts, they should have dropped
A word, and straight the play had stopped.

IV.

They, too, so beauteous! Each a queen
    By virtue of her brow and breast;
Not needing to be crowned, I mean,
    As I do. E'en when I was dressed,
Had either of them spoke, instead
Of glancing sideways with still head!

V.

But no: they let me laugh, and sing
    My birthday song quite through, adjust

The last rose in my garland, fling
 A last look on the mirror, trust
My arms to each an arm of theirs,
And so descend the castle-stairs—

VI.

And come out on the morning-troop
 Of merry friends who kissed my cheek,
And called me queen, and made me stoop
 Under the canopy—(a streak
That pierced it, of the outside sun,
Powdered with gold its gloom's soft dun)—

VII.

And they could let me take my state
 And foolish throne amid applause
Of all come there to celebrate
 My queen's-day—Oh I think the cause
Of much was, they forgot no crowd
Makes up for parents in their shroud!

VIII.

However that be, all eyes were bent
 Upon me, when my cousins cast
Theirs down; 'twas time I should present
 The victor's crown, but . . . there, 'twill last
No long time . . . the old mist again
Blinds me as then it did. How vain!

IX.

See! Gismond's at the gate, in talk
 With his two boys: I can proceed.
Well, at that moment, who should stalk
 Forth boldly—to my face, indeed—
But. Gauthier, and he thundered, "Stay!"
And all stayed. "Bring no crowns, I say!

X.

"Bring torches! Wind the penance-sheet
 About her! Let her shun the chaste,
Or lay herself before their feet!
 Shall she whose body I embraced
A night long, queen it in the day?
For honor's sake no crowns, I say!"

XI.

I? What I answered? As I live,
    I never fancied such a thing
As answer possible to give.
    What says the body when they spring
Some monstrous torture-engine's whole
Strength on it? No more says the soul.

XII.

Till out strode Gismond; then I knew
    That I was saved. I never met
His face before, but, at first view,
    I felt quite sure that God had set
Himself to Satan; who would spend
A minute's mistrust on the end?

XIII.

He strode to Gauthier, in his throat
    Gave him the lie, then struck his mouth
With one back-handed blow that wrote
    In blood men's verdict there. North, South,
East, West, I looked. The lie was dead,
And damned, and truth stood up instead.

XIV.

This glads me most, that I enjoyed
    The heart of the joy, with my content
In watching Gismond unalloyed
    By any doubt of the event:
God took that on him—I was bid
Watch Gismond for my part: I did.

XV.

Did I not watch him while he let
    His armorer just brace his greaves,
Rivet his hauberk, on the fret
    The while! His foot . . . my memory leaves
No least stamp out, nor how anon
He pulled his ringing gauntlets on.

XVI.

And e'en before the trumpet's sound
    Was finished, prone lay the false knight,
Prone as his lie, upon the ground:
    Gismond flew at him, used no sleight
O' the sword, but open-breasted drove,
Cleaving till out the truth he clove.

XVII.

Which done, he dragged him to my feet
  And said, "Here die, but end thy breath
In full confession, lest thou fleet
  From my first, to God's second death!
Say, hast thou lied?" And, "I have lied
To God and her," he said, and died.

XVIII.

Then Gismond, kneeling to me, asked
  —What safe my heart holds, though no word
Could I repeat now, if I tasked
  My powers forever, to a third
Dear even as you are. Pass the rest
Until I sank upon his breast.

XIX.

Over my head his arm he flung
  Against the world; and scarce I felt
His sword (that dripped by me and swung)
  A little shifted in its belt:
For he began to say the while
How South our home lay many a mile.

XX.

So 'mid the shouting multitude
  We two walked forth to never more
Return. My cousins have pursued
  Their life, untroubled as before
I vexed them. Gauthier's dwelling-place
God lighten! May his soul find grace!

XXI.

Our elder boy has got the clear
  Great brow; though when his brother's black
Full eye shows scorn, it . . . Gismond here?
  And have you brought my tercel back?
I just was telling Adela
How many birds it struck since May.

THE BOY AND THE ANGEL

MORNING, evening, noon and night,
"Praise God!" sang Theocrite.

Then to his poor trade he turned,
Whereby the daily meal was earned.

Hard he labored, long and well;
O'er his work the boy's curls fell.

But ever, at each period,
He stopped and sang, "Praise God!"

Then back again his curls he threw,
And cheerful turned to work anew.

Said Blaise, the listening monk, "Well done;
I doubt not thou art heard, my son:

"As well as if thy voice to-day
Were praising God, the Pope's great way.

"This Easter Day, the Pope at Rome
Praises God from Peter's dome."

Said Theocrite, "Would God that I
Might praise him, that great way, and die!"

Night passed, day shone,
And Theocrite was gone.

With God a day endures alway,
A thousand years are but a day.

God said in heaven, "Nor day nor night
Now brings the voice of my delight."

Then Gabriel, like a rainbow's birth,
Spread his wings and sank to earth;

Entered, in flesh, the empty cell,
Lived there, and played the craftsman well;

And morning, evening, noon and night,
Praised God in place of Theocrite.

And from a boy, to youth he grew:
The man put off the stripling's hue:

The man matured and fell away
Into the season of decay:

And ever o'er the trade he bent,
And ever lived on earth content.

(He did God's will; to him, all one
If on the earth or in the sun.)

God said, "A praise is in mine ear;
There is no doubt in it, no fear:

"So sing old worlds, and so
New worlds that from my footstool go.

"Clearer loves sound other ways:
I miss my little human praise."

Then forth sprang Gabriel's wings, off fell
The flesh disguise, remained the cell.

'Twas Easter Day: he flew to Rome,
And paused above Saint Peter's dome.

In the tiring-room close by
The great outer gallery,

With his holy vestments dight,
Stood the new Pope, Theocrite:

And all his past career
Came back upon him clear,

Since when, a boy, he plied his trade,
Till on his life the sickness weighed;

And in his cell, when death drew near,
An angel in a dream brought cheer:

And rising from the sickness drear,
He grew a priest, and now stood here.

To the East with praise he turned,
And on his sight the angel burned.

"I bore thee from thy craftsman's cell,
And set thee here; I did not well.

"Vainly I left my angel-sphere,
Vain was thy dream of many a year.

"Thy voice's praise seemed weak; it dropped—
Creation's chorus stopped!

"Go back and praise again
The early way, while I remain.

"With that weak voice of our disdain,
Take up creation's pausing strain.

"Back to the cell and poor employ:
Resume the craftsman and the boy!"

Theocrite grew old at home;
A new Pope dwelt in Peter's dome.

One vanished as the other died:
They sought God side by side.

INSTANS TYRANNUS

I.

Of the million or two, more or less,
I rule and possess,
One man, for some cause undefined,
Was least to my mind.

II.

I struck him, he grovelled of course—
For, what was his force?
I pinned him to earth with my weight
And persistence of hate:
And he lay, would not moan, would not curse,
As his lot might be worse.

III.

"Were the object less mean, would he stand
At the swing of my hand!
For obscurity helps him and blots
The hole where he squats."

So, I set my five wits on the stretch
To inveigle the wretch.
All in vain! Gold and jewels I threw,
Still he couched there perdue;
I tempted his blood and his flesh,
Hid in roses my mesh,
Choicest cates and the flagon's best spilth:
Still he kept to his filth.

IV.

Had he kith now or kin, were access
To his heart, did I press:
Just a son or a mother to seize!
No such booty as these.
Were it simply a friend to pursue
'Mid my million or two,
Who could pay me in person or pelf
What he owes me himself!
No: I could not but smile through my chafe:
For the fellow lay safe
As his mates do, the midge and the nit,
—Through minuteness, to wit.

V.

Then a humor more great took its place
At the thought of his face,
The droop, the low cares of the mouth,
The trouble uncouth
'Twixt the brows, all that air one is fain
To put out of its pain.
And, "no!" I admonished myself,
"Is one mocked by an elf,
Is one baffled by toad or by rat?
The gravamen's in that!
How the lion, who crouches to suit
His back to my foot,
Would admire that I stand in debate!
But the small turns the great
If it vexes you,—that is the thing!
Toad or rat vex the king?
Though I waste half my realm to unearth
Toad or rat, 'tis well worth!"

VI.

So, I soberly laid my last plan
To extinguish the man.

Round his creep-hole, with never a break
Ran my fires for his sake;
Over-head, did my thunder combine
With my under-ground mine:
Till I looked from my labor content
To enjoy the event.

VII.

When sudden . . . how think ye, the end?
Did I say "without friend"?
Say rather, from marge to blue marge
The whole sky grew his targe
With the sun's self for visible boss,
While an Arm ran across
Which the earth heaved beneath like a breast
Where the wretch was safe prest!
Do you see? Just my vengeance complete,
The man sprang to his feet,
Stood erect, caught at God's skirts, and prayed!
—So, I was afraid!

MESMERISM

I.

ALL I believed is true!
    I am able yet
    All I want, to get
By a method as strange as new:
Dare I trust the same to you?

II.

If at night, when doors are shut,
    And the wood-worm picks,
    And the death-watch ticks,
And the bar has a flag of smut,
And a cat's in the water-butt—

III.

And the socket floats and flares,
    And the house-beams groan,
    And a foot unknown
Is surmised on the garret-stairs,
And the locks slip unawares—

IV.

And the spider, to serve his ends,
   By a sudden thread,
   Arms and legs outspread,
On the table's midst descends,
Comes to find, God knows what friends!—

V.

If since eve drew in, I say,
   I have sat and brought
   (So to speak) my thought
To bear on the woman away,
Till I felt my hair turn gray—

VI.

Till I seemed to have and hold,
   In the vacancy
   'Twixt the wall and me,
From the hair-plait's chestnut-gold
To the foot in its muslin fold—

VII.

Have and hold, then and there,
   Her, from head to foot,
   Breathing and mute,
Passive and yet aware,
In the grasp of my steady stare—

VIII.

Hold and have, there and then,
   All her body and soul
   That completes my whole,
All that women add to men,
In the clutch of my steady ken—

IX.

Having and holding, till
   I imprint her fast
   On the void at last
As the sun does whom he will
By the calotypist's skill—

X.

Then,—if my heart's strength serve,
   And through all and each
   Of the veils I reach
To her soul and never swerve,
Knitting an iron nerve—

XI.

Command her soul to advance
   And inform the shape
   Which has made escape
And before my countenance
Answers me glance for glance—

XII.

I, still with a gesture fit
   Of my hands that best
   Do my soul's behest,
Pointing the power from it,
While myself do steadfast sit—

XIII.

Steadfast and still the same
   On my object bent,
   While the hands give vent
To my ardor and my aim
And break into very flame—

XIV.

Then I reach, I must believe,
   Not her soul in vain,
   For to me again
It reaches, and past retrieve
Is wound in the toils I weave;

XV.

And must follow as I require,
   As befits a thrall,
   Bringing flesh and all,
Essence and earth-attire,
To the source of the tractile fire:

XVI.

Till the house called hers, not mine,
   With a growing weight
   Seems to suffocate
If she break not its leaden line
And escape from its close confine.

XVII.

Out of doors into the night!
   On to the maze
   Of the wild wood-ways,
Not turning to left nor right
From the pathway, blind with sight—

XVIII.

Making through rain and wind
 O'er the broken shrubs,
 'Twixt the stems and stubs,
With a still, composed, strong mind,
Nor a care for the world behind—

XIX.

Swifter and still more swift,
 As the crowding peace
 Doth to joy increase
In the wide blind eyes uplift
Through the darkness and the drift!

XX.

While I—to the shape, I too
 Feel my soul dilate
 Nor a whit abate,
And relax not a gesture due,
As I see my belief come true.

XXI.

For, there! have I drawn or no
 Life to that lip?
 Do my fingers dip
In a flame which again they throw
On the cheek that breaks a-glow?

XXII.

Ha! was the hair so first?
 What, unfilleted,
 Made alive, and spread
Through the void with a rich outburst,
Chestnut gold-interspersed?

XXIII.

Like the doors of a casket-shrine,
 See, on either side,
 Her two arms divide
Till the heart betwixt makes sign,
Take me, for I am thine!

XXIV.

"Now—now"—the door is heard!
 Hark, the stairs! and near—
 Nearer—and here—
"Now!" and at call the third
She enters without a word.

XXV.

On doth she march and on
    To the fancied shape;
    It is, past escape,
Herself, now: the dream is done
And the shadow and she are one.

XXVI.

First I will pray. Do Thou
    That ownest the soul,
    Yet wilt grant control
To another, nor disallow
For a time, restrain me now!

XXVII.

I admonish me while I may,
    Not to squander guilt,
    Since require Thou wilt
At my hand its price one day!
What the price is, who can say?

THE GLOVE

(Peter Ronsard *loquitur*)

"Heigho," yawned one day King Francis,
"Distance all value enhances!
When a man's busy, why, leisure
Strikes him as wonderful pleasure:
'Faith, and at leisure once is he?
Straightway he wants to be busy.
Here we've got peace; and aghast I'm
Caught thinking war the true pastime.
Is there a reason in metre?
Give us your speech, master Peter!"
I who, if mortal dare say so,
Ne'er am at loss with my Naso,
"Sire," I replied, "joys prove cloudlets:
Men are the merest Ixions"—
Here the King whistled aloud, "Let's
—Heigho—go look at our lions!"
Such are the sorrowful chances
If you talk fine to King Francis.

And so, to the courtyard proceeding,
Our company, Francis was leading,
Increased by new followers tenfold
Before he arrived at the penfold;
Lords, ladies, like clouds which bedizen
At sunset the western horizon.
And Sir De Lorge pressed 'mid the foremost
With the dame he professed to adore most.
Oh, what a face! One by fits eyed
Her, and the horrible pitside;
For the penfold surrounded a hollow
Which led where the eye scarce dared follow,
And shelved to the chamber secluded
Where Bluebeard, the great lion, brooded.
The King hailed his keeper, an Arab
As glossy and black as a scarab,
And bade him make sport and at once stir
Up and out of his den the old monster.
They opened a hole in the wire-work
Across it, and dropped there a firework,
And fled: one's heart's beating redoubled;
A pause, while the pit's mouth was troubled,
The blackness and silence so utter,
By the firework's slow sparkling and sputter;
Then earth in a sudden contortion
Gave out to our gaze her abortion.
Such a brute! Were I friend Clement Marot
(Whose experience of nature's but narrow,
And whose faculties move in no small mist
When he versifies David the Psalmist)
I should study that brute to describe you
Illum Juda Leonem de Tribu.

One's whole blood grew curdling and creepy
To see the black mane, vast and heapy,
The tail in the air stiff and straining,
The wide eyes, nor waxing nor waning,
As over the barrier which bounded
His platform, and us who surrounded
The barrier, they reached and they rested
On space that might stand him in best stead:
For who knew, he thought, what the amazement,
The eruption of clatter and blaze meant,
And if, in this minute of wonder,
No outlet, 'mid lightning and thunder,
Lay broad, and, his shackles all shivered,

The lion at last was delivered?
Ay, that was the open sky o'erhead!
And you saw by the flash on his forehead,
By the hope in those eyes wide and steady,
He was leagues in the desert already,
Driving the flocks up the mountain,
Or catlike couched hard by the fountain
To waylay the date-gathering negress:
So guarded he entrance or egress.
"How he stands!" quoth the King: "we may well swear,
(No novice, we've won our spurs elsewhere
And so can afford the confession,)
We exercise wholesome discretion
In keeping aloof from his threshold,
Once hold you, those jaws want no fresh hold,
Their first would too pleasantly purloin
The visitor's brisket or surloin:
But who's he would prove so fool-hardy?
Not the best man of Marignan, pardie!"

The sentence no sooner was uttered,
Than over the rails a glove fluttered,
Fell close to the lion, and rested:
The dame 'twas, who flung it and jested
With life so, De Lorge had been wooing
For months past; he sat there pursuing
His suit, weighing out with nonchalance
Fine speeches like gold from a balance.

Sound the trumpet, no true knight's a tarrier!
De Lorge made one leap at the barrier,
Walked straight to the glove,—while the lion
Ne'er moved, kept his far-reaching eye on
The palm-tree-edged desert-spring's sapphire,
And the musky oiled skin of the Kaffir,—
Picked it up, and as calmly retreated,
Leaped back where the lady was seated,
And full in the face of its owner
Flung the glove.

"Your heart's queen, you dethrone her?
So should I!"—cried the King—"'twas mere vanity,
Not love, set that task to humanity!"
Lords and ladies alike turned with loathing
From such a proved wolf in sheep's clothing.

Not so, I; for I caught an expression
In her brow's undisturbed self-possession
Amid the Court's scoffing and merriment,—
As if from no pleasing experiment
She rose, yet of pain not much heedful
So long as the process was needful,—
As if she had tried in a crucible,
To what "speeches like gold" were reducible,
And, finding the finest prove copper,
Felt the smoke in her face was but proper;
To know what she had *not* to trust to,
Was worth all the ashes and dust too.
She went out 'mid hooting and laughter;
Clement Marot stayed; I followed after,
And asked, as a grace, what it all meant?
If she wished not the rash deed's recallment?
"For I"—so I spoke—"am a poet:
Human nature,—behoves that I know it!"

She told me, "Too long had I heard
Of the deed proved alone by the word:
For my love—what De Lorge would not dare!
With my scorn—what De Lorge could compare!
And the endless descriptions of death
He would brave when my lip formed a breath,
I must reckon as braved, or, of course,
Doubt his word—and moreover, perforce,
For such gifts as no lady could spurn,
Must offer my love in return.
When I looked on your lion, it brought
All the dangers at once to my thought,
Encountered by all sorts of men,
Before he was lodged in his den,—
From the poor slave whose club or bare hands
Dug the trap, set the snare on the sands,
With no King and no Court to applaud,
By no shame, should he shrink, overawed,
Yet to capture the creature made shift,
That his rude boys might laugh at the gift,
—To the page who last leaped o'er the fence
Of the pit, on no greater pretence
Than to get back the bonnet he dropped,
Lest his pay for a week should be stopped.
So, wiser I judged it to make
One trial what 'death for my sake'
Really meant, while the power was yet mine,

Than to wait until time should define
Such a phrase not so simply as I,
Who took it to mean just 'to die.'
The blow a glove gives is but weak:
Does the mark yet discolor my cheek?
But when the heart suffers a blow,
Will the pain pass so soon, do you know?"

I looked, as away she was sweeping,
And saw a youth eagerly keeping
As close as he dared to the doorway.
No doubt that a noble should more weigh
His life than befits a plebeian;
And yet, had our brute been Nemean—
(I judge by a certain calm fervor
The youth stepped with, forward to serve her)
—He'd have scarce thought you did him the worst turn
If you whispered, "Friend, what you'd get, first earn!"
And when, shortly after, she carried
Her shame from the Court, and they married,
To that marriage some happiness, maugre
The voice of the Court, I dared augur.

For De Lorge, he made women with men vie,
Those in wonder and praise, these in envy;
And in short stood so plain a head taller
That he wooed and won . . . how do you call her?
The beauty, that rose in the sequel
To the King's love, who loved her a week well.
And 'twas noticed he never would honor
De Lorge (who looked daggers upon her)
With the easy commission of stretching
His legs in the service, and fetching
His wife, from her chamber, those straying
Sad gloves she was always mislaying,
While the King took the closet to chat in,—
But of course this adventure came pat in.
And never the King told the story,
How bringing a glove brought such glory,
But the wife smiled—"His nerves are grown firmer:
Mine he brings now and utters no murmur."

Venienti occurrite morbo!
With which moral I drop my theorbo.

TIME'S REVENGES

I'VE a Friend, over the sea;
I like him, but he loves me.
It all grew out of the books I write;
They find such favor in his sight
That he slaughters you with savage looks
Because you don't admire my books.
He does himself though,—and if some vein
Were to snap to-night in this heavy brain,
To-morrow month, if I lived to try,
Round should I just turn quietly,
Or out of the bedclothes stretch my hand
Till I found him, come from his foreign land
To be my nurse in this poor place,
And make my broth and wash my face
And light my fire and, all the while,
Bear with his old good-humored smile
That I told him "Better have kept away
Than come and kill me, night and day,
With, worse than fever throbs and shoots,
The creaking of his clumsy boots."
I am as sure that this he would do,
As that Saint Paul's is striking two.
And I think I rather . . . woe is me!

—Yes, rather should see him than not see,
If lifting a hand could seat him there
Before me in the empty chair
To-night, when my head aches indeed,
And I can neither think nor read,
Nor make these purple fingers hold
The pen; this garret's freezing cold!

And I've a Lady—there he wakes,
The laughing fiend and prince of snakes
Within me, at her name, to pray
Fate send some creature in the way
Of my love for her, to be down-torn,
Upthrust and outward-borne,
So I might prove myself that sea
Of passion which I needs must be!
Call my thoughts false and my fancies quaint
And my style infirm and its figures faint,

All the critics say, and more blame yet,
And not one angry word you get.
But, please you, wonder I would put
My cheek beneath that lady's foot
Rather than trample under mine
The laurels of the Florentine,
And you shall see how the devil spends
A fire God gave for other ends!
I tell you, I stride up and down
This garret, crowned with love's best crown,
And feasted with love's perfect feast,
To think I kill for her, at least,
Body and soul and peace and fame,
Alike youth's end and manhood's aim,
—So is my spirit, as flesh with sin,
Filled full, eaten out and in
With the face of her, the eyes of her,
The lips, the little chin, the stir
Of shadow round her mouth; and she
—I'll tell you—calmly would decree
That I should roast at a slow fire,
If that would compass her desire
And make her one whom they invite
To the famous ball to-morrow night.

There may be heaven; there must be hell;
Meantime, there is our earth here—well!

THE ITALIAN IN ENGLAND

THAT second time they hunted me
From hill to plain, from shore to sea,
And Austria, hounding far and wide
Her blood-hounds through the country-side,
Breathed hot and instant on my trace,—
I made six days a hiding-place
Of that dry green old aqueduct
Where I and Charles, when boys, have plucked
The fire-flies from the roof above,
Bright creeping through the moss they love:
—How long it seems since Charles was lost!
Six days the soldiers crossed and crossed
The country in my very sight;
And when that peril ceased at night,
The sky broke out in red dismay

With signal fires; well, there I lay
Close covered o'er in my recess,
Up to the neck in ferns and cress,
Thinking on Metternich our friend,
And Charles's miserable end,
And much beside, two days; the third,
Hunger o'ercame me when I heard
The peasants from the village go
To work among the maize; you know,
With us in Lombardy, they bring
Provisions packed on mules, a string
With little bells that cheer their task,
And casks, and boughs on every cask
To keep the sun's heat from the wine;
These I let pass in jingling line,
And, close on them, dear noisy crew,
The peasants from the village, too;
For at the very rear would troop
Their wives and sisters in a group
To help, I knew. When these had passed,
I threw my glove to strike the last,
Taking the chance: she did not start,
Much less cry out, but stooped apart,
One instant rapidly glanced round,
And saw me beckon from the ground:
A wild bush grows and hides my crypt;
She picked my glove up while she stripped
A branch off, then rejoined the rest
With that; my glove lay in her breast.
Then I drew breath; they disappeared:
It was for Italy I feared.

An hour, and she returned alone
Exactly where my glove was thrown.
Meanwhile came many thoughts: on me
Rested the hopes of Italy;
I had devised a certain tale
Which, when 'twas told her, could not fail
Persuade a peasant of its truth;
I meant to call a freak of youth
This hiding, and give hopes of pay,
And no temptation to betray.
But when I saw that woman's face,
Its calm simplicity of grace,
Our Italy's own attitude
In which she walked thus far, and stood,

Planting each naked foot so firm,
To crush the snake and spare the worm—
At first sight of her eyes, I said,
"I am that man upon whose head
They fix the price, because I hate
The Austrians over us: the State
Will give you gold—oh, gold so much!—
If you betray me to their clutch,
And be your death, for aught I know,
If once they find you saved their foe.
Now, you must bring me food and drink,
And also paper, pen and ink,
And carry safe what I shall write
To Padua, which you'll reach at night
Before the duomo shuts; go in,
And wait till Tenebræ begin;
Walk to the third confessional,
Between the pillar and the wall,
And kneeling whisper, *Whence comes peace?*
Say it a second time, then cease;
And if the voice inside returns,
*From Christ and Freedom; what concerns
The cause of Peace?*—for answer, slip
My letter where you placed your lip;
Then come back happy we have done
Our mother service—I, the son,
As you the daughter of our land!"

Three mornings more, she took her stand
In the same place, with the same eyes:
I was no surer of sunrise
Than of her coming. We conferred
Of her own prospects, and I heard
She had a lover—stout and tall,
She said—then let her eyelids fall,
"He could do much"—as if some doubt
Entered her heart,—then, passing out,
"She could not speak for others, who
Had other thoughts; herself she knew:"
And so she brought me drink and food.
After four days, the scouts pursued
Another path; at last arrived
The help my Paduan friends contrived
To furnish me: she brought the news.
For the first time I could not choose
But kiss her hand, and lay my own

Upon her head—"This faith was shown
To Italy, our mother; she
Uses my hand and blesses thee."
She followed down to the sea-shore;
I left and never saw her more.

How very long since I have thought
Concerning—much less wished for—aught
Beside the good of Italy,
For which I live and mean to die!
I never was in love; and since
Charles proved false, what shall now convince
My inmost heart I have a friend?
However, if I pleased to spend
Real wishes on myself—say, three—
I know at least what one should be.
I would grasp Metternich until
I felt his red wet throat distil
In blood through these two hands. And next,
—Nor much for that am I perplexed—
Charles, perjured traitor, for his part,
Should die slow of a broken heart
Under his new employers. Last
—Ah, there, what should I wish? For fast
Do I grow old and out of strength.
If I resolved to seek at length
My father's house again, how scared
They all would look, and unprepared!
My brothers live in Austria's pay
—Disowned me long ago, men say;
And all my early mates who used
To praise me so—perhaps induced
More than one early step of mine—
Are turning wise: while some opine
"Freedom grows license," some suspect
"Haste breeds delay," and recollect
They always said, such premature
Beginnings never could endure!
So, with a sullen "All's for best,"
The land seems settling to its rest.
I think then, I should wish to stand
This evening in that dear, lost land,
Over the sea the thousand miles,
And know if yet that woman smiles
With the calm smile; some little farm
She lives in there, no doubt: what harm

If I sat on the door-side bench,
And, while her spindle made a trench
Fantastically in the dust,
Inquired of all her fortunes—just
Her children's ages and their names,
And what may be the husband's aims
For each of them. I'd talk this out,
And sit there, for an hour about,
Then kiss her hand once more, and lay
Mine on her head, and go my way.

   So much for idle wishing—how
It steals the time! To business now.

THE ENGLISHMAN IN ITALY

PIANO DI SORRENTO

Fortù, Fortù, my beloved one,
   Sit here by my side,
On my knees put up both little feet!
   I was sure, if I tried,
I could make you laugh spite of Scirocco.
   Now, open your eyes,
Let me keep you amused till he vanish
   In black from the skies,
With telling my memories over
   As you tell your beads;
All the Plain saw me gather, I garland
   —The flowers or the weeds.
Time for rain! for your long hot dry Autumn
   Had net-worked with brown
The white skin of each grape on the bunches,
   Marked like a quail's crown,
Those creatures you make such account of,
   Whose heads,—speckled white
Over brown like a great spider's back,
   As I told you last night,—
Your mother bites off for her supper.
   Red-ripe as could be,
Pomegranates were chapping and splitting
   In halves on the tree:
And betwixt the loose walls of great flintstone,
   Or in the thick dust

On the path, or straight out of the rock-side,
  Wherever could thrust
Some burnt sprig of bold hardy rock-flower
  Its yellow face up,
For the prize were great butterflies fighting,
  Some five for one cup.
So, I guessed, ere I got up this morning,
  What change was in store,
By the quick rustle-down of the quail-nets
  Which woke me before
I could open my shutter, made fast
  With a bough and a stone,
And look through the twisted dead vine-twigs,
  Sole lattice that's known.
Quick and sharp rang the rings down the net-poles,
  While, busy beneath,
Your priest and his brother tugged at them,
  The rain in their teeth.
And out upon all the flat house-roofs
  Where split figs lay drying,
The girls took the frails under cover:
  Nor use seemed in trying
To get out the boats and go fishing,
  For, under the cliff,
Fierce the black water frothed o'er the blind-rock.
  No seeing our skiff
Arrive about noon from Amalfi,
  —Our fisher arrive,
And pitch down his basket before us,
  All trembling alive
With pink and gray jellies, your sea-fruit;
  You touch the strange lumps,
And mouths gape there, eyes open, all manner
  Of horns and of humps,
Which only the fisher looks grave at,
  While round him like imps
Cling screaming the children as naked
  And brown as his shrimps;
Himself too as bare to the middle
  —You see round his neck
The string and its brass coin suspended,
  That saves him from wreck.
But to-day not a boat reached Salerno,
  So back, to a man,
Came our friends, with whose help in the vineyards
  Grape-harvest began.

In the vat, halfway up in our house-side,
   Like blood the juice spins,
While your brother all bare-legged is dancing
   Till breathless he grins
Dead-beaten in effort on effort
   To keep the grapes under,
Since still when he seems all but master,
   In pours the fresh plunder
From girls who keep coming and going
   With basket on shoulder,
And eyes shut against the rain's driving;
   Your girls that are older,—
For under the hedges of aloe,
   And where, on its bed
Of the orchard's black mould, the love-apple
   Lies pulpy and red,
All the young ones are kneeling and filling
   Their laps with the snails
Tempted out by this first rainy weather,—
   Your best of regales,
As to-night will be proved to my sorrow,
   When, supping in state,
We shall feast our grape-gleaners (two dozen,
   Three over one plate)
With lasagne so tempting to swallow
   In slippery ropes,
And gourds fried in great purple slices,
   That color of popes.
Meantime, see the grape bunch they've brought you,
   The rain-water slips
O'er the heavy blue bloom on each globe
   Which the wasp to your lips
Still follows with fretful persistence:
   Nay, taste, while awake,
This half of a curd-white smooth cheese-ball
   That peels, flake by flake,
Like an onion, each smoother and whiter;
   Next, sip this weak wine
From the thin green glass flask, with its stopper,
   A leaf of the vine;
And end with the prickly-pear's red flesh
   That leaves through its juice
The stony black seeds on your pearl-teeth.
   Scirocco is loose!
Hark, the quick, whistling pelt of the olives
   Which, thick in one's track,

Tempt the stranger to pick up and bite them,
  Though not yet half black!
How the old twisted olive trunks shudder,
  The medlars let fall
Their hard fruit, and the brittle great fig-trees
  Snap off, figs and all,
For here comes the whole of the tempest!
  No refuge, but creep
Back again to my side and my shoulder,
  And listen or sleep.
O, how will your country show next week,
  When all the vine-boughs
Have been stripped of their foliage to pasture
  The mules and the cows?
Last eve, I rode over the mountains;
  Your brother, my guide,
Soon left me, to feast on the myrtles
  That offered, each side,
Their fruit-balls, black, glossy and luscious,—
  Or strip from the sorbs
A treasure, or, rosy and wondrous,
  Those hairy gold orbs!
But my mule picked his sure sober path out,
  Just stopping to neigh,
When he recognized down in the valley
  His mates on their way
With the faggots and barrels of water;
  And soon we emerged
From the plain, where the woods could scarce follow;
  And still as we urged
Our way, the woods wondered, and left us,
  As up still we trudged,
Though the wild path grew wilder each instant,
  And place was e'en grudged
'Mid the rock-chasms and piles of loose stones
  Like the loose broken teeth
Of some monster which climbed there to die
  From the ocean beneath—
Place was grudged to the silver-gray fume-weed
  That clung to the path,
And dark rosemary ever a-dying
  That, 'spite the wind's wrath,
So loves the salt rock's face to seaward,
  And lentisks as staunch
To the stone where they root and bear berries,
  And . . . what shows a branch

Coral-colored, transparent, with circlets
  Of pale seagreen leaves;
Over all trod my mule with the caution
  Of gleaners o'er sheaves,
Still, foot after foot like a lady,
  Till, round after round,
He climbed to the top of Calvano,
  And God's own profound
Was above me, and round me the mountains,
  And under, the sea,
And within me my heart to bear witness
  What was and shall be.
Oh, heaven and the terrible crystal!
  No rampart excludes
Your eye from the life to be lived
  In the blue solitudes.
Oh, those mountains, their infinite movement!
  Still moving with you;
For, ever some new head and breast of them
  Thrusts into view
To observe the intruder; you see it
  If quickly you turn
And, before they escape you, surprise them.
  They grudge you should learn
How the soft plains they look on, lean over
  And love (they pretend)
—Cower beneath them, the flat sea-pine crouches,
  The wild fruit-trees bend,
E'en the myrtle-leaves curl, shrink and shut:
  All is silent and grave:
'Tis a sensual and timorous beauty,
  How fair! but a slave.
So, I turned to the sea; and there slumbered
  As greenly as ever
Those isles of the siren, your Galli;
  No ages can sever
The Three, nor enable their sister
  To join them,—halfway
On the voyage, she looked at Ulysses—
  No farther to-day,
Though the small one, just launched in the wave,
  Watches breast-high and steady
From under the rock, her bold sister
  Swum halfway already.
Fortù, shall we sail there together
  And see from the sides

Quite new rocks show their faces, new haunts
  Where the siren abides?
Shall we sail round and round them, close over
  The rocks, though unseen,
That ruffle the gray glassy water
  To glorious green?
Then scramble from splinter to splinter,
  Reach land and explore,
On the largest, the strange square black turret
  With never a door,
Just a loop to admit the quick lizards;
  Then, stand there and hear
The birds' quiet singing, that tells us
  What life is, so clear?
—The secret they sang to Ulysses
  When, ages ago,
He heard and he knew this life's secret
  I hear and I know.

Ah, see! The sun breaks o'er Calvano;
  He strikes the great gloom
And flutters it o'er the mount's summit
  In airy gold fume.
All is over. Look out, see the gypsy,
  Our tinker and smith,
Has arrived, set up bellows and forge,
  And down-squatted forthwith
To his hammering, under the wall there;
  One eye keeps aloof
The urchins that itch to be putting
  His jews'-harps to proof,
While the other, through locks of curled wire,
  Is watching how sleek
Shines the hog, come to share in the windfall
  —Chew abbot's own cheek!
All is over. Wake up and come out now,
  And down let us go,
And see the fine things got in order
  At church for the show
Of the Sacrament, set forth this evening;
  To-morrow's the Feast
Of the Rosary's Virgin, by no means
  Of Virgins the least,
As you'll hear in the off-hand discourse
  Which (all nature, no art)
The Dominican brother, these three weeks.

Was getting by heart.
Not a pillar nor post but is dizened
  With red and blue papers;
All the roof waves with ribbons, each altar
  Ablaze with long tapers;
But the great masterpiece is the scaffold
  Rigged glorious to hold
All the fiddlers and fifers and drummers
  And trumpeters bold,
Not afraid of Bellini nor Auber,
  Who, when the priest's hoarse,
Will strike us up something that's brisk
  For the feast's second course.
And then will the flaxen-wigged Image
  Be carried in pomp
Through the Plain, while in gallant procession
  The priests mean to stomp.
All round the glad church lie old bottles
  With gunpowder stopped,
Which will be, when the Image re-enters,
  Religiously popped;
And at night from the crest of Calvano
  Great bonfires will hang,
On the Plain will the trumpets join chorus,
  And more poppers bang.
At all events, come—to the garden
  As far as the wall;
See me tap with a hoe on the plaster
  Till out there shall fall
A scorpion with wide angry nippers!

—"Such trifles!" you say?
Fortù, in my England at home,
  Men meet gravely to-day
And debate, if abolishing Corn-laws
  Be righteous and wise
—If 'twere proper, Scirocco should vanish
  In black from the skies!

IN A GONDOLA

He sings

I SEND my heart up to thee, all my heart
  In this my singing.
For the stars help me, and the sea bears part;
  The very night is clinging

Closer to Venice' streets to leave one space
  Above me, whence thy face
May light my joyous heart to thee its dwelling-place.

She speaks

Say after me, and try to say
My very words, as if each word
Came from you of your own accord,
In your own voice, in your own way:
"This woman's heart and soul and brain
Are mine as much as this gold chain
She bids me wear; which" (say again)
"I choose to make by cherishing
A precious thing, or choose to fling
Over the boat-side, ring by ring."
And yet once more say . . . no word more!
Since words are only words. Give o'er!

Unless you call me, all the same,
Familiarly by my pet name,
Which if the Three should hear you call,
And me reply to, would proclaim
At once our secret to them all.
Ask of me, too, command me, blame—
Do, break down the partition-wall
'Twixt us, the daylight world beholds
Curtained in dusk and splendid folds!
What's left but—all of me to take?
I am the Three's: prevent them, slake
Your thirst! 'Tis said, the Arab sage,
In practising with gems, can loose
Their subtle spirit in his cruce
And leave but ashes: so, sweet mage,
Leave them my ashes when thy use
Sucks out my soul, thy heritage!

He sings

I.

Past we glide, and past, and past!
  What's that poor Agnese doing
Where they make the shutters fast?
  Gray Zanobi's just a-wooing
To his couch the purchased bride:
  Past we glide!

II.

Past we glide, and past, and past!
  Why's the Pucci Palace flaring
Like a beacon to the blast?
  Guests by hundreds, not one caring
If the dear host's neck were wried:
  Past we glide!

She sings

I.

The moth's kiss, first!
Kiss me as if you made believe
You were not sure, this eve,
How my face, your flower, had pursed
Its petals up; so, here and there
You brush it, till I grow aware
Who wants me, and wide ope I burst.

II.

The bee's kiss, now!
Kiss me as if you entered gay
My heart at some noonday,
A bud that dares not disallow
The claim, so all is rendered up,
And passively its shattered cup
Over your head to sleep I bow.

He sings

I.

What are we two?
I am a Jew,
And carry thee, farther than friends can pursue,
To a feast of our tribe;
Where they need thee to bribe
The devil that blasts them unless he imbibe
Thy . . . Scatter the vision forever! And now,
As of old, I am I, thou art thou!

II.

Say again, what we are?
The sprite of a star,
I lure thee above where the destinies bar
My plumes their full play
Till a ruddier ray

Than my pale one announce there is withering away
Some . . . Scatter the vision forever! And now,
As of old, I am I, thou art thou!

He muses

Oh, which were best, to roam or rest?
The land's lap or the water's breast?
To sleep on yellow millet-sheaves,
Or swim in lucid shallows just
Eluding water-lily leaves,
An inch from Death's black fingers, thrust
To lock you, whom release he must;
Which life were best on Summer eves?

He speaks, musing

Lie back; could thought of mine improve you?
From this shoulder let there spring
A wing; from this, another wing;
Wings, not legs and feet, shall move you!
Snow-white must they spring, to blend
With your flesh, but I intend
They shall deepen to the end,
Broader, into burning gold,
Till both wings crescent-wise enfold
Your perfect self, from 'neath your feet
To o'er your head, where, lo, they meet
As if a million sword-blades hurled
Defiance from you to the world!

Rescue me thou, the only real!
And scare away this mad ideal
That came, nor motions to depart!
Thanks! Now, stay ever as thou art!

Still he muses

I.

What if the Three should catch at last
Thy serenader? While there's cast
Paul's cloak about my head, and fast
Gian pinions me, Himself has past
His stylet through my back; I reel;
And . . . is it thou I feel?

II.

They trail me, these three godless knaves,
Past every church that saints and saves,
Nor stop till, where the cold sea raves
By Lido's wet accursed graves,
They scoop mine, roll me to its brink,
And . . . on thy breast I sink!

She replies, musing

Dip your arm o'er the boat-side, elbow-deep,
As I do: thus: were death so unlike sleep,
Caught this way? Death's to fear from flame or steel,
Or poison doubtless; but from water—feel!

Go find the bottom! Would you stay me? There!
Now pluck a great blade of that ribbon-grass
To plait in where the foolish jewel was,
I flung away: since you have praised my hair,
'Tis proper to be choice in what I wear.

He speaks

Row home? must we row home? Too surely
Know I where its front's demurely
Over the Giudecca piled;
Window just with window mating,
Door on door exactly waiting,
All's the set face of a child:
But behind it, where's a trace
Of the staidness and reserve,
And formal lines without a curve,
In the same child's playing-face?
No two windows look one way
O'er the small sea-water thread
Below them. Ah, the autumn day
I, passing, saw you overhead!
First, out a cloud of curtain blew,
Then a sweet cry, and last came you—
To catch your lory that must needs
Escape just then, of all times then,
To peck a tall plant's fleecy seeds,
And make me happiest of men.
I scarce could breathe to see you reach
So far back o'er the balcony
To catch him ere he climbed too high
Above you in the Smyrna peach,

That quick the round smooth cord of gold,
This coiled hair on your head, unrolled,
Fell down you like a gorgeous snake
The Roman girls were wont, of old,
When Rome there was, for coolness' sake
To let lie curling o'er their bosoms.
Dear lory, may his beak retain
Ever its delicate rose stain
As if the wounded lotus-blossoms
Had marked their thief to know again!

Stay longer yet, for others' sake
Than mine! What should your chamber do?
—With all its rarities that ache
In silence while day lasts, but wake
At night-time and their life renew,
Suspended just to pleasure you
Who brought against their will together
These objects, and, while day lasts, weave
Around them such a magic tether
That dumb they look: your harp, believe,
With all the sensitive tight strings
Which dare not speak, now to itself
Breathes slumberously, as if some elf
Went in and out the chords, his wings
Make murmur wheresoe'er they graze,
As an angel may, between the maze
Of midnight palace-pillars, on
And on, to sow God's plagues, have gone
Through guilty glorious Babylon.
And while such murmurs flow, the nymph
Bends o'er the harp-top from her shell
As the dry limpet for the lymph
Come with a tune he knows so well.
And how your statues' hearts must swell!
And how your pictures must descend
To see each other, friend with friend!
Oh, could you take them by surprise,
You'd find Schidone's eager Duke
Doing the quaintest courtesies
To that prim saint by Haste-thee-Luke!
And, deeper into her rock den,
Bold Castelfranco's Magdelen
You'd find retreated from the ken
Of that robed counsel-keeping Ser—
As if the Tizian thinks of her,

And is not, rather, gravely bent
On seeing for himself what toys
Are these, his progeny invent,
What litter now the board employs
Whereon he signed a document
That got him murdered! Each enjoys
Its night so well, you cannot break
The sport up, so, indeed must make
More stay with me, for others' sake.

She speaks

I.

To-morrow, if a harp-string, say,
Is used to tie the jasmine back
That overfloods my room with sweets,
Contrive your Zorzi somehow meets
  My Zanze! If the ribbon's black,
The Three are watching: keep away!

II.

Your gondola—let Zorzi wreathe
A mesh of water-weeds about
Its prow, as if he unaware
Had struck some quay or bridge-foot stair!
That I may throw a paper out
As you and he go underneath.

There's Zanze's vigilant taper; safe are we.
Only one minute more to-night with me?
Resume your past self of a month ago!
Be you the bashful gallant, I will be
The lady with the colder breast than snow.
Now bow you, as becomes, nor touch my hand
More than I touch yours when I step to land,
And say, "All thanks, Siora!"—
                               Heart to heart
And lips to lips! Yet once more, ere we part,
Clasp me and make me thine, as mine thou art!

He is surprised, and stabbed

It was ordained to be so, sweet!—and best
Comes now, beneath thine eyes, upon thy breast.
Still kiss me! Care not for the cowards! Care
Only to put aside thy beauteous hair
My blood will hurt! The Three, I do not scorn

To death, because they never lived: but I
Have lived indeed, and so—(yet one more kiss)—can die!

WARING

I.

I.

WHAT's become of Waring
Since he gave us all the slip,
Chose land-travel or seafaring,
Boots and chest or staff and scrip,
Rather than pace up and down
Any longer London town?

II.

Who'd have guessed it from his lip
Or his brow's accustomed bearing,
On the night he thus took ship
Or started landward?—little caring
For us, it seems, who supped together
(Friends of his too, I remember)
And walked home through the merry weather,
The snowiest in all December.
I left his arm that night myself
For what's-his-name's, the new prose-poet
Who wrote the book there, on the shelf—
How, forsooth, was I to know it
If Waring meant to glide away
Like a ghost at break of day?
Never looked he half so gay!

III.

He was prouder than the devil:
How he must have cursed our revel!
Ay and many other meetings,
Indoor visits, outdoor greetings,
As up and down he paced this London,
With no work done, but great works undone,
Where scarce twenty knew his name.
Why not, then, have earlier spoken,
Written, bustled? Who's to blame
If your silence kept unbroken?
"True, but there were sundry jottings,
Stray-leaves, fragments, blurs and blottings,

Certain first steps were achieved
Already which"—(is that your meaning?)
"Had well borne out whoe'er believed
In more to come!" But who goes gleaning
Hedge-side chance-blades, while full-sheaved
Stand cornfields by him? Pride, o'erweening
Pride alone, puts forth such claims
O'er the day's distinguished names.

IV.

Meantime, how much I loved him,
I find out now I've lost him.
I who cared not if I moved him,
Who could so carelessly accost him,
Henceforth never shall get free
Of his ghostly company,
His eyes that just a little wink
As deep I go into the merit
Of this and that distinguished spirit—
His cheeks' raised color, soon to sink,
As long I dwell on some stupendous
And tremendous (Heaven defend us!)
Monstr'-inform'-ingens-horrend-ous
Demoniaco-seraphic
Penman's latest piece of graphic.
Nay, my very wrist grows warm
With his dragging weight of arm.
E'en so, swimmingly appears,
Through one's after-supper musings,
Some lost lady of old years
With her beauteous vain endeavor
And goodness unrepaid as ever;
The face, accustomed to refusings,
We, puppies that we were . . . Oh **never**
Surely, nice of conscience, scrupled
Being aught like false, forsooth, to?
Telling aught but honest truth to?
What a sin, had we centupled
Its possessor's grace and sweetness!
No! she heard in its completeness
Truth, for truth's a weighty matter,
And truth, at issue, we can't flatter!
Well, 'tis done with; she's exempt
From damning us through such a sally;
And so she glides, as down a valley,
Taking up with her contempt,

Past our reach; and, in the flowers
Shut her unregarded hours.

v.

Oh, could I have him back once more,
This Waring, but one half-day more!
Back, with the quiet face of yore,
So hungry for acknowledgment
Like mine! I'd fool him to his bent.
Feed, should not he, to heart's content?
I'd say, "to only have conceived,
Planned your great works, apart from progress,
Surpasses little works achieved!"
I'd lie so, I should be believed.
I'd make such havoc of the claims
Of the day's distinguished names
To feast him with, as feasts an ogress
Her feverish sharp-toothed gold-crowned child!
Or as one feasts a creature rarely
Captured here, unreconciled
To capture; and completely gives
Its pettish humors license, barely
Requiring that it lives.

vi.

Ichabod, Ichabod,
The glory is departed!
Travels Waring East away?
Who, of knowledge, by hearsay,
Reports a man upstarted
Somewhere as a god,
Hordes grown European-hearted,
Millions of the wild made tame
On a sudden at his fame?
In Vishnu-land what Avatar?
Or who in Moscow, toward the Czar,
With the demurest of footfalls
Over the Kremlin's pavement bright
With serpentine and syenite,
Steps, with five other Generals
That simultaneously take snuff,
For each to have pretext enough
And kerchiefwise unfold his sash
Which, softness' self, is yet the stuff
To hold fast where a steel chain snaps,

And leave the grand white neck no gash?
Waring in Moscow, to those rough
Cold northern natures born perhaps,
Like the lambwhite maiden dear
From the circle of mute kings
Unable to repress the tear,
Each as his sceptre down he flings,
To Dian's fane at Taurica,
Where now a captive priestess, she alway
Mingles her tender grave Hellenic speech
With theirs, tuned to the hailstone-beaten beach
As pours some pigeon, from the myrrhy lands
Rapt by the whirlblast to fierce Scythian strands
Where breed the swallows, her melodious cry
Amid their barbarous twitter!
In Russia? Never! Spain were fitter!
Ay, most likely 'tis in Spain
That we and Waring meet again.
Now, while he turns down that cool narrow lane
Into the blackness, out of grave Madrid
All fire and shine, abrupt as when there's slid
Its stiff gold blazing pall
From some black coffin-lid.
Or, best of all,
I love to think
The leaving us was just a feint;
Back here to London did he slink,
And now works on without a wink
Of sleep, and we are on the brink
Of something great in fresco-paint:
Some garret's ceiling, walls and floor,
Up and down and o'er and o'er
He splashes, as none splashed before
Since great Caldara Polidore.
Or Music means this land of ours
Some favor yet, to pity won
By Purcell from his Rosy Bowers,—
"Give me my so-long promised son,
Let Waring end what I begun!"
Then down he creeps and out he steals
Only when the night conceals
His face; in Kent 'tis cherry-time,
Or hops are picking: or at prime
Of March he wanders as, too happy,
Years ago when he was young,

Some mild eve when woods grew sappy
And the early moths had sprung
To life from many a trembling sheath
Woven the warm boughs beneath;
While small birds said to themselves
What should soon be actual song,
And young gnats, by tens and twelves,
Made as if they were the throng
That crowd around and carry aloft
The sound they have nursed, so sweet and pure,
Out of a myriad noises soft,
Into a tone that can endure
Amid the noise of a July noon
When all God's creatures crave their boon,
All at once and all in tune,
And get it, happy as Waring then,
Having first within his ken
What a man might do with men:
And far too glad, in the even-glow,
To mix with the world he meant to take
Into his hand, he told you, so—
And out of it his world to make,
To contract and to expand
As he shut or oped his hand.
O Waring, what's to really be?
A clear stage and a crowd to see!
Some Garrick, say, out shall not he
The heart of Hamlet's mystery pluck?
Or, where most unclean beasts are rife,
Some Junius—am I right?—shall tuck
His sleeve, and forth with flaying-knife!
Some Chatterton shall have the luck
Of calling Rowley into life!
Some one shall somehow run a-muck
With this old world for want of strife
Sound asleep. Contrive, contrive
To rouse us, Waring! Who's alive?
Our men scarce seem in earnest now.
Distinguished names!—but 'tis, somehow,
As if they played at being names
Still more distinguished, like the games
Of children. Turn our sport to earnest
With a visage of the sternest!
Bring the real times back, confessed
Still better than our very best!

II.

I.

"When I last saw Waring . . ."
(How all turned to him who spoke!
You saw Waring? Truth or joke?
In land-travel or sea-faring?)

II.

"We were sailing by Triest
Where a day or two we harbored:
A sunset was in the West,
When, looking over the vessel's side,
One of our company espied
A sudden speck to larboard.
And as a sea-duck flies and swims
At once, so came the light craft up,
With its sole lateen sail that trims
And turns (the water round its rims
Dancing, as round a sinking cup)
And by us like a fish it curled,
And drew itself up close beside,
Its great sail on the instant furled,
And o'er its thwarts a shrill voice cried,
(A neck as bronzed as a Lascar's)
'Buy wine of us, you English brig?
Or fruit, tobacco and cigars?
A pilot for you to Triest?
Without one, look you ne'er so big,
They'll never let you up the bay!
We natives should know best.'
I turned, and 'just those fellows' way,'
Our captain said, 'The 'long-shore thieves
Are laughing at us in their sleeves.'

III.

"In truth, the boy leaned laughing back;
And one, half-hidden by his side
Under the furled sail, soon I spied,
With great grass hat and kerchief black,
Who looked up with his kingly throat
Said somewhat, while the other shook
His hair back from his eyes to look
Their longest at us; then the boat,
I know not how, turned sharply round,

Laying her whole side on the sea
As a leaping fish does; from the lee
Into the weather, cut somehow
Her sparkling path beneath our bow
And so went off, as with a bound,
Into the rosy and golden half
O' the sky, to overtake the sun
And reach the shore, like the sea-calf
Its singing cave; yet I caught one
Glance ere away the boat quite passed,
And neither time nor toil could mar
Those features: so I saw the last
Of Waring!"—You? Oh, never star
Was lost here but it rose afar!
Look East, where whole new thousands are!
In Vishnu-land what Avatar?

THE TWINS

"Give" and "It-shall-be-given-unto-you."

I.

GRAND rough old Martin Luther
    Bloomed fables—flowers on furze,
The better the uncouther:
    Do roses stick like burrs?

II.

A beggar asked an alms
    One day at an abbey-door,
Said Luther; but, seized with qualms,
    The Abbot replied, "We're poor!

III.

"Poor, who had plenty once,
    When gifts fell thick as rain:
But they give us nought, for the nonce,
    And how should we give again?"

IV.

Then the beggar, "See your sins!
    Of old, unless I err,
Ye had brothers for inmates, twins,
    Date and Dabitur.

V.

"While Date was in good case
Dabitur flourished too:
For Dabitur's lenten face
No wonder if Date rue.

VI.

"Would ye retrieve the one?
Try and make plump the other!
When Date's penance is done,
Dabitur helps his brother.

VII.

"Only, beware relapse!"
The Abbot hung his head.
This beggar might be perhaps
An angel, Luther said.

A LIGHT WOMAN

I.

So FAR as our story approaches the end,
Which do you pity the most of us three?—
My friend, or the mistress of my friend
With her wanton eyes, or me?

II.

My friend was already too good to lose,
And seemed in the way of improvement yet,
When she crossed his path with her hunting-noose,
And over him drew her net.

III.

When I saw him tangled in her toils,
A shame, said I, if she adds just him
To her nine-and-ninety other spoils,
The hundredth for a whim!

IV.

And before my friend be wholly hers,
How easy to prove to him, I said,
An eagle's the game her pride prefers,
Though she snaps at a wren instead!

v.

So, I gave her eyes my own eyes to take,
　My hand sought hers as in earnest need,
And round she turned for my noble sake,
　And gave me herself indeed.

vi.

The eagle am I, with my fame in the world,
　The wren is he, with his maiden face.
—You look away and your lip is curled?
　Patience, a moment's space!

vii.

For see, my friend goes shaking and white;
　He eyes me as the basilisk:
I have turned, it appears, his day to night,
　Eclipsing his sun's disk.

viii.

And I did it, he thinks, as a very thief:
　"Though I love her—that, he comprehends—
One should master one's passions, (love, in chief)
　And be loyal to one's friends!"

ix.

And she,—she lies in my hand as tame
　As a pear late basking over a wall;
Just a touch to try and off it came;
　'Tis mine,—can I let it fall?

x.

With no mind to eat it, that's the worst!
　Were it thrown in the road, would the case assist?
'T was quenching a dozen blue-flies' thirst
　When I gave its stalk a twist.

xi.

And I,—what I seem to my friend, you see:
　What I soon shall seem to his love, you guess:
What I seem to myself, do you ask of me?
　No hero, I confess.

xii.

'Tis an awkward thing to play with souls,
　And matter enough to save one's own:
Yet think of my friend, and the burning coals
　He played with for bits of stone!

XIII.

One likes to show the truth for the truth;
  That the woman was light is very true:
But suppose she says,—Never mind that youth!
  What wrong have I done to you?

XIV.

Well, anyhow, here the story stays,
  So far at least as I understand;
And, Robert Browning, you writer of plays,
  Here's a subject made to your hand!

THE LAST RIDE TOGETHER

I.

I SAID—Then, dearest, since 'tis so,
Since now at length my fate I know,
Since nothing all my love avails,
Since all, my life seemed meant for, fails,
  Since this was written and needs must be—
My whole heart rises up to bless
Your name in pride and thankfulness!
Take back the hope you gave,—I claim
Only a memory of the same,
—And this beside, if you will not blame,
  Your leave for one more last ride with me.

II.

My mistress bent that brow of hers;
Those deep dark eyes where pride demurs
When pity would be softening through,
Fixed me a breathing-while or two
  With life or death in the balance: right!
The blood replenished me again;
My last thought was at least not vain:
I and my mistress, side by side
Shall be together, breathe and ride,
So, one day more am I deified.
  Who knows but the world may end to-night?

III.

Hush! if you saw some western cloud
All billowy-bosomed, over-bowed
By many benedictions—sun's
And moon's and evening-star's at once—
  And so, you, looking and loving best,

Conscious grew, your passion drew
Cloud, sunset, moonrise, star-shine too,
Down on you, near and yet more near,
Till flesh must fade for heaven was here!—
Thus leant she and lingered—joy and fear!
   Thus lay she a moment on my breast.

IV.

Then we began to ride. My soul
Smoothed itself out, a long-cramped scroll
Freshening and fluttering in the wind.
Past hopes already lay behind.
   What need to strive with a life awry?
Had I said that, had I done this,
So might I gain, so might I miss.
Might she have loved me? just as well
She might have hated, who can tell!
Where had I been now if the worst befell?
   And here we are riding, she and I.

V.

Fail I alone, in words and deeds?
Why, all men strive, and who succeeds?
We rode; it seemed my spirit flew,
Saw other regions, cities new,
   As the world rushed by on either side.
I thought,—All labor, yet no less
Bear up beneath their unsuccess.
Look at the end of work, contrast
The petty done, the undone vast,
This present of theirs with the hopeful past!
   I hoped she would love me; here we ride.

VI.

What hand and brain went ever paired?
What heart alike conceived and dared?
What act proved all its thought had been?
What will but felt the fleshy screen?
   We ride and I see her bosom heave.
There's many a crown for who can reach.
Ten lines, a statesman's life in each!
The flag stuck on a heap of bones,
A soldier's doing! what atones?
They scratch his name on the Abbey-stones.
   My riding is better, by their leave.

VII.

What does it all mean, poet? Well,
Your brains beat into rhythm, you tell
What we felt only; you expressed
You hold things beautiful the best,
 And place them in rhyme so, side by side.
'Tis something, nay 'tis much: but then,
Have you yourself what's best for men?
Are you—poor, sick, old ere your time—
Nearer one whit your own sublime
Than we who never have turned a rhyme?
 Sing, riding's a joy! For me, I ride.

VIII.

And you, great sculptor—so, you gave
A score of years to Art, her slave,
And that's your Venus, whence we turn
To yonder girl that fords the burn!
 You acquiesce, and shall I repine?
What, man of music, you grown gray
With notes and nothing else to say,
Is this your sole praise from a friend,.
"Greatly his opera's strains intend,
But in music we know how fashions end!"
 I gave my youth; but we ride, in fine.

IX.

Who knows what's fit for us? Had fate
Proposed bliss here should sublimate
My being—had I signed the bond—
Still one must lead some life beyond,
 Have a bliss to die with, dim-descried.
This foot once planted on the goal,
This glory-garland round my soul,
Could I descry such? Try and test!
I sink back shuddering from the quest.
Earth being so good, would heaven seem best?
 Now, heaven and she are beyond this ride.

X.

And yet—she has not spoke so long!
What if heaven be that, fair and strong
At life's best, with our eyes upturned
Whither life's flower is first discerned,
 We, fixed so, ever should so abide?
What if we still ride on, we two,

With life forever old yet new,
Changed not in kind but in degree,
The instant made eternity,—
And heaven just prove that I and she
Ride, ride together, forever ride?

THE PIED PIPER OF HAMELIN

A Child's Story

(Written for, and Inscribed to, W. M. the Younger)

I.

HAMELIN Town's in Brunswick,
By famous Hanover city;
The river Weser, deep and wide,
Washes its wall on the southern side;
A pleasanter spot you never spied;
But, when begins my ditty,
Almost five hundred years ago,
To see the townsfolk suffer so
From vermin, was a pity.

II.

Rats!
They fought the dogs and killed the cats,
And bit the babies in the cradles,
And ate the cheeses out of the vats,
And licked the soup from the cooks' own ladles,
Split open the kegs of salted sprats,
Made nests inside men's Sunday hats,
And even spoiled the women's chats,
By drowning their speaking
With shrieking and squeaking
In fifty different sharps and flats.

III.

At last the people in a body
To the Town Hall came flocking:
" 'Tis clear," cried they, "our Mayor's a noddy;
And as for our Corporation—shocking
To think we buy gowns lined with ermine
For dolts that can't or won't determine
What's best to rid us of our vermin!
You hope, because you're old and obese,

To find in the furry civic robe ease?
Rouse up, sirs! Give your brains a racking
To find the remedy we're lacking,
Or, sure as fate, we'll send you packing!"
At this the Mayor and Corporation
Quaked with a mighty consternation.

IV.

An hour they sat in council;
    At length the Mayor broke silence:
"For a guilder I'd my ermine gown sell,
    I wish I were a mile hence!
It's easy to bid one rack one's brain—
I'm sure my poor head aches again,
I've scratched it so, and all in vain.
Oh for a trap, a trap, a trap!"
Just as he said this, what should hap
At the chamber-door but a gentle tap?
"Bless us," cried the Mayor, "what's that?"
(With the Corporation as he sat,
Looking little though wondrous fat;
Nor brighter was his eye, nor moister
Than a too-long-opened oyster,
Save when at noon his paunch grew mutinous
For a plate of turtle green and glutinous)
"Only a scraping of shoes on the mat?
Anything like the sound of a rat
Makes my heart go pit-a-pat!"

V.

"Come in!"—the Mayor cried, looking bigger:
And in did come the strangest figure!
His queer long coat from heel to head
Was half of yellow and half of red,
And he himself was tall and thin,
With sharp blue eyes, each like a pin,
And light loose hair, yet swarthy skin,
No tuft on cheek nor beard on chin,
But lips where smiles went out and in;
There was no guessing his kith and kin:
And nobody could enough admire
The tall man and his quaint attire.
Quoth one: "It's as my great-grandsire,
Starting up at the Trump of Doom's tone,
Had walked this way from his painted tomb-stone!"

VI.

He advanced to the council-table:
And, "Please your honors," said he, "I'm able,
By means of a secret charm, to draw
All creatures living beneath the sun,
That creep or swim or fly or run,
After me so as you never saw!
And I chiefly use my charm
On creatures that do people harm,
The mole and toad and newt and viper;
And people call me the Pied Piper."
(And here they noticed round his neck
A scarf of red and yellow stripe,
To match with his coat of the self-same cheque;
And at the scarf's end hung a pipe;
And his fingers, they noticed, were ever straying
As if impatient to be playing
Upon this pipe, as low it dangled
Over his vesture so old-fangled.)
"Yet," said he, "poor piper as I am,
In Tartary I freed the Cham,
Last June, from his huge swarms of gnats;
I eased in Asia the Nizam
Of a monstrous brood of vampire-bats:
And as for what your brain bewilders,
If I can rid your town of rats
Will you give me a thousand guilders?"
"One? fifty thousand!"—was the exclamation
Of the astonished Mayor and Corporation.

VII.

Into the street the Piper stept,
  Smiling first a little smile,
As if he knew what magic slept
  In his quiet pipe the while;
Then, like a musical adept,
To blow the pipe his lips he wrinkled,
And green and blue his sharp eyes twinkled,
Like a candle-flame where salt is sprinkled;
And ere three shrill notes the pipe uttered,
You heard as if an army muttered;
And the muttering grew to a grumbling;
And the grumbling grew to a mighty rumbling;
And out of the houses the rats came tumbling.
Great rats, small rats, lean rats, brawny rats,

Brown rats, black rats, gray rats, tawny rats,
Grave old plodders, gay young friskers,
  Fathers, mothers, uncles, cousins,
Cocking tails and pricking whiskers,
  Families by tens and dozens,
Brothers, sisters, husbands, wives—
Followed the Piper for their lives.
From street to street he piped advancing,
And step for step they followed dancing,
Until they came to the river Weser,
Wherein all plunged and perished!
—Save one who, stout as Julius Cæsar,
Swam across and lived to carry
(As he, the manuscript he cherished)
To Rat-land home his commentary:
Which was, "At the first shrill notes of the pipe,
I heard a sound as of scraping tripe,
And putting apples, wondrous ripe,
Into a cider-press's gripe:
And a moving away of pickle-tub-boards,
And a leaving ajar of conserve-cupboards,
And a drawing the corks of train-oil-flasks,
And a breaking the hoops of butter-casks:
And it seemed as if a voice
(Sweeter far than by harp or by psaltery
Is breathed) called out, 'Oh rats, rejoice!
The world is grown to one vast drysaltery!
So munch on, crunch on, take your nuncheon,
Breakfast, supper, dinner, luncheon!'
And just as a bulky sugar-puncheon,
All ready staved, like a great sun shone
Glorious scarce an inch before me,
Just as methought it said, 'Come, bore me!'
—I found the Weser rolling o'er me."

VIII.

You should have heard the Hamelin people
Ringing the bells till they rocked the steeple.
"Go," cried the Mayor, "and get long poles,
Poke out the nests and block up the holes!
Consult with carpenters and builders,
And leave in our town not even a trace
Of the rats!"—when suddenly, up the face
Of the Piper perked in the market-place,
With a, "First, if you please, my thousand guilders!"

IX.

A thousand guilders! The Mayor looked blue;
So did the Corporation too.
For council dinners made rare havoc
With Claret, Moselle, Vin-de-Grave, Hock;
And half the money would replenish
Their cellar's biggest butt with Rhenish.
To pay this sum to a wandering fellow
With a gypsy coat of red and yellow!
"Beside," quoth the Mayor with a knowing wink,
"Our business was done at the river's brink;
We saw with our eyes the vermin sink,
And what's dead can't come to life, I think.
So, friend, we're not the folks to shrink
From the duty of giving you something for drink,
And a matter of money to put in your poke;
But as for the guilders, what we spoke
Of them, as you very well know, was in joke.
Beside, our losses have made us thrifty.
A thousand guilders! Come, take fifty!"

X.

The Piper's face fell, and he cried
"No trifling! I can't wait, beside!
I've promised to visit by dinner time
Bagdat, and accept the prime
Of the Head-Cook's pottage, all he's rich in,
For having left, in the Caliph's kitchen,
Of a nest of scorpions no survivor:
With him I proved no bargain-driver,
With you, don't think I'll bate a stiver!
And folks who put me in a passion
May find me pipe after another fashion."

XI.

"How?" cried the Mayor, "d'ye think I brook
Being worse treated than a Cook?
Insulted by a lazy ribald
With idle pipe and vesture piebald?
You threaten us, fellow? Do your worst,
Blow your pipe there till you burst!"

XII.

Once more he stept into the street,
    And to his lips again
Laid his long pipe of smooth straight cane;

And ere he blew three notes (such sweet
Soft notes as yet musician's cunning
   Never gave the enraptured air)
There was a rustling that seemed like a bustling
Of merry crowds justling at pitching and hustling;
Small feet were pattering, wooden shoes clattering,
Little hands clapping and little tongues chattering,
And, like fowls in a farm-yard when barley is scattering,
Out came the children running.
All the little boys and girls,
With rosy cheeks and flaxen curls,
And sparkling eyes and teeth like pearls,
Tripping and skipping, ran merrily after
The wonderful music with shouting and laughter.

XIII.

The Mayor was dumb, and the Council stood
As if they were changed into blocks of wood,
Unable to move a step, or cry
To the children merrily skipping by,
—Could only follow with the eye
That joyous crowd at the Piper's back.
But how the Mayor was on the rack,
And the wretched Council's bosoms beat,
As the Piper turned from the High Street
To where the Weser rolled its waters
Right in the way of their sons and daughters!
However, he turned from South to West,
And to Koppelberg Hill his steps addressed,
And after him the children pressed;
Great was the joy in every breast.
"He never can cross that mighty top!
He's forced to let the piping drop,
And we shall see our children stop!"
When, lo, as they reached the mountain-side,
A wondrous portal opened wide,
As if a cavern was suddenly hollowed;
And the Piper advanced and the children followed,
And when all were in to the very last,
The door in the mountain-side shut fast.
Did I say, all? No! One was lame,
And could not dance the whole of the way;
And in after years, if you would blame
His sadness, he was used to say,—
"It's dull in our town since my playmates left!
I can't forget that I'm bereft

Of all the pieasant sights they see,
Which the Piper also promised me.
For he led us, he said, to a joyous land,
Joining the town and just at hand,
Where waters gushed and fruit-trees grew,
And flowers put forth a fairer hue,
And everything was strange and new;
The sparrows were brighter than peacocks here,
And their dogs outran our fallow deer,
And honey-bees had lost their stings,
And horses were born with eagles' wings:
And just as I became assured
My lame foot would be speedily cured,
The music stopped and I stood still,
And found myself outside the hill,
Left alone against my will,
To go now limping as before,
And never hear of that country more!"

XIV.

Alas, alas for Hamelin!
    There came into many a burgher's pate
    A text which says that heaven's gate
    Opes to the rich at as easy rate
As the needle's eye takes a camel in!
The Mayor sent East, West, North and South,
To offer the Piper, by word of mouth,
    Wherever it was men's lot to find him,
Silver and gold to his heart's content,
If he'd only return the way he went,
    And bring the children behind him.
But when they saw 'twas a lost endeavor,
And Piper and dancers were gone forever,
They made a decree that lawyers never
    Should think their records dated duly
If, after the day of the month and year,
These words did not as well appear,
"And so long after what happened here
    On the Twenty-second of July,
Thirteen hundred and seventy-six:"
And the better in memory to fix
The place of the children's last retreat,
They called it, the Pied Piper's Street—
Where any one playing on pipe or tabor
Was sure for the future to lose his labor.
Nor suffered they hostelry or tavern

To shock with mirth a street so solemn;
But opposite the place of the cavern
They wrote the story on a column,
And on the great church-window painted
The same, to make the world acquainted
How their children were stolen away,
And there it stands to this very day.
And I must not omit to say
That in Transylvania there's a tribe
Of alien people who ascribe
The outlandish ways and dress
On which their neighbors lay such stress,
To their fathers and mothers having risen
Out of some subterraneous prison
Into which they were trepanned
Long time ago in a mighty band
Out of Hamelin town in Brunswick land,
But how or why, they don't understand.

xv.

So, Willy, let me and you be wipers
Of scores out with all men—especially pipers!
And, whether they pipe us free fróm rats or fróm mice,
If we've promised them aught, let us keep our promise!

A GRAMMARIAN'S FUNERAL

Shortly after the Revival of Learning in Europe

Let us begin and carry up this corpse,
    Singing together.
Leave we the common crofts, the vulgar thorpes,
    Each in its tether
Sleeping safe on the bosom of the plain,
    Cared-for till cock-crow:
Look out if yonder be not day again
    Rimming the rock-row!
That's the appropriate country; there, man's thought,
    Rarer, intenser,
Self-gathered for an outbreak, as it ought,
    Chafes in the censer.
Leave we the unlettered plain its herd and crop;
    Seek we sepulture

On a tall mountain, citied to the top,
  Crowded with culture!
All the peaks soar, but one the rest excels;
  Clouds overcome it;
No! yonder sparkle is the citadel's
  Circling its summit.
Thither our path lies; wind we up the heights:
  Wait ye the warning?
Our low life was the level's and the night's;
  He's for the morning.
Step to a tune, square chests, erect each head,
  'Ware the beholders!
This is our master, famous, calm and dead,
  Borne on our shoulders.

Sleep, crop and herd! sleep, darkling thorpe and croft,
  Safe from the weather!
He, whom we convoy to his grave aloft,
  Singing together,
He was a man born with thy face and throat,
  Lyric Apollo!
Long he lived nameless: how should Spring take note
  Winter would follow?
Till lo, the little touch, and youth was gone!
  Cramped and diminished,
Moaned he, "New measures, other feet anon!
  My dance is finished?"
No, that's the world's way: (keep the mountain-side,
  Make for the city!)
He knew the signal, and stepped on with pride
  Over men's pity;
Left play for work, and grappled with the world
  Bent on escaping:
"What's in the scroll," quoth he, "thou keepest furled?
  Show me their shaping,
Theirs who most studied man, the bard and sage,—
  Give!"—So, he gowned him,
Straight got by heart that book to its last page:
  Learned, we found him.
Yea, but we found him bald too, eyes like lead,
  Accents uncertain:
"Time to taste life," another would have said,
  "Up with the curtain!"
This man said rather, "Actual life comes next?
  Patience a moment!

Grant I have mastered learning's crabbed text,
    Still there's the comment.
Let me know all! Prate not of most or least,
    Painful or easy!
Even to the crumbs I'd fain eat up the feast,
    Ay, nor feel queasy."
Oh, such a life as he resolved to live,
    When he had learned it,
When he had gathered all books had to give!
    Sooner, he spurned it.
Image the whole, then execute the parts—
    Fancy the fabric
Quite, ere you build, ere steel strike fire from quartz,
    Ere mortar dab brick!

(Here's the town-gate reached: there's the market-place
    Gaping before us.)
Yea, this in him was the peculiar grace
    (Hearten our chorus!)
That before living he'd learn how to live—
    No end to learning:
Earn the means first—God surely will contrive
    Use for our earning.
Others mistrust and say, "But time escapes:
    Live now or never!"
He said, "What's time? Leave Now for dogs and apes!
    Man has Forever."
Back to his book then: deeper drooped his head:
    Calculus racked him:
Leaden before, his eyes grew dross of lead:
    Tussis attacked him.
"Now, master, take a little rest!"—not he!
    (Caution redoubled,
Step two abreast, the way winds narrowly!)
    Not a whit troubled,
Back to his studies, fresher than at first,
    Fierce as a dragon
He (soul-hydroptic with a sacred thirst)
    Sucked at the flagon.
Oh, if we draw a circle premature,
    Heedless of far gain,
Greedy for quick returns of profit, sure
    Bad is our bargain!
Was it not great? did not he throw on God,
    (He loves the burthen)—

God's task to make the heavenly period
    Perfect the earthen?
Did not he magnify the mind, show clear
    Just what it all meant?
He would not discount life, as fools do here,
    Paid by instalment.
He ventured neck or nothing—heaven's success
    Found, or earth's failure:
"Wilt thou trust death or not?" He answered "Yes!
    Hence with life's pale lure!"
That low man seeks a little thing to do,
    Sees it and does it:
This high man, with a great thing to pursue,
    Dies ere he knows it.
That low man goes on adding one to one,
    His hundred's soon hit:
This high man, aiming at a million,
    Misses an unit.
That, has the world here—should he need the next,
    Let the world mind him!
This, throws himself on God, and unperplexed
    Seeking shall find him.
So, with the throttling hands of death at strife,
    Ground he at grammar;
Still, through the rattle, parts of speech were rife:
    While he could stammer
He settled *Hoti's* business—let it be!—
    Properly based *Oun*—
Gave us the doctrine of the enclitic *De,*
    Dead from the waist down.
Well, here's the platform, here's the proper place:
    Hail to your purlieus,
All ye highfliers of the feathered race,
    Swallows and curlews!
Here's the top-peak; the multitude below
    Live, for they can, there:
This man decided not to Live but Know—
    Bury this man there?
Here—here's his place, where meteors shoot, clouds form,
    Lightnings are loosened,
Stars come and go! Let joy break with the storm,
    Peace let the dew send!
Lofty designs must close in like effects:
    Loftily lying,
Leave him—still loftier than the world suspects,
    Living and dying.

THE HERETIC'S TRAGEDY

A Middle-Age Interlude

Rosa Mundi; Seu, Fulcite Me Floribus. A Conceit of Master Gysbrecht, Canon-Regular of Saint Jodocus-by-the-Bar, Ypres City. Cantuque, Virgilius. And Hath Often Been Sung at Hock-Tide and Festivals. Gavisus Eram, Jessides.

(It would seem to be a glimpse from the burning of Jacques du Bourg-Molay, at Paris, A.D. 1314; as distorted by the refraction from Flemish brain to brain, during the course of a couple of centuries.)

I.

Preadmonisheth the Abbot Deodaet

The Lord, we look to once for all,
   Is the Lord we should look at, all at once:
He knows not to vary, saith Saint Paul,
   Nor the shadow of turning, for the nonce.
See him no other than as he is!
   Give both the infinitudes their due—
Infinite mercy, but, I wis,
   As infinite a justice too.
              [*Organ: plagal-cadence.*
   As infinite a justice too.

II.

One Singeth

John, Master of the Temple of God,
   Falling to sin the Unknown Sin,
What he bought of Emperor Aldabrod,
   He sold it to Sultan Saladin:
Till, caught by Pope Clement, a-buzzing there,
   Hornet-prince of the mad wasps' hive,
And clipt of his wings in Paris square,
   They bring him now to be burned alive.
     [*And wanteth there grace of lute or clavicithern, ye
       shall say to confirm him who singeth—*
   We bring John now to be burned alive.

III.

In the midst is a goodly gallows built;
  'Twixt fork and fork, a stake is stuck;
But first they set divers tumbrils a-tilt,
  Make a trench all round with the city muck;
Inside they pile log upon log, good store;
  Fagots not few, blocks great and small,
Reach a man's mid-thigh, no less, no more,—
  For they mean he should roast in the sight of all.

CHORUS

  We mean he should roast in the sight of all.

IV.

Good sappy bavins that kindle forthwith;
  Billets that blaze substantial and slow;
Pine-stump split deftly, dry as pith;
  Larch-heart that chars to a chalk-white glow:
Then up they hoist me John in a chafe,
  Sling him fast like a hog to scorch,
Spit in his face, then leap back safe,
  Sing "Laudes" and bid clap-to the torch.

CHORUS

  Laus Deo—who bids clap-to the torch.

V.

John of the Temple, whose fame so bragged,
  Is burning alive in Paris square!
How can he curse, if his mouth is gagged?
  Or wriggle his neck, with a collar there?
Or heave his chest, which a band goes round?
  Or threat with his fist, since his arms are spliced?
Or kick with his feet, now his legs are bound?
  —Thinks John, I will call upon Jesus Christ.

                    [*Here one crosseth himself.*

VI.

Jesus Christ—John had bought and sold,
  Jesus Christ—John had eaten and drunk;
To him, the Flesh meant silver and gold.
  (*Salva reverentia.*)
Now it was, "Saviour, bountiful lamb,
  I have roasted thee Turks, though men roast me!
See thy servant, the plight wherein I am!
  Art thou a saviour? Save thou me!"

CHORUS

  'Tis John the mocker cries, "Save thou me!"

VII.

Who maketh God's menace an idle word?
    —Saith, it no more means what it proclaims,
Than a damsel's threat to her wanton bird?—
    For she too prattles of ugly names.
—Saith, he knoweth but one thing,—what he knows?
    That God is good and the rest is breath;
Why else is the same styled Sharon's rose?
    Once a rose, ever a rose, he saith.
CHORUS
    Oh, John shall yet find a rose, he saith!

VIII.

Alack, there be roses and roses, John!
    Some, honeyed of taste like your leman's tongue:
Some, bitter; for why? (roast gayly on!)
    Their tree struck root in devil's dung.
When Paul once reasoned of righteousness
    And of temperance and of judgment to come,
Good Felix trembled, he could no less:
    John, snickering, crook'd his wicked thumb.
CHORUS
    What cometh to John of the wicked thumb?

IX.

Ha ha, John plucketh now at his rose
    To rid himself of a sorrow at heart!
Lo,—petal on petal, fierce rays unclose;
    Anther on anther, sharp spikes outstart;
And with blood for dew, the bosom boils;
    And a gust of sulphur is all its smell;
And lo, he is horribly in the toils
    Of a coal-black giant flower of hell!
CHORUS
    What maketh heaven, That maketh hell.

X.

So, as John called now, through the fire amain,
    On the Name, he had cursed with, all his life—
To the Person, he bought and sold again—
    For the Face, with his daily buffets rife—
Feature by feature It took its place:
    And his voice, like a mad dog's choking bark,
At the steady whole of the Judge's face—
    Died. Forth John's soul flared into the dark.
SUBJOINETH THE ABBOT DEODAET
    God help all poor souls lost in the dark!

HOLY-CROSS DAY

On Which the Jews Were Forced to Attend an Annual Christian Sermon in Rome

["Now was come about Holy-Cross Day, and now must my lord preach his first sermon to the Jews: as it was of old cared for in the merciful bowels of the Church, that, so to speak, a crumb at least from her conspicuous table here in Rome, should be, though but once yearly, cast to the famishing dogs, under-trampled and bespitten-upon beneath the feet of the guests. And a moving sight in truth, this, of so many of the besotted blind restif and ready-to-perish Hebrews! now maternally brought—nay, (for He saith, 'Compel them to come in') haled, as it were, by the head and hair, and against their obstinate hearts, to partake of the heavenly grace. What awakening, what striving with tears, what working of a yeasty conscience! Nor was my lord wanting to himself on so apt an occasion; witness the abundance of conversions which did incontinently reward him: though not to my lord be altogether the glory."—*Diary by the Bishop's Secretary, 1600.*]

What the Jews really said, on thus being driven to church, was rather to this effect:—

I.

Fee, faw, fum! bubble and squeak!
Blessedest Thursday's the fat of the week.
Rumble and tumble, sleek and rough,
Stinking and savory, smug and gruff,
Take the church-road, for the bell's due chime
Gives us the summons—'tis sermon-time!

II.

Boh, here's Barnabas! Job, that's you?
Up stumps Solomon—bustling too?
Shame, man! greedy beyond your years
To handsel the bishop's shaving-shears?
Fair play's a jewel! Leave friends in the lurch?
Stand on a line ere you start for the church!

III.

Higgledy piggledy, packed we lie,
Rats in a hamper, swine in a sty,
Wasps in a bottle, frogs in a sieve,
Worms in a carcass, fleas in a sleeve.
Hist! square shoulders, settle your thumbs
And buzz for the bishop—here he comes.

IV.

Bow, wow, wow—a bone for the dog!
I liken his Grace to an acorned hog.
What, a boy at his side, with the bloom of a lass,
To help and handle my lord's hour-glass!
Didst ever behold so lithe a chime?
His cheek hath laps like a fresh-singed swine.

V.

Aaron's asleep—shove hip to haunch,
Or somebody deal him a dig in the paunch!
Look at the purse with the tassel and knob,
And the gown with the angel and thingumbob!
What's he at, quotha? reading his text!
Now you've his curtsey—and what comes next?

VI.

See to our converts—you doomed black dozen—
No stealing away—nor cog nor cozen!
You five, that were thieves, deserve it fairly;
You seven, that were beggars, will live less sparely;
You took your turn and dipped in the hat,
Got fortune—and fortune gets you; mind that!

VII.

Give your first groan—compunction's at work;
And soft! from a Jew you mount to a Turk.
Lo, Micah,—the selfsame beard on chin
He was four times already converted in!
Here's a knife, clip quick—it's a sign of grace—
Or he ruins us all with his hanging-face.

VIII.

Whom now is the bishop a-leering at?
I know a point where his text falls pat.
I'll tell him to-morrow, a word just now
Went to my heart and made me vow
I meddle no more with the worst of trades—
Let somebody else pay his serenades.

IX.

Groan all together now, whee—hee—hee!
It's a-work, it's a-work, ah, woe is me!
It began, when a herd of us, picked and placed,
Were spurred through the Corso, stripped to the waist;
Jew brutes, with sweat and blood well spent
To usher in worthily Christian Lent.

X.

It grew, when the hangman entered our bounds,
Yelled, pricked us out to his church like hounds:
It got to a pitch, when the hand indeed
Which gutted my purse, would throttle my creed:
And it overflows, when, to even the odd,
Men I helped to their sins, help me to their God.

XI.

But now, while the scapegoats leave our flock,
And the rest sit silent and count the clock,
Since forced to muse the appointed time
On these precious facts and truths sublime,—
Let us fitly employ it, under our breath,
In saying Ben Ezra's Song of Death.

XII.

For Rabbi Ben Ezra, the night he died,
Called sons and sons' sons to his side,
And spoke, "This world has been harsh and strange;
Something is wrong: there needeth a change.
But what, or where? at the last or first?
In one point only we sinned, at worst.

XIII.

"The Lord will have mercy on Jacob yet,
And again in his border see Israel set.
When Judah beholds Jerusalem,
The stranger-seed shall be joined to them:
To Jacob's House shall the Gentiles cleave.
So the Prophet saith and his sons believe.

XIV.

"Ay, the children of the chosen race
Shall carry and bring them to their place:
In the land of the Lord shall lead the same,
Bondsmen and handmaids. Who shall blame,
When the slaves enslave, the oppressed ones o'er
The oppressor triumph forevermore?

XV.

"God spoke, and gave us the word to keep:
Bade never fold the hands nor sleep
'Mid a faithless world,—at watch and ward,
Till Christ at the end relieve our guard.
By his servant Moses the watch was set:
Though near upon cock-crow, we keep it yet.

XVI.

"Thou! if thou wast he, who at mid-watch came,
By the starlight, naming a dubious name!
And if, too heavy with sleep—too rash
With fear—O thou, if that martyr-gash
Fell on thee coming to take thine own,
And we gave the Cross, when we owed the Throne—

XVII.

"Thou art the Judge. We are bruised thus.
But, the Judgment over, join sides with us!
Thine too is the cause! and not more thine
Than ours, is the work of these dogs and swine,
Whose life laughs through and spits at their creed,
Who maintain thee in word, and defy thee in deed!

XVIII.

"We withstood Christ then? Be mindful how
At least we withstand Barabbas now!
Was our outrage sore? But the worst we spared,
To have called these—Christians, had we dared!
Let defiance to them pay mistrust of thee,
And Rome make amends for Calvary!

XIX.

"By the torture, prolonged from age to age,
By the infamy, Israel's heritage,
By the Ghetto's plague, by the garb's disgrace,
By the badge of shame, by the felon's place,
By the branding-tool, the bloody whip,
And the summons to Christian fellowship,—

XX.

"We boast our proof that at least the Jew
Would wrest Christ's name from the Devil's crew.
Thy face took never so deep a shade
But we fought them in it, God our aid!
A trophy to bear, as we march, thy band,
South, East, and on to the Pleasant Land!"*

PROTUS

AMONG these latter busts we count by scores,
Half-emperors and quarter-emperors,
Each with his bay-leaf fillet, loose-thonged vest,
Loric and low-browed Gorgon on the breast,—

*Pope Gregory XVI. abolished this bad business of the Sermon.—R. B.

One loves a baby face, with violets there,
Violets instead of laurel in the hair,
As those were all the little locks could bear.

Now read here. "Protus ends a period
Of empery beginning with a god;
Born in the porphyry chamber at Byzant,
Queens by his cradle, proud and ministrant:
And if he quickened breath there, 'twould like fire
Pantingly through the dim vast realm transpire.
A fame that he was missing spread afar:
The world, from its four corners, rose in war,
Till he was borne out on a balcony
To pacify the world when it should see.
The captains ranged before him, one, his hand
Made baby points at, gained the chief command.
And day by day more beautiful he grew
In shape, all said, in feature and in hue,
While young Greek sculptors gazing on the child,
Became, with old Greek sculpture, reconciled.
Already sages labored to condense
In easy tomes a life's experience:
And artists took grave counsel to impart
In one breath and one hand-sweep, all their art—
To make his graces prompt as blossoming
Of plentifully-watered palms in spring:
Since well beseems it, whoso mounts the throne,
For beauty, knowledge, strength, should stand alone,
And mortals love the letters of his name."

—Stop! Have you turned two pages? Still the same
New reign, same date. The scribe goes on to say
How that same year, on such a month and day,
"John the Pannonian, groundedly believed
A blacksmith's bastard, whose hard hand reprieved
The Empire from its fate the year before,—
Came, had a mind to take the crown, and wore
The same for six years, (during which the Huns
Kept off their fingers from us), till his sons
Put something in his liquor"—and so forth.
Then a new reign. Stay—"Take at its just worth"
(Subjoins an annotator) "what I give
As hearsay. Some think, John let Protus live
And slip away. 'Tis said, he reached man's age
At some blind northern court; made, first a page,
Then tutor to the children; last, of use

About the hunting-stables. I deduce
He wrote the little tract 'On worming dogs,'
Whereof the name in sundry catalogues
Is extant yet. A Protus of the race
Is rumored to have died a monk in Thrace,—
And if the same, he reached senility."

Here's John the Smith's rough-hammered head. Great eye,
Gross jaw and griped lips do what granite can
To give you the crown-grasper. What a man!

THE STATUE AND THE BUST

There's a palace in Florence, the world knows well,
And a statue watches it from the square,
And this story of both do our townsmen tell.

Ages ago, a lady there,
At the farthest window facing the East
Asked, "Who rides by with the royal air?"

The bridesmaids' prattle around her ceased;
She leaned forth, one on either hand;
They saw how the blush of the bride increased—

They felt by its beats her heart expand—
As one at each ear and both in a breath
Whispered, "The Great-Duke Ferdinand."

That selfsame instant, underneath,
The Duke rode past in his idle way,
Empty and fine like a swordless sheath.

Gay he rode, with a friend as gay,
Till he threw his head back—"Who is she?"
—"A bride the Riccardi brings home to-day."

Hair in heaps lay heavily
Over a pale brow spirit-pure—
Carved like the heart of the coal-black tree,

Crisped like a war-steed's encolure—
And vainly sought to dissemble her eyes
Of the blackest black our eyes endure.

And lo, a blade for a knight's emprise
Filled the fine empty sheath of a man,—
The Duke grew straightway brave and wise.

He looked at her, as a lover can;
She looked at him, as one who awakes:
The past was a sleep, and her life began.

Now, love so ordered for both their sakes,
A feast was held that selfsame night
In the pile which the mighty shadow makes.

(For Via Larga is three-parts light,
But the palace overshadows one,
Because of a crime, which may God requite!

To Florence and God the wrong was done,
Through the first republic's murder there
By Cosimo and his cursed son.)

The Duke (with the statue's face in the square)
Turned in the midst of his multitude
At the bright approach of the bridal pair.

Face to face the lovers stood
A single minute and no more,
While the bridegroom bent as a man subdued—

Bowed till his bonnet brushed the floor—
For the Duke on the lady a kiss conferred,
As the courtly custom was of yore.

In a minute can lovers exchange a word?
If a word did pass, which I do not think,
Only one out of the thousand heard.

That was the bridegroom. At day's brink
He and his bride were alone at last
In a bed chamber by a taper's blink.

Calmly he said that her lot was cast,
That the door she had passed was shut on her
Till the final catafalk repassed.

The world meanwhile, its noise and stir,
Through a certain window facing the East
She could watch like a convent's chronicler.

Since passing the door might lead to a feast,
And a feast might lead to so much beside,
He, of many evils, chose the least.

"Freely I choose too," said the bride—
"Your window and its world suffice,"
Replied the tongue, while the heart replied—

"If I spend the night with that devil twice,
May his window serve as my loop of hell
Whence a damned soul looks on paradise!

"I fly to the Duke who loves me well,
Sit by his side and laugh at sorrow
Ere I count another ave-bell.

" 'Tis only the coat of a page to borrow,
And tie my hair in a horse-boy's trim,
And I save my soul—but not to-morrow"—

(She checked herself and her eye grew dim)
"My father tarries to bless my state:
I must keep it one day more for him.

"Is one day more so long to wait?
Moreover the Duke rides past, I know;
We shall see each other, sure as fate."

She turned on her side and slept. Just so!
So we resolve on a thing and sleep:
So did the lady, ages ago.

That night the Duke said, "Dear or cheap
As the cost of this cup of bliss may prove
To body or soul, I will drain it deep."

And on the morrow, bold with love,
He beckoned the bridegroom (close on call,
As his duty bade, by the Duke's alcove)

And smiled " 'Twas a very funeral,
Your lady will think, this feast of ours,—
A shame to efface, whate'er befall!

"What if we break from the Arno bowers,
And try if Petraja, cool and green,
Cure last night's fault with this morning's flowers?"

The bridegroom, not a thought to be seen
On his steady brow and quiet mouth,
Said, "Too much favor for me so mean!

"But, alas! my lady leaves the South;
Each wind that comes from the Apennine
Is a menace to her tender youth:

"Nor a way exists, the wise opine,
If she quits her palace twice this year,
To avert the flower of life's decline."

Quoth the Duke, "A sage and a kindly fear.
Moreover Petraja is cold this spring:
Be our feast to-night as usual here!"

And then to himself—"Which night shall bring
Thy bride to her lover's embraces, fool—
Or I am the fool, and thou art the king!

"Yet my passion must wait a night, nor cool—
For to-night the Envoy arrives from France
Whose heart I unlock with thyself, my tool.

"I need thee still and might miss perchance.
To-day is not wholly lost, beside,
With its hope of my lady's countenance:

"For I ride—what should I do but ride?
And passing her palace, if I list,
May glance at its window—well betide!"

So said, so done: nor the lady missed
One ray that broke from the ardent brow,
Nor a curl of the lips where the spirit kissed.

Be sure that each renewed the vow,
No morrow's sun should arise and set
And leave them then as it left them now.

But next day passed, and next day yet,
With still fresh cause to wait one day more
Ere each leaped over the parapet.

And still, as love's brief morning wore,
With a gentle start, half smile, half sigh,
They found love not as it seemed before.

They thought it would work infallibly,
But not in despite of heaven and earth:
The rose would blow when the storm passed by.

Meantime they could profit in winter's dearth
By store of fruits that supplant the rose:
The world and its ways have a certain worth:

And to press a point while these oppose
Were simple policy; better wait:
We lose no friends and we gain no foes.

Meantime, worse fates than a lover's fate,
Who daily may ride and pass and look
Where his lady watches behind the grate!

And she—she watched the square like a book
Holding one picture and only one,
Which daily to find she undertook:

When the picture was reached the book was done,
And she turned from the picture at night to scheme
Of tearing it out for herself next sun.

So weeks grew months, years; gleam by gleam
The glory dropped from their youth and love,
And both perceived they had dreamed a dream;

Which hovered as dreams do, still above:
But who can take a dream for a truth?
Oh, hide our eyes from the next remove!

One day as the lady saw her youth
Depart, and the silver thread that streaked
Her hair, and, worn by the serpent's tooth,

The brow so puckered, the chin so peaked,—
And wondered who the woman was,
Hollow-eyed and haggard-cheeked,

Fronting her silent in the glass—
"Summon here," she suddenly said,
"Before the rest of my old self pass,

"Him, the Carver, a hand to aid,
Who fashions the clay no love will change,
And fixes a beauty never to fade.

"Let Robbia's craft so apt and strange
  Arrest the remains of young and fair,
  And rivet them while the seasons range.

"Make me a face on the window there,
  Waiting as ever, mute the while,
  My love to pass below in the square!

"And let me think that it may beguile
  Dreary days which the dead must spend
  Down in their darkness under the aisle,

"To say, 'What matters it at the end?
  I did no more while my heart was warm
  Than does that image, my pale-faced friend.'

"Where is the use of the lip's red charm,
  The heaven of hair, the pride of the brow,
  And the blood that blues the inside arm—

"Unless we turn, as the soul knows how,
  The earthly gift to an end divine?
  A lady of clay is as good, I trow."

But long ere Robbia's cornice, fine,
  With flowers and fruits which leaves enlace,
  Was set where now is the empty shrine—

(And, leaning out of a bright blue space,
  As a ghost might lean from a chink of sky,
  The passionate pale lady's face—

Eying ever, with earnest eye
  And quick-turned neck at its breathless stretch,
  Some one who ever is passing by—)

The Duke had sighed like the simplest wretch
  In Florence, "Youth—my dream escapes!
  Will its record stay?" And he bade them fetch

Some subtle moulder of brazen shapes—
  "Can the soul, the will, die out of a man
  Ere his body find the grave that gapes?

"John of Douay shall effect my plan,
  Set me on horseback here aloft,
  Alive, as the crafty sculptor can,

"In the very square I have crossed so oft:
That men may admire, when future suns
Shall touch the eyes to a purpose soft,

"While the mouth and the brow stay brave in bronze—
Admire and say, 'When he was alive
How he would take his pleasure once!'

"And it shall go hard but I contrive
To listen the while, and laugh in my tomb
At idleness which aspires to strive."

So! While these wait the trump of doom,
How do their spirits pass, I wonder,
Nights and days in the narrow room?

Still, I suppose, they sit and ponder
What a gift life was, ages ago,
Six steps out of the chapel yonder.

Only they see not God, I know,
Nor all that chivalry of his,
The soldier-saints who, row on row,

Burn upward each to his point of bliss—
Since, the end of life being manifest,
He had burned his way through the world to this.

I hear you reproach, "But delay was best,
For their end was a crime."—Oh, a crime will do
As well, I reply, to serve for a test,

As a virtue golden through and through,
Sufficient to vindicate itself
And prove its worth at a moment's view!

Must a game be played for the sake of pelf?
Where a button goes, 'twere an epigram
To offer the stamp of the very Guelph.

The true has no value beyond the sham:
As well the counter as coin, I submit,
When your table's a hat, and your prize, a dram.

Stake your counter as boldly every whit,
Venture as warily, use the same skill,
Do your best, whether winning or losing it,

If you choose to play!—is my principle.
Let a man contend to the uttermost
For his life's set prize, be it what it will!

The counter our lovers staked was lost
As surely as if it were lawful coin:
And the sin I impute to each frustrate ghost

Is—the unlit lamp and the ungirt loin,
Though the end in sight was a vice, I say.
You of the virtue (we issue join)
How strive you? *De te, fabula!*

PORPHYRIA'S LOVER

THE rain set early in to-night,
    The sullen wind was soon awake,
It tore the elm-tops down for spite,
    And did its worst to vex the lake:
I listened with heart fit to break.
When glided in Porphyria; straight
    She shut the cold out and the storm,
And kneeled and made the cheerless grate
    Blaze up, and all the cottage warm;
Which done, she rose, and from her form
Withdrew the dripping cloak and shawl,
    And laid her soiled gloves by, untied
Her hat and let the damp hair fall,
    And, last, she sat down by my side
And called me. When no voice replied,
She put my arm about her waist,
    And made her smooth white shoulder **bare,**
And all her yellow hair displaced,
    And, stooping, made my cheek lie **there,**
And spread, o'er all, her yellow hair,
Murmuring how she loved me—she
    Too weak, for all her heart's endeavor,
To set its struggling passion free
    From pride, and vainer ties dissever,
And give herself to me forever.
But passion sometimes would prevail,
    Nor could to-night's gay feast **restrain**
A sudden thought of one so pale
    For love of her, and all in vain:

So, she was come through wind and rain.
Be sure I looked up at her eyes
　　Happy and proud; at last I knew
Porphyria worshipped me; surprise
　　Made my heart swell, and still it **grew**
While I debated what to do.
That moment she was mine, mine, fair,
　　Perfectly pure and good: I found
A thing to do, and all her hair
　　In one long yellow string I wound
Three times her little throat around,
And strangled her. No pain felt she;
　　I am quite sure she felt no pain.
As a shut bud that holds a bee,
　　I warily oped her lids: again
Laughed the blue eyes without a stain.
And I untightened next the tress
　　About her neck; her cheek once more
Blushed bright beneath my burning kiss:
　　I propped her head up as before,
Only, this time my shoulder bore
Her head, which droops upon it still:
　　The smiling rosy little head,
So glad it has its utmost will,
　　That all it scorned at once is fled,
And I, its love, am gained instead!
Porphyria's love: she guessed not how
　　Her darling one wish would be heard.
And thus we sit together now,
　　And all night long we have not stirred,
And yet God has not said a word!

"CHILDE ROLAND TO THE DARK TOWER CAME"

(SEE EDGAR'S SONG IN "LEAR.")

I.

MY FIRST THOUGHT was, he lied in every word,
　　That hoary cripple, with malicious eye
　　Askance to watch the working of his lie
On mine, and mouth scarce able to afford
Suppression of the glee, that pursed and scored
　　Its edge, at one more victim gained thereby.

II.

What else should he be set for, with his staff?
  What, save to waylay with his lies, ensnare
  All travellers who might find him posted there,
And ask the road? I guessed what skull-like laugh
Would break, what crutch 'gin write my epitaph
  For pastime in the dusty thoroughfare,

III.

If at his counsel I should turn aside
  Into that ominous tract which, all agree,
  Hides the Dark Tower. Yet acquiescingly
I did turn as he pointed: neither pride
Nor hope rekindling at the end descried,
  So much as gladness that some end might be.

IV.

For, what with my whole world-wide wandering,
  What with my search drawn out through years, my hope
  Dwindled into a ghost not fit to cope
With that obstreperous joy success would bring,—
I hardly tried now to rebuke the spring
  My heart made, finding failure in its scope.

V.

As when a sick man very near to death
  Seems dead indeed, and feels begin and end
  The tears, and takes the farewell of each friend,
And hears one bid the other go, draw breath
Freelier outside, ("since all is o'er," he saith,
  "And the blow fallen no grieving can amend;")

VI.

While some discuss if near the other graves
  Be room enough for this, and when a day
  Suits best for carrying the corpse away,
With care about the banners, scarves and staves:
And still the man hears all, and only craves
  He may not shame such tender love and stay.

VII.

Thus, I had so long suffered in this quest,
  Heard failure prophesied so oft, been writ
  So many times among "The Band"—to wit,
The knights who to the Dark Tower's search addressed
Their steps—that just to fail as they, seemed best,
  And all the doubt was now—should I be fit?

VIII.

So, quiet as despair, I turned from him,
  That hateful cripple, out of his highway
  Into the path he pointed. All the day
Had been a dreary one at best, and dim
Was settling to its close, yet shot one grim
  Red leer to see the plain catch its estray.

IX.

For mark! no sooner was I fairly found
  Pledged to the plain, after a pace or two,
  Than, pausing to throw backward a last view
O'er the safe road, 'twas gone; gray plain all round:
Nothing but plain to the horizon's bound.
  I might go on; nought else remained to do.

X.

So, on I went. I think I never saw
  Such starved ignoble nature; nothing throve:
  For flowers—as well expect a cedar grove!
But cockle, spurge, according to their law
Might propagate their kind, with none to awe,
  You'd think; a burr had been a treasure trove.

XI.

No! penury, inertness and grimace,
  In some strange sort, were the land's portion. "See
  Or shut your eyes," said Nature peevishly,
"It nothing skills: I cannot help my case:
'Tis the Last Judgment's fire must cure this place,
  Calcine its clods and set my prisoners free."

XII.

If there pushed any ragged thistle-stalk
  Above its mates, the head was chopped; the bents
  Were jealous else. What made those holes and rents
In the dock's harsh swarth leaves, bruised as to balk
All hope of greenness? 'tis a brute must walk
  Pashing their life out, with a brute's intents.

XIII.

As for the grass, it grew as scant as hair
  In leprosy; thin dry blades pricked the mud
  Which underneath looked kneaded up with blood.
One stiff blind horse, his every bone a-stare,
Stood stupefied, however he came there:
  Thrust out past service from the devil's stud!

XIV.

Alive? he might be dead for aught I know,
  With that red gaunt and colloped neck a-strain,
  And shut eyes underneath the rusty mane;
Seldom went such grotesqueness with such woe;
I never saw a brute I hated so;
  He must be wicked to deserve such pain.

XV.

I shut my eyes and turned them on my heart.
  As a man calls for wine before he fights,
  I asked one draught of earlier, happier sights,
Ere fitly I could hope to play my part.
Think first, fight afterwards—the soldier's art:
  One taste of the old time sets all to rights.

XVI.

Not it! I fancied Cuthbert's reddening face
  Beneath its garniture of curly gold,
  Dear fellow, till I almost felt him fold
An arm in mine to fix me to the place,
That way he used. Alas, one night's disgrace!
  Out went my heart's new fire and left it cold.

XVII.

Giles then, the soul of honor—there he stands
  Frank as ten years ago when knighted first.
  What honest man should dare (he said) he durst.
Good—but the scene shifts—faugh! what hangman hands
Pin to his breast a parchment? His own bands
  Read it. Poor traitor, spit upon and curst!

XVIII.

Better this present than a past like that;
  Back therefore to my darkening path again!
  No sound, no sight as far as eye could strain.
Will the night send a howlet or a bat?
I asked: when something on the dismal flat
  Came to arrest my thoughts and change their train.

XIX.

A sudden little river crossed my path
  As unexpected as a serpent comes.
  No sluggish tide congenial to the glooms;
This, as it frothed by, might have been a bath
For the fiend's glowing hoof—to see the wrath
  Of its black eddy bespate with flakes and spumes.

xx.

So petty yet so spiteful! All along,
   Low scrubby alders kneeled down over it;
   Drenched willows flung them headlong in a fit
Of mute despair, a suicidal throng:
The river which had done them all the wrong,
   Whate'er that was, rolled by, deterred no whit.

xxi.

Which, while I forded,—good saints, how I feared
   To set my foot upon a dead man's cheek,
   Each step, or feel the spear I thrust to seek
For hollows, tangled in his hair or beard!
—It may have been a water-rat I speared,
   But, ugh! it sounded like a baby's shriek.

xxii.

Glad was I when I reached the other bank.
   Now for a better country. Vain presage!
   Who were the strugglers, what war did they wage,
Whose savage trample thus could pad the dank
Soil to a plash? Toads in a poisoned tank,
   Or wild cats in a red-hot iron cage—

xxiii.

The fight must so have seemed in that fell cirque.
   What penned them there, with all the plain to choose?
   No footprint leading to that horrid mews,
None out of it. Mad brewage set to work
Their brains, no doubt, like galley-slaves the Turk
   Pits for his pastime, Christians against Jews.

xxiv.

And more than that—a furlong on—why, there!
   What bad use was that engine for, that wheel,
   Or brake, not wheel—that harrow fit to reel
Men's bodies out like silk? with all the air
Of Tophet's tool, on earth left unaware,
   Or brought to sharpen its rusty teeth of steel.

xxv.

Then came a bit of stubbed ground, once a wood,
   Next a marsh, it would seem, and now mere earth
   Desperate and done with; (so a fool finds mirth,
Makes a thing and then mars it, till his mood
Changes and off he goes!) within a rood—
   Bog, clay and rubble, sand and stark black dearth.

XXVI.

Now blotches rankling, colored gay and grim,
   Now patches where some leanness of the soil's
   Broke into moss or substances like boils;
Then came some palsied oak, a cleft in him
Like a distorted mouth that splits its rim
   Gaping at death, and dies while it recoils.

XXVII.

And just as far as ever from the end!
   Nought in the distance but the evening, nought
   To point my footstep further! At the thought,
A great black bird, Apollyon's bosom-friend,
Sailed past, nor beat his wide wing dragon-penned
   That brushed my cap—perchance the guide I sought.

XXVIII.

For, looking up, aware I somehow grew,
   'Spite of the dusk, the plain had given place
   All round to mountains—with such name to grace
Mere ugly heights and heaps now stolen in view.
How thus they had surprised me,—solve it, you!
   How to get from them was no clearer case.

XXIX.

Yet half I seemed to recognize some trick
   Of mischief happened to me, God knows when—
   In a bad dream perhaps. Here ended, then,
Progress this way. When, in the very nick
Of giving up, one time more, came a click
   As when a trap shuts—you're inside the den!

XXX.

Burningly it came on me all at once,
   This was the place! those two hills on the right,
   Crouched like two bulls locked horn in horn in fight;
While to the left, a tall scalped mountain . . . Dunce,
Dotard, a-dozing at the very nonce,
   After a life spent training for the sight!

XXXI.

What in the midst lay but the Tower itself?
   The round squat turret, blind as the fool's heart,
   Built of brown stone, without a counterpart
In the whole world. The tempest's mocking elf
Points to the shipman thus the unseen shelf
   He strikes on, only when the timbers start.

XXXII.

Not see? because of night perhaps?—why, day
  Came back again for that! before it left,
  The dying sunset kindled through a cleft:
The hills, like giants at a hunting, lay,
Chin upon hand, to see the game at bay,—
  "Now stab and end the creature—to the heft!"

XXXIII.

Not hear? when noise was everywhere! it tolled
  Increasing like a bell. Names in my ears,
  Of all the lost adventurers my peers,—
How such a one was strong, and such was bold,
And such was fortunate, yet each of old
  Lost, lost! one moment knelled the woe of years.

XXXIV.

There they stood, ranged along the hillsides, met
  To view the last of me, a living frame
  For one more picture! in a sheet of flame
I saw them and I knew them all. And yet
Dauntless the slug-horn to my lips I set,
  And blew. *"Childe Roland to the Dark Tower came."*

CHRISTMAS-EVE

FLORENCE, 1850

I.

Out of the little chapel I burst
Into the fresh night-air again.
Five minutes full, I waited first
In the doorway, to escape the rain
That drove in gusts down the common's centre
At the edge of which the chapel stands,
Before I plucked up heart to enter.
Heaven knows how many sorts of hands
Reached past me, groping for the latch
Of the inner door that hung on catch
More obstinate the more they fumbled,
Till, giving way at last with a scold
Of the crazy hinge, in squeezed or tumbled
One sheep more to the rest in fold,
And left me irresolute, standing sentry
In the sheepfold's lath-and-plaster entry,

Four feet long by two feet wide,
Partitioned off from the vast inside—
I blocked up half of it at least.
No remedy; the rain kept driving.
They eyed me much as some wild beast,
That congregation, still arriving,
Some of them by the main road, white
A long way past me into the night,
Skirting the common, then diverging;
Not a few suddenly emerging
From the common's self through the paling-gaps,
—They house in the gravel-pits perhaps,
Where the road stops short with its safeguard border
Of lamps, as tired of such disorder;—
But the most turned in yet more abruptly
From a certain squalid knot of alleys,
Where the town's bad blood once slept corruptly,
Which now the little chapel rallies
And leads into day again,—its priestliness
Lending itself to hide their beastliness
So cleverly (thanks in part to the mason),
And putting so cheery a whitewashed face on
Those neophytes too much in lack of it,
That, where you cross the common as I did,
And meet the party thus presided,
"Mount Zion" with Love-lane at the back of it,
They front you as little disconcerted
As, bound for the hills, her fate averted,
And her wicked people made to mind him,
Lot might have marched with Gomorrah behind him.

II.

Well, from the road, the lanes or the common,
In came the flock: the fat weary woman,
Panting and bewildered, down-clapping
Her umbrella with a mighty report,
Grounded it by me, wry and flapping,
A wreck of whalebones; then, with a snort,
Like a startled horse, at the interloper
(Who humbly knew himself improper,
But could not shrink up small enough)
—Round to the door, and in,—the gruff
Hinge's invariable scold
Making my very blood run cold.
Prompt in the wake of her, up-pattered
On broken clogs, the many-tattered

Little old-faced peaking sister-turned-mother
Of the sickly babe she tried to smother
Somehow up, with its spotted face,
From the cold, on her breast, the one warm place;
She too must stop, wring the poor ends dry
Of a draggled shawl, and add thereby
Her tribute to the door-mat, sopping
Already from my own clothes' dropping,
Which yet she seemed to grudge I should stand on:
Then, stooping down to take off her pattens,
She bore them defiantly, in each hand one,
Planted together before her breast
And its babe, as good as a lance in rest.
Close on her heels, the dingy satins
Of a female something, past me flitted,
With lips as much too white, as a streak
Lay far too red on each hollow cheek;
And it seemed the very door-hinge pitied
All that was left of a woman once,
Holding at least its tongue for the nonce.
Then a tall yellow man, like the Penitent Thief,
With his jaw bound up in a handkerchief,
And eyelids screwed together tight,
Led himself in by some inner light.
And, except from him, from each that entered,
I got the same interrogation—
"What, you the alien, you have ventured
To take with us, the elect, your station?
A carer for none of it, a Gallio!"—
Thus, plain as print, I read the glance
At a common prey, in each countenance
As of huntsman giving his hounds the tallyho.
And, when the door's cry drowned their wonder,
The draught, it always sent in shutting,
Made the flame of the single tallow candle
In the cracked square lantern I stood under,
Shoot its blue lip at me, rebutting
As it were, the luckless cause of scandal:
I verily fancied the zealous light
(In the chapel's secret, too!) for spite
Would shudder itself clean off the wick,
With the airs of a Saint John's Candlestick.
There was no standing it much longer.
"Good folks," thought I, as resolve grew stronger,
"This way you perform the Grand-Inquisitor
When the weather sends you a chance visitor?

You are the men, and wisdom shall die with you,
And none of the old Seven Churches vie with you!
But still, despite the pretty perfection
To which you carry your trick of exclusiveness,
And, taking God's word under wise protection,
Correct its tendency to diffusiveness,
And bid one reach it over hot ploughshares,—
Still, as I say, though you've found salvation,
If I should choose to cry, as now, 'Shares!'—
See if the best of you bars me my ration!
I prefer, if you please, for my expounder
Of the laws of the feast, the feast's own Founder;
Mine's the same right with your poorest and sickliest
Supposing I don the marriage vestiment:
So, shut your mouth and open your Testament,
And carve me my portion at your quickliest!"
Accordingly, as a shoemaker's lad
With wizened face in want of soap,
And wet apron wound round his waist like a rope,
(After stopping outside, for his cough was bad,
To get the fit over, poor gentle creature,
And so avoid disturbing the preacher)
—Passed in, I sent my elbow spikewise
At the shutting door, and entered likewise,
Received the hinge's accustomed greeting,
And crossed the threshold's magic pentacle,
And found myself in full conventicle,
—To wit, in Zion Chapel Meeting,
On the Christmas-Eve of 'Forty-nine,
Which, calling its flock to their special clover,
Found all assembled and one sheep over,
Whose lot, as the weather pleased, was mine.

III.

I very soon had enough of it.
The hot smell and the human noises,
And my neighbor's coat, the greasy cuff of it,
Were a pebble-stone that a child's hand poises,
Compared with the pig-of-lead-like pressure
Of the preaching man's immense stupidity,
As he poured his doctrine forth, full measure,
To meet his audience's avidity.
You needed not the wit of the Sibyl
To guess the cause of it all, in a twinkling:
No sooner had our friend got an inkling
Of treasure hid in the Holy Bible,

(Whene'er 'twas that the thought first struck him,
How death, at unawares, might duck him
Deeper than the grave, and quench
The gin-shop's light in hell's grim drench)
Than he handled it so, in fine irreverence,
As to hug the book of books to pieces:
And, a patchwork of chapters and texts in severance,
Not improved by the private dog's-ears and creases,
Having clothed his own soul with, he'd fain see equipt yours,—
So tossed you again your Holy Scriptures.
And you picked them up, in a sense, no doubt:
Nay, had but a single face of my neighbors
Appeared to suspect that the preacher's labors
Were help which the world could be saved without,
'Tis odds but I might have borne in quiet
A qualm or two at my spiritual diet,
Or (who can tell?) perchance even mustered
Somewhat to urge in behalf of the sermon:
But the flock sat on, divinely flustered,
Sniffing, methought, its dew of Hermon
With such content in every snuffle,
As the devil inside us loves to ruffle.
My old fat woman purred with pleasure,
And thumb round thumb went twirling faster,
While she, to his periods keeping measure,
Maternally devoured the pastor.
The man with the handkerchief untied it,
Showed us a horrible wen inside it,
Gave his eyelids yet another screwing,
And rocked himself as the woman was doing.
The shoemaker's lad, discreetly choking,
Kept down his cough. 'Twas too provoking!
My gorge rose at the nonsense and stuff of it;
So, saying like Eve when she plucked the apple,
"I wanted a taste, and now there's enough of it,"
I flung out of the little chapel.

IV.

There was a lull in the rain, a lull
In the wind too; the moon was risen,
And would have shone out pure and full,
But for the ramparted cloud-prison,
Block on block built up in the West,
For what purpose the wind knows best,
Who changes his mind continually.
And the empty other half of the sky

Seemed in its silence as if it knew
What, any moment, might look through
A chance gap in that fortress massy:—
Through its fissures you got hints
Of the flying moon, by the shifting tints,
Now, a dull lion-color, now, brassy
Burning to yellow, and whitest yellow,
Like furnace-smoke just ere flames bellow,
All a-simmer with intense strain
To let her through,—then blank again,
At the hope of her appearance failing.
Just by the chapel, a break in the railing
Shows a narrow path directly across;
'Tis ever dry walking there, on the moss—
Besides, you go gently all the way up-hill.
I stooped under and soon felt better;
My head grew lighter, my limbs more supple,
As I walked on, glad to have slipt the fetter.
My mind was full of the scene I had left,
That placid flock, that pastor vociferant,
—How this outside was pure and different!
The sermon, now—what a mingled weft
Of good and ill! Were either less,
Its fellow had colored the whole distinctly;
But alas for the excellent earnestness,
And the truths, quite true if stated succinctly,
But as surely false, in their quaint presentment,
However to pastor and flock's contentment!
Say rather, such truths looked false to your eyes.
With his provings and parallels twisted and twined,
Till how could you know them, grown double their size
In the natural fog of the good man's mind,
Like yonder spots of our roadside lamps,
Haloed about with the common's damps?
Truth remains true, the fault's in the prover;
The zeal was good, and the aspiration;
And yet, and yet, yet, fifty times over,
Pharaoh received no demonstration,
By his Baker's dream of Baskets Three,
Of the doctrine of the Trinity,—
Although, as our preacher thus embellished it,
Apparently his hearers relished it
With so unfeigned a gust—who knows if
They did not prefer our friend to Joseph?
But so it is everywhere, one way with all of them!
These people have really felt, no doubt,

A something, the motion they style the Call of them;
And this is their method of bringing about,
By a mechanism of words and tones,
(So many texts in so many groans)
A sort of reviving and reproducing,
More or less perfectly, (who can tell?)
Of the mood itself, that strengthens by using;
And how that happens, I understand well.
A tune was born in my head last week,
Out of the thump-thump and shriek-shriek
Of the train, as I came by it, up from Manchester;
And when, next week, I take it back again,
My head will sing to the engine's clack again,
While it only makes my neighbor's haunches stir,
—Finding no dormant musical sprout
In him, as in me, to be jolted out.
'Tis the taught already that profits by teaching;
He gets no more from the railway's preaching
Than, from this preacher who does the rail's office, I:
Whom therefore the flock cast a jealous eye on.
Still, why paint over their door "Mount Zion,"
To which all flesh shall come, saith the prophecy?

v.

But wherefore be harsh on a single case?
After how many modes, this Christmas-Eve,
Does the self-same weary thing take place?
The same endeavor to make you believe,
And with much the same effect, no more:
Each method abundantly convincing,
As I say, to those convinced before,
But scarce to be swallowed without wincing
By the not-as-yet-convinced. For me,
I have my own church equally:
And in this church my faith sprang first!
(I said, as I reached the rising ground,
And the wind began again, with a burst
Of rain in my face, and a glad rebound
From the heart beneath, as if, God speeding me,
I entered his church-door, nature leading me)
—In youth I looked to these very skies,
And probing their immensities,
I found God there, his visible power;
Yet felt in my heart, amid all its sense
Of the power, an equal evidence

That his love, there too, was the nobler dower.
For the loving worm within its clod
Were diviner than a loveless god
Amid his worlds, I will dare to say.
You know what I mean: God's all, man's nought:
But also, God, whose pleasure brought
Man into being, stands away
As it were a handbreadth off, to give
Room for the newly-made to live,
And look at him from a place apart,
And use his gifts of brain and heart,
Given, indeed, but to keep forever.
Who speaks of man, then, must not sever
Man's very elements from man,
Saying, "But all is God's"—whose plan
Was to create man and then leave him
Able, his own word saith, to grieve him,
But able to glorify him too,
As a mere machine could never do,
That prayed or praised, all unaware
Of its fitness for aught but praise and prayer,
Made perfect as a thing of course.
Man, therefore, stands on his own stock
Of love and power as a pin-point rock:
And, looking to God who ordained divorce
Of the rock from his boundless continent,
Sees, in his power made evident,
Only excess by a million-fold
O'er the power God gave man in the mould.
For, note: man's hand, first formed to carry
A few pounds' weight, when taught to marry
Its strength with an engine's, lifts a mountain,
—Advancing in power by one degree;
And why count steps through eternity?
But love is the ever-springing fountain:
Man may enlarge or narrow his bed
For the water's play, but the water-head—
How can he multiply or reduce it?
As easy create it, as cause it to cease;
He may profit by it, or abuse it,
But 'tis not a thing to bear increase
As power does: be love less or more
In the heart of man, he keeps it shut
Or opes it wide, as he pleases, but
Love's sum remains what it was before.

So, gazing up, in my youth, at love
As seen through power, ever above
All modes which make it manifest,
My soul brought all to a single test—
That he, the Eternal First and Last,
Who, in his power, had so surpassed
All man conceives of what is might,—
Whose wisdom, too, showed infinite,
—Would prove as infinitely good;
Would never, (my soul understood,)
With power to work all love desires,
Bestow e'en less than man requires;
That he who endlessly was teaching,
Above my spirit's utmost reaching,
What love can do in the leaf or stone,
(So that to master this alone,
This done in the stone or leaf for me,
I must go on learning endlessly)
Would never need that I, in turn,
Should point him out defect unheeded,
And show that God had yet to learn
What the meanest human creature needed,
—Not life, to wit, for a few short years,
Tracking his way through doubts and fears,
While the stupid earth on which I stay
Suffers no change, but passive adds
Its myriad years to myriads,
Though I, he gave it to, decay,
Seeing death come and choose about me,
And my dearest ones depart without me.
No: love which, on earth, amid all the shows of it,
Has ever been seen the sole good of life in it,
The love, ever growing there, spite of the strife in it,
Shall arise, made perfect, from death's repose of it.
And I shall behold thee, face to face,
O God, and in thy light retrace
How in all I loved here, still wast thou!
Whom pressing to, then, as I fain would now,
I shall find as able to satiate
The love, thy gift, as my spirit's wonder
Thou art able to quicken and sublimate,
With this sky of thine, that I now walk under,
And glory in thee for, as I gaze
Thus, thus! Oh, let men keep their ways
Of seeking thee in a narrow shrine—
Be this my way! And this is mine!

VI.

For lo, what think you? suddenly
The rain and the wind ceased, and the sky
Received at once the full fruition
Of the moon's consummate apparition.
The black cloud-barricade was riven,
Ruined beneath her feet, and driven
Deep in the West; while, bare and breathless,
North and South and East lay ready
For a glorious thing that, dauntless, deathless,
Sprang across them and stood steady.
'Twas a moon-rainbow, vast and perfect,
From heaven to heaven extending, perfect
As the mother-moon's self, full in face.
It rose, distinctly at the base
With its seven proper colors chorded,
Which still, in the rising, were compressed,
Until at last they coalesced,
And supreme the spectral creature lorded
In a triumph of whitest white,—
Above which intervened the night.
But above night too, like only the next,
The second of a wondrous sequence,
Reaching in rare and rarer frequence,
Till the heaven of heavens were circumflexed,
Another rainbow rose, a mightier,
Fainter, flushier and flightier,—
Rapture dying along its verge.
Oh, whose foot shall I see emerge,
Whose, from the straining topmost dark,
On to the keystone of that arc?

VII.

This sight was shown me, there and then,—
Me, one out of a world of men,
Singled forth, as the chance might hap
To another if, in a thunderclap
Where I heard noise and you saw flame,
Some one man knew God called his name.
For me, I think I said, "Appear!
Good were it to be ever here.
If thou wilt, let me build to thee
Service-tabernacles three,
Where, forever in thy presence,
In ecstatic acquiescence,
Far alike from thriftless learning

And ignorance's undiscerning,
I may worship and remain!"
Thus at the show above me, gazing
With upturned eyes, I felt my brain
Glutted with the glory, blazing
Throughout its whole mass, over and under,
Until at length it burst asunder
And out of it bodily there streamed,
The too-much glory, as it seemed,
Passing from out me to the ground,
Then palely serpentining round
Into the dark with mazy error.

VIII.

All at once I looked up with terror.
He was there.
He himself with his human air.
On the narrow pathway, just before.
I saw the back of him, no more—
He had left the chapel, then, as I.
I forgot all about the sky.
No face: only the sight
Of a sweepy garment, vast and white,
With a hem that I could recognize.
I felt terror, no surprise;
My mind filled with the cataract
At one bound of the mighty fact.
"I remember, he did say
Doubtless that, to this world's end,
Where two or three should meet and pray,
He would be in the midst, their friend;
Certainly he was there with them!"
And my pulses leaped for joy
Of the golden thought without alloy,
That I saw his very vesture's hem.
Then rushed the blood back, cold and clear,
With a fresh enhancing shiver of fear;
And I hastened, cried out while I pressed
To the salvation of the vest,
"But not so, Lord! It cannot be
That thou, indeed, art leaving me—
Me, that have despised thy friends!
Did my heart make no amends?
Thou art the love of God—above
His power, didst hear me place his love,
And that was leaving the world for thee.

Therefore thou must not turn from me
As I had chosen the other part!
Folly and pride o'ercame my heart.
Our best is bad, nor bears thy test;
Still, it should be our very best.
I thought it best that thou, the spirit,
Be worshipped in spirit and in truth,
And in beauty, as even we require it—
Not in the forms burlesque, uncouth,
I left but now, as scarcely fitted
For thee: I knew not what I pitied.
But, all I felt there, right or wrong,
What is it to thee, who curest sinning?
Am I not weak as thou art strong?
I have looked to thee from the beginning,
Straight up to thee through all the world
Which, like an idle scroll, lay furled
To nothingness on either side:
And since the time thou wast descried,
Spite of the weak heart, so have I
Lived ever, and so fain would die,
Living and dying, thee before!
But if thou leavest me"—

IX.

Less or more,
I suppose that I spoke thus.
When,—have mercy, Lord, on us!
The whole face turned upon me full.
And I spread myself beneath it,
As when the bleacher spreads, to seethe it
In the cleansing sun, his wool,—
Steeps in the flood of noontide whiteness
Some defiled, discolored web—
So lay I, saturate with brightness.
And when the flood appeared to ebb,
Lo, I was walking, light and swift,
With my senses settling fast and steadying,
But my body caught up in the whirl and drift
Of the vesture's amplitude, still eddying
On, just before me, still to be followed,
As it carried me after with its motion:
What shall I say?—as a path were hollowed
And a man went weltering through the ocean,
Sucked along in the flying wake
Of the luminous water-snake.

Darkness and cold were cloven, as through
I passed, upborne yet walking too.
And I turned to myself at intervals,—
"So he said, so it befalls.
God who registers the cup
Of mere cold water, for his sake
To a disciple rendered up,
Disdains not his own thirst to slake
At the poorest love was ever offered:
And because my heart I proffered,
With true love trembling at the brim,
He suffers me to follow him
Forever, my own way,—dispensed
From seeking to be influenced
By all the less immediate ways
That earth, in worships manifold,
Adopts to reach, by prayer and praise,
The garment's hem, which, lo, I hold!"

x.

And so we crossed the world and stopped.
For where am I, in city or plain,
Since I am 'ware of the world again?
And what is this that rises propped
With pillars of prodigious girth?
Is it really on the earth,
This miraculous Dome of God?
Has the angel's measuring-rod
Which numbered cubits, gem from gem,
'Twixt the gates of the New Jerusalem,
Meted it out,—and what he meted,
Have the sons of men completed?
—Binding, ever as he bade,
Columns in the colonnade
With arms wide open to embrace
The entry of the human race
To the breast of . . . what is it, yon building,
Ablaze in front, all paint and gilding,
With marble for brick, and stones of price
For garniture of the edifice?
Now I see; it is no dream;
It stands there and it does not seem:
Forever, in pictures, thus it looks,
And thus I have read of it in books
Often in England, leagues away,

And wondered how these fountains play,
Growing up eternally
Each to a musical water-tree,
Whose blossoms drop, a glittering boon,
Before my eyes, in the light of the moon,
To the granite lavers underneath.
Liar and dreamer in your teeth!
I, the sinner that speak to you,
Was in Rome this night, and stood, and knew
Both this and more. For see, for see,
The dark is rent, mine eye is free
To pierce the crust of the outer wall,
And I view inside, and all there, all,
As the swarming hollow of a hive,
The whole Basilica alive!
Men in the chancel, body and nave,
Men on the pillars' architrave,
Men on the statues, men on the tombs
With popes and kings in their porphyry wombs,
All famishing in expectation
Of the main-altar's consummation.
For see, for see, the rapturous moment
Approaches, and earth's best endowment
Blends with heaven's; the taper-fires
Pant up, the winding brazen spires
Heave loftier yet the baldachin;
The incense-gaspings, long kept in,
Suspire in clouds; the organ blatant
Holds his breath and grovels latent,
As if God's hushing finger grazed him,
(Like Behemoth when he praised him)
At the silver bell's shrill tinkling,
Quick cold drops of terror sprinkling
On the sudden pavement strewed
With faces of the multitude.
Earth breaks up, time drops away,
In flows heaven, with its new day
Of endless life, when He who trod,
Very man and very God,
This earth in weakness, shame and pain,
Dying the death whose signs remain
Up yonder on the accursed tree,—
Shall come again, no more to be
Of captivity the thrall,
But the one God, All in all,
King of kings, Lord of lords,

As His servant John received the words,
"I died, and live forevermore!"

XI.

Yet I was left outside the door.
"Why sit I here on the threshold-stone,
Left till He return, alone
Save for the garment's extreme fold
Abandoned still to bless my hold?"
My reason, to my doubt, replied,
As if a book were opened wide,
And at a certain page I traced
Every record undefaced,
Added by successive years,—
The harvestings of truth's stray ears
Singly gleaned, and in one sheaf
Bound together for belief.
Yes, I said—that he will go
And sit with these in turn, I know.
Their faith's heart beats, though her head swims
Too giddily to guide her limbs,
Disabled by their palsy-stroke
From propping mine. Though Rome's gross yoke
Drops off, no more to be endured,
Her teaching is not so obscured
By errors and perversities,
That no truth shines athwart the lies:
And he, whose eye detects a spark
Even where, to man's, the whole seems dark,
May well see flame where each beholder
Acknowledges the embers smoulder.
But I, a mere man, fear to quit
The clue God gave me as most fit
To guide my footsteps through life's maze,
Because himself discerns all ways
Open to reach him: I, a man
Able to mark where faith began
To swerve aside, till from its summit
Judgment drops her damning plummet,
Pronouncing such a fatal space
Departed from the founder's base:
He will not bid me enter too,
But rather sit, as now I do,
Awaiting his return outside.
—'Twas thus my reason straight replied

And joyously I turned, and pressed
The garment's skirt upon my breast,
Until, afresh its light suffusing me,
My heart cried—"What has been abusing me
That I should wait here lonely and coldly,
Instead of rising, entering boldly,
Baring truth's face, and letting drift
Her veils of lies as they choose to shift?
Do these men praise him? I will raise
My voice up to their point of praise!
I see the error; but above
The scope of error, see the love.—
Oh, love of those first Christian days!
—Fanned so soon into a blaze,
From the spark preserved by the trampled sect,
That the antique sovereign Intellect
Which then sat ruling in the world,
Like a change in dreams, was hurled
From the throne he reigned upon:
You looked up and he was gone.
Gone, his glory of the pen!
—Love, with Greece and Rome in ken,
Bade her scribes abhor the trick
Of poetry and rhetoric,
And exult with hearts set free,
In blessed imbecility
Scrawled, perchance, on some torn sheet
Leaving Sallust incomplete.
Gone, his pride of sculptor, painter!
—Love, while able to acquaint her
While the thousand statues yet
Fresh from chisel, pictures wet
From brush, she saw on every side,
Chose rather with an infant's pride
To frame those portents which impart
Such unction to true Christian Art.
Gone, music too! The air was stirred
By happy wings: Terpander's bird
(That, when the cold came, fled away)
Would tarry not the wintry day,—
As more-enduring sculpture must,
Till filthy saints rebuked the gust
With which they chanced to get a sight
Of some dear naked Aphrodite
They glanced a thought above the toes of,
By breaking zealously her nose off.

Love, surely, from that music's lingering,
Might have filched her organ-fingering,
Nor chosen rather to set prayings
To hog-grunts, praises to horse-neighings.
Love was the startling thing, the new:
Love was the all-sufficient too;
And seeing that, you see the rest:
As a babe can find its mother's breast
As well in darkness as in light,
Love shut our eyes, and all seemed right.
True, the world's eyes are open now:
—Less need for me to disallow
Some few that keep Love's zone unbuckled,
Peevish as ever to be suckled,
Lulled by the same old baby-prattle
With intermixture of the rattle,
When she would have them creep, stand steady
Upon their feet, or walk already,
Not to speak of trying to climb.
I will be wise another time,
And not desire a wall between us,
When next I see a church-roof cover
So many species of one genus,
All with foreheads bearing *lover*
Written above the earnest eyes of them;
All with breasts that beat for beauty,
Whether sublimed, to the surprise of them,
In noble daring, steadfast duty,
The heroic in passion, or in action,—
Or, lowered for sense's satisfaction,
To the mere outside of human creatures,
Mere perfect form and faultless features.
What? with all Rome here, whence to levy
Such contributions to their appetite,
With women and men in a gorgeous bevy,
They take, as it were, a padlock, clap it tight
On their southern eyes, restrained from feeding
On the glories of their ancient reading,
On the beauties of their modern singing,
On the wonders of the builder's bringing,
On the majesties of Art around them,—
And, all these loves, late struggling incessant,
When faith has at last united and bound them,
They offer up to God for a present?
Why, I will, on the whole, be rather proud of it,—
And, only taking the act in reference

To the other recipients who might have allowed it,
I will rejoice that God had the preference."

XII.

So I summed up my new resolves:
Too much love there can never be.
And where the intellect devolves
Its function on love exclusively,
I, a man who possesses both,
Will accept the provision, nothing loth,
—Will feast my love, then depart elsewhere,
That my intellect may find its share.
And ponder, O soul, the while thou departest,
And see thou applaud the great heart of the artist,
Who, examining the capabilities
Of the block of marble he has to fashion
Into a type of thought or passion,—
Not always, using obvious facilities,
Shapes it, as any artist can,
Into a perfect symmetrical man,
Complete from head to foot of the life-size,
Such as old Adam stood in his wife's eyes,—
But, now and then, bravely aspires to consummate
A Colossus by no means so easy to come at,
And uses the whole of his block for the bust,
Leaving the mind of the public to finish it,
Since cut it ruefully short he must:
On the face alone he expends his devotion,
He rather would mar than resolve to diminish it,
—Saying, "Applaud me for this grand notion
Of what a face may be! As for completing it
In breast and body and limbs, do that, you!"
All hail! I fancy how, happily meeting it,
A trunk and legs would perfect the statue,
Could man carve so as to answer volition.
And how much nobler than petty cavils,
Were a hope to find, in my spirit-travels,
Some artist of another ambition,
Who having a block to carve, no bigger,
Has spent his power on the opposite quest,
And believed to begin at the feet was best—
For so may I see, ere I die, the whole figure!

XIII.

No sooner said than out in the night!
My heart beat lighter and more light:

And still, as before, I was walking swift,
With my senses settling fast and steadying,
But my body caught up in the whirl and drift
Of the vesture's amplitude, still eddying
On just before me, still to be followed,
As it carried me after with its motion,
—What shall I say?—as a path were hollowed,
And a man went weltering through the ocean,
Sucked along in the flying wake
Of the luminous water-snake.

XIV.

Alone! I am left alone once more—
(Save for the garment's extreme fold
Abandoned still to bless my hold)
Alone, beside the entrance-door
Of a sort of temple,—perhaps a college,
—Like nothing I ever saw before
At home in England, to my knowledge.
The tall old quaint irregular town!
It may be . . . though which, I can't affirm . . . any
Of the famous middle-age towns of Germany;
And this flight of stairs where I sit down,
Is it Halle, Weimar, Cassel, Frankfort,
Or Göttingen, I have to thank for 't?
It may be Göttingen,—most likely.
Through the open door I catch obliquely
Glimpses of a lecture-hall;
And not a bad assembly neither,
Ranged decent and symmetrical
On benches, waiting what's to see there;
Which, holding still by the vesture's hem,
I also resolve to see with them,
Cautious this time how I suffer to slip
The chance of joining in fellowship
With any that call themselves his friends;
As these folks do, I have a notion.
But hist—a buzzing and emotion!
All settle themselves, the while ascends
By the creaking rail to the lecture-desk,
Step by step, deliberate
Because of his cranium's over-freight,
Three parts sublime to one grotesque,
If I have proved an accurate guesser,
The hawk-nosed, high-cheekboned Professor.
I felt at once as if there ran

A shoot of love from my heart to the man—
That sallow virgin-minded studious
Martyr to mild enthusiasm,
As he uttered a kind of cough-preludious
That woke my sympathetic spasm,
(Beside some spitting that made me sorry)
And stood, surveying his auditory
With a wan pure look, wellnigh celestial,—
Those blue eyes had survived so much!
While, under the foot they could not smutch,
Lay all the fleshly and the bestial.
Over he bowed, and arranged his notes,
Till the auditory's clearing of throats
Was done with, died into a silence;
And, when each glance was upward sent,
Each bearded mouth composed intent,
And a pin might be heard drop half a mile hence,—
He pushed back higher his spectacles,
Let the eyes stream out like lamps from cells,
And giving his head of hair—a hake
Of undressed tow, for color and quantity—
One rapid and impatient shake,
(As our own young England adjusts a jaunty tie
When about to impart, on mature digestion,
Some thrilling view of the surplice-question)
—The Professor's grave voice, sweet though hoarse,
Broke into his Christmas-Eve discourse.

xv.

And he began it by observing
How reason dictated that men
Should rectify the natural swerving,
By a reversion, now and then,
To the well-heads of knowledge, few
And far away, whence rolling grew
The life-stream wide whereat we drink,
Commingled, as we needs must think,
With waters alien to the source;
To do which, aimed this eve's discourse;
Since, where could be a fitter time
For tracing backward to its prime,
This Christianity, this lake,
This reservoir, whereat we slake,
From one or other bank, our thirst?
So, he proposed inquiring first
Into the various sources whence

This Myth of Christ is derivable;
Demanding from the evidence,
(Since plainly no such life was livable)
How these phenomena should class?
Whether 'twere best opine Christ was,
Or never was at all, or whether
He was and was not, both together—
It matters little for the name,
So the idea be left the same.
Only, for practical purpose' sake,
'Twas obviously as well to take
The popular story,—understanding
How the ineptitude of the time,
And the penman's prejudice, expanding
Fact into fable fit for the clime,
Had, by slow and sure degrees, translated it
Into this myth, this Individuum,—
Which, when reason had strained and abated it
Of foreign matter, left, for residuum,
A Man!—a right true man, however,
Whose work was worthy a man's endeavor:
Work, that gave warrant almost sufficient
To his disciples, for rather believing
He was just omnipotent and omniscient,
As it gives to us, for as frankly receiving
His word, their tradition,—which, though it meant
Something entirely different
From all that those who only heard it,
In their simplicity thought and averred it,
Had yet a meaning quite as respectable:
For, among other doctrines delectable,
Was he not surely the first to insist on
The natural sovereignty of our race?—
Here the lecturer came to a pausing-place.
And while his cough, like a droughty piston,
Tried to dislodge the husk that grew to him,
I seized the occasion of bidding adieu to him,
The vesture still within my hand.

XVI.

I could interpret its command.
This time he would not bid me enter
The exhausted air-bell of the Critic.
Truth's atmosphere may grow mephitic
When Papist struggles with Dissenter,
Impregnating its pristine clarity,

—One, by his daily fare's vulgarity,
Its gust of broken meat and garlic;
—One, by his soul's too-much presuming
To turn the frankincense's fuming
And vapors of the candle starlike
Into the cloud her wings she buoys on.
Each, that thus sets the pure air seething,
May poison it for healthy breathing—
But the Critic leaves no air to poison;
Pumps out with ruthless ingenuity
Atom by atom, and leaves you—vacuity.
Thus much of Christ does he reject?
And what retain? His intellect?
What is it I must reverence duly?
Poor intellect for worship, truly,
Which tells me simply what was told
(If mere morality, bereft
Of the God in Christ, be all that's left)
Elsewhere by voices manifold;
With this advantage, that the stater
Made nowise the important stumble
Of adding, he, the sage and humble,
Was also one with the Creator.
You urge Christ's followers' simplicity:
But how does shifting blame evade it?
Have wisdom's words no more felicity?
The stumbling-block, his speech—who laid it?
How comes it that for one found able
To sift the truth of it from fable,
Millions believe it to the letter?
Christ's goodness, then—does that fare better?
Strange goodness, which upon the score
Of being goodness, the mere due
Of man to fellow-man, much more
To God—should take another view
Of its possessor's privilege,
And bid him rule his race! You pledge
Your fealty to such rule? What, all—
From heavenly John and Attic Paul,
And that brave weather-battered Peter,
Whose stout faith only stood completer
For buffets, sinning to be pardoned,
As, more his hands hauled nets, they hardened,—
All, down to you, the man of men,
Professing here at Göttingen,
Compose Christ's flock! They, you and I,

Are sheep of a good man! And why?
The goodness,—how did he acquire it?
Was it self-gained, did God inspire it?
Choose which; then tell me, on what ground
Should its possessor dare propound
His claim to rise o'er us an inch?
Were goodness all some man's invention,
Who arbitrarily made mention
What we should follow, and whence flinch,—
What qualities might take the style
Of right and wrong,—and had such guessing
Met with as general acquiescing
As graced the alphabet erewhile,
When A got leave an Ox to be,
No Camel (quoth the Jews) like G,—
For thus inventing thing and title
Worship were that man's fit requital.
But if the common conscience must
Be ultimately judge, adjust
Its apt name to each quality
Already known,—I would decree
Worship for such mere demonstration
And simple work of nomenclature,
Only the day I praised, not nature,
But Harvey, for the circulation.
I would praise such a Christ, with pride
And joy, that he, as none beside,
Had taught us how to keep the mind
God gave him, as God gave his kind,
Freer than they from fleshly taint:
I would call such a Christ our Saint,
As I declare our Poet, him
Whose insight makes all others dim:
A thousand poets pried at life,
And only one amid the strife
Rose to be Shakespeare: each shall take
His crown, I'd say, for the world's sake—
Though some objected—"Had we seen
The heart and head of each, what screen
Was broken there to give them light,
While in ourselves it shuts the sight,
We should no more admire, perchance,
That these found truth out at a glance,
Than marvel how the bat discerns
Some pitch-dark cavern's fifty turns,
Led by a finer tact, a gift

He boasts, which other birds must shift
Without, and grope as best they can."
No, freely I would praise the man,—
Nor one whit more, if he contended
That gift of his from God descended.
Ah friend, what gift of man's does not?
No nearer something, by a jot,
Rise an infinity of nothings
Than one: take Euclid for your teacher:
Distinguish kinds: do crownings, clothings,
Make that creator which was creature?
Multiply gifts upon man's head,
And what, when all's done, shall be said
But—the more gifted he, I ween!
That one's made Christ, this other, Pilate,
And this might be all that has been,—
So what is there to frown or smile at?
What is left for us, save, in growth
Of soul, to rise up, far past both,
From the gift looking to the giver,
And from the cistern to the river,
And from the finite to infinity,
And from man's dust to God's divinity?

XVII.

Take all in a word: the truth in God's breast
Lies trace for trace upon ours impressed:
Though he is so bright and we so dim,
We are made in his image to witness him:
And were no eye in us to tell,
Instructed by no inner sense,
The light of heaven from the dark of hell,
That light would want its evidence,—
Though justice, good and truth were still
Divine, if, by some demon's will,
Hatred and wrong had been proclaimed
Law through the worlds, and right misnamed.
No mere exposition of morality
Made or in part or in totality,
Should win you to give it worship, therefore:
And, if no better proof you will care for,
—Whom do you count the worst man upon earth?
Be sure, he knows, in his conscience, more
Of what right is, than arrives at birth
In the best man's acts that we bow before:
This last knows better—true, but my fact is,

'Tis one thing to know, and another to practise.
And thence I conclude that the real God-function
Is to furnish a motive and injunction
For practising what we know already.
And such an injunction and such a motive
As the God in Christ, do you waive, and "heady,
High-minded," hang your tablet-votive
Outside the fane on a finger-post?
Morality to the uttermost,
Supreme in Christ as we all confess,
Why need we prove would avail no jot
To make him God, if God he were not?
What is the point where himself lays stress?
Does the precept run "Believe in good,
In justice, truth, now understood
For the first time"?—or, "Believe in me,
Who lived and died, yet essentially
Am Lord of Life"? Whoever can take
The same to his heart and for mere love's sake
Conceive of the love,—that man obtains
A new truth; no conviction gains
Of an old one only, made intense
By a fresh appeal to his faded sense.

XVIII.

Can it be that he stays inside?
Is the vesture left me to commune with?
Could my soul find aught to sing in tune with
Even at this lecture, if she tried?
Oh, let me at lowest sympathize
With the lurking drop of blood that lies
In the desiccated brain's white roots
Without throb for Christ's attributes,
As the lecturer makes his special boast!
If love's dead there, it has left a ghost.
Admire we, how from heart to brain
(Though to say so strike the doctors dumb)
One instinct rises and falls again,
Restoring the equilibrium.
And how when the Critic had done his best,
And the pearl of price, at reason's test,
Lay dust and ashes levigable
On the Professor's lecture-table,—
When we looked for the inference and monition
That our faith, reduced to such condition,
Be swept forthwith to its natural dust-hole,—

He bids us, when we least expect it,
Take back our faith,—if it be not just whole,
Yet a pearl indeed, as his tests affect it,
Which fact pays damage done rewardingly,
So, prize we our dust and ashes accordingly!
"Go home and venerate the myth
I thus have experimented with—
This man, continue to adore him
Rather than all who went before him,
And all who ever followed after!"—
Surely for this I may praise you, my brother!
Will you take the praise in tears or laughter?
That's one point gained: can I compass another?
Unlearned love was safe from spurning—
Can't we respect your loveless learning?
Let us at least give learning honor!
What laurels had we showered upon her,
Girding her loins up to perturb
Our theory of the Middle Verb;
Or Turk-like brandishing a scimitar
O'er anapæsts in comic-trimeter;
Or curing the halt and maimed "Iketides,"
While we lounged on at our indebted ease:
Instead of which, a tricksy demon
Sets her at Titus or Philemon!
When ignorance wags his ears of leather
And hates God's word, 'tis altogether;
Nor leaves he his congenial thistles
To go and browse on Paul's Epistles.
—And you, the audience, who might ravage
The world wide, enviably savage,
Nor heed the cry of the retriever,
More than Herr Heine (before his fever),—
I do not tell a lie so arrant
As say my passion's wings are furled up,
And, without plainest heavenly warrant,
I were ready and glad to give the world up—
But still, when you rub brow meticulous,
And ponder the profit of turning holy
If not for God's, for your own sake solely,
—God forbid I should find you ridiculous!
Deduce from this lecture all that eases you,
Nay, call yourselves, if the calling pleases you,
"Christians,"—abhor the deist's pravity,—
Go on, you shall no more move my gravity
Than, when I see boys ride a-cockhorse,

I find it in my heart to embarrass them
By hinting that their stick's a mock horse,
And they really carry what they say carries them.

XIX.

So sat I talking with my mind.
I did not long to leave the door
And find a new church, as before,
But rather was quiet and inclined
To prolong and enjoy the gentle resting
From further tracking and trying and testing.
"This tolerance is a genial mood!"
(Said I, and a little pause ensued.)
"One trims the bark 'twixt shoal and shelf,
And sees, each side, the good effects of it,
A value for religion's self,
A carelessness about the sects of it.
Let me enjoy my own conviction,
Not watch my neighbor's faith with fretfulness,
Still spying there some dereliction
Of truth, perversity, forgetfulness!
Better a mild indifferentism,
Teaching that both our faiths (though duller
His shine through a dull spirit's prism)
Originally had one color!
Better pursue a pilgrimage
Through ancient and through modern times
To many peoples, various climes,
Where I may see saint, savage, sage
Fuse their respective creeds in one
Before the general Father's throne!"

XX.

—'Twas the horrible storm began afresh!
The black night caught me in his mesh,
Whirled me up, and flung me prone.
I was left on the college-step alone.
I looked, and far there, ever fleeting
Far, far away, the receding gesture,
And looming of the lessening vesture!—
Swept forward from my stupid hand,
While I watched my foolish heart expand
In the lazy glow of benevolence,
O'er the various modes of man's belief.
I sprang up with fear's vehemence.
Needs must there be one way, our chief

Best way of worship: let me strive
To find it, and when found, contrive
My fellows also take their share!
This constitutes my earthly care:
God's is above it and distinct.
For I, a man, with men am linked
And not a brute with brutes; no gain
That I experience, must remain
Unshared: but should my best endeavor
To share it, fail—subsisteth ever
God's care above, and I exult
That God, by God's own ways occult,
May—doth, I will believe—bring back
All wanderers to a single track.
Meantime, I can but testify
God's care for me—no more, can I—
It is but for myself I know;
The world rolls witnessing around me
Only to leave me as it found me;
Men cry there, but my ear is slow:
Their races flourish or decay
—What boots it, while yon lucid way
Loaded with stars divides the vault?
But soon my soul repairs its fault
When, sharpening sense's hebetude,
She turns on my own life! So viewed,
No mere mote's-breadth but teems immense
With witnessings of providence:
And woe to me if when I look
Upon that record, the sole book
Unsealed to me, I take no heed
Of any warning that I read!
Have I been sure, this Christmas-Eve,
God's own hand did the rainbow weave,
Whereby the truth from heaven slid
Into my soul?—I cannot bid
The world admit he stooped to heal
My soul, as if in a thunder-peal
Where one heard noise, and one saw flame,
I only knew he named my name:
But what is the world to me, for sorrow
Or joy in its censure, when to-morrow
It drops the remark, with just-turned head,
Then, on again, "That man is dead"?
Yes, but for me—my name called,—drawn
As a conscript's lot from the lap's black yawn,

He has dipt into on a battle-dawn:
Bid out of life by a nod, a glance,—
Stumbling, mute-mazed, at nature's chance,—
With a rapid finger circled round,
Fixed to the first poor inch of ground
To fight from, where his foot was found;
Whose ear but a minute since lay free
To the wide camp's buzz and gossipry—
Summoned, a solitary man,
To end his life where his life began,
From the safe glad rear, to the dreadful van!
Soul of mine, hadst thou caught and held
By the hem of the vesture!—

XXI.

And I caught
At the flying robe, and unrepelled
Was lapped again in its folds full-fraught
With warmth and wonder and delight,
God's mercy being infinite.
For scarce had the words escaped my tongue,
When, at a passionate bound, I sprung
Out of the wandering world of rain,
Into the little chapel again.

XXII.

How else was I found there, bolt upright
On my bench, as if I had never left it?
—Never flung out on the common at night,
Nor met the storm and wedge-like cleft it,
Seen the raree-show of Peter's successor,
Or the laboratory of the Professor!
For the Vision, that was true, I wist,
True as that heaven and earth exist.
There sat my friend, the yellow and tall,
With his neck and its wen in the selfsame place;
Yet my nearest neighbor's cheek showed gall.
She had slid away a contemptuous space:
And the old fat woman, late so placable,
Eyed me with symptoms, hardly mistakable,
Of her milk of kindness turning rancid.
In short, a spectator might have fancied
That I had nodded, betrayed by slumber,
Yet kept my seat, a warning ghastly,
Through the heads of the sermon, nine in number,
And woke up now at the tenth and lastly.

But again, could such disgrace have happened?
Each friend at my elbow had surely nudged it;
And, as for the sermon, where did my nap end?
Unless I heard it, could I have judged it?
Could I report as I do at the close,
First, the preacher speaks through his nose:
Second, his gesture is too emphatic:
Thirdly, to waive what's pedagogic,
The subject-matter itself lacks logic:
Fourthly, the English is ungrammatic.
Great news! the preacher is found no Pascal,
Whom, if I pleased, I might to the task call
Of making square to a finite eye
The circle of infinity,
And find so all-but-just-succeeding!
Great news! the sermon proves no reading
Where bee-like in the flowers I bury me,
Like Taylor's the immortal Jeremy!
And now that I know the very worst of him,
What was it I thought to obtain at first of him?
Ha! Is God mocked, as he asks?
Shall I take on me to change his tasks,
And dare, dispatched to a river-head
For a simple draught of the element,
Neglect the thing for which he sent,
And return with another thing instead?—
Saying, "Because the water found
Welling up from underground,
Is mingled with the taints of earth,
While thou, I know, dost laugh at dearth,
And couldst, at wink or word, convulse
The world with the leap of a river-pulse,—
Therefore I turned from the oozings muddy,
And bring thee a chalice I found, instead:
See the brave veins in the breccia ruddy!
One would suppose that the marble bled.
What matters the water? A hope I have nursed:
The waterless cup will quench my thirst."
—Better have knelt at the poorest stream
That trickles in pain from the straitest rift!
For the less or the more is all God's gift,
Who blocks up or breaks wide the granite-seam.
And here, is there water or not, to drink?
I then, in ignorance and weakness,
Taking God's help, have attained to think
My heart does best to receive in meekness

That mode of worship, as most to his mind,
Where earthly aids being cast behind,
His All in All appears serene
With the thinnest human veil between,
Letting the mystic lamps, the seven,
The many motions of his spirit,
Pass, as they list, to earth from heaven.
For the preacher's merit or demerit,
It were to be wished the flaws were fewer
In the earthen vessel, holding treasure
Which lies as safe in a golden ewer;
But the main thing is, does it hold good measure?
Heaven soon sets right all other matters!—
Ask, else, these ruins of humanity,
This flesh worn out to rags and tatters,
This soul at struggle with insanity,
Who thence take comfort—can I doubt?—
Which an empire gained, were a loss without.
May it be mine! And let us hope
That no worse blessing befall the Pope,
Turn'd sick at last of to-day's buffoonery,
Of posturings and petticoatings,
Beside his Bourbon bully's gloatings
In the bloody orgies of drunk poltroonery!
Nor may the Professor forego its peace
At Göttingen presently, when, in the dusk
Of his life, if his cough, as I fear, should increase,
Prophesied of by that horrible husk—
When thicker and thicker the darkness fills
The world through his misty spectacles,
And he gropes for something more substantial
Than a fable, myth or personification,—
May Christ do for him what no mere man shall,
And stand confessed as the God of salvation!
Meantime, in the still recurring fear
Lest myself, at unawares, be found,
While attacking the choice of my neighbors round,
With none of my own made—I choose here!
The giving out of the hymn reclaims me;
I have done: and if any blames me,
Thinking that merely to touch in brevity
The topics I dwell on, were unlawful,—
Or worse, that I trench, with undue levity,
On the bounds of the holy and the awful,—
I praise the heart, and pity the head of him,
And refer myself to THEE, instead of him,

Who head and heart alike discernest,
Looking below light speech we utter,
When frothy spume and frequent sputter
Prove that the soul's depths boil in earnest!
May truth shine out, stand ever before us!
I put up pencil and join chorus
To Hepzibah Tune, without further apology,
The last five verses of the third section
Of the seventeenth hymn of Whitfield's Collection,
To conclude with the doxology.

MEN AND WOMEN

☆

HOW IT STRIKES A CONTEMPORARY

I ONLY knew one poet in my life:
And this, or something like it, was his way.

You saw go up and down Valladolid,
A man of mark, to know next time you saw.
His very serviceable suit of black
Was courtly once and conscientious still,
And many might have worn it, though none did:
The cloak, that somewhat shone and showed the threads,
Had purpose, and the ruff, significance.
He walked and tapped the pavement with his cane,
Scenting the world, looking it full in face,
An old dog, bald and blindish, at his heels.
They turned up, now, the alley by the church,
That leads no whither; now, they breathed themselves
On the main promenade just at the wrong time:
You'd come upon his scrutinizing hat,
Making a peaked shade blacker than itself
Against the single window spared some house
Intact yet with its mouldered Moorish work,—
Or else surprise the ferrel of his stick
Trying the mortar's temper 'tween the chinks
Of some new shop a-building, French and fine.
He stood and watched the cobbler at his trade,
The man who slices lemons into drink,
The coffee-roaster's brazier, and the boys
That volunteer to help him turn its winch.
He glanced o'er books on stalls with half an eye,
And fly-leaf ballads on the vender's string,

And broad-edge bold-print posters by the wall.
He took such cognizance of men and things,
If any beat a horse, you felt he saw;
If any cursed a woman, he took note;
Yet stared at nobody,—you stared at him,
And found, less to your pleasure than surprise,
He seemed to know you and expect as much.
So, next time that a neighbor's tongue was loosed,
It marked the shameful and notorious fact,
We had among us, not so much a spy,
As a recording chief-inquisitor,
The town's true master if the town but knew!
We merely kept a governor for form,
While this man walked about and took account
Of all thought, said and acted, then went home,
And wrote it fully to our Lord the King
Who has an itch to know things, he knows why,
And reads them in his bedroom of a night.
Oh, you might smile! there wanted not a touch,
A tang of . . . well, it was not wholly ease
As back into your mind the man's look came.
Stricken in years a little,—such a brow
His eyes had to live under!—clear as flint
On either side the formidable nose
Curved, cut and colored like an eagle's claw.
Had he to do with A's surprising fate?
When altogether old B disappeared
And young C got his mistress,—was 't our friend,
His letter to the King, that did it all?
What paid the bloodless man for so much pains?
Our Lord the King has favorites manifold,
And shifts his ministry some once a month;
Our city gets new governors at whiles,—
But never word or sign, that I could hear,
Notified to this man about the streets
The King's approval of those letters conned
The last thing duly at the dead of night.
Did the man love his office? Frowned our Lord,
Exhorting when none heard—"Beseech me not!
Too far above my people,—beneath me!
I set the watch,—how should the people know?
Forget them, keep me all the more in mind!"
Was some such understanding 'twixt the two?

    I found no truth in one report at least—
That if you tracked him to his home, down lanes

Beyond the Jewry, and as clean to pace,
You found he ate his supper in a room
Blazing with lights, four Titians on the wall,
And twenty naked girls to change his plate!
Poor man, he lived another kind of life
In that new stuccoed third house by the bridge,
Fresh-painted, rather smart than otherwise!
The whole street might o'erlook him as he sat,
Leg crossing leg, one foot on the dog's back,
Playing a decent cribbage with his maid
(Jacynth, you're sure her name was) o'er the cheese
And fruit, three red halves of starved winter-pears,
Or treat of radishes in April. Nine,
Ten, struck the church clock, straight to bed went he.

My father, like the man of sense he was,
Would point him out to me a dozen times;
" 'St—'st," he'd whisper, "the Corregidor!"
I had been used to think that personage
Was one with lacquered breeches, lustrous belt,
And feathers like a forest in his hat,
Who blew a trumpet and proclaimed the news,
Announced the bull-fights, gave each church its turn,
And memorized the miracle in vogue!
He had a great observance from us boys;
We were in error; that was not the man.

I'd like now, yet had haply been afraid,
To have just looked, when this man came to die,
And seen who lined the clean gay garret-sides
And stood about the neat low truckle-bed,
With the heavenly manner of relieving guard.
Here had been, mark, the general-in-chief,
Through a whole campaign of the world's life and death,
Doing the King's work all the dim day long,
In his old coat and up to knees in mud,
Smoked like a herring, dining on a crust,—
And, now the day was won, relieved at once!
No further show or need for that old coat,
You are sure, for one thing! Bless us, all the while
How sprucely we are dressed out, you and I!
A second, and the angels alter that.
Well, I could never write a verse,—could you?
Let's to the Prado and make the most of time.

FRA LIPPO LIPPI

I AM poor brother Lippo, by your leave!
You need not clap your torches to my face.
Zooks, what's to blame? you think you see a monk!
What, 'tis past midnight, and you go the rounds,
And here you catch me at an alley's end
Where sportive ladies leave their doors ajar?
The Carmine's my cloister: hunt it up,
Do,—harry out, if you must show your zeal,
Whatever rat, there, haps on his wrong hole,
And nip each softling of a wee white mouse,
Weke, weke, that's crept to keep him company!
Aha, you know your betters! Then, you'll take
Your hand away that's fiddling on my throat,
And please to know me likewise. Who am I?
Why, one, sir, who is lodging with a friend
Three streets off—he's a certain . . . how d'ye call?
Master—a . . . Cosimo of the Medici,
I' the house that caps the corner. Boh! you were best!
Remember and tell me, the day you're hanged,
How you affected such a gullet's-gripe!
But you, sir, it concerns you that your knaves
Pick up a manner nor discredit you:
Zooks, are we pilchards, that they sweep the streets
And count fair prize what comes into their net?
He's Judas to a tittle, that man is!
Just such a face! Why, sir, you make amends.
Lord, I'm not angry! Bid your hangdogs go
Drink out this quarter-florin to the health
Of the munificent House that harbors me
(And many more beside, lads! more beside!)
And all's come square again. I'd like his face—
His, elbowing on his comrade in the door
With the pike and lantern,—for the slave that holds
John Baptist's head a-dangle by the hair
With one hand ("Look you, now," as who should say)
And his weapon in the other, yet unwiped!
It's not your chance to have a bit of chalk,
A wood-coal or the like? or you should see!
Yes, I'm the painter, since you style me so.
What, brother Lippo's doings, up and down,
You know them and they take you? like enough!
I saw the proper twinkle in your eye—
'Tell you, I liked your looks at very first.

Let's sit and set things straight now, hip to haunch.
Here's spring come, and the nights one makes up bands
To roam the town and sing out carnival,
And I've been three weeks shut within my mew,
A-painting for the great man, saints and saints
And saints again. I could not paint all night—
Ouf! I leaned out of window for fresh air.
There came a hurry of feet and little feet,
A sweep of lute-strings, laughs, and whifts of song,—
Flower o' the broom,
Take away love, and our earth is a tomb!
Flower o' the quince,
I let Lisa go, and what good in life since?
Flower o' the thyme—and so on. Round they went.
Scarce had they turned the corner when a titter
Like the skipping of rabbits by moonlight,—three slim shapes,
And a face that looked up . . . zooks, sir, flesh and blood,
That's all I'm made of! Into shreds it went,
Curtain and counterpane and coverlet,
All the bed-furniture—a dozen knots,
There was a ladder! Down I let myself,
Hands and feet, scrambling somehow, and so dropped,
And after them. I came up with the fun
Hard by Saint Laurence, hail fellow, well met,—
Flower o' the rose,
If I've been merry, what matter who knows?
And so as I was stealing back again
To get to bed and have a bit of sleep
Ere I rise up to-morrow and go work
On Jerome knocking at his poor old breast
With his great round stone to subdue the flesh,
You snap me of the sudden. Ah, I see!
Though your eye twinkles still, you shake your head—
Mine's shaved--a monk, you say—the sting's in that!
If Master Cosimo announced himself,
Mum's the word naturally; but a monk!
Come, what am I a beast for? tell us, now!
I was a baby when my mother died
And father died and left me in the street.
I starved there, God knows how, a year or two
On fig-skins, melon-parings, rinds and shucks,
Refuse and rubbish. One fine frosty day,
My stomach being empty as your hat,
The wind doubled me up and down I went.
Old Aunt Lapaccia trussed me with one hand,
(Its fellow was a stinger as I knew)

And so along the wall, over the bridge,
By the straight cut to the convent. Six words there,
While I stood munching my first bread that month:
"So, boy, you're minded," quoth the good fat father
Wiping his own mouth, 'twas refection-time,—
"To quit this very miserable world?
Will you renounce" . . . "the mouthful of bread?" thought I;
By no means! Brief, they made a monk of me;
I did renounce the world, its pride and greed,
Palace, farm, villa, shop, and banking-house,
Trash, such as these poor devils of Medici
Have given their hearts to—all at eight years old.
Well, sir, I found in time, you may be sure,
'Twas not for nothing—the good bellyful,
The warm serge and the rope that goes all round,
And day-long blessed idleness beside!
"Let's see what the urchin's fit for"—that came next.
Not overmuch their way, I must confess.
Such a to-do! They tried me with their books:
Lord, they'd have taught me Latin in pure waste!
Flower o' the clove,
All the Latin I construe is, "amo" I love!
But, mind you, when a boy starves in the streets
Eight years together, as my fortune was,
Watching folk's faces to know who will fling
The bit of half-stripped grape-bunch he desires,
And who will curse or kick him for his pains,—
Which gentleman processional and fine,
Holding a candle to the Sacrament,
Will wink and let him lift a plate and catch
The droppings of the wax to sell again,
Or holla for the Eight and have him whipped,—
How say I?—nay, which dog bites, which lets drop
His bone from the heap of offal in the street,—
Why, soul and sense of him grow sharp alike,
He learns the look of things, and none the less
For admonition from the hunger-pinch.
I had a store of such remarks, be sure,
Which, after I found leisure, turned to use.
I drew men's faces on my copy-books,
Scrawled them within the antiphonary's marge,
Joined legs and arms to the long music-notes,
Found eyes and nose and chin for A's and B's,
And made a string of pictures of the world
Betwixt the ins and outs of verb and noun,
On the wall, the bench, the door. The monks looked black.

"Nay," quoth the Prior, "turn him out, d'ye say?
In no wise. Lose a crow and catch a lark.
What if at last we get our man of parts,
We Carmelites, like those Camaldolese
And Preaching Friars, to do our church up fine
And put the front on it that ought to be!"
And hereupon he bade me daub away.
Thank you! my head being crammed, the walls a blank,
Never was such prompt disemburdening.
First, every sort of monk, the black and white,
I drew them, fat and lean: then, folk at church,
From good old gossips waiting to confess
Their cribs of barrel-droppings, candle-ends,—
To the breathless fellow at the altar-foot,
Fresh from his murder, safe and sitting there
With the little children round him in a row
Of admiration, half for his beard and half
For that white anger of his victim's son
Shaking a fist at him with one fierce arm,
Signing himself with the other because of Christ
(Whose sad face on the cross sees only this
After the passion of a thousand years)
Till some poor girl, her apron o'er her head,
(Which the intense eyes looked through) came at eve
On tiptoe, said a word, dropped in a loaf,
Her pair of earrings and a bunch of flowers
(The brute took growling), prayed, and so was gone.
I painted all, then cried " 'Tis ask and have;
Choose, for more's ready!"—laid the ladder flat,
And showed my covered bit of cloister-wall.
The monks closed in a circle and praised loud
Till checked, taught what to see and not to see,
Being simple bodies,—"That's the very man!
Look at the boy who stoops to pat the dog!
That woman's like the Prior's niece who comes
To care about his asthma: it's the life!"
But there my triumph's straw-fire flared and funked;
Their betters took their turn to see and say:
The Prior and the learned pulled a face
And stopped all that in no time. "How? what's here?
Quite from the mark of painting, bless us all!
Faces, arms, legs, and bodies like the true
As much as pea and pea! it's devil's-game!
Your business is not to catch men with show,
With homage to the perishable clay,
But lift them over it, ignore it all,

Make them forget there's such a thing as flesh.
Your business is to paint the souls of men—
Man's soul, and it's a fire, smoke . . . no, it's not . . .
It's vapor done up like a new-born babe—
(In that shape when you die it leaves your mouth)
It's . . . well, what matters talking, it's the soul!
Give us no more of body than shows soul!
Here's Giotto, with his Saint a-praising God,
That sets us praising,—why not stop with him?
Why put all thoughts of praise out of our head
With wonder at lines, colors, and what not?
Paint the soul, never mind the legs and arms!
Rub all out, try at it a second time.
Oh, that white smallish female with the breasts,
She's just my niece . . . Herodias, I would say,—
Who went and danced and got men's heads cut off!
Have it all out!" Now, is this sense, I ask?
A fine way to paint soul, by painting body
So ill, the eye can't stop there, must go further
And can't fare worse! Thus, yellow does for white
When what you put for yellow's simply black,
And any sort of meaning looks intense
When all beside itself means and looks nought.
Why can't a painter lift each foot in turn,
Left foot and right foot, go a double step,
Make his flesh liker and his soul more like,
Both in their order? Take the prettiest face,
The Prior's niece . . . patron-saint—is it so pretty
You can't discover if it means hope, fear,
Sorrow or joy? won't beauty go with these?
Suppose I've made her eyes all right and blue,
Can't I take breath and try to add life's flash,
And then add soul and heighten them threefold?
Or say there's beauty with no soul at all—
(I never saw it—put the case the same—)
If you get simple beauty and nought else,
You get about the best thing God invents:
That's somewhat: and you'll find the soul you have missed,
Within yourself, when you return him thanks.
"Rub all out!" Well, well, there's my life, in short,
And so the thing has gone on ever since.
I'm grown a man no doubt, I've broken bounds:
You should not take a fellow eight years old
And make him swear to never kiss the girls.
I'm my own master, paint now as I please—
Having a friend, you see, in the Corner-house!

Lord, it's fast holding by the rings in front—
Those great rings serve more purposes than just
To plant a flag in, or tie up a horse!
And yet the old schooling sticks, the old grave eyes
Are peeping o'er my shoulder as I work,
The heads shake still—"It's art's decline, my son!
You're not of the true painters, great and old;
Brother Angelico's the man, you'll find;
Brother Lorenzo stands his single peer:
Fag on at flesh, you'll never make the third!"
Flower o' the pine,
You keep your mistr . . . manners, and I'll stick to mine!
I'm not the third, then: bless us, they must know!
Don't you think they're the likeliest to know,
They with their Latin? So, I swallow my rage,
Clench my teeth, suck my lips in tight, and paint
To please them—sometimes do and sometimes don't;
For, doing most, there's pretty sure to come
A turn, some warm eve finds me at my saints—
A laugh, a cry, the business of the world—
(*Flower o' the peach,*
Death for us all, and his own life for each!)
And my whole soul revolves, the cup runs over,
The world and life's too big to pass for a dream,
And I do these wild things in sheer despite,
And play the fooleries you catch me at,
In pure rage! The old mill-horse, out at grass
After hard years, throws up his stiff heels so,
Although the miller does not preach to him
The only good of grass is to make chaff.
What would men have? Do they like grass or no—
May they or mayn't they? all I want's the thing
Settled forever one way. As it is,
You tell too many lies and hurt yourself:
You don't like what you only like too much,
You do like what, if given you at your word,
You find abundantly detestable.
For me, I think I speak as I was taught;
I always see the garden and God there
A-making man's wife: and, my lesson learned,
The value and significance of flesh,
I can't unlearn ten minutes afterwards.

You understand me: I'm a beast, I know.
But see, now—why, I see as certainly
As that the morning-star's about to shine,

What will hap some day. We've a youngster here
Comes to our convent, studies what I do,
Slouches and stares and lets no atom drop:
His name is Guidi—he'll not mind the monks—
They call him Hulking Tom, he lets them talk—
He picks my practice up—he'll paint apace,
I hope so—though I never live so long,
I know what's sure to follow. You be judge!
You speak no Latin more than I, belike;
However, you're my man, you've seen the world
—The beauty and the wonder and the power,
The shapes of things, their colors, lights and shades,
Changes, surprises,—and God made it all!
—For what? Do you feel thankful, ay or no,
For this fair town's face, yonder river's line,
The mountain round it and the sky above,
Much more the figures of man, woman, child,
These are the frame to? What's it all about?
To be passed over, despised? or dwelt upon,
Wondered at? oh, this last of course!—you say.
But why not do as well as say,—paint these
Just as they are, careless what comes of it?
God's works—paint any one, and count it crime
To let a truth slip. Don't object, "His works
Are here already; nature is complete:
Suppose you reproduce her—(which you can't)
There's no advantage! you must beat her, then."
For, don't you mark? we're made so that we love
First when we see them painted, things we have passed
Perhaps a hundred times nor cared to see;
And so they are better, painted—better to us,
Which is the same thing. Art was given for that;
God uses us to help each other so,
Lending our minds out. Have you noticed, now,
Your cullion's hanging face? A bit of chalk,
And trust me but you should, though! How much more,
If I drew higher things with the same truth!
That were to take the Prior's pulpit-place,
Interpret God to all of you! Oh, oh,
It makes me mad to see what men shall do
And we in our graves! This world's no blot for us,
Nor blank; it means intensely, and means good:
To find its meaning is my meat and drink.
"Ay, but you don't so instigate to prayer!"
Strikes in the Prior: "when your meaning's plain
It does not say to folk—remember matins,

Or, mind you fast next Friday!" Why, for this
What need of art at all? A skull and bones,
Two bits of stick nailed crosswise, or, what's best,
A bell to chime the hour with, does as well.
I painted a Saint Laurence six months since
At Prato, splashed the fresco in fine style:
"How looks my painting, now the scaffold 's down?"
I ask a brother: "Hugely," he returns—
"Already not one phiz of your three slaves
Who turn the Deacon off his toasted side,
But's scratched and prodded to our heart's content,
The pious people have so eased their own
With coming to say prayers there in a rage:
We get on fast to see the bricks beneath.
Expect another job this time next year,
For pity and religion grow i' the crowd—
Your painting serves its purpose!" Hang the fools

    —That is—you'll not mistake an idle word
Spoke in a huff by a poor monk, God wot,
Tasting the air this spicy night which turns
The unaccustomed head like Chianti wine!
Oh, the church knows! don't misreport me, now!
It's natural a poor monk out of bounds
Should have his apt word to excuse himself:
And hearken how I plot to make amends.
I have bethought me: I shall paint a piece
. . . There's for you! Give me six months, then go, see
Something in Sant' Ambrogio's! Bless the nuns!
They want a cast o' my office. I shall paint
God in the midst, Madonna and her babe,
Ringed by a bowery, flowery angel-brood,
Lilies and vestments and white faces, sweet
As puff on puff of grated orris-root
When ladies crowd to church at midsummer.
And then i' the front, of course a saint or two—
Saint John, because he saves the Florentines,
Saint Ambrose, who puts down in black and white
The convent's friends and gives them a long day,
And Job, I must have him there past mistake,
The man of Uz (and Us without the z,
Painters who need his patience). Well, all these
Secured at their devotion, up shall come
Out of a corner when you least expect,
As one by a dark stair into a great light,
Music and talking, who but Lippo! I!—

Mazed, motionless, and moonstruck—I'm the man!
Back I shrink—what is this I see and hear?
I, caught up with my monk's-things by mistake,
My old serge gown and rope that goes all round,
I, in this presence, this pure company!
Where 's a hole, where 's a corner for escape?
Then steps a sweet angelic slip of a thing
Forward, puts out a soft palm—"Not so fast!"
—Addresses the celestial presence, "nay—
He made you and devised you, after all,
Though he's none of you! Could Saint John there draw—
His camel-hair make up a painting-brush?
We come to brother Lippo for all that,
Iste perfecit opus!" So, all smile—
I shuffle sideways with my blushing face
Under the cover of a hundred wings
Thrown like a spread of kirtles when you're gay
And play hot cockles, all the doors being shut,
Till, wholly unexpected, in there pops
The hothead husband! Thus I scuttle off
To some safe bench behind, not letting go
The palm of her, the little lily thing
That spoke the good word for me in the nick,
Like the Prior's niece . . . Saint Lucy, I would say.
And so all's saved for me, and for the church
A pretty picture gained. Go, six months hence!
Your hand, sir, and good-bye: no lights, no lights!
The street's hushed, and I know my own way back,
Don't fear me! There's the gray beginning. Zooks!

ANDREA DEL SARTO

CALLED "THE FAULTLESS PAINTER"

BUT do not let us quarrel any more,
No, my Lucrezia; bear with me for once:
Sit down and all shall happen as you wish.
You turn your face, but does it bring your heart?
I'll work then for your friend's friend, never fear,
Treat his own subject after his own way,
Fix his own time, accept too his own price,
And shut the money into this small hand
When next it takes mine. Will it? tenderly?
Oh, I'll content him,—but to-morrow, Love!
I often am much wearier than you think,

This evening more than usual, and it seems
As if—forgive now—should you let me sit
Here by the window with your hand in mine
And look a half-hour forth on Fiesole,
Both of one mind, as married people use,
Quietly, quietly the evening through,
I might get up to-morrow to my work
Cheerful and fresh as ever. Let us try.
To-morrow, how you shall be glad for this!
Your soft hand is a woman of itself,
And mine the man's bared breast she curls inside.
Don't count the time lost, neither; you must serve
For each of the five pictures we require:
It saves a model. So! keep looking so—
My serpentining beauty, rounds on rounds!
—How could you ever prick those perfect ears,
Even to put the pearl there! oh, so sweet—
My face, my moon, my everybody's moon,
Which everybody looks on and calls his,
And, I suppose, is looked on by in turn,
While she looks—no one's: very dear, no less.
You smile? why, there 's my picture ready made,
There 's what we painters call our harmony!
A common grayness silvers everything,—
All in a twilight, you and I alike
—You, at the point of your first pride in me
(That 's gone you know),—but I, at every point;
My youth, my hope, my art, being all toned **down**
To yonder sober pleasant Fiesole.
There 's the bell clinking from the chapel-top;
That length of convent-wall across the way
Holds the trees safer, huddled more inside;
The last monk leaves the garden; days decrease,
And autumn grows, autumn in everything.
Eh? the whole seems to fall into a shape
As if I saw alike my work and self
And all that I was born to be and do,
A twilight-piece. Love, we are in God's hand.
How strange now looks the life he makes us lead;
So free we seem, so fettered fast we are!
I feel he laid the fetter: let it lie!
This chamber for example—turn your head—
All that 's behind us! You don't understand
Nor care to understand about my art,
But you can hear at least when people speak:
And that cartoon, the second from the door

—It is the thing, Love! so such things should be—
Behold Madonna!—I am bold to say.
I can do with my pencil what I know,
What I see, what at bottom of my heart
I wish for, if I ever wish so deep—
Do easily, too—what I say, perfectly,
I do not boast, perhaps: yourself are judge,
Who listened to the Legate's talk last week,
And just as much they used to say in France.
At any rate 't is easy, all of it!
No sketches first, no studies, that 's long past:
I do what many dream of all their lives,
—Dream? strive to do, and agonize to do,
And fail in doing. I could count twenty such
On twice your fingers, and not leave this town,
Who strive—you don't know how the others strive
To paint a little thing like that you smeared
Carelessly passing with your robes afloat,—
Yet do much less, so much less, Someone says,
(I know his name, no matter)—so much less!
Well, less is more, Lucrezia: I am judged.
There burns a truer light of God in them,
In their vexed beating stuffed and stopped-up brain,
Heart, or whate'er else, than goes on to prompt
This low-pulsed forthright craftsman's hand of mine.
Their works drop groundward, but themselves, I know,
Reach many a time a heaven that 's shut to me,
Enter and take their place there sure enough,
Though they come back and cannot tell the world.
My works are nearer heaven, but I sit here.
The sudden blood of these men! at a word—
Praise them, it boils, or blame them, it boils too.
I, painting from myself and to myself,
Know what I do, am unmoved by men's blame
Or their praise either. Somebody remarks
Morello's outline there is wrongly traced,
His hue mistaken; what of that? or else,
Rightly traced and well ordered; what of that?
Speak as they please, what does the mountain care?
Ah, but a man's reach should exceed his grasp,
Or what 's a heaven for? All is silver-gray
Placid and perfect with my art: the worse!
I know both what I want and what might gain,
And yet how profitless to know, to sigh
"Had I been two, another and myself,
Our head would have o'erlooked the world!" No doubt.

Yonder 's a work now, of that famous youth
The Urbinate who died five years ago.
('T is copied, George Vasari sent it me.)
Well, I can fancy how he did it all,
Pouring his soul, with kings and popes to see,
Reaching, that heaven might so replenish him,
Above and through his art—for it gives way;
That arm is wrongly put—and there again—
A fault to pardon in the drawing's lines,
Its body, so to speak: its soul is right,
He means right—that, a child may understand.
Still, what an arm! and I could alter it:
But all the play, the insight and the stretch—
Out of me, out of me! And wherefore out?
Had you enjoined them on me, given me soul,
We might have risen to Rafael, I and you!
Nay, Love, you did give all I asked, I think—
More than I merit, yes, by many times.
But had you—oh, with the same perfect brow,
And perfect eyes, and more than perfect mouth,
And the low voice my soul hears, as a bird
The fowler's pipe, and follows to the snare—
Had you, with these the same, but brought a mind!
Some women do so. Had the mouth there urged,
"God and the glory! never care for gain.
The present by the future, what is that?
Live for fame, side by side with Agnolo!
Rafael is waiting: up to God, all three!"
I might have done it for you. So it seems:
Perhaps not. All is as God overrules.
Besides, incentives come from the soul's self;
The rest avail not. Why do I need you?
What wife had Rafael, or has Agnolo?
In this world, who can do a thing, will not;
And who would do it, cannot, I perceive:
Yet the will 's somewhat—somewhat, too, the power—
And thus we half-men struggle. At the end,
God, I conclude, compensates, punishes.
'T is safer for me, if the award be strict,
That I am something underrated here,
Poor this long while, despised, to speak the truth.
I dared not, do you know, leave home all day,
For fear of chancing on the Paris lords.
The best is when they pass and look aside;
But they speak sometimes; I must bear it all.
Well may they speak! That Francis, that first time,

And that long festal year at Fontainebleau!
I surely then could sometimes leave the ground,
Put on the glory, Rafael's daily wear,
In that humane great monarch's golden look,—
One finger in his beard or twisted curl
Over his mouth's good mark that made the smile,
One arm about my shoulder, round my neck,
The jingle of his gold chain in my ear,
I painting proudly with his breath on me,
All his court round him, seeing with his eyes,
Such frank French eyes, and such a fire of souls
Profuse, my hand kept plying by those hearts,—
And, best of all, this, this, this face beyond,
This in the background, waiting on my work,
To crown the issue with a last reward!
A good time, was it not, my kingly days?
And had you not grown restless . . . but I know—
'T is done and past; 't was right, my instinct said;
Too live the life grew, golden and not gray,
And I'm the weak-eyed bat no sun should tempt
Out of the grange whose four walls make his world.
How could it end in any other way?
You called me, and I came home to your heart.
The triumph was—to reach and stay there; since
I reached it ere the triumph, what is lost?
Let my hands frame your face in your hair's gold,
You beautiful Lucrezia that are mine!
"Rafael did this, Andrea painted that;
The Roman's is the better when you pray,
But still the other's Virgin was his wife"—
Men will excuse me. I am glad to judge
Both pictures in your presence; clearer grows
My better fortune, I resolve to think.
For, do you know, Lucrezia, as God lives,
Said one day Agnolo, his very self,
To Rafael . . . I have known it all these years . . .
(When the young man was flaming out his thoughts
Upon a palace-wall for Rome to see,
Too lifted up in heart because of it)
"Friend, there 's a certain sorry little scrub
Goes up and down our Florence, none cares how,
Who, were he set to plan and execute
As you are, pricked on by your popes and kings,
Would bring the sweat into that brow of yours!"
To Rafael's!—And indeed the arm is wrong.
I hardly dare . . . yet, only you to see,

Give the chalk here—quick, thus the line should go!
Ay, but the soul! he 's Rafael! rub it out!
Still, all I care for, if he spoke the truth,
(What he? why, who but Michel Agnolo?
Do you forget already words like those?)
If really there was such a chance, so lost,—
Is, whether you 're—not grateful—but more pleased.
Well, let me think so. And you smile indeed!
This hour has been an hour! Another smile?
If you would sit thus by me every night
I should work better, do you comprehend?
I mean that I should earn more, give you more.
See, it is settled dusk now; there 's a star;
Morello 's gone, the watch-lights show the wall,
The cue-owls speak the name we call them by.
Come from the window, Love,—come in, at last,
Inside the melancholy little house
We built to be so gay with. God is just.
King Francis may forgive me: oft at nights
When I look up from painting, eyes tired out,
The walls become illumined, brick from brick
Distinct, instead of mortar, fierce bright gold,
That gold of his I did cement them with!
Let us but love each other. Must you go?
That Cousin here again? he waits outside?
Must see you—you, and not with me? Those loans?
More gaming debts to pay? you smiled for that?
Well, let smiles buy me! have you more to spend?
While hand and eye and something of a heart
Are left me, work 's my ware, and what 's it worth?
I'll pay my fancy. Only let me sit
The gray remainder of the evening out,
Idle, you call it, and muse perfectly
How I could paint, were I but back in France,
One picture, just one more—the Virgin's face,
Not yours this time! I want you at my side
To hear them—that is, Michel Agnolo—
Judge all I do and tell you of its worth.
Will you? To-morrow, satisfy your friend.
I take the subjects for his corridor,
Finish the portrait out of hand—there, there,
And throw him in another thing or two
If he demurs; the whole should prove enough
To pay for this same Cousin's freak. Beside,
What 's better and what 's all I care about,
Get you the thirteen scudi for the ruff!

Love, does that please you? Ah, but what does he,
The Cousin! what does he to please you more?

I am grown peaceful as old age to-night.
I regret little, I would change still less.
Since there my past life lies, why alter it?
The very wrong to Francis!—it is true
I took his coin, was tempted and complied,
And built this house and sinned, and all is said.
My father and my mother died of want.
Well, had I riches of my own? you see
How one gets rich! Let each one bear his lot.
They were born poor, lived poor, and poor they died:
And I have labored somewhat in my time
And not been paid profusely. Some good son
Paint my two hundred pictures—let him try!
No doubt, there's something strikes a balance. Yes,
You loved me quite enough, it seems to-night.
This must suffice me here. What would one have?
In heaven, perhaps, new chances, one more chance—
Four great walls in the New Jerusalem,
Meted on each side by the angel's reed,
For Leonard, Rafael, Agnolo and me
To cover—the three first without a wife,
While I have mine! So—still they overcome
Because there's still Lucrezia,—as I choose.

Again the Cousin's whistle! Go, my Love.

THE BISHOP ORDERS HIS TOMB AT SAINT PRAXED'S CHURCH

ROME, 15—

VANITY, saith the preacher, vanity!
Draw round my bed: is Anselm keeping back?
Nephews—sons mine . . . ah God, I know not! Well—
She, men would have to be your mother once,
Old Gandolf envied me, so fair she was!
What's done is done, and she is dead beside,
Dead long ago, and I am Bishop since,
And as she died so must we die ourselves,
And thence ye may perceive the world's a dream.
Life, how and what is it? As here I lie
In this state-chamber, dying by degrees,

Hours and long hours in the dead night, I ask
"Do I live, am I dead?" Peace, peace seems all.
Saint Praxed's ever was the church for peace;
And so, about this tomb of mine. I fought
With tooth and nail to save my niche, ye know:
—Old Gandolf cozened me, despite my care;
Shrewd was that snatch from out the corner South
He graced his carrion with, God curse the same!
Yet still my niche is not so cramped but thence
One sees the pulpit o' the epistle-side,
And somewhat of the choir, those silent seats,
And up into the aery dome where live
The angels, and a sunbeam 's sure to lurk:
And I shall fill my slab of basalt there,
And 'neath my tabernacle take my rest,
With those nine columns round me, two and two,
The odd one at my feet where Anselm stands:
Peach-blossom marble all, the rare, the ripe
As fresh-poured red wine of a mighty pulse.
—Old Gandolf with his paltry onion-stone,
Put me where I may look at him! True peach,
Rosy and flawless: how I earned the prize!
Draw close: that conflagration of my church
—What then? So much was saved if aught were missed!
My sons, ye would not be my death? Go dig
The white-grape vineyard where the oil-press stood,
Drop water gently till the surface sink,
And if ye find . . . Ah God, I know not, I! . . .
Bedded in store of rotten fig-leaves soft,
And corded up in a tight olive-frail,
Some lump, ah God, of *lapis lazuli*,
Big as a Jew's head cut off at the nape,
Blue as a vein o'er the Madonna's breast . . .
Sons, all have I bequeathed you, villas, all,
That brave Frascati villa with its bath,
So, let the blue lump poise between my knees,
Like God the Father's globe on both his hands
Ye worship in the Jesu Church so gay,
For Gandolf shall not choose but see and burst!
Swift as a weaver's shuttle fleet our years:
Man goeth to the grave, and where is he?
Did I say basalt for my slab, sons? Black—
'T was ever antique-black I meant! How else
Shall ye contrast my frieze to come beneath?
The bas-relief in bronze ye promised me,
Those Pans and Nymphs ye wot of, and perchance

Some tripod, thyrsus, with a vase or so,
The Saviour at his sermon on the mount,
Saint Praxed in a glory, and one Pan
Ready to twitch the Nymph's last garment off,
And Moses with the tables . . . but I know
Ye mark me not! What do they whisper thee,
Child of my bowels, Anselm? Áh, ye hope
To revel down my villas while I gasp
Bricked o'er with beggar's mouldy travertine
Which Gandolf from his tomb-top chuckles at!
Nay, boys, ye love me—all of jasper, then!
'T is jasper ye stand pledged to, lest I grieve.
My bath must needs be left behind, alas!
One block, pure green as a pistachio-nut,
There 's plenty jasper somewhere in the world—
And have I not Saint Praxed's ear to pray
Horses for ye, and brown Greek manuscripts,
And mistresses with great smooth marbly limbs?
—That 's if ye carve my epitaph aright,
Choice Latin, picked phrase, Tully's every word,
No gaudy ware like Gandolf's second line—
Tully, my masters? Ulpian serves his need!
And then how I shall lie through centuries,
And hear the blessed mutter of the mass,
And see God made and eaten all day long,
And feel the steady candle-flame, and taste
Good strong thick stupefying incense-smoke!
For as I lie here, hours of the dead night,
Dying in state and by such slow degrees,
I fold my arms as if they clasped a crook,
And stretch my feet forth straight as stone can point,
And let the bedclothes, for a mortcloth, drop
Into great laps and folds of sculptor's-work.
And as yon tapers dwindle, and strange thoughts
Grow, with a certain humming in my ears,
About the life before I lived this life,
And this life too, popes, cardinals and priests,
Saint Praxed at his sermon on the mount,
Your tall pale mother with her talking eyes,
And new-found agate urns as fresh as day,
And marble's language, Latin pure, discreet,
—Aha, ELUCESCEBAT quoth our friend?
No Tully, said I, Ulpian at the best!
Evil and brief hath been my pilgrimage.
All *lapis*, all, sons! Else I give the Pope
My villas! Will ye ever eat my heart?

Ever your eyes were as a lizard's quick,
They glitter like your mother's for my soul,
Or ye would heighten my impoverished frieze,
Piece out its starved design, and fill my vase
With grapes, and add a visor and a Term,
And to the tripod ye would tie a lynx
That in his struggle throws the thyrsus down,
To comfort me on my entablature
Whereon I am to lie till I must ask
"Do I live, am I dead?" There, leave me, there!
For ye have stabbed me with ingratitude
To death—ye wish it—God, ye wish it! Stone—
Gritstone, a-crumble! Clammy squares which sweat
As if the corpse they keep were oozing through—
And no more *lapis* to delight the world!
Well, go! I bless ye. Fewer tapers there,
But in a row: and, going, turn your backs
—Ay, like departing altar-ministrants,
And leave me in my church, the church for peace,
That I may watch at leisure if he leers—
Old Gandolf, at me, from his onion-stone,
As still he envied me, so fair she was!

BISHOP BLOUGRAM'S APOLOGY

No MORE WINE? then we'll push back chairs and talk.
A final glass for me, though: cool, i' faith!
We ought to have our Abbey back, you see.
It's different, preaching in basilicas,
And doing duty in some masterpiece
Like this of brother Pugin's, bless his heart!
I doubt if they're half baked, those chalk rosettes,
Ciphers and stucco-twiddlings everywhere;
It's just like breathing in a lime-kiln: eh?
These hot long ceremonies of our church
Cost us a little—oh, they pay the price,
You take me—amply pay it! Now, we'll talk.

So, you despise me, Mr. Gigadibs.
No deprecation,—nay, I beg you, sir!
Beside 'tis our engagement: don't you know,
I promised, if you'd watch a dinner out,
We'd see truth dawn together?—truth that peeps
Over the glasses' edge when dinner's done,
And body gets its sop and holds its noise

And leaves soul free a little. Now's the time:
'Tis break of day! You do despise me then.
And if I say, "despise me,"—never fear!
I know you do not in a certain sense—
Not in my arm-chair, for example: here,
I well imagine you respect my place
(*Status, entourage,* worldly circumstance)
Quite to its value—very much indeed:
—Are up to the protesting eyes of you
In pride at being seated here for once—
You'll turn it to such capital account!
When somebody, through years and years to come,
Hints of the bishop,—names me—that's enough:
"Blougram? I knew him"—(into it you slide)
"Dined with him once, a Corpus Christi Day,
All alone, we two; he's a clever man:
And after dinner,—why, the wine you know,—
Oh, there was wine, and good!—what with the wine . . .
'Faith, we began upon all sorts of talk!
He's no bad fellow, Blougram; he had seen
Something of mine he relished, some review:
He's quite above their humbug in his heart,
Half-said as much, indeed—the thing's his trade.
I warrant, Blougram's sceptical at times:
How otherwise? I liked him, I confess!"
Che che, my dear sir, as we say at Rome,
Don't you protest now! It's fair give and take;
You have had your turn and spoken your home-truths.
The hand's mine now, and here you follow suit.

Thus much conceded, still the first fact stays—
You do despise me; your ideal of life
Is not the bishop's: you would not be I.
You would like better to be Goethe, now,
Or Buonaparte, or, bless me, lower still,
Count D'Orsay,—so you did what you preferred,
Spoke as you thought, and, as you cannot help,
Believed or disbelieved, no matter what,
So long as on that point, whate'er it was,
You loosed your mind, were whole and sole yourself.
—That, my ideal never can include,
Upon that element of truth and worth
Never be based! for say they make me Pope—
(They can't—suppose it for our argument!)
Why, there I'm at my tether's end, I've reached
My height, and not a height which pleases you:

An unbelieving Pope won't do, you say.
It's like those eerie stories nurses tell,
Of how some actor on a stage played Death,
With pasteboard crown, sham orb and tinselled dart,
And called himself the monarch of the world;
Then, going in the tire-room afterward,
Because the play was done, to shift himself,
Got touched upon the sleeve familiarly,
The moment he had shut the closet door,
By Death himself. Thus God might touch a Pope
At unawares, ask what his baubles mean,
And whose part he presumed to play just now?
Best be yourself, imperial, plain and true!

So, drawing comfortable breath again,
You weigh and find, whatever more or less
I boast of my ideal realized,
Is nothing in the balance when opposed
To your ideal, your grand simple life,
Of which you will not realize one jot.
I am much, you are nothing; you would be all,
I would be merely much: you beat me there.

No, friend, you do not beat me: hearken why!
The common problem, yours, mine, every one's,
Is—not to fancy what were fair in life
Provided it could be,—but, finding first
What may be, then find how to make it fair
Up to our means: a very different thing!
No abstract intellectual plan of life
Quite irrespective of life's plainest laws,
But one, a man, who is man and nothing more,
May lead within a world which (by your leave)
Is Rome or London, not Fool's-paradise.
Embellish Rome, idealize away,
Make paradise of London if you can,
You're welcome, nay, you're wise.

                            A simile!
We mortals cross the ocean of this world
Each in his average cabin of a life;
The best's not big, the worst yields elbow-room.
Now for our six months' voyage—how prepare?
You come on shipboard with a landsman's list
Of things he calls convenient: so they are!

An India screen is pretty furniture,
A piano-forte is a fine resource,
All Balzac's novels occupy one shelf,
The new edition fifty volumes long;
And little Greek books, with the funny type
They get up well at Leipsic, fill the next:
Go on! slabbed marble, what a bath it makes!
And Parma's pride, the Jerome, let us add!
'Twere pleasant could Correggio's fleeting glow
Hang full in face of one where'er one roams,
Since he more than the others brings with him
Italy's self,—the marvellous Modenese!—
Yet was not on your list before, perhaps.
—Alas, friend, here's the agent . . . is't the name?
The captain, or whoever's master here—
You see him screw his face up; what's his cry
Ere you set foot on shipboard? "Six feet square!"
If you won't understand what six feet mean,
Compute and purchase stores accordingly—
And if, in pique because he overhauls
Your Jerome, piano, bath, you come on board
Bare—why, you cut a figure at the first
While sympathetic landsmen see you off;
Not afterward, when long ere half seas over,
You peep up from your utterly naked boards
Into some snug and well-appointed berth,
Like mine for instance (try the cooler jug—
Put back the other, but don't jog the ice!)
And mortified you mutter, "Well and good;
He sits enjoying his sea-furniture;
'Tis stout and proper, and there's store of it:
Though I've the better notion, all agree,
Of fitting rooms up. Hang the carpenter,
Neat ship-shape fixings and contrivances—
I would have brought my Jerome, frame and all!"
And meantime you bring nothing: never mind—
You've proved your artist-nature: what you don't
You might bring, so despise me, as I say.

Now come, let's backward to the starting-place.
See my way: we're two college friends, suppose.
Prepare together for our voyage, then;
Each note and check the other in his work,—
Here's mine, a bishop's outfit; criticise!
What's wrong? why won't you be a bishop too?

Why first, you don't believe, you don't and can't,
(Not statedly, that is, and fixedly
And absolutely and exclusively)
In any revelation called divine.
No dogmas nail your faith; and what remains
But say so, like the honest man you are?
First, therefore, overhaul theology!
Nay, I too, not a fool, you please to think,
Must find believing every whit as hard:
And if I do not frankly say as much,
The ugly consequence is clear enough.

Now wait, my friend: well, I do not believe—
If you'll accept no faith that is not fixed,
Absolute and exclusive, as you say.
You're wrong—I mean to prove it in due time.
Meanwhile, I know where difficulties lie
I could not, cannot solve, nor ever shall,
So give up hope accordingly to solve—
(To you, and over the wine). Our dogmas then
With both of us, though in unlike degree,
Missing full credence—overboard with them!
I mean to meet you on your own premise:
Good, there go mine in company with yours!

And now what are we? unbelievers both,
Calm and complete, determinedly fixed
To-day, to-morrow, and forever, pray?
You'll guarantee me that? Not so, I think!
In no wise! all we've gained is, that belief,
As unbelief before, shakes us by fits,
Confounds us like its predecessor. Where's
The gain? how can we guard our unbelief,
Make it bear fruit to us?—the problem here.
Just when we are safest, there's a sunset-touch,
A fancy from a flower-bell, some one's death,
A chorus-ending from Euripides,—
And that's enough for fifty hopes and fears
As old and new at once as nature's self,
To rap and knock and enter in our soul,
Take hands and dance there, a fantastic ring,
Round the ancient idol, on his base again,—
The grand Perhaps! We look on helplessly.
There the old misgivings, crooked questions are—
This good God,—what he could do, if he would,

Would, if he could—then must have done long since:
If so, when, where and how? some way must be,—
Once feel about, and soon or late you hit
Some sense, in which it might be, after all.
Why not, "The Way, the Truth, the Life?"

—That way

Over the mountain, which who stands upon
Is apt to doubt if it be meant for a road;
While, if he views it from the waste itself,
Up goes the line there, plain from base to brow,
Not vague, mistakable! what's a break or two
Seen from the unbroken desert either side?
And then (to bring in fresh philosophy)
What if the breaks themselves should prove at last
The most consummate of contrivances
To train a man's eye, teach him what is faith?
And so we stumble at truth's very test!
All we have gained then by our unbelief
Is a life of doubt diversified by faith,
For one of faith diversified by doubt:
We called the chess-board white,—we call it black.

"Well," you rejoin, "the end's no worse, at least;
We've reason for both colors on the board:
Why not confess then, where I drop the faith
And you the doubt, that I'm as right as you?"

Because, friend, in the next place, this being so,
And both things even,—faith and unbelief
Left to a man's choice,—we'll proceed a step,
Returning to our image, which I like.

A man's choice, yes—but a cabin-passenger's—
The man made for the special life o' the world—
Do you forget him? I remember though!
Consult our ship's conditions and you find
One and but one choice suitable to all;
The choice, that you unluckily prefer,
Turning things topsy-turvy—they or it
Going to the ground. Belief or unbelief
Bears upon life, determines its whole course,
Begins at its beginning. See the world
Such as it is,—you made it not, nor I;
I mean to take it as it is,—and you,
Not so you'll take it,—though you get nought else.

I know the special kind of life I like,
What suits the most my idiosyncrasy,
Brings out the best of me and bears me fruit
In power, peace, pleasantness and length of days.
I find that positive belief does this
For me, and unbelief, no whit of this.
—For you, it does, however?—that, we'll try!
'Tis clear, I cannot lead my life, at least,
Induce the world to let me peaceably,
Without declaring at the outset, "Friends,
I absolutely and peremptorily
Believe!"—I say, faith is my waking life:
One sleeps, indeed, and dreams at intervals,
We know, but waking's the main point with us
And my provision's for life's waking part.
Accordingly, I use heart, head and hand
All day, I build, scheme, study, and make friends;
And when night overtakes me, down I lie,
Sleep, dream a little, and get done with it,
The sooner the better, to begin afresh.
What's midnight doubt before the dayspring's faith?
You, the philosopher, that disbelieve,
That recognize the night, give dreams their weight—
To be consistent you should keep your bed,
Abstain from healthy acts that prove you man,
For fear you drowse perhaps at unawares!
And certainly at night you'll sleep and dream,
Live through the day and bustle as you please.
And so you live to sleep as I to wake,
To unbelieve as I to still believe?
Well, and the common sense o' the world calls you
Bed-ridden,—and its good things come to me.
Its estimation, which is half the fight,
That's the first-cabin comfort I secure:
The next . . . but you perceive with half an eye!
Come, come, it's best believing, if we may;
You can't but own that!

                       Next, concede again,
If once we choose belief, on all accounts
We can't be too decisive in our faith,
Conclusive and exclusive in its terms,
To suit the world which gives us the good things.
In every man's career are certain points
Whereon he dares not be indifferent;
The world detects him clearly. if he dare,

As baffled at the game, and losing life.
He may care little or he may care much
For riches, honor, pleasure, work, repose,
Since various theories of life and life's
Success are extant which might easily
Comport with either estimate of these;
And whoso chooses wealth or poverty,
Labor or quiet, is not judged a fool
Because his fellow would choose otherwise:
We let him choose upon his own account
So long as he's consistent with his choice.
But certain points, left wholly to himself,
When once a man has arbitrated on,
We say he must succeed there or go hang.
Thus, he should wed the woman he loves most
Or needs most, whatsoe'er the love or need—
For he can't wed twice. Then, he must avouch,
Or follow, at the least, sufficiently,
The form of faith his conscience holds the best,
Whate'er the process of conviction was:
For nothing can compensate his mistake
On such a point, the man himself being judge:
He cannot wed twice, nor twice lose his soul.

Well now, there's one great form of Christian faith
I happened to be born in—which to teach
Was given me as I grew up, on all hands,
As best and readiest means of living by;
The same on examination being proved
The most pronounced moreover, fixed, precise
And absolute form of faith in the whole world—
Accordingly, most potent of all forms
For working on the world. Observe, my friend!
Such as you know me, I am free to say,
In these hard latter days which hamper one,
Myself—by no immoderate exercise
Of intellect and learning, but the tact
To let external forces work for me,
—Bid the street's stones be bread and they are bread;
Bid Peter's creed, or rather, Hildebrand's,
Exalt me o'er my fellows in the world
And make my life an ease and joy and pride;
It does so,—which for me's a great point gained,
Who have a soul and body that exact
A comfortable care in many ways.
There's power in me and will to dominate

Which I must exercise, they hurt me else:
In many ways I need mankind's respect,
Obedience, and the love that's born of fear:
While at the same time, there's a taste I have,
A toy of soul, a titillating thing,
Refuses to digest these dainties crude.
The naked life is gross till clothed upon:
I must take what men offer, with a grace
As though I would not, could I help it, take!
An uniform I wear though over-rich—
Something imposed on me, no choice of mine;
No fancy-dress worn for pure fancy's sake
And despicable therefore! now folk kneel
And kiss my hand—of course the Church's hand.
Thus I am made, thus life is best for me,
And thus that it should be I have procured;
And thus it could not be another way,
I venture to imagine.

               You'll reply,
So far my choice, no doubt, is a success;
But were I made of better elements,
With nobler instincts, purer tastes, like you,
I hardly would account the thing success
Though it did all for me I say.

                   But, friend,
We speak of what is; not of what might be,
And how 'twere better if 'twere otherwise.
I am the man you see here plain enough:
Grant I'm a beast, why, beasts must lead beasts' lives!
Suppose I own at once to tail and claws;
The tailless man exceeds me: but being tailed
I'll lash out lion fashion, and leave apes
To dock their stump and dress their haunches up.
My business is not to remake myself,
But make the absolute best of what God made.
Or—our first simile—though you prove me doomed
To a viler berth still, to the steerage-hole,
The sheep-pen or the pig-sty, I should strive
To make what use of each were possible;
And as this cabin gets upholstery,
That hutch should rustle with sufficient straw.

   But, friend, I don't acknowledge quite so fast
I fail of all your manhood's lofty tastes

Enumerated so complacently,
On the mere ground that you forsooth can find
In this particular life I choose to lead
No fit provision for them. Can you not?
Say you, my fault is I address myself
To grosser estimators than should judge?
And that's no way of holding up the soul,
Which, nobler, needs men's praise perhaps, yet knows
One wise man's verdict outweighs all the fools'—
Would like the two, but, forced to choose, takes that.
I pine among my million imbeciles
(You think) aware some dozen men of sense
Eye me and know me, whether I believe
In the last winking Virgin, as I vow,
And am a fool, or disbelieve in her
And am a knave,—approve in neither case,
Withhold their voices though I look their way:
Like Verdi when, at his worst opera's end
(The thing they gave at Florence,—what's its name?)
While the mad houseful's plaudits near out-bang
His orchestra of salt-box, tongs, and bones,
He looks through all the roaring and the wreaths
Where sits Rossini patient in his stall.

    Nay, friend, I meet you with an answer here—
That even your prime men who appraise their kind
Are men still, catch a wheel within a wheel,
See more in a truth than the truth's simple self,
Confuse themselves. You see lads walk the street
Sixty the minute; what's to note in that?
You see one lad o'erstride a chimney-stack;
Him you must watch—he's sure to fall, yet stands!
Our interest's on the dangerous edge of things.
The honest thief, the tender murderer,
The superstitious atheist, demirep
That loves and saves her soul in new French books—
We watch while these in equilibrium keep
The giddy line midway: one step aside,
They're classed and done with. I, then, keep the line
Before your sages,—just the men to shrink
From the gross weights, coarse scales and labels broad
You offer their refinement. Fool or knave?
Why needs a bishop be a fool or knave
When there's a thousand diamond weights between?
So, I enlist them. Your picked twelve, you'll find,
Profess themselves indignant, scandalized

At thus being held unable to explain
How a superior man who disbelieves
May not believe as well: that's Schelling's way!
It's through my coming in the tail of time,
Nicking the minute with a happy tact.
Had I been born three hundred years ago
They'd say, "What's strange? Blougram of course believes;"
And, seventy years since, "disbelieves of course."
But now, "He may believe; and yet, and yet
How can he?" All eyes turn with interest.
Whereas, step off the line on either side—
You, for example, clever to a fault,
The rough and ready man who write apace,
Read somewhat seldomer, think perhaps even less—
You disbelieve! Who wonders and who cares?
Lord So-and-so—his coat bedropped with wax,
All Peter's chains about his waist, his back
Brave with the needlework of Noodledom—
Believes! Again, who wonders and who cares?
But I, the man of sense and learning too,
The able to think yet act, the this, the that,
I, to believe at this late time of day!
Enough; you see, I need not fear contempt.

—Except it's yours! Admire me as these may
You don't. But whom at least do you admire?
Present your own perfection, your ideal,
Your pattern man for a minute—oh, make haste!
Is it Napoleon you would have us grow?
Concede the means; allow his head and hand,
(A large concession, clever as you are)
Good! In our common primal element
Of unbelief (we can't believe, you know—
We're still at that admission, recollect!)
Where do you find—apart from, towering o'er
The secondary temporary aims
Which satisfy the gross taste you despise—
Where do you find his star?—his crazy trust
God knows through what or in what? it's alive
And shines and leads him, and that's all we want.
Have we aught in our sober night shall point
Such ends as his were, and direct the means
Of working out our purpose straight as his,
Nor bring a moment's trouble on success
With after-care to justify the same?
—Be a Napoleon, and yet disbelieve—

Why, the man's mad, friend, take his light away!
What's the vague good o' the world, for which you dare
With comfort to yourself blow millions up?
We neither of us see it! we do see
The blown-up millions—spatter of their brains
And writhing of their bowels and so forth,
In that bewildering entanglement
Of horrible eventualities
Past calculation to the end of time!
Can I mistake for some clear word of God
(Which were my ample warrant for it all)
His puff of hazy instinct, idle talk,
"The State, that's I," quack-nonsense about crowns,
And (when one beats the man to his last hold)
A vague idea of setting things to rights,
Policing people efficaciously,
More to their profit, most of all to his own;
The whole to end that dismallest of ends
By an Austrian marriage, cant to us the Church,
And resurrection of the old régime?
Would I, who hope to live a dozen years,
Fight Austerlitz for reasons such and such?
No: for, concede me but the merest chance
Doubt may be wrong—there's judgment, life to come!
With just that chance, I dare not. Doubt proves right?
This present life is all?—you offer me
Its dozen noisy years, without a chance
That wedding an archduchess, wearing lace,
And getting called by divers new-coined names,
Will drive off ugly thoughts and let me dine,
Sleep, read and chat in quiet as I like!
Therefore I will not.

                        Take another case;
Fit up the cabin yet another way.
What say you to the poets? shall we write
Hamlet, Othello—make the world our own,
Without a risk to run of either sort?
I can't!—to put the strongest reason first.
"But try," you urge, "the trying shall suffice;
The aim, if reached or not, makes great the life:
Try to be Shakespeare, leave the rest to fate!"
Spare my self-knowledge—there's no fooling me!
If I prefer remaining my poor self,
I say so not in self-dispraise but praise.
If I'm a Shakespeare, let the well alone;

Why should I try to be what now I am?
If I'm no Shakespeare, as too probable,—
His power and consciousness and self-delight
And all we want in common, shall I find—
Trying forever? while on points of taste
Wherewith, to speak it humbly, he and I
Are dowered alike—I'll ask you, I or he,
Which in our two lives realizes most?
Much, he imagined—somewhat, I possess.
He had the imagination; stick to that!
Let him say, "In the face of my soul's works
Your world is worthless and I touch it not
Lest I should wrong them"—I'll withdraw my plea.
But does he say so? look upon his life!
Himself, who only can, gives judgment there.
He leaves his towers and gorgeous palaces
To build the trimmest house in Stratford town;
Saves money, spends it, owns the worth of things,
Giulio Romano's pictures, Dowland's lute;
Enjoys a show, respects the puppets, too,
And none more, had he seen its entry once,
Than "Pandulph, of fair Milan cardinal."
Why then should I who play that personage,
The very Pandulph Shakespeare's fancy made,
Be told that had the poet chanced to start
From where I stand now (some degree like mine
Being just the goal he ran his race to reach)
He would have run the whole race back, forsooth,
And left being Pandulph, to begin write plays?
Ah, the earth's best can be but the earth's best!
Did Shakespeare live, he could but sit at home
And get himself in dreams the Vatican,
Greek busts, Venetian paintings, Roman walls,
And English books, none equal to his own,
Which I read, bound in gold (he never did).
—Terni's fall, Naples' bay, and Gothard's top—
Eh, friend? I could not fancy one of these;
But, as I pour this claret, there they are:
I've gained them—crossed St. Gothard last July
With ten mules to the carriage and a bed
Slung inside; is my hap the worse for that?
We want the same things, Shakespeare and myself,
And what I want, I have: he, gifted more,
Could fancy he too had them when he liked,
But not so thoroughly that, if fate allowed,
He would not have them also in my sense.

We play one game; I send the ball aloft
No less adroitly that of fifty strokes
Scarce five go o'er the wall so wide and high
Which sends them back to me: I wish and get.
He struck balls higher and with better skill,
But at a poor fence level with his head,
And hit—his Stratford house, a coat of arms,
Successful dealings in his grain and wool,—
While I receive heaven's incense in my nose
And style myself the cousin of Queen Bess.
Ask him, if this life's all, who wins the game?

Believe—and our whole argument breaks up.
Enthusiasm's the best thing, I repeat;
Only, we can't command it; fire and life
Are all, dead matter's nothing, we agree:
And be it a mad dream or God's very breath,
The fact's the same,—belief's fire, once in us,
Makes of all else mere stuff to show itself:
We penetrate our life with such a glow
As fire lends wood and iron—this turns steel,
That burns to ash—all's one, fire proves its power
For good or ill, since men call flare success.
But paint a fire, it will not therefore burn.
Light one in me, I'll find it food enough!
Why, to be Luther—that's a life to lead,
Incomparably better than my own.
He comes, reclaims God's earth for God, he says,
Sets up God's rule again by simple means,
Reopens a shut book, and all is done.
He flared out in the flaring of mankind;
Such Luther's luck was: how shall such be mine?
If he succeeded, nothing's left to do:
And if he did not altogether—well,
Strauss is the next advance. All Strauss should be
I might be also. But to what result?
He looks upon no future: Luther did.
What can I gain on the denying side?
Ice makes no conflagration. State the facts,
Read the text right, emancipate the world—
The emancipated world enjoys itself
With scarce a thank-you: Blougram told it first
It could not owe a farthing,—not to him
More than Saint Paul! 'twould press its pay, you think?
Then add there's still that plaguy hundredth chance

Strauss may be wrong. And so a risk is run—
For what gain? not for Luther's, who secured
A real heaven in his heart throughout his life,
Supposing death a little altered things.

"Ay, but since really you lack faith," you cry,
"You run the same risk really on all sides,
In cool indifference as bold unbelief.
As well be Strauss as swing 'twixt Paul and him.
It's not worth having, such imperfect faith,
No more available to do faith's work
Than unbelief like mine. Whole faith, or none!"

Softly, my friend! I must dispute that point.
Once own the use of faith, I'll find you faith.
We're back on Christian ground. You call for faith:
I show you doubt, to prove that faith exists.
The more of doubt, the stronger faith, I say,
If faith o'ercomes doubt. How I know it does?
By life and man's free will, God gave for that!
To mould life as we choose it, shows our choice:
That's our one act, the previous work's his own.
You criticise the soul? it reared this tree—
This broad life and whatever fruit it bears!
What matter though I doubt at every pore,
Head-doubts, heart-doubts, doubts at my fingers' ends,
Doubts in the trivial work of every day,
Doubts at the very bases of my soul
In the grand moments when she probes herself—
If finally I have a life to show,
The thing I did, brought out in evidence
Against the thing done to me underground
By hell and all its brood, for aught I know?
I say, whence sprang this? shows it faith or doubt?
All's doubt in me; where's break of faith in this?
It is the idea, the feeling and the love,
God means mankind should strive for and show forth
Whatever be the process to that end,—
And not historic knowledge, logic sound,
And metaphysical acumen, sure!
"What think ye of Christ," friend? when all's done and said
Like you this Christianity or not?
It may be false, but will you wish it true?
Has it your vote to be so if it can?
Trust you an instinct silenced long ago

That will break silence and enjoin you love
What mortified philosophy is hoarse,
And all in vain, with bidding you despise?
If you desire faith—then you've faith enough:
What else seeks God—nay, what else seek ourselves?
You form a notion of me, we'll suppose,
On hearsay; it's a favorable one:
"But still" (you add), "there was no such good man,
Because of contradiction in the facts.
One proves, for instance, he was born in Rome,
This Blougram; yet throughout the tales of him
I see he figures as an Englishman."
Well, the two things are reconcilable.
But would I rather you discovered that,
Subjoining—"Still, what matter though they be?
Blougram concerns me nought, born here or there."

Pure faith indeed—you know not what you ask!
Naked belief in God the Omnipotent,
Omniscient, Omnipresent, sears too much
The sense of conscious creatures to be borne.
It were the seeing him, no flesh shall dare.
Some think, Creation's meant to show him forth:
I say it's meant to hide him all it can,
And that's what all the blessed evil's for.
Its use in Time is to environ us,
Our breath, our drop of dew, with shield enough
Against that sight till we can bear its stress.
Under a vertical sun, the exposed brain
And lidless eye and disemprisoned heart
Less certainly would wither up at once
Than mind, confronted with the truth of him.
But time and earth case-harden us to live;
The feeblest sense is trusted most; the child
Feels God a moment, ichors o'er the place,
Plays on and grows to be a man like us.
With me, faith means perpetual unbelief
Kept quiet like the snake 'neath Michael's foot
Who stands calm just because he feels it writhe.
Or, if that's too ambitious,—here's my box—
I need the excitation of a pinch
Threatening the torpor of the inside-nose
Nigh on the imminent sneeze that never comes.
"Leave it in peace," advise the simple folk:
Make it aware of peace by itching-fits,
Say I—let doubt occasion still more faith!

You'll say, once all believed, man, woman, child,
In that dear middle-age these noodles praise.
How you'd exult if I could put you back
Six hundred years, blot out cosmogony,
Geology, ethnology, what not
(Greek endings, each the little passing-bell
That signifies some faith's about to die),
And set you square with Genesis again,—
When such a traveller told you his last news,
He saw the ark a-top of Ararat
But did not climb there since 'twas getting dusk
And robber-bands infest the mountain's foot!
How should you feel, I ask, in such an age,
How act? As other people felt and did;
With soul more blank than this decanter's knob,
Believe—and yet lie, kill, rob, fornicate,
Full in belief's face, like the beast you'd be!

No, when the fight begins within himself,
A man's worth something. God stoops o'er his head,
Satan looks up between his feet—both tug—
He's left, himself, i' the middle: the soul wakes
And grows. Prolong that battle through his life!
Never leave growing till the life to come!
Here, we've got callous to the Virgin's winks
That used to puzzle people wholesomely:
Men have outgrown the shame of being fools.
What are the laws of nature, not to bend
If the Church bid them?—brother Newman asks.
Up with the Immaculate Conception, then—
On to the rack with faith!—is my advice.
Will not that hurry us upon our knees,
Knocking our breasts, "It can't be—yet it shall!
Who am I, the worm, to argue with my Pope?
Low things confound the high things!" and so forth.
That's better than acquitting God with grace
As some folk do. He's tried—no case is proved,
Philosophy is lenient—he may go!

You'll say, the old system's not so obsolete
But men believe still: ay, but who and where?
King Bomba's lazzaroni foster yet
The sacred flame, so Antonelli writes;
But even of these, what ragamuffin-saint
Believes God watches him continually,

As he believes in fire that it will burn,
Or rain that it will drench him? Break fire's law,
Sin against rain, although the penalty
Be just a singe or soaking? "No," he smiles;
"Those laws are laws that can enforce themselves."

The sum of all is—yes, my doubt is great,
My faith's still greater, then my faith's enough.
I have read much, thought much, experienced much,
Yet would die rather than avow my fear
The Naples' liquefaction may be false,
When set to happen by the palace-clock
According to the clouds or dinner-time.
I hear you recommend, I might at least
Eliminate, decrassify my faith
Since I adopt it; keeping what I must
And leaving what I can—such points as this.
I won't—that is, I can't throw one away.
Supposing there's no truth in what I hold
About the need of trial to man's faith,
Still, when you bid me purify the same,
To such a process I discern no end.
Clearing off one excrescence to see two,
There's ever a next in size, now grown as big,
That meets the knife: I cut and cut again!
First cut the Liquefaction, what comes last
But Fichte's clever cut at God himself?
Experimentalize on sacred things!
I trust nor hand nor eye nor heart nor brain
To stop betimes: they all get drunk alike.
The first step, I am master not to take.

You'd find the cutting-process to your taste
As much as leaving growths of lies unpruned,
Nor see more danger in it,—you retort.
Your taste's worth mine; but my taste proves more wise
When we consider that the steadfast hold
On the extreme end of the chain of faith
Gives all the advantage, makes the difference
With the rough purblind mass we seek to rule:
We are their lords, or they are free of us,
Just as we tighten or relax our hold.
So, other matters equal, we'll revert
To the first problem—which, if solved my way

And thrown into the balance, turns the scale—
How we may lead a comfortable life,
How suit our luggage to the cabin's size.

Of course you are remarking all this time
How narrowly and grossly I view life,
Respect the creature-comforts, care to rule
The masses, and regard complacently
"The cabin," in our old phrase. Well, I do.
I act for, talk for, live for this world now,
As this world prizes action, life and talk:
No prejudice to what next world may prove,
Whose new laws and requirements, my best pledge
To observe then, is that I observe these now,
Shall do hereafter what I do meanwhile.
Let us concede (gratuitously though)
Next life relieves the soul of body, yields
Pure spiritual enjoyment: well, my friend,
Why lose this life i' the meantime, since its use
May be to make the next life more intense?

Do you know, I have often had a dream
(Work it up in your next month's article)
Of man's poor spirit in its progress, still
Losing true life forever and a day
Through ever trying to be and ever being—
In the evolution of successive spheres—
Before its actual sphere and place of life,
Halfway into the next, which having reached,
It shoots with corresponding foolery
Halfway into the next still, on and off!
As when a traveller, bound from North to South,
Scouts fur in Russia: what's its use in France?
In France spurns flannel: where's its need in Spain?
In Spain drops cloth, too cumbrous for Algiers!
Linen goes next, and last the skin itself,
A superfluity at Timbuctoo.
When, through his journey, was the fool at ease?
I'm at ease now, friend; worldly in this world,
I take and like its way of life; I think
My brothers, who administer the means,
Live better for my comfort—that's good too;
And God, if he pronounce upon such life,
Approves my service, which is better still.
If he keep silence,—why, for you or me

Or that brute beast pulled-up in to-day's "Times,"
What odds is 't, save to ourselves, what life we lead?

    You meet me at this issue: you declare,—
All special-pleading done with—truth is truth,
And justifies itself by undreamed ways.
You don't fear but it's better, if we doubt,
To say so, act up to our truth perceived
However feebly. Do then,—act away!
'Tis there I'm on the watch for you. How one acts
Is, both of us agree, our chief concern:
And how you'll act is what I fain would see
If, like the candid person you appear,
You dare to make the most of your life's scheme
As I of mine, live up to its full law
Since there's no higher law that counterchecks.
Put natural religion to the test
You've just demolished the revealed with—quick,
Down to the root of all that checks your will,
All prohibition to lie, kill and thieve,
Or even to be an atheistic priest!
Suppose a pricking to incontinence—
Philosophers deduce you chastity
Or shame, from just the fact that at the first
Whoso embraced a woman in the field,
Threw club down and forewent his brains beside,
So, stood a ready victim in the reach
Of any brother savage, club in hand;
Hence saw the use of going out of sight
In wood or cave to prosecute his loves:
I read this in a French book t'other day.
Does law so analyzed coerce you much?
Oh, men spin clouds of fuzz where matters end,
But you who reach where the first thread begins,
You'll soon cut that!—which means you can, but won't,
Through certain instincts, blind, unreasoned-out,
You dare not set aside, you can't tell why,
But there they are, and so you let them rule.
Then, friend, you seem as much a slave as I,
A liar, conscious coward and hypocrite,
Without the good the slave expects to get,
In case he has a master after all!
You own your instincts? why, what else do I,
Who want, am made for, and must have a God
Ere I can be aught, do aught?—no mere name
Want, but the true thing with what proves its truth,

To wit, a relation from that thing to me,
Touching from head to foot—which touch I feel,
And with it take the rest, this life of ours!
I live my life here; yours you dare not live.

—Not as I state it, who (you please subjoin)
Disfigure such a life and call it names,
While, to your mind, remains another way
For simple men: knowledge and power have rights,
But ignorance and weakness have rights too.
There needs no crucial effort to find truth
If here or there or anywhere about:
We ought to turn each side, try hard and see,
And if we can't, be glad we've earned at least
The right, by one laborious proof the more,
To graze in peace earth's pleasant pasturage.
Men are not angels, neither are they brutes:
Something we may see, all we cannot see.
What need of lying? I say, I see all,
And swear to each detail the most minute
In what I think a Pan's face—you, mere cloud:
I swear I hear him speak and see him wink,
For fear, if once I drop the emphasis,
Mankind may doubt there's any cloud at all.
You take the simple life—ready to see,
Willing to see (for no cloud's worth a face)—
And leaving quiet what no strength can move,
And which, who bids you move? who has the right?
I bid you; but you are God's sheep, not mine:
"Pastor est tui Dominus." You find
In this the pleasant pasture of our life
Much you may eat without the least offence,
Much you don't eat because your maw objects,
Much you would eat but that your fellow-flock
Open great eyes at you and even butt,
And thereupon you like your mates so well
You cannot please yourself, offending them;
Though when they seem exorbitantly sheep,
You weigh your pleasure with their butts and bleats
And strike the balance. Sometimes certain fears
Restrain you, real checks since you find them so;
Sometimes you please yourself and nothing checks:
And thus you graze through life with not one lie,
And like it best.
                    But do you, in truth's name?
If so, you beat—which means you are not I—

Who needs must make earth mine and feed my fill
Not simply unbutted at, unbickered with,
But motioned to the velvet of the sward
By those obsequious wethers' very selves.
Look at me, sir; my age is double yours:
At yours, I knew beforehand, so enjoyed,
What now I should be—as, permit the word,
I pretty well imagine your whole range
And stretch of tether twenty years to come.
We both have minds and bodies much alike:
In truth's name, don't you want my bishopric,
My daily bread, my influence, and my state?
You're young. I'm old; you must be old one day;
Will you find then, as I do hour by hour,
Women their lovers kneel to, who cut curls
From your fat lap-dog's ear to grace a brooch—
Dukes, who petition just to kiss your ring—
With much beside you know or may conceive?
Suppose we die to-night: well, here am I,
Such were my gains, life bore this fruit to me,
While writing all the same my articles
On music, poetry, the fictile vase
Found at Albano, chess, Anacreon's Greek.
But you—the highest honor in your life,
The thing you'll crown yourself with, all your days,
Is—dining here and drinking this last glass
I pour you out in sign of amity
Before we part forever. Of your power
And social influence, worldly worth in short,
Judge what's my estimation by the fact,
I do not condescend to enjoin, beseech,
Hint secrecy on one of all these words!
You're shrewd and know that should you publish one
The world would brand the lie—my enemies first,
Who'd sneer—"the bishop's an arch-hypocrite
And knave perhaps, but not so frank a fool."
Whereas I should not dare for both my ears
Breathe one such syllable, smile one such smile,
Before the chaplain who reflects myself—
My shade's so much more potent than your flesh.
What's your reward, self-abnegating friend?
Stood you confessed of those exceptional
And privileged great natures that dwarf mine—
A zealot with a mad ideal in reach,
A poet just about to print his ode,
A statesman with a scheme to stop this war,

An artist whose religion is his art—
I should have nothing to object: such men
Carry the fire, all things grow warm to them,
Their drugget's worth my purple, they beat me.
But you,—you're just as little those as I—
You, Gigadibs, who, thirty years of age,
Write stately for Blackwood's Magazine,
Believe you see two points in Hamlet's soul
Unseized by the Germans yet—which view you'll print—
Meantime the best you have to show being still
That lively lightsome article we took
Almost for the true Dickens,—what's its name?
"The Slum and Cellar, or Whitechapel life
Limned after dark!" it made me laugh, I know,
And pleased a month, and brought you in ten pounds.
—Success I recognize and compliment,
And therefore give you, if you choose, three words
(The card and pencil-scratch is quite enough)
Which whether here, in Dublin or New York,
Will get you, prompt as at my eyebrow's wink,
Such terms as never you aspired to get
In all our own reviews and some not ours.
Go write your lively sketches! be the first
"Blougram, or The Eccentric Confidence"—
Or better simply say, "The Outward-bound."
Why, men as soon would throw it in my teeth
As copy and quote the infamy chalked broad
About me on the church-door opposite.
You will not wait for that experience though,
I fancy, howsoever you decide,
To discontinue—not detesting, not
Defaming, but at least—despising me!

———

    Over his wine so smiled and talked his hour
Sylvester Blougram, styled *in partibus*
Episcopus, nec non—(the deuce knows what
It's changed to by our novel hierarchy)
With Gigadibs the literary man,
Who played with spoons, explored his plate's design,
And ranged the olive-stones about its edge,
While the great bishop rolled him out a mind
Long crumpled, till creased consciousness lay smooth.

    For Blougram, he believed, say, half he spoke.
The other portion, as he shaped it thus
For argumentatory purposes,

He felt his foe was foolish to dispute.
Some arbitrary accidental thoughts
That crossed his mind, amusing because new,
He chose to represent as fixtures there,
Invariable convictions (such they seemed
Beside his interlocutor's loose cards
Flung daily down, and not the same way twice),
While certain hell-deep instincts, man's weak tongue
Is never bold to utter in their truth
Because styled hell-deep ('tis an old mistake
To place hell at the bottom of the earth);
He ignored these,—not having in readiness
Their nomenclature and philosophy:
He said true things, but called them by wrong names.
"On the whole," he thought, "I justify myself
On every point where cavillers like this
Oppugn my life: he tries one kind of fence,
I close, he's worsted, that's enough for him.
He's on the ground: if ground should break away
I take my stand on, there's a firmer yet
Beneath it, both of us may sink and reach.
His ground was over mine and broke the first:
So, let him sit with me this many a year!"

He did not sit five minutes. Just a week
Sufficed his sudden healthy vehemence.
Something had struck him in the "Outward-bound"
Another way than Blougram's purpose was:
And having bought, not cabin-furniture
But settler's-implements (enough for three)
And started for Australia—there, I hope,
By this time he has tested his first plough,
And studied his last chapter of St. John.

DRAMATIS PERSONÆ

1864

ABT VOGLER

(After He Has Been Extemporizing upon the Musical Instrument of His Invention)

I.

WOULD that the structure brave, the manifold music I build,
  Bidding my organ obey, calling its keys to their work,
Claiming each slave of the sound, at a touch, as when Solomon willed

Armies of angels that soar, legions of demons that lurk,
Man, brute, reptile, fly,—alien of end and of aim,
  Adverse, each from the other heaven-high, hell-deep removed,—
Should rush into sight at once as he named the ineffable Name,
  And pile him a palace straight, to pleasure the princess he loved!

II.

Would it might tarry like his, the beautiful building of mine,
  This which my keys in a crowd pressed and importuned to raise!
Ah, one and all, how they helped, would dispart now and now combine,
  Zealous to hasten the work, heighten their master his praise!
And one would bury his brow with a blind plunge down to hell,
  Burrow awhile and build, broad on the roots of things,
Then up again swim into sight, having based me my palace well,
  Founded it, fearless of flame, flat on the nether springs.

III.

And another would mount and march, like the excellent minion he was,
  Ay, another and yet another, one crowd but with many a crest,
Raising my rampired walls of gold as transparent as glass,
  Eager to do and die, yield each his place to the rest:
For higher still and higher (as a runner tips with fire,
  When a great illumination surprises a festal night—
Outlining round and round Rome's dome from space to spire)
  Up, the pinnacled glory reached, and the pride of my soul was in sight.

IV.

In sight? Not half! for it seemed, it was certain, to match man's birth,
  Nature in turn conceived, obeying an impulse as I;
And the emulous heaven yearned down, made effort to reach the earth,
  As the earth had done her best, in my passion, to scale the sky:
Novel splendors burst forth, grew familiar and dwelt with mine,
  Not a point nor peak but found and fixed its wandering star;
Meteor-moons, balls of blaze: and they did not pale nor pine,
  For earth had attained to heaven, there was no more near nor far.

V.

Nay more; for there wanted not who walked in the glare and glow,
  Presences plain in the place; or, fresh from the Protoplast,
Furnished for ages to come, when a kindlier wind should blow,
  Lured now to begin and live, in a house to their liking at last;
Or else the wonderful Dead who have passed through the body and gone,
  But were back once more to breathe in an old world worth their new:
What never had been, was now; what was, as it shall be anon;
  And what is,—shall I say, matched both? for I was made perfect too.

VI.

All through my keys that gave their sounds to a wish of my soul,
   All through my soul that praised as its wish flowed visibly forth,
All through music and me! For think, had I painted the whole,
   Why, there it had stood, to see, nor the process so wonder-worth:
Had I written the same, made verse—still, effect proceeds from cause,
   Ye know why the forms are fair, ye hear how the tale is told;
It is all triumphant art, but art in obedience to laws,
   Painter and poet are proud in the artist-list enrolled:—

VII.

But here is the finger of God, a flash of the will that can,
   Existent behind all laws, that made them and, lo, they are!
And I know not if, save in this, such gift be allowed to man,
   That out of three sounds he frame, not a fourth sound, but a star.
Consider it well: each tone of our scale in itself is nought;
   It is everywhere in the world—loud, soft, and all is said:
Give it to me to use! I mix it with two in my thought:
   And, there! Ye have heard and seen: consider and bow the head!

VIII.

Well, it is gone at last, the palace of music I reared;
   Gone! and the good tears start, the praises that come too slow;
For one is assured at first, one scarce can say that he feared,
   That he even gave it a thought, the gone thing was to go.
Never to be again! But many more of the kind
   As good, nay, better perchance: is this your comfort to me?
To me, who must be saved because I cling with my mind
   To the same, same self, same love, same God: ay, what was, shall be.

IX.

Therefore to whom turn I but to Thee, the ineffable Name?
   Builder and maker, Thou, of houses not made with hands!
What, have fear of change from Thee who art ever the same?
   Doubt that Thy power can fill the heart that Thy power expands?
There shall never be one lost good! What was, shall live as before;
   The evil is null, is nought, is silence implying sound;
What was good, shall be good, with, for evil, so much good more;
   On the earth the broken arcs; in the heaven, a perfect round.

X.

All we have willed or hoped or dreamed of good, shall exist;
   Not its semblance, but itself; no beauty, nor good, nor power
Whose voice has gone forth, but each survives for the melodist
   When eternity affirms the conception of an hour.
The high that proved too high, the heroic for earth too hard,

The passion that left the ground to lose itself in the sky,
Are music sent up to God by the lover and the bard;
  Enough that he heard it once: we shall hear it by-and-by.

XI.

And what is our failure here but a triumph's evidence
  For the fulness of the days? Have we withered or agonized?
Why else was the pause prolonged but that singing might issue **thence?**
  Why rushed the discords in, but that harmony should be **prized?**
Sorrow is hard to bear, and doubt is slow to clear,
  Each sufferer says his say, his scheme of the weal and woe:
But God has a few of us whom he whispers in the ear;
  The rest may reason and welcome: 't is we musicians know.

XII.

Well, it is earth with me; silence resumes her reign:
  I will be patient and proud, and soberly acquiesce.
Give me the keys. I feel for the common chord again,
  Sliding by semitones, till I sink to the minor,—yes,
And I blunt it into a ninth, and I stand on alien ground,
  Surveying awhile the heights I rolled from into the deep;
Which, hark, I have dared and done, for my resting-place is **found,**
  The C Major of this life: so, now I will try to sleep.

RABBI BEN EZRA

I.

Grow old along with me!
The best is yet to be,
The last of life, for which the first was made:
Our times are in His hand
Who saith, "A whole I planned,
Youth shows but half; trust God: see all, nor be afraid!"

II.

Not that, amassing flowers,
Youth sighed, "Which rose make ours,
Which lily leave and then as best recall?"
Not that, admiring stars,
It yearned, "Nor Jove, nor Mars;
Mine be some figured flame which blends, transcends them all!"

III.

Not for such hopes and fears
Annulling youth's brief years,

Do I remonstrate: folly wide the mark!
Rather I prize the doubt
Low kinds exist without,
Finished and finite clods, untroubled by a spark.

IV.

Poor vaunt of life indeed,
Were man but formed to feed
On joy, to solely seek and find and feast;
Such feasting ended, then
As sure an end to men;
Irks care the crop-full bird? Frets doubt the maw-crammed beast?

V.

Rejoice we are allied
To That which doth provide
And not partake, effect and not receive!
A spark disturbs our clod;
Nearer we hold of God
Who gives, than of His tribes that take, I must believe.

VI.

Then, welcome each rebuff
That turns earth's smoothness rough,
Each sting that bids nor sit nor stand but go!
Be our joys three-parts pain!
Strive, and hold cheap the strain;
Learn, nor account the pang; dare, never grudge the throe!

VII.

For thence,—a paradox
Which comforts while it mocks,—
Shall life succeed in that it seems to fail:
What I aspired to be,
And was not, comforts me:
A brute I might have been, but would not sink i' the scale.

VIII.

What is he but a brute
Whose flesh hath soul to suit,
Whose spirit works lest arms and legs want play?
To man, propose this test—
Thy body at its best,
How far can that project thy soul on its lone way?

IX.

Yet gifts should prove their use:
I own the Past profuse
Of power each side, perfection every turn:
Eyes, ears took in their dole,
Brain treasured up the whole;
Should not the heart beat once "How good to live and learn"?

X.

Not once beat "Praise be Thine!
I see the whole design,
I, who saw power, see now Love perfect too:
Perfect I call Thy plan:
Thanks that I was a man!
Maker, remake, complete,—I trust what Thou shalt do!"

XI.

For pleasant is this flesh;
Our soul, in its rose-mesh
Pulled ever to the earth, still yearns for rest:
Would we some prize might hold
To match those manifold
Possessions of the brute,—gain most, as we did best!

XII.

Let us not always say,
"Spite of this flesh to-day
I strove, made head, gained ground upon the whole!"
As the bird wings and sings,
Let us cry, "All good things
Are ours, nor soul helps flesh more, now, than flesh helps soul!"

XIII.

Therefore I summon age
To grant youth's heritage,
Life's struggle having so far reached its term:
Thence shall I pass, approved
A man, for aye removed
From the developed brute; a God though in the germ.

XIV.

And I shall thereupon
Take rest, ere I be gone
Once more on my adventure brave and new:
Fearless and unperplexed,
When I wage battle next,
What weapons to select. what armor to indue.

xv.

Youth ended, I shall try
My gain or loss thereby;
Leave the fire-ashes, what survives is gold:
And I shall weigh the same,
Give life its praise or blame:
Young, all lay in dispute; I shall know, being old.

xvi.

For note, when evening shuts,
A certain moment cuts
The deed off, calls the glory from the gray:
A whisper from the west
Shoots—"Add this to the rest,
Take it and try its worth: here dies another day."

xvii.

So, still within this life,
Though lifted o'er its strife,
Let me discern, compare, pronounce at last,
"This rage was right i' the main,
That acquiescence vain:
The Future I may face now I have proved the Past."

xviii.

For more is not reserved
To man, with soul just nerved
To act to-morrow what he learns to-day:
Here, work enough to watch
The Master work, and catch
Hints of the proper craft, tricks of the tool's true play.

xix.

As it was better, youth
Should strive, through acts uncouth,
Toward making, than repose on aught found made:
So, better, age, exempt
From strife, should know, than tempt
Further. Thou waitedst age: wait death nor be afraid!

xx.

Enough now, if the Right
And Good and Infinite
Be named here, as thou callest thy hand thine own,
With knowledge absolute,
Subject to no dispute
From fools that crowded youth, nor let thee feel alone.

XXI.

Be there, for once and all,
Severed great minds from small,
Announced to each his station in the Past!
Was I, the world arraigned,
Were they, my soul disdained,
Right? Let age speak the truth and give us peace at last!

XXII.

Now, who shall arbitrate?
Ten men love what I hate,
Shun what I follow, slight what I receive;
Ten, who in ears and eyes
Match me: we all surmise,
They this thing, and I that: whom shall my soul believe?

XXIII.

Not on the vulgar mass
Called "work," must sentence pass,
Things done, that took the eye and had the price;
O'er which, from level stand,
The low world laid its hand,
Found straightway to its mind, could value in a trice:

XXIV.

But all, the world's coarse thumb
And finger failed to plumb,
So passed in making up the main account;
All instincts immature,
All purposes unsure,
That weighed not as his work, yet swelled the man's amount:

XXV.

Thoughts hardly to be packed
Into a narrow act,
Fancies that broke through language and escaped;
All I could never be,
All, men ignored in me,
This, I was worth to God, whose wheel the pitcher shaped.

XXVI.

Ay, note that Potter's wheel,
That metaphor! and feel
Why time spins fast, why passive lies our clay,—
Thou, to whom fools propound,
When the wine makes its round,
"Since life fleets, all is change; the Past gone, seize to-day!"

XXVII.

Fool! All that is, at all,
Lasts ever, past recall;
Earth changes, but thy soul and God stand sure:
What entered into thee,
That was, is, and shall be:
Time's wheel runs back or stops: Potter and clay endure.

XXVIII.

He fixed thee 'mid this dance
Of plastic circumstance,
This Present, thou, forsooth, wouldst fain arrest:
Machinery just meant
To give thy soul its bent,
Try thee and turn thee forth, sufficiently impressed.

XXIX.

What though the earlier grooves,
Which ran the laughing loves
Around thy base, no longer pause and press?
What though, about thy rim,
Scull-things in order grim
Grow out, in graver mood, obey the sterner stress?

XXX.

Look not thou down but up!
To uses of a cup,
The festal board, lamp's flash and trumpet's peal,
The new wine's foaming flow,
The Master's lips aglow!
Thou, heaven's consummate cup, what needst thou with earth's wheel?

XXXI.

But I need, now as then,
Thee, God, who mouldest men;
And since, not even while the whirl was worst,
Did I—to the wheel of life
With shapes and colors rife,
Bound dizzily—mistake my end, to slake Thy thirst:

XXXII.

So, take and use Thy work:
Amend what flaws may lurk,
What strain o' the stuff, what warpings past the aim!
My times be in Thy hand!
Perfect the cup as planned!
Let age approve of youth, and death complete the same!

CALIBAN UPON SETEBOS

OR,

NATURAL THEOLOGY IN THE ISLAND

"Thou thoughtest that I was altogether such an one as thyself."

['WILL sprawl, now that the heat of day is best,
Flat on his belly in the pit's much mire,
With elbows wide, fists clenched to prop his chin.
And, while he kicks both feet in the cool slush,
And feels about his spine small eft-things course,
Run in and out each arm, and make him laugh:
And while above his head a pompion-plant,
Coating the cave-top as a brow its eye,
Creeps down to touch and tickle hair and beard,
And now a flower drops with a bee inside,
And now a fruit to snap at, catch and crunch,—
He looks out o'er yon sea which sunbeams cross
And recross till they weave a spider-web,
(Meshes of fire, some great fish breaks at times,)
And talks to his own self, howe'er he please,
Touching that other, whom his dam called God.
Because to talk about Him, vexes—ha,
Could He but know! and time to vex is now,
When talk is safer than in winter-time.
Moreover Prosper and Miranda sleep
In confidence he drudges at their task,
And it is good to cheat the pair, and gibe,
Letting the rank tongue blossom into speech.]

Setebos, Setebos, and Setebos!
'Thinketh, He dwelleth i' the cold o' the moon.

'Thinketh He made it, with the sun to match,
But not the stars; the stars came otherwise;
Only made clouds, winds, meteors, such as that:
Also this isle, what lives and grows thereon,
And snaky sea which rounds and ends the same.

'Thinketh, it came of being ill at ease:
He hated that He cannot change His cold,
Nor cure its ache. 'Hath spied an icy fish
That longed to 'scape the rock-stream where she lived,

And thaw herself within the lukewarm brine
O' the lazy sea her stream thrusts far amid,
A crystal spike 'twixt two warm walls of wave;
Only, she ever sickened, found repulse
At the other kind of water, not her life,
(Green-dense and dim-delicious, bred o' the sun,)
Flounced back from bliss she was not born to breathe,
And in her old bounds buried her despair,
Hating and loving warmth alike: so He.

'Thinketh, He made thereat the sun, this isle,
Trees and the fowls here, beast and creeping thing.
Yon otter, sleek-wet, black, lithe as a leech;
Yon auk, one fire-eye in a ball of foam,
That floats and feeds; a certain badger brown
He hath watched hunt with that slant white-wedge eye
By moonlight; and the pie with the long tongue
That pricks deep into oakwarts for a worm,
And says a plain word when she finds her prize,
But will not eat the ants; the ants themselves
That build a wall of seeds and settled stalks
About their hole—He made all these and more,
Made all we see, and us, in spite: how else?
He could not, Himself, make a second self
To be His mate; as well have made Himself:
He would not make what He mislikes or slights,
An eyesore to Him, or not worth His pains:
But did, in envy, listlessness or sport,
Make what Himself would fain, in a manner, be—
Weaker in most points, stronger in a few,
Worthy, and yet mere playthings all the while,
Things He admires and mocks too,—that is it.
Because, so brave, so better though they be,
It nothing skills if He begin to plague.
Look now, I melt a gourd-fruit into mash,
Add honeycomb and pods, I have perceived,
Which bite like finches when they bill and kiss,—
Then, when froth rises bladdery, drink up all,
Quick, quick, till maggots scamper through my brain;
Last, throw me on my back i' the seeded thyme,
And wanton, wishing I were born a bird.
Put case, unable to be what I wish,
I yet could make a live bird out of clay:
Would not I take clay, pinch my Caliban
Able to fly?—for, there, see, he hath wings,
And great comb like the hoopoe's to admire,

And there, a sting to do his foes offence,
There, and I will that he begin to live,
Fly to yon rock-top, nip me off the horns
Of grigs high up that make the merry din,
Saucy through their veined wings, and mind me not.
In which feat, if his leg snapped, brittle clay,
And he lay stupid-like,—why, I should laugh;
And if he, spying me, should fall to weep,
Beseech me to be good, repair his wrong,
Bid his poor leg smart less or grow again,—
Well, as the chance were, this might take or else
Not take my fancy: I might hear his cry,
And give the manikin three sound legs for one,
Or pluck the other off, leave him like an egg,
And lessoned he was mine and merely clay.
Were this no pleasure, lying in the thyme,
Drinking the mash, with brain become alive,
Making and marring clay at will? So He.

'Thinketh, such shows nor right nor wrong in Him,
Nor kind, nor cruel: He is strong and Lord.
'Am strong myself compared to yonder crabs
That march now from the mountain to the sea;
'Let twenty pass, and stone the twenty-first,
Loving not, hating not, just choosing so.
'Say, the first straggler that boasts purple spots
Shall join the file, one pincer twisted off;
'Say, this bruised fellow shall receive a worm,
And two worms he whose nippers end in red;
As it likes me each time, I do: so He.

Well then, 'supposeth He is good i' the main,
Placable if His mind and ways were guessed,
But rougher than His handiwork, be sure!
Oh, He hath made things worthier than Himself,
And envieth that, so helped, such things do more
Than He who made them! What consoles but this?
That they, unless through Him, do nought at all,
And must submit: what other use in things?
'Hath cut a pipe of pithless elder-joint
That, blown through, gives exact the scream o' the jay
When from her wing you twitch the feathers blue:
Sound this, and little birds that hate the jay
Flock within stone's throw, glad their foe is hurt:
Put case such pipe could prattle and boast forsooth,
"I catch the birds, I am the crafty thing,

I make the cry my maker cannot make
With his great round mouth; he must blow **through mine!**"
Would not I smash it with my foot? So He.
But wherefore rough, why cold and ill at ease?
Aha, that is a question! Ask, for that,
What knows,—the something over Setebos
That made Him, or He, may be, found and **fought,**
Worsted, drove off and did to nothing, perchance.
There may be something quiet o'er His head,
Out of His reach, that feels nor joy nor grief,
Since both derive from weakness in some **way.**
I joy because the quails come; would not joy
Could I bring quails here when I have a mind:
This Quiet, all it hath a mind to, doth.
'Esteemeth stars the outposts of its couch,
But never spends much thought nor care that **way.**
It may look up, work up,—the worse for those
It works on! 'Careth but for Setebos
The many-handed as a cuttle-fish,
Who, making Himself feared through what **He does,**
Looks up, first, and perceives he cannot soar
To what is quiet and hath happy life;
Next looks down here, and out of very spite
Makes this a bauble-world to ape yon real,
These good things to match those as hips do **grapes.**
'T is solace making baubles, ay, and sport.
Himself peeped late, eyed Prosper at his books
Careless and lofty, lord now of the isle:
Vexed, 'stitched a book of broad leaves, arrow-shaped,
Wrote thereon, he knows what, prodigious words;
Has peeled a wand and called it by a name;
Weareth at whiles for an enchanter's robe
The eyed skin of a supple ocelot;
And hath an ounce sleeker than youngling mole,
A four-legged serpent he makes cower and **couch,**
Now snarl, now hold its breath and mind his **eye,**
And saith she is Miranda and my wife:
'Keeps for his Ariel a tall pouch-bill crane
He bids go wade for fish and straight disgorge;
Also a sea-beast, lumpish, which he snared,
Blinded the eyes of, and brought somewhat **tame,**
And split its toe-webs, and now pens the drudge
In a hole o' the rock and calls him Caliban;
A bitter heart that bides its time and bites.
'Plays thus at being Prosper in a way,
Taketh his mirth with make-believes: so He.

His dam held that the Quiet made all things
Which Setebos vexed only: 'holds not so.
Who made them weak, meant weakness He might **vex.**
Had He meant other, while His hand was in,
Why not make horny eyes no thorn could prick,
Or plate my scalp with bone against the snow,
Or overscale my flesh 'neath joint and joint,
Like an orc's armor? Ay,—so spoil His sport!
He is the One now: only He doth all.

'Saith, He may like, perchance, what profits Him.
Ay, himself loves what does him good; but why?
'Gets good no otherwise. This blinded beast
Loves whoso places flesh-meat on his nose,
But, had he eyes, would want no help, but hate
Or love, just as it liked him: He hath eyes.
Also it pleaseth Setebos to work,
Use all His hands, and exercise much craft,
By no means for the love of what is worked.
'Tasteth, himself, no finer good i' the world
When all goes right, in this safe summer-time,
And he wants little, hungers, aches not much,
Than trying what to do with wit and strength.
'Falls to make something: 'piled yon pile of turfs,
And squared and stuck there squares of soft white **chalk,**
And, with a fish-tooth, scratched a moon on each,
And set up endwise certain spikes of tree,
And crowned the whole with a sloth's skull a-top,
Found dead i' the woods, too hard for one to kill.
No use at all i' the work, for work's sole sake;
'Shall some day knock it down again: so He.

'Saith He is terrible: watch His feats in proof!
One hurricane will spoil six good months' hope.
He hath a spite against me, that I know,
Just as He favors Prosper, who knows why?
So it is, all the same, as well I find.
'Wove wattles half the winter, fenced them firm
With stone and stake to stop she-tortoises
Crawling to lay their eggs here: well, one wave,
Feeling the foot of Him upon its neck,
Gaped as a snake does, lolled out its large tongue,
And licked the whole labor flat: so much for spite.

'Saw a ball flame down late (yonder it lies)
Where, half an hour before, I slept i' the shade:

Often they scatter sparkles: there is force!
'Dug up a newt He may have envied once
And turned to stone, shut up inside a stone.
Please Him and hinder this?—What Prosper **does?**
Aha, if He would tell me how! Not He!
There is the sport: discover how or die!
All need not die, for of the things o' the isle
Some flee afar, some dive, some run up trees;
Those at His mercy,—why, they please Him most
When . . . when . . . well, never try the same **way twice**
Repeat what act has pleased, He may grow wroth.
You must not know His ways, and play Him off,
Sure of the issue. 'Doth the like himself:
'Spareth a squirrel that it nothing fears
But steals the nut from underneath my thumb,
And when I threat, bites stoutly in defence:
'Spareth an urchin that contrariwise,
Curls up into a ball, pretending death
For fright at my approach: the two ways please.
But what would move my choler more than this,
That either creature counted on its life
To-morrow and next day and all days to come,
Saying, forsooth, in the inmost of its heart,
"Because he did so yesterday with me,
And otherwise with such another brute,
So much he do henceforth and always."—Ay?
Would teach the reasoning couple what "must" **means!**
'Doth as he likes, or wherefore Lord? So He.

Conceiveth all things will continue thus,
And we shall have to live in fear of Him
So long as He lives, keeps His strength: **no change,**
If He have done His best, make no new world
To please Him more, so leave off watching this,—
If He surprise not even the Quiet's self
Some strange day,—or, suppose, grow into it
As grubs grow butterflies: else, here are we,
And there is He, and nowhere help at all.

'Believeth with the life, the pain shall stop.
His dam held different, that after death
He both plagued enemies and feasted friends:
Idly! He doth His worst in this our life,
Giving just respite lest we die through pain,

Saving last pain for worst,—with which, an end.
Meanwhile, the best way to escape His ire
Is, not to seem too happy. 'Sees, himself,
Yonder two flies, with purple films and pink,
Bask on the pompion-bell above: kills both.
'Sees two black painful beetles roll their ball
On head and tail as if to save their lives:
Moves them the stick away they strive to clear.

Even so, 'would have Him misconceive, suppose
This Caliban strives hard and ails no less,
And always, above all else, envies Him;
Wherefore he mainly dances on dark nights,
Moans in the sun, gets under holes to laugh,
And never speaks his mind save housed as now:
Outside, 'groans, curses. If He caught me here,
O'erheard this speech, and asked "What chucklest at?"
'Would, to appease Him, cut a finger off,
Or of my three kid yearlings burn the best,
Or let the toothsome apples rot on tree,
Or push my tame beast for the orc to taste:
While myself lit a fire, and made a song
And sung it, "*What I hate, be consecrate*
To celebrate Thee and Thy state, no mate
For Thee; what see for envy in poor me?"
Hoping the while, since evils sometimes mend,
Warts rub away and sores are cured with slime,
That some strange day, will either the Quiet catch
And conquer Setebos, or likelier He
Decrepit may doze, doze, as good as die.

[What, what? A curtain o'er the world at once!
Crickets stop hissing; not a bird—or, yes,
There scuds His raven that has told Him all!
It was fool's play, this prattling! Ha! The wind
Shoulders the pillared dust, death's house o' the move,
And fast invading fires begin! White blaze—
A tree's head snaps—and there, there, there, there, there,
His thunder follows! Fool to gibe at Him!
Lo! 'Lieth flat and loveth Setebos!
'Maketh his teeth meet through his upper lip,
Will let those quails fly, will not eat this month
One little mess of whelks, so he may 'scape!]

CONFESSIONS

I.

WHAT is he buzzing in my ears?
　"Now that I come to die,
Do I view the world as a vale of tears?"
　Ah, reverend sir, not I!

II.

What I viewed there once, what I view again
　Where the physic bottles stand
On the table's edge,—is a suburb lane,
　With a wall to my bedside hand.

III.

That lane sloped, much as the bottles do,
　From a house you could descry
O'er the garden-wall: is the curtain blue
　Or green to a healthy eye?

IV.

To mine, it serves for the old June weather
　Blue above lane and wall;
And that farthest bottle labelled "Ether"
　Is the house o'ertopping all.

V.

At a terrace, somewhere near the stopper,
　There watched for me, one June,
A girl: I know, sir, it's improper,
　My poor mind's out of tune.

VI.

Only, there was a way . . . you crept
　Close by the side, to dodge
Eyes in the house, two eyes except:
　They styled their house "The Lodge."

VII.

What right had a lounger up their lane?
　But, by creeping very close,
With the good wall's help,—their eyes might strain
　And stretch themselves to Oes,

VIII.

Yet never catch her and me together,
　As she left the attic, there,
By the rim of the bottle labelled "Ether,"
　And stole from stair to stair,

IX.

And stood by the rose-wreathed gate. Alas,
　We loved, sir—used to meet:
How sad and bad and mad it was—
　But then, how it was sweet!

PROSPICE

FEAR DEATH?—to feel the fog in my throat,
　The mist in my face,
When the snows begin, and the blasts denote
　I am nearing the place,
The power of the night, the press of the storm,
　The post of the foe;
Where he stands, the Arch Fear in a visible form,
　Yet the strong man must go:
For the journey is done and the summit attained,
　And the barriers fall,
Though a battle 's to fight ere the guerdon be gained,
　The reward of it all.
I was ever a fighter, so—one fight more,
　The best and the last!
I would hate that death bandaged my eyes, and forbore,
　And bade me creep past.
No! let me taste the whole of it, fare like my peers
　The heroes of old,
Bear the brunt, in a minute pay glad life's arrears
　Of pain, darkness and cold.
For sudden the worst turns the best to the brave,
　The black minute's at end,
And the elements' rage, the fiend-voices that rave,
　Shall dwindle, shall blend,
Shall change, shall become first a peace out of pain,
　Then a light, then thy breast,
O thou soul of my soul! I shall clasp thee again,
　And with God be the rest!

YOUTH AND ART

I.

It once might have been, once only:
  We lodged in a street together,
You, a sparrow on the housetop lonely,
  I, a lone she-bird of his feather.

II.

Your trade was with sticks and clay,
  You thumbed, thrust, patted and polished,
Then laughed "They will see some day
  Smith made, and Gibson demolished."

III.

My business was song, song, song;
  I chirped, cheeped, trilled and twittered,
"Kate Brown's on the boards ere long,
  And Grisi's existence embittered!"

IV.

I earned no more by a warble
  Than you by a sketch in plaster;
You wanted a piece of marble,
  I needed a music-master.

V.

We studied hard in our styles,
  Chipped each at a crust like Hindoos,
For air, looked out on the tiles,
  For fun, watched each other's windows.

VI.

You lounged, like a boy of the South,
  Cap and blouse—nay, a bit of beard too;
Or you got it, rubbing your mouth
  With fingers the clay adhered to.

VII.

And I—soon managed to find
  Weak points in the flower-fence facing,
Was forced to put up a blind
  And be safe in my corset-lacing.

VIII.

No harm! It was not my fault
　If you never turned your eye's tail up
As I shook upon E *in alt.,*
　Or ran the chromatic scale up:

IX.

For spring bade the sparrows pair,
　And the boys and girls gave guesses,
And stalls in our street looked rare
　With bulrush and watercresses.

X.

Why did not you pinch a flower
　In a pellet of clay and fling it?
Why did not I put a power
　Of thanks in a look, or sing it?

XI.

I did look, sharp as a lynx,
　(And yet the memory rankles,)
When models arrived, some minx
　Tripped up-stairs, she and her ankles.

XII.

But I think I gave you as good!
　"That foreign fellow,—who can know
How she pays, in a playful mood,
　For his tuning her that piano?"

XIII.

Could you say so, and never say,
　"Suppose we join hands and fortunes,
And I fetch her from over the way,
　Her, piano, and long tunes and short tunes"?

XIV.

No, no: you would not be rash,
　Nor I rasher and something over:
You've to settle yet Gibson's hash,
　And Grisi yet lives in clover.

XV.

But you meet the Prince at the Board,
　I'm queen myself at *bals-paré,*
I've married a rich old lord,
　And you're dubbed knight and an R. A.

XVI.

Each life unfulfilled, you see;
 It hangs still, patchy and scrappy:
We have not sighed deep, laughed free,
 Starved, feasted, despaired,—been happy.

XVII.

And nobody calls you a dunce,
 And people suppose me clever:
This could but have happened once,
 And we missed it, lost it forever.

A FACE

IF ONE could have that little head of hers
Painted upon a background of pale gold,
Such as the Tuscan's early art prefers!
No shade encroaching on the matchless mould
Of those two lips, which should be opening soft
In the pure profile; not as when she laughs,
For that spoils all: but rather as if aloft
Yon hyacinth, she loves so, leaned its staff's
Burden of honey-colored buds to kiss
And capture 'twixt the lips apart for this.
Then her lithe neck, three fingers might surround,
How it should waver on the pale gold ground
Up to the fruit-shaped, perfect chin it lifts!
I know, Correggio loves to mass, in rifts
Of heaven, his angel faces, orb on orb
Breaking its outline, burning shades absorb:
But these are only massed there, I should think,
Waiting to see some wonder momently
Grow out, stand full, fade slow against the sky
(That's the pale ground you'd see this sweet face by),
All heaven, meanwhile, condensed into one eye
Which fears to lose the wonder, should it wink.

A LIKENESS

SOME people hang portraits up
In a room where they dine or sup:
And the wife clinks tea-things under,
And her cousin, he stirs his cup,
Asks, "Who was the lady, I wonder?"

" 'T is a daub John bought at a sale,"
Quoth the wife,—looks black as thunder.
"What a shade beneath her nose!
Snuff-taking, I suppose,"—
Adds the cousin, while John's corns ail.

Or else, there's no wife in the case,
But the portrait's queen of the place,
Alone 'mid the other spoils
Of youth,—masks, gloves and foils,
And pipe-sticks, rose, cherry-tree, jasmine,
And the long whip, the tandem-lasher,
And the cast from a fist ("not, alas! mine,
But my master's, the Tipton Slasher"),
And the cards where pistol-balls mark ace,
And a satin shoe used for cigar-case,
And the chamois-horns ("shot in the Chablais"),
And prints—Rarey drumming on Cruiser,
And Sayers, our champion, the bruiser,
And the little edition of Rabelais:
Where a friend, with both hands in his pockets,
May saunter up close to examine it,
And remark a good deal of Jane Lamb in it,
"But the eyes are half out of their sockets;
That hair's not so bad, where the gloss is,
But they've made the girl's nose a proboscis:
Jane Lamb, that we danced with at Vichy!
What, is not she Jane? Then, who is she?"
All that I own is a print,
An etching, a mezzotint;
'T is a study, a fancy, a fiction,
Yet a fact (take my conviction)
Because it has more than a hint
Of a certain face, I never
Saw elsewhere touch or trace of
In women I've seen the face of:
Just an etching, and, so far, clever.

I keep my prints, an imbroglio,
Fifty in one portfolio.
When somebody tries my claret,
We turn round chairs to the fire,
Chirp over days in a garret,
Chuckle o'er increase of salary,
Taste the good fruits of our leisure.
Talk about pencil and lyre,

And the National Portrait Gallery:
Then I exhibit my treasure.
After we've turned over twenty,
And the debt of wonder my crony owes
Is paid to my Marc Antonios,
He stops me—"*Festina lentè!*
What's that sweet thing there, the etching?"
How my waistcoat-strings want stretching,
How my cheeks grow red as tomatoes,
How my heart leaps! But hearts, after leaps, ache.

"By the by, you must take, for a keepsake,
That other, you praised, of Volpato's."
The fool! would he try a flight further and say—
He never saw, never before to-day,
What was able to take his breath away,
A face to lose youth for, to occupy age
With the dream of, meet death with,—why, I'll not engage
But that, half in a rapture and half in a rage,
I should toss him the thing's self—" 'T is only a duplicate,
A thing of no value! Take it, I supplicate!"

MR. SLUDGE, "THE MEDIUM"

Now, don't, sir! Don't expose me! Just this once!
This was the first and only time, I'll swear,—
Look at me,—see, I kneel,—the only time,
I swear, I ever cheated,—yes, by the soul
Of Her who hears—(your sainted mother, sir!)
All, except this last accident, was truth—
This little kind of slip!—and even this,
It was your own wine, sir, the good champagne,
(I took it for Catawba, you're so kind,)
Which put the folly in my head!

                                        "Get up?"
You still inflict on me that terrible face?
You show no mercy?—Not for Her dear sake,
The sainted spirit's, whose soft breath even now
Blows on my cheek—(don't you feel something, sir?)
You'll tell?

                    Go tell, then! Who the devil cares
What such a rowdy chooses to . . .
                                        Aie—aie—aie!
Please, sir! your thumbs are through my windpipe, sir!
Ch—ch!

Well, sir, I hope you've done it now!
Oh Lord! I little thought, sir, yesterday,
When your departed mother spoke those words
Of peace through me, and moved you, sir, so much,
You gave me—(very kind it was of you)
These shirt-studs—(better take them back again,
Please, sir)—yes, little did I think so soon
A trifle of trick, all through a glass too much
Of his own champagne, would change my best of friends
Into an angry gentleman!

                              Though, 't was wrong.
I don't contest the point; your anger's just:
Whatever put such folly in my head,
I know 't was wicked of me. There's a thick
Dusk undeveloped spirit (I've observed)
Owes me a grudge—a negro's, I should say,
Or else an Irish emigrant's; yourself
Explained the case so well last Sunday, sir,
When we had summoned Franklin to clear up
A point about those shares i' the telegraph:
Ay, and he swore . . . or might it be Tom Paine? . . .
Thumping the table close by where I crouched,
He'd do me soon a mischief: that's come true!
Why, now your face clears! I was sure it would!
Then, this one time . . . don't take your hand away,
Through yours I surely kiss your mother's hand . . .
You'll promise to forgive me?—or, at least,
Tell nobody of this? Consider, sir!
What harm can mercy do? Would but the shade
Of the venerable dead-one just vouchsafe
A rap or tip! What bit of paper's here?
Suppose we take a pencil, let her write,
Make the least sign, she urges on her child
Forgiveness? There now! Eh? Oh! 'T was your foot,
And not a natural creak, sir?

                              Answer, then!
Once, twice, thrice . . . see, I'm waiting to say "thrice!"
All to no use? No sort of hope for me?
It's all to post to Greeley's newspaper?

What? If I told you all about the tricks?
Upon my soul!—the whole truth, and nought else,
And how there's been some falsehood—for your part,
Will you engage to pay my passage out,

And hold your tongue until I'm safe on board?
England's the place, not Boston—no offence!
I see what makes you hesitate: don't fear!
I mean to change my trade and cheat no more,
Yes, this time really it's upon my soul!
Be my salvation!—under Heaven, of course.
I'll tell some queer things. Sixty Vs must do.
A trifle, though, to start with! We'll refer
The question to this table?

       How you're changed!
Then split the difference; thirty more, we'll say.
Ay, but you leave my presents! Else I'll swear
'T was all through those: you wanted yours again,
So, picked a quarrel with me, to get them back!
Tread on a worm, it turns, sir! If I turn,
Your fault! 'T is you'll have forced me! Who's obliged
To give up life yet try no self-defence?
At all events, I'll run the risk. Eh?

         Done!
May I sit, sir? This dear old table, now!
Please, sir, a parting eggnog and cigar!
I've been so happy with you! Nice stuffed chairs,
And sympathetic sideboards; what an end
To all the instructive evenings! (It's alight.)
Well, nothing lasts, as Bacon came and said.
Here goes,—but keep your temper, or I'll scream!

Fol-lol-the-rido-liddle-iddle-ol!
You see, sir, it's your own fault more than mine;
It's all your fault, you curious gentlefolk!
You're prigs,—excuse me,—like to look so spry,
So clever, while you cling by half a claw
To the perch whereon you puff yourselves at roost,
Such piece of self-conceit as serves for perch
Because you chose it, so it must be safe.
Oh, otherwise you're sharp enough! You spy
Who slips, who slides, who holds by help of wing,
Wanting real foothold,—who can't keep upright
On the other perch, your neighbor chose, not you:
There's no outwitting you respecting him!
For instance, men love money—that, you know—
And what men do to gain it: well, suppose
A poor lad, say a help's son in your house,
Listening at keyholes, hears the company

Talk grand of dollars, V-notes, and so forth,
How hard they are to get, how good to hold,
How much they buy,—if, suddenly, in pops he—
"*I*'ve got a V-note!"—what do you say to him?
What's your first word which follows your last kick?
"Where did you steal it, rascal?" That's because
He finds you, fain would fool you, off your perch,
Not on the special piece of nonsense, sir,
Elected your parade-ground: let him try
Lies to the end of the list,—"He picked it up,
His cousin died and left it him by will,
The President flung it to him, riding by,
An actress trucked it for a curl of his hair,
He dreamed of luck and found his shoe enriched,
He dug up clay, and out of clay made gold"—
How would you treat such possibilities?
Would not you, prompt, investigate the case
With cowhide? "Lies, lies, lies," you'd shout: and why?
Which of the stories might not prove mere truth?
This last, perhaps, that clay was turned to coin!

Let's see, now, give him me to speak for him!
How many of your rare philosophers,
In plaguy books I've had to dip into,
Believed gold could be made thus, saw it made,
And made it? Oh, with such philosophers
You're on your best behavior! While the lad—
With him, in a trice, you settle likelihoods,
Nor doubt a moment how he got his prize:
In his case, you hear, judge and execute,
All in a breath: so would most men of sense.

But let the same lad hear you talk as grand
At the same keyhole, you and company,
Of signs and wonders, the invisible world;
How wisdom scouts our vulgar unbelief
More than our vulgarest credulity;
How good men have desired to see a ghost,
What Johnson used to say, what Wesley did,
Mother Goose thought, and fiddle-diddle-dee:—
If he break in with, "Sir, *I* saw a ghost!"
Ah, the ways change! He finds you perched and prim;
It's a conceit of yours that ghosts may be:
There's no talk now of cowhide. "Tell it out!
Don't fear us! Take your time and recollect!
Sit down first: try a glass of wine, my boy!

And, David, (is not that your Christian name?)
Of all things, should this happen twice—it may—
Be sure, while fresh in mind, you let us know!"
Does the boy blunder, blurt out this, blab that,
Break down in the other, as beginners will?
All's candor, all's considerateness—"No haste!
Pause and collect yourself! We understand!
That's the bad memory, or the natural shock,
Or the unexplained *phenomena!*"

                        Egad,
The boy takes heart of grace; finds, never fear,
The readiest way to ope your own heart wide,
Show—what I call your peacock-perch, pet post
To strut, and spread the tail, and squawk upon!
"Just as you thought, much as you might expect!
There be more things in heaven and earth, Horatio," . . .
And so on. Shall not David take the hint,
Grow bolder, stroke you down at quickened rate?
If he ruffle a feather, it's, "Gently, patiently!
Manifestations are so weak at first!
Doubting, moreover, kills them, cuts all short,
Cures with a vengeance!"

                    There, sir, that's your style
You and your boy—such pains bestowed on him,
Or any headpiece of the average worth,
To teach, say, Greek, would perfect him apace,
Make him a Person ("Porson?" thank you, sir!)
Much more, proficient in the art of lies.
You never leave the lesson! Fire alight,
Catch you permitting it to die! You've friends;
There's no withholding knowledge,—least from those
Apt to look elsewhere for their souls' supply:
Why should not you parade your lawful prize?
Who finds a picture, digs a medal up,
Hits on a first edition,—he henceforth
Gives it his name, grows notable: how much more,
Who ferrets out a "medium"? "David's yours,
You highly-favored man? Then, pity souls
Less privileged! Allow us share your luck!"
So, David holds the circle, rules the roast,
Narrates the vision, peeps in the glass ball,
Sets-to the spirit-writing, hears the raps,
As the case may be.

Now mark! To be precise—
Though I say, "lies" all these, at this first stage,
'T is just for science' sake: I call such grubs
By the name of what they'll turn to, dragon-flies.
Strictly, it's what good people style untruth;
But yet, so far, not quite the full-grown thing:
It's fancying, fable-making, nonsense-work—
What never meant to be so very bad—
The knack of story-telling, brightening up
Each dull old bit of fact that drops its shine.
One does see somewhat when one shuts one's eyes,
If only spots and streaks; tables do tip
In the oddest way of themselves: and pens, good Lord,
Who knows if you drive them or they drive you?
'Tis but a foot in the water and out again;
Not that duck-under which decides your dive.
Note this, for it's important: listen why.

I'll prove, you push on David till he dives
And ends the shivering. Here's your circle, now:
Two-thirds of them, with heads like you their host,
Turn up their eyes, and cry, as you expect,
"Lord, who'd have thought it!" But there's always one
Looks wise, compassionately smiles, submits,
"Of your veracity no kind of doubt,
But—do you feel so certain of that boy's?
Really, I wonder! I confess myself
More chary of my faith!" That's galling, sir!
What, he the investigator, he the sage,
When all's done? Then, you just have shut your eyes,
Opened your mouth, and gulped down David whole,
You! Terrible were such catastrophe!
So, evidence is redoubled, doubled again,
And doubled besides; once more, "He heard, we heard,
You and they heard, your mother and your wife,
Your children and the stranger in your gates:
Did they or did they not?" So much for him,
The black sheep, guest without the wedding-garb,
The doubting Thomas! Now's your turn to crow:
"He's kind to think you such a fool: Sludge cheats?
Leave you alone to take precautions!"

Straight
The rest join chorus. Thomas stands abashed,
Sips silent some such beverage as this,
Considers if it be harder, shutting eyes

And gulping David in good fellowship,
Than going elsewhere, getting, in exchange,
With no eggnog to lubricate the food,
Some just as tough a morsel. Over the way,
Holds Captain Sparks his court: is it better there?
Have not you hunting-stories, scalping-scenes,
And Mexican War exploits to swallow plump
If you'd be free o' the stove-side, rocking-chair,
And trio of affable daughters?

                         Doubt succumbs!
Victory! All your circle's yours again!
Out of the clubbing of submissive wits,
David's performance rounds, each chink gets patched,
Every protrusion of a point's filed fine,
All's fit to set a-rolling round the world,
And then return to David finally,
Lies seven feet thick about his first half-inch.
Here's a choice birth o' the supernatural,
Poor David's pledged to! You've employed no tool
That laws exclaim at, save the devil's own,
Yet screwed him into henceforth gulling you
To the top o' your bent,—all out of one half-lie!

You hold, if there's one half or a hundredth part
Of a lie, that's his fault,—his be the penalty!
I dare say! You'd prove firmer in his place?
You'd find the courage,—that first flurry over,
That mild bit of romancing-work at end,—
To interpose with "It gets serious, this;
Must stop here. Sir, I saw no ghost at all.
Inform your friends I made . . . well, fools of them,
And found you ready made. I've lived in clover
These three weeks: take it out in kicks of me!"
I doubt it. Ask your conscience! Let me know,
Twelve months hence, with how few embellishments
You've told almighty Boston of this passage
Of arms between us, your first taste o' the foil
From Sludge who could not fence, sir! Sludge, your boy!
I lied, sir,—there! I got up from my gorge
On offal in the gutter, and preferred
Your canvas-backs: I took their carver's size,
Measured his modicum of intelligence,
Tickled him on the cockles of his heart
With a raven feather, and next week found myself
Sweet and clean, dining daintily, dizened smart,

Set on a stool buttressed by ladies' knees,
Every soft smiler calling me her pet,
Encouraging my story to uncoil
And creep out from its hole, inch after inch,
"How last night, I no sooner snug in bed,
Tucked up, just as they left me,—than came raps!
While a light whisked" . . . "Shaped somewhat like a star?"
"Well, like some sort of stars, ma'am."—"So we thought!
And any voice? Not yet? Try hard, next time,
If you can't hear a voice; we think you may:
At least, the Pennsylvanian 'mediums' did."
Oh, next time comes the voice! "Just as we hoped!"
Are not the hopers proud now, pleased, profuse
O' the natural acknowledgment?

                                  Of course!
So, off we push, illy-oh-yo, trim the boat,
On we sweep with a cataract ahead,
We're midway to the Horse-shoe: stop, who can.
The dance of bubbles gay about our prow!
Experiences become worth waiting for,
Spirits now speak up, tell their inmost mind,
And compliment the "medium" properly,
Concern themselves about his Sunday coat,
See rings on his hand with pleasure. Ask yourself
How you'd receive a course of treats like these!
Why, take the quietest hack and stall him up,
Cram him with corn a month, then out with him
Among his mates on a bright April morn,
With the turf to tread; see if you find or no
A caper in him, if he bucks or bolts!
Much more a youth whose fancies sprout as rank
As toadstool-clump from melon-bed. 'Tis soon,
"Sirrah, you spirit, come, go, fetch and carry,
Read, write, rap, rub-a-dub, and hang yourself!"
I'm spared all further trouble; all's arranged;
Your circle does my business; I may rave
Like an epileptic dervish in the books,
Foam, fling myself flat, rend my clothes to shreds;
No matter: lovers, friends and countrymen
Will lay down spiritual laws, read wrong things right
By the rule o' reverse. If Francis Verulam
Styles himself Bacon, spells the name beside
With a *y* and a *k*, says he drew breath in York,
Gave up the ghost in Wales when Cromwell reigned,
(As, sir, we somewhat fear he was apt to say,

Before I found the useful book that knows)—
Why, what harm's done? The circle smiles apace,
"It was not Bacon, after all, you see!
We understand, the trick's but natural:
Such spirits' individuality
Is hard to put in evidence: they incline
To gibe and jeer, these undeveloped sorts.
You see, their world's much like a jail broke loose,
While this of ours remains shut, bolted, barred,
With a single window to it. Sludge, our friend,
Serves as this window, whether thin or thick,
Or stained or stainless; he's the medium-pane
Through which, to see us and be seen, they peep:
They crowd each other, hustle for a chance,
Tread on their neighbor's kibes, play tricks enough!
Does Bacon, tired of waiting, swerve aside?
Up in his place jumps Barnum—'I'm your man,
I'll answer you for Bacon!' Try once more!"

Or else it's—"What's a 'medium'? He's a means,
Good, bad, indifferent, still the only means
Spirits can speak by; he may misconceive,
Stutter and stammer,—he's their Sludge and drudge,
Take him or leave him; they must hold their peace,
Or else, put up with having knowledge strained
To half-expression through his ignorance.
Suppose the spirit Beethoven wants to shed
New music he's brimful of; why, he turns
The handle of this organ, grinds with Sludge,
And what he poured in at the mouth o' the mill
As a Thirty-third Sonata, (fancy now!)
Comes from the hopper as bran-new Sludge, nought else,
The Shakers' Hymn in G, with a natural F,
Or the 'Stars and Stripes' set to consecutive fourths."

Sir, where's the scrape you did not help me through,
You that are wise? And for the fools, the folk
Who came to see,—the guests, (observe that word!)
Pray do you find guests criticise your wine,
Your furniture, your grammar, or your nose?
Then, why your "medium"? What's the difference?
Prove your madeira red-ink and gamboge,—
Your Sludge, a cheat—then, somebody's a goose
For vaunting both as genuine. "Guests!" Don't fear!
They'll make a wry face, nor too much of that,
And leave you in your glory.

                              "No, sometimes
They doubt and say as much!" Ay, doubt they do!
And what's the consequence? "Of course they doubt"—
(You triumph)—"that explains the hitch at once!
Doubt posed our 'medium,' puddled his pure mind;
He gave them back their rubbish: pitch chaff in,
Could flour come out o' the honest mill?" So, prompt
Applaud the faithful: cases flock in point,
"How, when a mocker willed a 'medium' once
Should name a spirit James whose name was George,
'James,' cried the 'medium,'—'twas the test of truth!"
In short, a hit proves much, a miss proves more.
Does this convince? The better: does it fail?
Time for the double-shotted broadside, then—
The grand means, last resource. Look black and big!
"You style us idiots, therefore—why stop short?
Accomplices in rascality: this we hear
In our own house, from our invited guest
Found brave enough to outrage a poor boy
Exposed by our good faith! Have you been heard?
Now, then, hear us; one man's not quite worth twelve.
You see a cheat? Here's some twelve see an ass:
Excuse me if I calculate: good day!"
Out slinks the sceptic, all the laughs explode,
Sludge waves his hat in triumph!

                              Or—he don't.
There's something in real truth (explain who can!)
One casts a wistful eye at, like the horse
Who mopes beneath stuffed hay-racks and won't munch
Because he spies a corn-bag: hang that truth,
It spoils all dainties proffered in its place!
I've felt at times when, cockered, cosseted
And coddled by the aforesaid company,
Bidden enjoy their bullying,—never fear,
But o'er their shoulders spit at the flying man,—
I've felt a child; only, a fractious child
That, dandled soft by nurse, aunt, grandmother,
Who keep him from the kennel, sun and wind,
Good fun and wholesome mud,—enjoined be sweet,
And comely and superior,—eyes askance
The ragged sons o' the gutter at their game,
Fain would be down with them i' the thick o' the filth,
Making dirt-pies, laughing free, speaking plain,
And calling granny the gray old cat she is.
I've felt a spite, I say, at you, at them,

Huggings and humbug—gnashed my teeth to mark
A decent dog pass! It's too bad, I say,
Ruining a soul so!

               But what's "so," what's fixed,
Where may one stop? Nowhere! The cheating's nursed
Out of the lying, softly and surely spun
To just your length, sir! I'd stop soon enough:
But you're for progress. "All old, nothing new?
Only the usual talking through the mouth,
Or writing by the hand? I own, I thought
This would develop, grow demonstrable,
Make doubt absurd, give figures we might see,
Flowers we might touch. There's no one doubts you, Sludge!
You dream the dreams, you see the spiritual sights,
The speeches come in your head, beyond dispute.
Still, for the sceptics' sake, to stop all mouths,
We want some outward manifestation!—well,
The Pennsylvanians gained such; why not Sludge?
He may improve with time!"

                    Ay, that he may!
He sees his lot: there's no avoiding fate.
'T is a trifle at first. "Eh, David? Did you hear?
You jogged the table, your foot caused the squeak,
This time you're . . . joking, are you not, my boy?"
"N-n-no!"—and I'm done for, bought and sold henceforth
The old good easy jog-trot way, the . . . eh?
The . . . not so very false, as falsehood goes,
The spinning out and drawing fine, you know,—
Really mere novel-writing of a sort,
Acting, or improvising, make-believe,
Surely not downright cheatery,—anyhow,
'Tis done with and my lot cast; Cheat's my name:
The fatal dash of brandy in your tea
Has settled what you'll have the souchong's smack:
The caddy gives way to the dram-bottle.

Then, it's so cruel easy! Oh, those tricks
That can't be tricks, those feats by sleight of hand,
Clearly no common conjuror's—no, indeed!
A conjuror? Choose me any craft i' the world
A man puts hand to; and with six months' pains,
I'll play you twenty tricks miraculous
To people untaught the trade: have you seen glass blown,
Pipes pierced? Why, just this biscuit that I chip,

Did you ever watch a baker toss one flat
To the oven? Try and do it! Take my word,
Practise but half as much, while limbs are lithe,
To turn, shove, tilt a table, crack your joints,
Manage your feet, dispose your hands aright,
Work wires that twitch the curtains, play the glove
At end o' your slipper,—then put out the lights
And . . . there, there, all you want you'll get, I hope!
I found it slip, easy as an old shoe.

Now, lights on table again! I've done my part,
You take my place while I give thanks and rest.
"Well, Judge Humgruffin, what's your verdict, sir?
You, hardest head in the United States,—
Did you detect a cheat here? Wait! Let's see!
Just an experiment first, for candor's sake!
I'll try and cheat you, Judge! The table tilts:
Is it I that move it? Write! I'll press your hand:
Cry when I push, or guide your pencil, Judge!"
Sludge still triumphant! "That a rap, indeed?
That, the real writing? Very like a whale!
Then, if, sir, you—a most distinguished man,
And, were the Judge not here, I'd say, . . . no matter!
Well, sir, if you fail, you can't take us in,—
There's little fear that Sludge will!"

                                        Won't he, ma'am?
But what if our distinguished host, like Sludge,
Bade God bear witness that he played no trick,
While you believed that what produced the raps
Was just a certain child who died, you know,
And whose last breath you thought your lips had felt?
Eh? That's a capital point, ma'am: Sludge begins
At your entreaty with your dearest dead,
The little voice set lisping once again,
The tiny hand made feel for yours once more,
The poor lost image brought back, plain as dreams,
Which image, if a word had chanced recall,
The customary cloud would cross your eyes,
Your heart return the old tick, pay its pang!
A right mood for investigation, this!
One's at one's ease with Saul and Jonathan,
Pompey and Cæsar: but one's own lost child . . .
I wonder, when you heard the first clod drop
From the spadeful at the grave-side, felt you free
To investigate who twitched your funeral scarf

Or brushed your flounces? Then, it came of course,
You should be stunned and stupid; then (how else?)
Your breath stopped with your blood, your brain struck work.
But now, such causes fail of such effects,
All's changed,—the little voice begins afresh,
Yet you, calm, consequent, can test and try
And touch the truth. "Tests? Didn't the creature tell
Its nurse's name, and say it lived six years,
And rode a rocking-horse? Enough of tests!
Sludge never could learn that!"

        He could not, eh?
You compliment him. "Could not?" Speak for yourself!
I'd like to know the man I ever saw
Once,—never mind where, how, why, when,—once saw,
Of whom I do not keep some matter in mind
He'd swear I "could not" know, sagacious soul!
What? Do you live in this world's blow of blacks,
Palaver, gossipry, a single hour
Nor find one smut has settled on your nose,
Of a smut's worth, no more, no less?—one fact
Out of the drift of facts, whereby you learn
What someone was, somewhere, somewhen, somewhy?
You don't tell folk—"See what has stuck to me!
Judge Humgruffin, our most distinguished man,
Your uncle was a tailor, and your wife
Thought to have married Miggs, missed him, hit you!"—
Do you, sir, though you see him twice a-week?
"No," you reply, "what use retailing it?
Why should I?" But, you see, one day you *should*,
Because one day there's much use,—when this fact
Brings you the Judge upon both gouty knees
Before the supernatural; proves that Sludge
Knows, as you say, a thing he "could not" know:
Will not Sludge thenceforth keep an outstretched face,
The way the wind drives?

      "Could not!" Look you now,
I'll tell you a story! There's a whiskered chap,
A foreigner, that teaches music here
And gets his bread,—knowing no better way:
He says, the fellow who informed of him
And made him fly his country and fall West,
Was a hunchback cobbler, sat, stitched soles and sang,
In some outlandish place, the city Rome,
In a cellar by their Broadway, all day long;

Never asked questions, stopped to listen or look,
Nor lifted nose from lapstone; let the world
Roll round his three-legged stool, and news run in
The ears he hardly seemed to keep pricked up.
Well, that man went on Sundays, touched his pay,
And took his praise from government, you see;
For something like two dollars every week,
He'd engage tell you some one little thing
Of some one man, which led to many more,
(Because one truth leads right to the world's end,)
And make you that man's master—when he dined
And on what dish, where walked to keep his health
And to what street. His trade was, throwing thus
His sense out, like an ant-eater's long tongue,
Soft, innocent, warm, moist, impassible,
And when 'twas crusted o'er with creatures—slick,
Their juice enriched his palate. "Could not Sludge!"

I'll go yet a step further, and maintain,
Once the imposture plunged its proper depth
I' the rotten of your natures, all of you,—
(If one's not mad nor drunk, and hardly then)
It's impossible to cheat—that's, be found out!
Go tell your brotherhood this first slip of mine,
All to-day's tale, how you detected Sludge,
Behaved unpleasantly, till he was fain confess,
And so has come to grief! You'll find, I think,
Why Sludge still snaps his fingers in your face.
There now, you've told them! What's their prompt reply?
"Sir, did that youth confess he had cheated me,
I'd disbelieve him. He may cheat at times;
That's in the 'medium'-nature, thus they're made,
Vain and vindictive, cowards, prone to scratch.
And so all cats are; still, a cat's the beast
You coax the strange electric sparks from out,
By rubbing back its fur; not so a dog,
Nor lion, nor lamb: 'tis the cat's nature, sir!
Why not the dog's? Ask God, who made them beasts!
D'ye think the sound, the nicely-balanced man
(Like me,"—aside)—"like you yourself,"—(aloud)
"—He's stuff to make a 'medium'? Bless your soul,
'Tis these hysteric, hybrid half-and-halfs,
Equivocal, worthless vermin yield the fire!
We take such as we find them, 'ware their tricks,
Wanting their service. Sir, Sludge took in you—
How, I can't say, not being there to watch:

He was tried, was tempted by your easiness,—
He did not take in me!"

                       Thank you for Sludge!
I'm to be grateful to such patrons, eh,
When what you hear's my best word? 'Tis a challenge,
"Snap at all strangers, half-tamed prairie-dog,
So you cower duly at your keeper's beck!
Cat, show what claws were made for, muffling them
Only to me! Cheat others if you can,
Me, if you dare!" And, my wise sir, I dared—
Did cheat you first, made you cheat others next,
And had the help o' your vaunted manliness
To bully the incredulous. You used me?
Have not I used you, taken full revenge,
Persuaded folk they knew not their own name,
And straight they'd own the error! Who was the fool
When, to an awe-struck wide-eyed open-mouthed
Circle of sages, Sludge would introduce
Milton composing baby-rhymes, and Locke
Reasoning in gibberish, Homer writing Greek
In noughts and crosses, Asaph setting psalms
To crotchet and quaver? I've made a spirit squeak
In sham voice for a minute, then outbroke
Bold in my own, defying the imbeciles—
Have copied some ghost's pothooks, half a page,
Then ended with my own scrawl undisguised.
"All right! The ghost was merely using Sludge,
Suiting itself from his imperfect stock!"
Don't talk of gratitude to me! For what?
For being treated as a showman's ape,
Encouraged to be wicked and make sport,
Fret or sulk, grin or whimper, any mood
So long as the ape be in it and no man—
Because a nut pays every mood alike.
Curse your superior, superintending sort,
Who, since you hate smoke, send up boys that climb
To cure your chimney, bid a "medium" lie
To sweep you truth down! Curse your women too,
Your insolent wives and daughters, that fire up
Or faint away if a male hand squeeze theirs,
Yet, to encourage Sludge, may play with Sludge
As only a "medium," only the kind of thing
They must humor, fondle . . . oh, to misconceive
Were too preposterous! But I've paid them out!
They've had their wish—called for the naked truth,

And in she tripped, sat down and bade them stare:
They had to blush a little and forgive!
"The fact is, children talk so; in next world
All our conventions are reversed,—perhaps
Made light of: something like old prints, my dear!
The Judge has one, he brought from Italy,
A metropolis in the background,—o'er a bridge,
A team of trotting roadsters,—cheerful groups
Of wayside travellers, peasants at their work,
And, full in front, quite unconcerned, why not?
Three nymphs conversing with a cavalier,
And never a rag among them: 'fine,' folk cry—
And heavenly manners seem not much unlike!
Let Sludge go on; we'll fancy it's in print!"
If such as came for wool, sir, went home shorn,
Where is the wrong I did them? 'Twas their choice;
They tried the adventure, ran the risk, tossed up
And lost, as some one's sure to do in games;
They fancied I was made to lose,—smoked glass
Useful to spy the sun through, spare their eyes:
And had I proved a red-hot iron plate
They thought to pierce, and, for their pains, grew blind,
Whose were the fault but theirs? While, as things go,
Their loss amounts to gain, the more's the shame!
They've had their peep into the spirit-world,
And all this world may know it! They've fed fat
Their self-conceit which else had starved: what chance
Save this, of cackling o'er a golden egg
And compassing distinction from the flock,
Friends of a feather? Well, they paid for it,
And not prodigiously; the price o' the play,
Not counting certain pleasant interludes,
Was scarce a vulgar play's worth. When you buy
The actor's talent, do you dare propose
For his soul beside? Whereas, my soul you buy!
Sludge acts Macbeth, obliged to be Macbeth,
Or you'll not hear his first word! Just go through
That slight formality, swear himself's the Thane,
And henceforth he may strut and fret his hour,
Spout, spawl, or spin his target, no one cares!
Why hadn't I leave to play tricks, Sludge as Sludge?
Enough of it all! I've wiped out scores with you—
Vented your fustian, let myself be streaked
Like tom-fool with your ochre and carmine,
Worn patchwork your respectable fingers sewed
To metamorphose somebody,—yes, I've earned

My wages, swallowed down my bread of shame,
And shake the crumbs off—where but in your face?

As for religion—why, I served it, sir!
I'll stick to that! With my *phenomena*
I laid the atheist sprawling on his back,
Propped up Saint Paul, or, at least, Swedenborg!
In fact, it's just the proper way to balk
These troublesome fellows—liars, one and all,
Are not these sceptics? Well, to baffle them,
No use in being squeamish: lie yourself!
Erect your buttress just as wide o' the line,
Your side, as they build up the wall on theirs;
Where both meet, midway in a point, is truth,
High overhead: so, take your room, pile bricks,
Lie! Oh, there's titillation in all shame!
What snow may lose in white, snow gains in rose!
Miss Stokes turns—Rahab,—nor a bad exchange!
Glory be on her, for the good she wrought,
Breeding belief anew 'neath ribs of death,
Browbeating now the unabashed before,
Ridding us of their whole life's gathered straws
By a live coal from the altar! Why, of old,
Great men spent years and years in writing books
To prove we've souls, and hardly proved it then:
Miss Stokes with her live coal, for you and me!
Surely, to this good issue, all was fair—
Not only fondling Sludge, but, even suppose
He let escape some spice of knavery,—well,
In wisely being blind to it! Don't you praise
Nelson for setting spy-glass to blind eye
And saying . . . what was it—that he could not see
The signal he was bothered with? Ay, indeed!
I'll go beyond: there's a real love of a lie,
Liars find ready-made for lies they make,
As hand for glove, or tongue for sugar-plum.
At best, 'tis never pure and full belief;
Those furthest in the quagmire,—don't suppose
They strayed there with no warning, got no chance
Of a filth-speck in their face, which they clenched teeth,
Bent brow against! Be sure they had their doubts,
And fears, and fairest challenges to try
The floor o' the seeming solid sand! But no!
Their faith was pledged, acquaintance too apprised,
All but the last step ventured, kerchiefs waved,

And Sludge called "pet:" 'twas easier marching on
To the promised land; join those who, Thursday next,
Meant to meet Shakespeare; better follow Sludge—
Prudent, oh sure!—on the alert, how else?
But making for the mid-bog, all the same!
To hear your outcries, one would think I caught
Miss Stokes by the scruff o' the neck, and pitched her flat,
Foolish-face-foremost! Hear these simpletons,
That's all I beg, before my work's begun,
Before I've touched them with my finger-tip!
Thus they await me (do but listen, now!
It's reasoning, this is,—I can't imitate
The baby voice, though),—"In so many tales
Must be some truth, truth though a pin-point big,
Yet, some: a single man's deceived, perhaps—
Hardly, a thousand: to suppose one cheat
Can gull all these, were more miraculous far
Than aught we should confess a miracle,"—
And so on. Then the Judge sums up—(it's rare)
Bids you respect the authorities that leap
To the judgment-seat at once,—why don't you note
The limpid nature, the unblemished life,
The spotless honor, indisputable sense
Of the first upstart with his story? What—
Outrage a boy on whom you ne'er till now
Set eyes, because he finds raps trouble him?

Fools, these are: ay, and how of their opposites
Who never did, at bottom of their hearts,
Believe for a moment?—Men emasculate,
Blank of belief, who played, as eunuchs use,
With superstition safely,—cold of blood,
Who saw what made for them i' the mystery,
Took their occasion, and supported Sludge
—As proselytes? No, thank you, far too shrewd!
—But promisers of fair play, encouragers
O' the claimant; who in candor needs must hoist
Sludge up on Mars' Hill, get speech out of Sludge
To carry off, criticize, and cant about!
Didn't Athens treat Saint Paul so?—at any rate,
It's "a new thing," philosophy fumbles at.
Then there's the other picker-out of pearl
From dungheaps,—ay, your literary man,
Who draws on his kid gloves to deal with Sludge
Daintily and discreetly,—shakes a dust

O' the doctrine, flavors thence, he well knows how,
The narrative or the novel,—half-believes,
All for the book's sake, and the public's stare,
And the cash that's God's sole solid in this world!
Look at him! Try to be too bold, too gross
For the master! Not you! He's the man for muck;
Shovel it forth, full-splash, he'll smooth your brown
Into artistic richness, never fear!
Find him the crude stuff; when you recognize
Your lie again, you'll doff your hat to it,
Dressed out for company! "For company,"
I say, since there's the relish of success:
Let all pay due respect, call the lie truth,
Save the soft silent smirking gentleman
Who ushered in the stranger: you must sigh
"How melancholy, he, the only one,
Fails to perceive the bearing of the truth
Himself gave birth to!"—There's the triumph's smack!
That man would choose to see the whole world roll
I' the slime o' the slough, so he might touch the tip
Of his brush with what I call the best of browns—
Tint ghost-tales, spirit-stories, past the power
Of the outworn umber and bistre!

                                        Yet I think
There's a more hateful form of foolery—
The social sage's, Solomon of saloons
And philosophic diner-out, the fribble
Who wants a doctrine for a chopping-block
To try the edge of his faculty upon,
Prove how much common sense he'll hack and hew
I' the critical minute 'twixt the soup and fish!
These were my patrons: these, and the like of them
Who, rising in my soul now, sicken it,—
These I have injured! Gratitude to these?
The gratitude, forsooth, of a prostitute
To the greenhorn and the bully—friends of hers,
From the wag that wants the queer jokes for his club,
To the snuffbox-decorator, honest man,
Who just was at his wits' end where to find
So genial a Pasiphae! All and each
Pay, compliment, protect from the police:
And how she hates them for their pains, like me!
So much for my remorse at thanklessness
Toward a deserving public!

But, for God?
Ay, that's a question! Well, sir, since you press—
(How you do tease the whole thing out of me!
I don't mean you, you know, when I say "them:"
Hate you, indeed! But that Miss Stokes, that Judge!
Enough, enough—with sugar: thank you, sir!)
Now for it, then! Will you believe me, though?
You've heard what I confess; I don't unsay
A single word: I cheated when I could,
Rapped with my toe-joints, set sham hands at work,
Wrote down names weak in sympathetic ink,
Rubbed odic lights with ends of phosphor-match,
And all the rest; believe that: believe this,
By the same token, though it seem to set
The crooked straight again, unsay the said,
Stick up what I've knocked down; I can't help that
It's truth! I somehow vomit truth to-day.
This trade of mine—I don't know, can't be sure
But there was something in it, tricks and all!
Really, I want to light up my own mind.
They were tricks,—true, but what I mean to add
Is also true. First,—don't it strike you, sir?
Go back to the beginning,—the first fact
We're taught is, there's a world beside this world,
With spirits, not mankind, for tenantry;
That much within that world once sojourned here,
That all upon this world will visit there,
And therefore that we, bodily here below,
Must have exactly such an interest
In learning what may be the ways o' the world
Above us, as the disembodied folk
Have (by all analogic likelihood)
In watching how things go in the old home
With us, their sons, successors, and what not.
Oh, yes, with added powers probably,
Fit for the novel state,—old loves grown pure,
Old interests understood aright,—they watch!
Eyes to see, ears to hear, and hands to help,
Proportionate to advancement: they're ahead,
That's all—do what we do, but nobler done—
Use plate, whereas we eat our meals off delf,
(To use a figure.)

Concede that, and I ask
Next what may be the mode of intercourse
Between us men here, and those once-men there?

First comes the Bible's speech; then, history
With the supernatural element,—you know—
All that we sucked in with our mothers' milk,
Grew up with, got inside of us at last,
Till it's found bone of bone and flesh of flesh.
See now, we start with the miraculous,
And know it used to be, at all events:
What's the first step we take, and can't but take,
In arguing from the known to the obscure?
Why this: "What was before, may be to-day.
Since Samuel's ghost appeared to Saul,—of course
My brother's spirit may appear to me."
Go tell your teacher that! What's his reply?
What brings a shade of doubt for the first time
O'er his brow late so luminous with faith?
"Such things have been," says he, "and there's no doubt
Such things may be: but I advise mistrust
Of eyes, ears, stomach, and, more than all, your brain,
Unless it be of your great-grandmother,
Whenever they propose a ghost to you!"
The end is, there's a composition struck;
'Tis settled, we've some way of intercourse
Just as in Saul's time; only, different:
How, when and where, precisely,—find it out!
I want to know, then, what's so natural
As that a person born into this world
And seized on by such teaching, should begin
With firm expectancy and a frank look-out
For his own allotment, his especial share
I' the secret,—his particular ghost, in fine?
I mean, a person born to look that way,
Since natures differ: take the painter-sort,
One man lives fifty years in ignorance
Whether grass be green or red,—"No kind of eye
For color," say you; while another picks
And puts away even pebbles, when a child,
Because of bluish spots and pinky veins—
"Give him forthwith a paint-box!" Just the same
Was I born . . . "medium," you won't let me say,—
Well, seer of the supernatural
Everywhen, everyhow, and everywhere,—
Will that do?

              I and all such boys of course
Started with the same stock of Bible-truth;
Only,—what in the rest you style their sense,

Instinct, blind reasoning but imperative,
This, betimes, taught them the old world had one law
And ours another: "New world, new laws," cried they:
"None but old laws, seen everywhere at work,"
Cried I, and by their help explained my life
The Jews' way, still a working way to me.
Ghosts made the noises, fairies waved the lights,
Or Santaclaus slid down on New Year's Eve
And stuffed with cakes the stocking at my bed,
Changed the worn shoes, rubbed clean the fingered slate
O' the sum that came to grief the day before.

This could not last long: soon enough I found
Who had worked wonders thus, and to what end:
But did I find all easy, like my mates?
Henceforth no supernatural any more?
Not a whit: what projects the billiard-balls?
"A cue," you answer. "Yes, a cue," said I;
"But what hand, off the cushion, moved the cue?
What unseen agency, outside the world,
Prompted its puppets to do this and that,
Put cakes and shoes and slates into their mind,
These mothers and aunts, nay even schoolmasters?"
Thus high I sprang, and there have settled since.
Just so I reason, in sober earnest still,
About the greater godsends, what you call
The serious gains and losses of my life.
What do I know or care about your world
Which either is or seems to be? This snap
O' my fingers, sir! My care is for myself;
Myself am whole and sole reality
Inside a raree-show and a market-mob
Gathered about it: that's the use of things.
'Tis easy saying they serve vast purposes,
Advantage their grand selves: be it true or false,
Each thing may have two uses. What's a star?
A world, or a world's sun: doesn't it serve
As taper also, timepiece, weather-glass,
And almanac? Are stars not set for signs
When we should shear our sheep, sow corn, prune trees?
The Bible says so.

Well, I add one use
To all the acknowledged uses, and declare
If I spy Charles's Wain at twelve to-night,
It warns me, "Go, nor lose another day,

And have your hair cut, Sludge!" You laugh: and why?
Were such a sign too hard for God to give?
No: but Sludge seems too little for such grace:
Thank you, sir! So you think, so does not Sludge!
When you and good men gape at Providence,
Go into history and bid us mark
Not merely powder-plots prevented, crowns
Kept on kings' heads by miracle enough,
But private mercies—oh, you've told me, sir,
Of such interpositions! How yourself
Once, missing on a memorable day
Your handkerchief—just setting out, you know,—
You must return to fetch it, lost the train,
And saved your precious self from what befell
The thirty-three whom Providence forgot.
You tell, and ask me what I think of this?
Well, sir, I think then, since you needs must know,
What matter had you and Boston city to boot
Sailed skyward, like burnt onion-peelings? Much
To you, no doubt: for me—undoubtedly
The cutting of my hair concerns me more,
Because, however sad the truth may seem,
Sludge is of all-importance to himself.
You set apart that day in every year
For special thanksgiving, were a heathen else:
Well, I who cannot boast the like escape,
Suppose I said, "I don't thank Providence
For my part, owing it no gratitude"?
"Nay, but you owe as much,"—you'd tutor me,
"You, every man alive, for blessings gained
In every hour o' the day, could you but know!
I saw my crowning mercy: all have such,
Could they but see!" Well, sir, why don't they see?
"Because they won't look,—or, perhaps, they can't."
Then, sir, suppose I can, and will, and do
Look, microscopically as is right,
Into each hour with its infinitude
Of influences at work to profit Sludge?
For that's the case: I've sharpened up my sight
To spy a providence in the fire's going out,
The kettle's boiling, the dime's sticking fast
Despite the hole i' the pocket. Call such facts
Fancies, too petty a work for Providence,
And those same thanks which you exact from me
Prove too prodigious payment: thanks for what,
If nothing guards and guides us little men?

No, no, sir! You must put away your pride,
Resolve to let Sludge into partnership!
I live by signs and omens: looked at the roof
Where the pigeons settle—"If the further bird,
The white, takes wing first, I'll confess when thrashed
Not, if the blue does,"—so I said to myself
Last week, lest you should take me by surprise:
Off flapped the white,—and I'm confessing, sir!
Perhaps 'tis Providence's whim and way
With only me, i' the world: how can you tell?
"Because unlikely!" Was it likelier, now,
That this our one out of all worlds beside,
The what-d'you-call-'em millions, should be just
Precisely chosen to make Adam for,
And the rest o' the tale? Yet the tale's true, you know
Such undeserving clod was graced so once;
Why not graced likewise undeserving Sludge?
Are we merit-mongers, flaunt we filthy rags?
All you can bring against my privilege
Is, that another way was taken with you,—
Which I don't question. It's pure grace, my luck:
I'm broken to the way of nods and winks,
And need no formal summoning. You've a help;
Holloa his name or whistle, clap your hands,
Stamp with your foot or pull the bell: all's one,
He understands you want him, here he comes.
Just so, I come at the knocking: you, sir, wait
The tongue o' the bell, nor stir before you catch
Reason's clear tingle, nature's clapper brisk,
Or that traditional peal was wont to cheer
Your mother's face turned heavenward: short of these
There's no authentic intimation, eh?
Well, when you hear, you'll answer them, start up
And stride into the presence, top of toe,
And there find Sludge beforehand, Sludge that sprang
At noise o' the knuckle on the partition-wall!
I think myself the more religious man.
Religion's all or nothing; it's no mere smile
O' contentment, sigh of aspiration, sir—
No quality o' the finelier-tempered clay
Like its whiteness or its lightness; rather, stuff
O' the very stuff, life of life, and self of self.
I tell you, men won't notice; when they do,
They'll understand. I notice nothing else:
I'm eyes, ears, mouth of me, one gaze and gape,
Nothing eludes me, everything's a hint,

Handle and help. It's all absurd, and yet
There's something in it all, I know: how much?
No answer! What does that prove? Man's still man,
Still meant for a poor blundering piece of work
When all's done; but, if somewhat's done, like this,
Or not done, is the case the same? Suppose
I blunder in my guess at the true sense
O' the knuckle-summons, nine times out of ten,—
What if the tenth guess happen to be right?
If the tenth shovel-load of powdered quartz
Yield me the nugget? I gather, crush, sift all,
Pass o'er the failure, pounce on the success.
To give you a notion, now—(let who wins, laugh!)
When first I see a man, what do I first?
Why, count the letters which make up his name,
And as their number chances, even or odd,
Arrive at my conclusion, trim my course:
Hiram H. Horsefall is your honored name,
And haven't I found a patron, sir, in you?
"Shall I cheat this stranger?" I take apple-pips,
Stick one in either *canthus* of my eye,
And if the left drops first—(your left, sir, stuck)
I'm warned, I let the trick alone this time.
You, sir, who smile, superior to such trash,
You judge of character by other rules:
Don't your rules sometimes fail you? Pray, what rule
Have you judged Sludge by hitherto?

                                      Oh, be sure,
You, everybody blunders, just as I,
In simpler things than these by far! For see:
I knew two farmers,—one, a wiseacre
Who studied seasons, rummaged almanacs,
Quoted the dew-point, registered the frost,
And then declared, for outcome of his pains,
Next summer must be dampish: 'twas a drought.
His neighbor prophesied such drought would fall,
Saved hay and corn, made cent. per cent. thereby,
And proved a sage indeed: how came his lore?
Because one brindled heifer, late in March,
Stiffened her tail of evenings, and somehow
He got into his head that drought was meant!
I don't expect all men can do as much:
Such kissing goes by favor. You must take
A certain turn of mind for this,—a twist
I' the flesh, as well. Be lazily alive,

Open-mouthed, like my friend the ant-eater,
Letting all nature's loosely-guarded motes
Settle and, slick, be swallowed! Think yourself
The one i' the world, the one for whom the world
Was made, expect it tickling at your mouth!
Then will the swarm of busy buzzing flies,
Clouds of coincidence, break egg-shell, thrive,
Breed, multiply, and bring you food enough.

I can't pretend to mind your smiling, sir!
Oh, what you mean is this! Such intimate way,
Close converse, frank exchange of offices,
Strict sympathy of the immeasurably great
With the infinitely small, betokened here
By a course of signs and omens, raps and sparks,—
How does it suit the dread traditional text
O' the "Great and Terrible Name"? Shall the Heaven of Heavens
Stoop to such child's play?

                              Please, sir, go with me
A moment, and I'll try to answer you.
The "*Magnum et terribile*" (is that right?)
Well, folk began with this in the early day;
And all the acts they recognized in proof
Were thunders, lightnings, earthquakes, whirlwinds, dealt
Indisputably on men whose death they caused.
There, and there only, folk saw Providence
At work,—and seeing it, 'twas right enough
All heads should tremble, hands wring hands amain,
And knees knock hard together at the breath
O' the Name's first letter; why, the Jews, I'm told,
Won't write it down, no, to this very hour,
Nor speak aloud: you know best if't be so.
Each ague-fit of fear at end, they crept
(Because somehow people once born must live)
Out of the sound, sight, swing and sway o' the Name,
Into a corner, the dark rest of the world,
And safe space where as yet no fear had reached;
'Twas there they looked about them, breathed again,
And felt indeed at home, as we might say.
The current o' common things, the daily life,
This had their due contempt; no Name pursued
Man from the mountain-top where fires abide,
To his particular mouse-hole at its foot
Where he ate, drank, digested, lived in short:
Such was man's vulgar business, far too small

To be worth thunder: "small," folk kept on, "small,"
With much complacency in those great days!
A mote of sand, you know, a blade of grass—
What was so despicable as mere grass,
Except perhaps the life o' the worm or fly
Which fed there? These were "small" and men were great.
Well, sir, the old way's altered somewhat since,
And the world wears another aspect now:
Somebody turns our spyglass round, or else
Puts a new lens in it: grass, worm, fly grow big:
We find great things are made of little things,
And little things go lessening till at last
Comes God behind them. Talk of mountains now?
We talk of mould that heaps the mountain, mites
That throng the mould, and God that makes the mites.
The Name comes close behind a stomach-cyst,
The simplest of creations, just a sac
That's mouth, heart, legs and belly at once, yet lives
And feels, and could do neither, we conclude,
If simplified still further one degree:
The small becomes the dreadful and immense!
Lightning, forsooth? No word more upon that!
A tin-foil bottle, a strip of greasy silk,
With a bit of wire and knob of brass, and there's
Your dollar's-worth of lightning! But the cyst—
The life of the least of the little things?

                         No, no!
Preachers and teachers try another tack,
Come near the truth this time: they put aside
Thunder and lightning. "That's mistake," they cry;
"Thunderbolts fall for neither fright nor sport,
But do appreciable good, like tides,
Changes o' the wind, and other natural facts—
'Good' meaning good to man, his body or soul.
Mediate, immediate, all things minister
To man,—that's settled: be our future text
'We are His children!' " So, they now harangue
About the intention, the contrivance, all
That keeps up an incessant play of love,—
See the Bridgewater book.

                       Amen to it!
Well, sir, I put this question: I'm a child?
I lose no time, but take you at your word:
How shall I act a child's part properly?

Your sainted mother, sir,—used you to live
With such a thought as this a-worrying you?
"She has it in her power to throttle me,
Or stab or poison: she may turn me out,
Or lock me in,—nor stop at this to-day,
But cut me off to-morrow from the estate
I look for"—(long may you enjoy it, sir!)
"In brief, she may unchild the child I am."
You never had such crotchets? Nor have I!
Who, frank confessing childship from the first,
Cannot both fear and take my ease at once,
So, don't fear,—know what might be, well enough,
But know too, child-like, that it will not be,
At least in my case, mine, the son and heir
O' the kingdom, as yourself proclaim my style.
But do you fancy I stop short at this?
Wonder if suit and service, son and heir
Needs must expect, I dare pretend to find?
If, looking for signs proper to such an one,
I straight perceive them irresistible?
Concede that homage is a son's plain right,
And, never mind the nods and raps and winks,
'Tis the pure obvious supernatural
Steps forward, does its duty: why, of course!
I have presentiments; my dreams come true:
I fancy a friend stands whistling all in white
Blithe as a boblink, and he's dead I learn.
I take dislike to a dog my favorite long,
And sell him; he goes mad next week and snaps.
I guess that stranger will turn up to-day
I have not seen these three years; there's his knock.
I wager "sixty peaches on that tree!"—
That I pick up a dollar in my walk,
That your wife's brother's cousin's name was George—
And win on all points. Oh, you wince at this?
You'd fain distinguish between gift and gift,
Washington's oracle and Sludge's itch
O' the elbow when at whist he ought to trump?
With Sludge it's too absurd? *Fine, draw the line
Somewhere, but, sir, your somewhere is not mine!*

Bless us, I'm turning poet! It's time to end.
How you have drawn me out, sir! All I ask
Is—am I heir or not heir? If I'm he,
Then, sir, remember, that same personage
(To judge by what we read i' the newspaper)

Requires, beside one nobleman in gold
To carry up and down his coronet,
Another servant, probably a duke,
To hold eggnog in readiness: why want
Attendance, sir, when helps in his father's house
Abound, I'd like to know?

                      Enough of talk!
My fault is that I tell too plain a truth.
Why, which of those who say they disbelieve,
Your clever people, but has dreamed his dream,
Caught his coincidence, stumbled on his fact
He can't explain, (he'll tell you smilingly,)
Which he's too much of a philosopher
To count as supernatural, indeed,
So calls a puzzle and problem, proud of it:
Bidding you still be on your guard, you know,
Because one fact don't make a system stand,
Nor prove this an occasional escape
Of spirit beneath the matter: that's the way!
Just so wild Indians picked up, piece by piece,
The fact in California, the fine gold
That underlay the gravel—hoarded these,
But never made a system stand, nor dug!
So wise men hold out in each hollowed palm
A handful of experience, sparkling fact
They can't explain; and since their rest of life
Is all explainable, what proof in this?
Whereas I take the fact, the grain of gold,
And fling away the dirty rest of life,
And add this grain to the grain each fool has found
O' the million other such philosophers,—
Till I see gold, all gold and only gold,
Truth questionless though unexplainable,
And the miraculous proved the commonplace!
The other fools believed in mud, no doubt—
Failed to know gold they saw: was that so strange?
Are all men born to play Bach's fiddle-fugues,
"Time" with the foil in carte, jump their own height,
Cut the mutton with the broadsword, skate a five,
Make the red hazard with the cue, clip nails
While swimming, in five minutes row a mile,
Pull themselves three feet up with the left arm,
Do sums of fifty figures in their head,
And so on, by the scores of instances?
The Sludge with luck, who sees the spiritual facts,

His fellows strive and fail to see, may rank
With these, and share the advantage.

                                          Ay, but share

The drawback! Think it over by yourself;
I have not heart, sir, and the fire's gone gray.
Defect somewhere compensates for success,
Every one knows that. Oh, we're equals, sir!
The big-legged fellow has a little arm
And a less brain, though big legs win the race:
Do you suppose I 'scape the common lot?
Say, I was born with flesh so sensitive,
Soul so alert, that, practice helping both,
I guess what's going on outside the veil,
Just as a prisoned crane feels pairing-time
In the islands where his kind are, so must fall
To capering by himself some shiny night,
As if your back-yard were a plot of spice—
Thus am I 'ware o' the spirit-world: while you,
Blind as a beetle that way,—for amends,
Why, you can double fist and floor me, sir!
Ride that hot hardmouthed horrid horse of yours,
Laugh while it lightens, play with the great dog,
Speak your mind though it vex some friend to hear,
Never brag, never bluster, never blush,—
In short, you've pluck, when I'm a coward—there!
I know it, I can't help it,—folly or no,
I'm paralyzed, my hand's no more a hand,
Nor my head, a head, in danger: you can smile
And change the pipe in your cheek. Your gift's not mine.
Would you swap for mine? No! but you'd add my gift
To yours: I dare say! I too sigh at times,
Wish I were stouter, could tell truth nor flinch,
Kept cool when threatened, did not mind so much
Being dressed gayly, making strangers stare,
Eating nice things; when I'd amuse myself,
I shut my eyes and fancy in my brain,
I'm—now the President, now Jenny Lind,
Now Emerson, now the Benicia Boy—
With all the civilized world a-wondering
And worshiping. I know it's folly and worse;
I feel such tricks sap, honeycomb the soul,
But I can't cure myself,—despond, despair,
And then, hey, presto, there's a turn o' the wheel,
Under comes uppermost, fate makes full amends;
Sludge knows and sees and hears a hundred things

You all are blind to,—I've my taste of truth,
Likewise my touch of falsehood,—vice no doubt,
But you've your vices also: I'm content.

What, sir? You won't shake hands? "Because I cheat!"
"You've found me out in cheating!" That's enough
To make an apostle swear! Why, when I cheat,
Mean to cheat, do cheat, and am caught in the act,
Are you, or rather, am I sure o' the fact?
(There's verse again, but I'm inspired somehow.)
Well then I'm not sure! I may be, perhaps,
Free as a babe from cheating: how it began,
My gift,—no matter; what 'tis got to be
In the end now, that's the question; answer that!
Had I seen, perhaps, what hand was holding mine,
Leading me whither, I had died of fright:
So, I was made believe I led myself.
If I should lay a six-inch plank from roof
To roof, you would not cross the street, one step,
Even at your mother's summons: but, being shrewd,
If I paste paper on each side the plank
And swear 'tis solid pavement, why, you'll cross
Humming a tune the while, in ignorance
Beacon Street stretches a hundred feet below:
I walked thus, took the paper-cheat for stone.
Some impulse made me set a thing o' the move
Which, started once, ran really by itself;
Beer flows thus, suck the siphon; toss the kite,
It takes the wind and floats of its own force.
Don't let truth's lump rot stagnant for the lack
Of a timely helpful lie to leaven it!
Put a chalk-egg beneath the clucking hen,
She'll lay a real one, laudably deceived,
Daily for weeks to come. I've told my lie,
And seen truth follow, marvels none of mine;
All was not cheating, sir, I'm positive!
I don't know if I move your hand sometimes
When the spontaneous writing spreads so far,
If my knee lifts the table all that height,
Why the inkstand don't fall off the desk a-tilt,
Why the accordion plays a prettier waltz
Than I can pick out on the pianoforte,
Why I speak so much more than I intend,
Describe so many things I never saw.
I tell you, sir, in one sense, I believe
Nothing at all,—that everybody can,

Will, and does cheat: but in another sense
I'm ready to believe my very self—
That every cheat's inspired, and every lie
Quick with a germ of truth.

                              You ask perhaps
Why I should condescend to trick at all
If I know a way without it? This is why!
There's a strange secret sweet self-sacrifice
In any desecration of one's soul
To a worthy end,—isn't it Herodotus
(I wish I could read Latin!) who describes
The single gift o' the land's virginity,
Demanded in those old Egyptian rites,
(I've but a hazy notion—help me, sir!)
For one purpose in the world, one day in a life,
One hour in a day—thereafter, purity,
And a veil thrown o'er the past forevermore!
Well now, they understood a many things
Down by Nile city, or wherever it was!
I've always vowed, after the minute's lie,
And the end's gain,—truth should be mine henceforth.
This goes to the root o' the matter, sir,—this plain
Plump fact: accept it and unlock with it
The wards of many a puzzle!

                              Or, finally,
Why should I set so fine a gloss on things?
What need I care? I cheat in self-defense,
And there's my answer to a world of cheats!
Cheat? To be sure, sir! What's the world worth else?
Who takes it as he finds, and thanks his stars?
Don't it want trimming, turning, furbishing up
And polishing over? Your so-styled great men,
Do they accept one truth as truth is found,
Or try their skill at tinkering? What's your world?
Here are you born, who are, I'll say at once,
Of the luckiest kind, whether in head and heart,
Body and soul, or all that helps them both.
Well, now, look back: what faculty of yours
Came to its full, had ample justice done
By growing when rain fell, biding its time,
Solidifying growth when earth was dead,
Spiring up, broadening wide, in seasons due?
Never! You shot up and frost nipped you off,
Settled to sleep when sunshine bade you sprout;

One faculty thwarted its fellow: at the end,
All you boast is, "I had proved a topping tree
In other climes,"—yet this was the right clime
Had you foreknown the seasons. Young, you've force
Wasted like well-streams: old,—oh, then indeed,
Behold a labyrinth of hydraulic pipes
Through which you'd play off wondrous waterwork;
Only, no water's left to feed their play.
Young,—you've a hope, an aim, a love; it's tossed
And crossed and lost: you struggle on, some spark
Shut in your heart against the puffs around,
Through cold and pain; these in due time subside,
Now then for age's triumph, the hoarded light
You mean to loose on the altered face of things,—
Up with it on the tripod! It's extinct.
Spend your life's remnant asking, which was best,
Light smothered up that never peeped forth once,
Or the cold cresset with full leave to shine?
Well, accept this too,—seek the fruit of it
Not in enjoyment, proved a dream on earth,
But knowledge, useful for a second chance,
Another life,—you've lost this world—you've gained
Its knowledge for the next.—What knowledge, sir,
Except that you know nothing? Nay, you doubt
Whether 't were better have made you man or brute,
If aught be true, if good and evil clash.
No foul, no fair, no inside, no outside,
There's your world!

                      Give it me! I slap it brisk
With harlequin's pasteboard sceptre: what's it now?
Changed like a rock-flat, rough with rusty weed,
At first wash-over o' the returning wave!
All the dry dead impracticable stuff
Starts into life and light again; this world
Pervaded by the influx from the next.
I cheat, and what's the happy consequence?
You find full justice straightway dealt you out,
Each want supplied, each ignorance set at ease,
Each folly fooled. No life-long labor now
As the price of worse than nothing! No mere film
Holding you chained in iron, as it seems,
Against the outstretch of your very arms
And legs i' the sunshine moralists forbid!
What would you have? Just speak and, there, you see!
You're supplemented, made a whole at last,

Bacon advises, Shakespeare writes you songs,
And Mary Queen of Scots embraces you.
Thus it goes on, not quite like life perhaps,
But so near, that the very difference piques,
Shows that e'en better than this best will be—
This passing entertainment in a hut
Whose bare walls take your taste since, one stage more,
And you arrive at the palace: all half real,
And you, to suit it, less than real beside,
In a dream, lethargic kind of death in life,
That helps the interchange of natures, flesh
Transfused by souls, and such souls! Oh, 'tis choice!
And if at whiles the bubble, blown too thin,
Seem nigh on bursting,—if you nearly see
The real world through the false,—what *do* you see?
Is the old so ruined? You find you're in a flock
O' the youthful, earnest, passionate—genius, beauty,
Rank and wealth also, if you care for these;
And all depose their natural rights, hail you
(That's me, sir) as their mate and yoke-fellow.
Participate in Sludgehood—nay, grow mine,
I veritably possess them—banish doubt,
And reticence and modesty alike!
Why, here's the Golden Age, old Paradise
Or new Utopia! Here's true life indeed,
And the world well won now, mine for the first time!

And all this might be, may be, and with good help
Of a little lying shall be: so, Sludge lies!
Why, he's at worst your poet who sings how Greeks
That never were, in Troy which never was,
Did this or the other impossible great thing!
He's Lowell—it's a world (you smile applause)
Of his own invention—wondrous Longfellow,
Surprising Hawthorne! Sludge does more than they,
And acts the books they write: the more his praise!

But why do I mount to poets? Take plain prose—
Dealers in common sense, set these at work,
What can they do without their helpful lies?
Each states the law and fact and face o' the thing
Just as he'd have them, finds what he thinks fit,
Is blind to what missuits him, just records
What makes his case out, quite ignores the rest.
It's a History of the World, the Lizard Age,
The Early Indians, the Old Country War,

Jerome Napoleon, whatsoever you please,
All as the author wants it. Such a scribe
You pay and praise for putting life in stones,
Fire into fog, making the past your world.
There's plenty of "How did you contrive to grasp
The thread which led you through this labyrinth?
How build such solid fabric out of air?
How on so slight foundation found this tale,
Biography, narrative?" or, in other words,
"How many lies did it require to make
The portly truth you here present us with?"
"Oh," quoth the penman, purring at your praise,
" 'Tis fancy all; no particle of fact:
I was poor and threadbare when I wrote that book
'Bliss in the Golden City.' I, at Thebes?
We writers paint out of our heads, you see!"
"—Ah, the more wonderful the gift in you,
The more creativeness and godlike craft!"
But I, do I present you with my piece,
It's "What, Sludge? When my sainted mother spoke
The verses Lady Jane Grey last composed
About the rosy bower in the seventh heaven
Where she and Queen Elizabeth keep house,—
You made the raps? 'Twas your invention that?
Cur, slave, and devil!"—eight fingers and two thumbs
Stuck in my throat!

                 Well, if the marks seem gone,
'Tis because stiffish cocktail, taken in time,
Is better for a bruise than arnica.
There, sir! I bear no malice: 'tis n't in me.
I know I acted wrongly: still, I've tried
What I could say in my excuse,—to show
The devil's not all devil . . . I don't pretend,
An angel, much less such a gentleman
As you, sir! And I've lost you, lost myself,
Lost all, l-l-l- . . .

                 No—are you in earnest, sir?
Oh, yours, sir, is an angel's part! I know
What prejudice prompts, and what's the common course
Men take to soothe their ruffled self-conceit:
Only you rise superior to it all!
No, sir, it don't hurt much; it's speaking long
That makes me choke a little: the marks will go!
What? Twenty V-notes more, and outfit too,

And not a word to Greeley? One—one kiss
O' the hand that saves me! You'll not let me speak,
I well know, and I've lost the right, too true!
But I must say, sir, if She hears (she does)
Your sainted . . . Well, sir,—be it so! That's, I think,
My bedroom candle. Good-night! Bl-l-less you, sir!

R-r-r, you brute-beast and blackguard! Cowardly scamp!
I only wish I dared burn down the house
And spoil your sniggering! Oh, what, you're the man?
You're satisfied at last? You've found out Sludge?
We'll see that presently: my turn, sir, next!
I too can tell my story: brute,—do you hear?—
You throttled your sainted mother, that old hag,
In just such a fit of passion: no, it was . . .
To get this house of hers, and many a note
Like these . . . I'll pocket them, however . . . five,
Ten, fifteen . . . ay, you gave her throat the twist,
Or else you poisoned her! Confound the cuss!
Where was my head? I ought to have prophesied
He'll die in a year and join her: that's the way.
I don't know where my head is: what had I done?
How did it all go? I said he poisoned her,
And hoped he'd have grace given him to repent,
Whereon he picked this quarrel, bullied me
And called me cheat: I thrashed him,—who could help?
He howled for mercy, prayed me on his knees
To cut and run and save him from disgrace:
I do so, and once off, he slanders me.
An end of him! Begin elsewhere anew!
Boston's a hole, the herring-pond is wide,
V-notes are something, liberty still more.
Beside, is he the only fool in the world?

APPARENT FAILURE

"We shall soon lose a celebrated building."
Paris Newspaper.

I.

No, for I'll save it! Seven years since,
    I passed through Paris, stopped a day
To see the baptism of your Prince;
    Saw, made my bow, and went my way:

Walking the heat and headache off,
   I took the Seine-side, you surmise,
Thought of the Congress, Gortschakoff,
   Cavour's appeal and Buol's replies,
So sauntered till—what met my eyes?

II.

Only the Doric little Morgue!
   The dead-house where you show your drowned:
Petrarch's Vaucluse makes proud the Sorgue,
   Your Morgue has made the Seine renowned.
One pays one's debt in such a case;
   I plucked up heart and entered,—stalked,
Keeping a tolerable face
   Compared with some whose cheeks were chalked:
Let them! No Briton's to be balked!

III.

First came the silent gazers; next,
   A screen of glass, we're thankful for;
Last, the sight's self, the sermon's text,
   The three men who did most abhor
Their life in Paris yesterday,
   So killed themselves: and now, enthroned
Each on his copper couch, they lay
   Fronting me, waiting to be owned.
I thought, and think, their sin's atoned.

IV.

Poor men, God made, and all for that!
   The reverence struck me; o'er each head
Religiously was hung its hat,
   Each coat dripped by the owner's bed,
Sacred from touch: each had his berth,
   His bounds, his proper place of rest,
Who last night tenanted on earth
   Some arch, where twelve such slept abreast,—
Unless the plain asphalte seemed best.

V.

How did it happen, my poor boy?
   You wanted to be Buonaparte
And have the Tuileries for toy,
   And could not, so it broke your heart?
You, old one by his side, I judge,
   Were, red as blood, a socialist,

A leveller! Does the Empire grudge
　　You've gained what no Republic missed?
Be quiet, and unclench your fist!

VI.

And this—why, he was red in vain,
　　Or black,—poor fellow that is blue!
What fancy was it, turned your brain?
　　Oh, women were the prize for you!
Money gets women, cards and dice
　　Get money, and ill-luck gets just
The copper couch and one clear nice
　　Cool squirt of water o'er your bust,
The right thing to extinguish lust!

VII.

It's wiser being good than bad;
　　It's safer being meek than fierce:
It's fitter being sane than mad.
　　My own hope is, a sun will pierce
The thickest cloud earth ever stretched;
　　That, after Last, returns the First,
Though a wide compass round be fetched;
　　That what began best, can't end worst,
Nor what God blessed once, prove accurst.

EPILOGUE

FIRST SPEAKER, *as David*

I.

ON THE first of the Feast of Feasts,
　　The Dedication Day,
When the Levites joined the Priests
　　At the Altar in robed array,
Gave signal to sound and say,—

II.

When the thousands, rear and van,
　　Swarming with one accord,
Became as a single man
　　(Look, gesture, thought and word)
In praising and thanking the Lord,—

III.

When the singers lift up their voice,
   And the trumpets made endeavor,
Sounding, "In God rejoice!"
   Saying, "In Him rejoice
Whose mercy endureth forever!"—

IV.

Then the Temple filled with a cloud,
   Even the House of the Lord;
Porch bent and pillar bowed:
   For the presence of the Lord,
In the glory of His cloud,
   Had filled the House of the Lord.

SECOND SPEAKER, *as Renan.*

Gone now! All gone across the dark so far,
   Sharpening fast, shuddering ever, shutting still,
Dwindling into the distance, dies that star
   Which came, stood, opened once! We gazed our fill
With upturned faces on as real a Face
   That, stooping from grave music and mild fire,
Took in our homage, made a visible place
   Through many a depth of glory, gyre on gyre,
For the dim human tribute. Was this true?
   Could man indeed avail, mere praise of his,
To help by rapture God's own rapture too,
   Thrill with a heart's red tinge that pure pale bliss?
Why did it end? Who failed to beat the breast,
   And shriek, and throw the arms protesting wide,
When a first shadow showed the star addressed
   Itself to motion, and on either side
The rims contracted as the rays retired;
   The music, like a fountain's sickening pulse,
Subsided on itself; awhile transpired
   Some vestige of a Face no pangs convulse,
No prayers retard; then even this was gone,
   Lost in the night at last. We, lone and left
Silent through centuries, ever and anon
   Venture to probe again the vault bereft
Of all now save the lesser lights, a mist
   Of multitudinous points, yet suns, men say—
And this leaps ruby, this lurks amethyst,
   But where may hide what came and loved our clay?
How shall the sage detect in yon expanse

The star which chose to stoop and stay for us?
Unroll the records! Hailed ye such advance
  Indeed, and did your hope vanish thus?
Watchers of twilight, is the worst averred?
  We shall not look up, know ourselves are seen,
Speak, and be sure that we again are heard,
  Acting or suffering, have the disk's serene
Reflect our life, absorb an earthly flame,
  Nor doubt that, were mankind inert and numb,
Its core had never crimsoned all the same,
  Nor, missing ours, its music fallen dumb?
Oh, dread succession to a dizzy post,
  Sad sway of sceptre whose mere touch appalls,
Ghastly dethronement, cursed by those the most
  On whose repugnant brow the crown next falls!

Third Speaker

I.

Witless alike of will and way divine,
How heaven's high with earth's low should intertwine!
Friends, I have seen through your eyes: now use mine!

II.

Take the least man of all mankind, as I;
Look at his head and heart, find how and why
He differs from his fellows utterly:

III.

Then, like me, watch when nature by degrees
Grows alive round him, as in Arctic seas
(They said of old) the instinctive water flees

IV.

Toward some elected point of central rock,
As though, for its sake only, roamed the flock
Of waves about the waste: awhile they mock

V.

With radiance caught for the occasion,—hues
Of blackest hell now, now such reds and blues
As only heaven could fitly interfuse,—

VI.

The mimic monarch of the whirlpool, king
O' the current for a minute: then they wring
Up by the roots and oversweep the thing,

VII.

And hasten off, to play again elsewhere
The same part, choose another peak as bare,
They find and flatter, feast and finish there.

VIII.

When you see what I tell you,—nature dance
About each man of us, retire, advance,
As though the pageant's end were to enhance

IX.

His worth, and—once the life, his product, gained—
Roll away elsewhere, keep the strife sustained,
And show thus real, a thing the North but feigned—

X.

When you acknowledge that one world could do
All the diverse work, old yet ever new,
Divide us, each from other, me from you,—

XI.

Why, where's the need of Temple, when the walls
O' the world are that? What use of swells and falls
From Levites' choir, Priests' cries, and trumpet-calls?

XII.

That one Face, far from vanish, rather grows,
Or decomposes but to recompose,
Become my universe that feels and knows!

AT THE "MERMAID"

The figure that thou here seest . . . Tut!
Was it for gentle Shakespeare put?
                    B. JONSON. (*Adapted.*)

I.

I—"NEXT POET?" No, my hearties,
  I nor am nor fain would be!
Choose your chiefs and pick your parties,
  Not one soul revolt to me!
I, forsooth, sow song-sedition?
  I, a schism in verse provoke?
I, blown up by bard's ambition,
  Burst—your bubble-king? You joke.

II.

Come, be grave! The sherris mantling
  Still about each mouth, mayhap,
Breeds you insight—just a scantling—
  Brings me truth out—just a scrap.
Look and tell me! Written, spoken,
  Here 's my life-long work: and where
—Where 's your warrant or my token
  I'm the dead king's son and heir?

III.

Here 's my work: does work discover—
  What was rest from work—my life?
Did I live man's hater, lover?
  Leave the world at peace, at strife?
Call earth ugliness or beauty?
  See things there in large or small?
Use to pay its Lord my duty?
  Use to own a lord at all?

IV.

Blank of such a record, truly,
  Here 's the work I hand, this scroll,
Yours to take or leave; as duly,
  Mine remains the unproffered soul.
So much, no whit more, my debtors—
  How should one like me lay claim
To that largess elders, betters
  Sell you cheap their souls for—fame?

V.

Which of you did I enable
  Once to slip inside my breast,
There to catalogue and label
  What I like least, what love best,
Hope and fear, believe and doubt of,
  Seek and shun, respect—deride?
Who has right to make a rout of
  Rarities he found inside?

VI.

Rarities or, as he 'd rather,
  Rubbish such as stocks his own:
Need and greed (O strange) the **Father**
  Fashioned not for him alone!

Whence—the comfort set a-strutting,
  Whence—the outcry "Haste, behold!
Bard's breast open wide, past shutting,
  Shows what brass we took for gold!"

VII.

Friends, I doubt not he'd display you
  Brass—myself call oreichalch,—
Furnish much amusement; pray you
  Therefore, be content I balk
Him and you, and bar my portal!
  Here's my work outside: opine
What's inside me mean and mortal!
  Take your pleasure, leave me mine!

VIII.

Which is—not to buy your laurel
  As last king did, nothing loth.
Tale adorned and pointed moral
  Gained him praise and pity both.
Out rushed sighs and groans by dozens,
  Forth by scores oaths, curses flew:
Proving you were cater-cousins,
  Kith and kindred, king and you!

IX.

Whereas do I ne'er so little
  (Thanks to sherris), leave ajar
Bosom's gate—no jot nor tittle
  Grow we nearer than we are.
Sinning, sorrowing, despairing,
  Body-ruined, spirit-wrecked,—
Should I give my woes an airing,—
  Where's one plague that claims respect?

X.

Have you found your life distasteful?
  My life did and does smack sweet.
Was your youth of pleasure wasteful?
  Mine I saved and hold complete.
Do your joys with age diminish?
  When mine fail me, I'll complain.
Must in death your daylight finish?
  My sun sets to rise again.

XI.

What, like you, he proved—your Pilgrim—
  This our world a wilderness,
Earth still gray and heaven still grim,
  Not a hand there his might press,
Not a heart his own might throb to,
  Men all rogues and women—say,
Dolls which boys' heads duck and bob to,
  Grown folk drop or throw away?

XII.

My experience being other,
  How should I contribute verse
Worthy of your king and brother?
  Balaam-like I bless, not curse.
I find earth not gray but rosy,
  Heaven not grim but fair of hue.
Do I stoop? I pluck a posy.
  Do I stand and stare? All 's blue.

XIII.

Doubtless I am pushed and shoved by
  Rogues and fools enough: the more
Good luck mine, I love, am loved by
  Some few honest to the core.
Scan the near high, scout the far low!
  "But the low come close:" what then?
Simpletons? My match is Marlowe;
  Sciolists? My mate is Ben.

XIV.

Womankind—"the cat-like nature,
  False and fickle, vain and weak"—
What of this sad nomenclature
  Suits my tongue, if I must speak?
Does the sex invite, repulse so,
  Tempt, betray, by fits and starts?
So becalm but to convulse so,
  Decking heads and breaking hearts?

XV.

Well may you blaspheme at fortune!
  I "threw Venus" (Ben, expound!)
Never did I need importune
  Her, of all the Olympian round.

Blessings on my benefactress!
  Cursings suit—for aught I know—
Those who twitched her by the back tress,
  Tugged and thought to turn her—so!

XVI.

Therefore, since no leg to stand on
  Thus I 'm left with,—joy or grief
Be the issue,—I abandon
  Hope or care you name me Chief!
Chief and king and Lord's anointed,
  I?—who never once have wished
Death before the day appointed:
  Lived and liked, not poohed and pished!

XVII.

"Ah, but so I shall not enter,
  Scroll in hand, the common heart—
Stopped at surface: since at centre
  Song should reach *Welt-schmerz*, world-smart!"
"Enter in the heart?" Its shelly
  Cuirass guard mine, fore and aft!
Such song "enters in the belly
  And is cast out in the draught."

XVIII.

Back then to our sherris-brewage!
  "Kingship" quotha? I shall wait—
Waive the present time: some new age . . .
  But let fools anticipate!
Meanwhile greet me—"friend, good fellow,
  Gentle Will," my merry men!
As for making Envy yellow
  With "Next Poet"—(Manners, Ben!)

HOUSE

I.

SHALL 1 sonnet-sing you about myself?
  Do I live in a house you would like to see?
Is it scant of gear, has it store of pelf?
  "Unlock my heart with a sonnet-key?"

II.

Invite the world, as my betters have done?
  "Take notice: this building remains on **view**,
Its suites of reception every one,
  Its private apartment and bedroom too;

III.

"For a ticket, apply to the Publisher."
  No: thanking the public, I must decline.
A peep through my window, if folk prefer;
  But, please you, no foot over threshold of mine!

IV.

I have mixed with a crowd and heard free talk
  In a foreign land where an earthquake chanced
And a house stood gaping, nought to balk
  Man's eye wherever he gazed or glanced.

V.

The whole of the frontage shaven sheer,
  The inside gaped: exposed to day,
Right and wrong and common and queer,
  Bare, as the palm of your hand, it lay.

VI.

The owner? Oh, he had been crushed, no doubt!
  "Odd tables and chairs for a man of wealth!
What a parcel of musty old books about!
  He smoked,—no wonder he lost his health!

VII.

"I doubt if he bathed before he dressed.
  A brasier?—the pagan, he burned perfumes!
You see it is proved, what the neighbors guessed:
  His wife and himself had separate rooms."

VIII.

Friends, the goodman of the house at least
  Kept house to himself till an earthquake came:
'T is the fall of its frontage permits you feast
  On the inside arrangement you praise or blame.

IX.

Outside should suffice for evidence:
  And whoso desires to penetrate
Deeper, must dive by the spirit-sense—
  No optics like yours, at any rate!

x.

"Hoity-toity! A street to explore,
    Your house the exception! *'With this same key
Shakespeare unlocked his heart,'* once more!"
    Did Shakespeare? If so, the less Shakespeare **he!**

SHOP

I.

So, FRIEND, your shop was all your **house!**
    Its front, astonishing the street,
Invited view from man and mouse
    To what diversity of treat
    Behind its glass—the single sheet!

II.

What gimcracks, genuine Japanese:
    Gape-jaw and goggle-eye, the frog;
Dragons, owls, monkeys, beetles, geese;
    Some crush-nosed human-hearted dog:
    Queer names, too, such a catalogue!

III.

I thought "And he who owns the wealth
    Which blocks the window's vastitude,
—Ah, could I peep at him by stealth
    Behind his ware, pass shop, intrude
    On house itself, what scenes were **viewed!**

IV.

"If wide and showy thus the shop,
    What must the habitation prove?
The true house with no name a-top—
    The mansion, distant one remove,
    Once get him off his traffic-groove!

V.

"Pictures he likes, or books perhaps;
    And as for buying most and best,
Commend me to these city chaps!
    Or else he's social, takes his rest
    On Sundays, with a Lord for guest.

VI.

"Some suburb-palace, parked about
    And gated grandly, built last year:

The four-mile walk to keep off gout;
    Or big seat sold by bankrupt peer:
    But then he takes the rail, that 's clear.

VII.

"Or, stop! I wager, taste selects
    Some out-o'-the-way, some all-unknown
Retreat: the neighborhood suspects
    Little that he who rambles lone
    Makes Rothschild tremble on his throne!"

VIII.

Nowise! Nor Mayfair residence
    Fit to receive and entertain,—
Nor Hampstead villa's kind defence
    From noise and crowd, from dust and drain,—
    Nor country-box was soul's domain!

IX.

Nowise! At back of all that spread
    Of merchandise, woe 's me, I find
A hole i' the wall where, heels by head,
    The owner couched, his ware behind,
    —In cupboard suited to his mind.

X.

For why? He saw no use of life
    But, while he drove a roaring trade,
To chuckle "Customers are rife!"
    To chafe "So much hard cash outlaid,
    Yet zero in my profits made!

XI.

"This novelty costs pains, but—takes?
    Cumbers my counter! Stock no more!
This article, no such great shakes,
    Fizzes like wild-fire? Underscore
    The cheap thing—thousands to the fore!"

XII.

'T was lodging best to live most nigh
    (Cramp, coffinlike as crib might be)
Receipt of Custom; ear and eye
    Wanted no outworld: "Hear and see
    The bustle in the shop!" quoth he.

XIII.

My fancy of a merchant-prince
　Was different. Through his wares we groped
Our darkling way to—not to mince
　The matter—no black den where moped
　The master if we interloped!

XIV.

Shop was shop only: household-stuff?
　What did he want with comforts there?
"Walls, ceiling, floor, stay blank and rough,
　So goods on sale show rich and rare!
　'Sell and scud home,' be shop's affair!"

XV.

What might he deal in? Gems, suppose!
　Since somehow business must be done
At cost of trouble,—see, he throws
　You choice of jewels, every one
　Good, better, best, star, moon, and sun!

XVI.

Which lies within your power of purse?
　This ruby that would tip aright
Solomon's sceptre? Oh, your nurse
　Wants simply coral, the delight
　Of teething baby,—stuff to bite!

XVII.

Howe'er your choice fell, straight you took
　Your purchase, prompt your money rang
On counter,—scarce the man forsook
　His study of the "Times," just swang
　Till-ward his hand that stopped the clang,—

XVIII.

Then off made buyer with a prize,
　Then seller to his "Times" returned;
And so did day wear, wear, till eyes
　Brightened apace, for rest was earned:
　He locked door long ere candle burned.

XIX.

And whither went he? Ask himself,
　Not me! To change of scene, I think.

Once sold the ware and pursed the pelf,
  Chaffer was scarce his meat and drink,
Nor all his music—money-chink.

XX.

Because a man has shop to mind
  In time and place, since flesh must live,
Needs spirit lack all life behind,
  All stray thoughts, fancies fugitive,
  All loves except what trade can give?

XXI.

I want to know a butcher paints,
  A baker rhymes for his pursuit,
Candlestick-maker much acquaints
  His soul with song, or, haply mute,
  Blows out his brains upon the flute!

XXII.

But—shop each day and all day long!
  Friend, your good angel slept, your star
Suffered eclipse, fate did you wrong!
  From where these sorts of treasures are,
  There should our hearts be—Christ, how far!

PISGAH–SIGHTS I

I.

Over the ball of it,
  Peering and prying,
How I see all of it,
  Life there, outlying!
Roughness and smoothness,
  Shine and defilement,
Grace and uncouthness:
  One reconcilement.

II.

Orbed as appointed,
  Sister with brother
Joins, ne'er disjointed
  One from the other.
All 's lend-and-borrow;
  Good, see, wants evil,
Joy demands sorrow,
  Angel weds devil!

III.

"Which things must—*why* be?"
  Vain our endeavor!
So shall things aye be
  As they were ever.
"Such things should *so* be!"
  Sage our desistence!
Rough-smooth let globe be,
  Mixed—man's existence!

IV.

Man—wise and foolish,
  Lover and scorner,
Docile and mulish—
  Keep each his corner!
Honey yet gall of it!
  There 's the life lying,
And I see all of it,
  Only, I 'm dying!

PISGAH–SIGHTS II

I.

Could I but live again
  Twice my life over,
Would I once strive again?
  Would not I cover
Quietly all of it—
  Greed and ambition—
So, from the pall of it,
  Pass to fruition?

II.

"Soft!" I 'd say, "Soul mine!
  Three-score and ten years,
Let the blind mole mine
  Digging out deniers!
Let the dazed hawk soar,
  Claim the sun's rights too!
Turf 't is thy walk 's o'er,
  Foliage thy flight 's to."

III.

Only a learner,
  Quick one or slow one,

Just a discerner,
  I would teach no one.
I am earth's native:
  No rearranging it!
I be creative,
  Chopping and changing it?

IV.

March, men, my fellows!
  Those who, above me,
(Distance so mellows)
  Fancy you love me:
Those who, below me,
  (Distance makes great so)
Free to forego me,
  Fancy you hate so!

V.

Praising, reviling,
  Worst head and best head,
Past me defiling,
  Never arrested,
Wanters, abounders,
  March, in gay mixture,
Men, my surrounders!
  I am the fixture.

VI.

So shall I fear thee,
  Mightiness yonder!
Mock-sun—more near thee,
  What is to wonder?
So shall I love thee,
Down in the dark,—lest
Glowworm I prove thee,
  Star that now sparklest!

FEARS AND SCRUPLES

I.

HERE's my case. Of old I used to love him,
  This same unseen friend, before I knew:
Dream there was none like him, none above him,—
  Wake to hope and trust my dream was true.

II.

Loved I not his letters full of beauty?
  Not his actions famous far and wide?
Absent, he would know I vowed him duty;
  Present, he would find me at his side.

III.

Pleasant fancy! for I had but letters,
  Only knew of actions by hearsay:
He himself was busied with my betters;
  What of that? My turn must come some day.

IV.

"Some day" proving—no day! Here's the puzzle.
  Passed and passed my turn is. Why complain?
He's so busied! If I could but muzzle
  People's foolish mouths that give me pain!

V.

"Letters?" (hear them!) "You a judge of writing?
  Ask the experts! How they shake the head
O'er these characters, your friend's inditing—
  Call them forgery from A to Z!

VI.

"Actions? Where's your certain proof?" (they bother)
  "He, of all you find so great and good,
He, he only, claims this, that, the other
  Action—claimed by men, a multitude?"

VII.

I can simply wish I might refute you,
  Wish my friend would,—by a word, a wink,—
Bid me stop that foolish mouth,—you brute you!
  He keeps absent,—why, I cannot think.

VIII.

Never mind! Though foolishness may flout me,
  One thing's sure enough: 'tis neither frost,
No, nor fire, shall freeze or burn from out me
  Thanks for truth—though falsehood, gained—though lost.

IX.

All my days, I'll go the softlier, sadlier,
  For that dream's sake! How forget the thrill
Through and through me as I thought "The gladlier
  Lives my friend because I love him still!"

X.

Ah, but there's a menace someone utters!
"What and if your friend at home play tricks?
Peep at hide-and-seek behind the shutters?
Mean your eyes should pierce through solid bricks?

XI.

"What and if he, frowning, wake you, dreamy?
Lay on you the blame that bricks—conceal?
Say '*At least I saw who did not see me,*
Does see now, and presently shall feel'?"

XII.

"Why, that makes your friend a monster!" say you:
"Had his house no window? At first nod,
Would you not have hailed him?" Hush, I pray you!
What if this friend happen to be—God?

HERVÉ RIEL

I.

ON THE SEA and at the Hogue, sixteen hundred ninety-two,
Did the English fight the French,—woe to France!
And, the thirty-first of May, helter-skelter through the blue,
Like a crowd of frightened porpoises a shoal of sharks pursue,
Came crowding ship on ship to St. Malo on the Rance,
With the English fleet in view.

II.

'Twas the squadron that escaped, with the victor in full chase;
First and foremost of the drove, in his great ship, Damfreville;
Close on him fled, great and small,
Twenty-two good ships in all;
And they signalled to the place
"Help the winners of a race!
Get us guidance, give us harbor, take us quick—or, quicker still,
Here's the English can and will!"

III.

Then the pilots of the place put out brisk and leapt on board;
"Why, what hope or chance have ships like these to pass?" laughed they:
"Rocks to starboard, rocks to port, all the passage scarred and scored,
Shall the '*Formidable*' here with her twelve and eighty guns
Think to make the river-mouth by the single narrow way,

Trust to enter where 'tis ticklish for a craft of twenty tons,
    And with flow at full beside?
    Now, 'tis slackest ebb of tide.
  Reach the mooring? Rather say,
While rock stands or water runs,
  Not a ship will leave the bay!"

IV.

Then was called a council straight.
Brief and bitter the debate:
"Here's the English at our heels; would you have them take in tow
All that's left us of the fleet, linked together stern and bow,
For a prize to Plymouth Sound?
Better run the ships aground!"
  (Ended Damfreville his speech).
"Not a minute more to wait!
  Let the Captains all and each
  Shove ashore, then blow up, burn the vessels on the beach!
France must undergo her fate.

V.

"Give the word!" But no such word
Was ever spoke or heard;
  For up stood, for out stepped, for in struck amid all these
—A Captain? A Lieutenant? A Mate—first, second, third?
  No such man of mark, and meet
  With his betters to compete!
  But a simple Breton sailor pressed by Tourville for the fleet,
A poor coasting-pilot he, Hervé Riel the Croisickese.

VI.

And "What mockery or malice have we here?" cries Hervé Riel:
  "Are you mad, you Malouins? Are you cowards, fools, or rogues?
Talk to me of rocks and shoals, me who took the soundings, tell
On my fingers every bank, every shallow, every swell
  'Twixt the offing here and Grève where the river disembogues?
Are you bought by English gold? Is it love the lying's for?
  Morn and eve, night and day,
  Have I piloted your bay,
Entered free and anchored fast at the foot of Solidor.
  Burn the fleet and ruin France? That were worse than fifty Hogues!
  Sirs, they know I speak the truth! Sirs, believe me there's a way!
Only let me lead the line,
  Have the biggest ship to steer,
  Get this 'Formidable' clear,
Make the others follow mine,

And I lead them, most and least, by a passage I know well,
  Right to Solidor past Grève,
    And there lay them safe and sound;
  And if one ship misbehave,
    —Keel so much as grate the ground,
Why, I've nothing but my life,—here's my head!" cries Hervé Riel.

VII.

Not a minute more to wait.
"Steer us in, then, small and great!
  Take the helm, lead the line, save the squadron!" cried its chief.
Captains, give the sailor place!
  He is Admiral, in brief.
Still the north-wind, by God's grace!
See the noble fellow's face
As the big ship, with a bound,
Clears the entry like a hound,
Keeps the passage as its inch of way were the wide sea's profound!
  See, safe through shoal and rock,
  How they follow in a flock,
Not a ship that misbehaves, not a keel that grates the ground,
  Not a spar that comes to grief!
The peril, see, is past,
All are harbored to the last,
And just as Hervé Riel hollas "Anchor!"—sure as fate,
Up the English come—too late!

VIII.

So, the storm subsides to calm:
  They see the green trees wave
  On the heights o'erlooking Grève.
Hearts that bled are stanched with balm.
"Just our rapture to enhance,
  Let the English rake the bay,
Gnash their teeth and glare askance
  As they cannonade away!
'Neath rampired Solidor pleasant riding on the Rance!"
How hope succeeds despair on each Captain's countenance!
Out burst all with one accord,
  "This is Paradise for Hell!
    Let France, let France's King
    Thank the man that did the thing!"
What a shout, and all one word,
  "Hervé Riel!"
As he stepped in front once more,
  Not a symptom of surprise

In the frank blue Breton eyes,
Just the same man as before.

IX.

Then said Damfreville, "My friend,
I must speak out at the end,
  Though I find the speaking hard.
Praise is deeper than the lips:
You have saved the King his ships,
  You must name your own reward.
'Faith, our sun was near eclipse!
Demand whate'er you will,
France remains your debtor still.
Ask to heart's content and have! or my name's not **Damfreville**."

X.

Then a beam of fun outbroke
On the bearded mouth that spoke,
As the honest heart laughed through
Those frank eyes of Breton blue:
"Since I needs must say my say,
  Since on board the duty's done,
  And from Malo Roads to Croisic Point, what is it but a run?—
Since 'tis ask and have, I may—
  Since the others go ashore—
Come! A good whole holiday!
  Leave to go and see my wife, whom I call the Belle Aurore!"
  That he asked and that he got,—nothing more.

XI.

Name and deed alike are lost:
Not a pillar nor a post
  In his Croisic keeps alive the feat as it befell;
Not a head in white and black
On a single fishing-smack,
In memory of the man but for whom had gone to wrack
  All that France saved from the fight whence England bore the bell.
Go to Paris: rank on rank
  Search the heroes flung pell-mell
On the Louvre, face and flank!
  You shall look long enough ere you come to Hervé Riel.
So, for better and for worse,
Hervé Riel, accept my verse!
In my verse, Hervé Riel, do thou once more
Save the squadron, honor France, love thy wife the Belle Aurore!

A FORGIVENESS

I AM indeed the personage you know.
As for my wife,—what happened long ago—
You have a right to question me, as I
Am bound to answer.

        "Son, a fit reply!"
The monk half spoke, half ground through his clenched teeth,
At the confession-grate I knelt beneath.

Thus then all happened, Father! Power and place
I had as still I have. I ran life's race,
With the whole world to see, as only strains
His strength some athlete whose prodigious gains
Of good appall him: happy to excess,—
Work freely done should balance happiness
Fully enjoyed; and, since beneath my roof
Housed she who made home heaven, in heaven's behoof
I went forth every day, and all day long
Worked for the world. Look, how the laborer's song
Cheers him! Thus sang my soul, at each sharp throe
Of laboring flesh and blood—"She loves me so!"

One day, perhaps such song so knit the nerve
That work grew play and vanished. "I deserve
Haply my heaven an hour before the time!"
I laughed, as silverly the clockhouse-chime
Surprised me passing through the postern-gate
—Not the main entry where the menials wait
And wonder why the world's affairs allow
The master sudden leisure. That was how
I took the private garden-way for once.

Forth from the alcove, I saw start, ensconce
Himself behind the porphyry vase, a man.

My fancies in the natural order ran:
"A spy,—perhaps a foe in ambuscade,—
A thief,—more like, a sweetheart of some maid
Who pitched on the alcove for tryst perhaps."

"Stand there!" I bid.
       Whereat my man but wraps
His face the closelier with uplifted arm
Whereon the cloak lies, strikes in blind alarm

This and that pedestal as,—stretch and stoop,—
Now in, now out of sight, he thrids the group
Of statues, marble god and goddess ranged
Each side the pathway, till the gate's exchanged
For safety: one step thence, the street, you know!

Thus far I followed with my gaze. Then, slow,
Near on admiringly, I breathed again,
And—back to that last fancy of the train—
"A danger risked for hope of just a word
With—which of all my nest may be the bird
This poacher covets for her plumage, pray?
Carmen? Juana? Carmen seems too gay
For such adventure, while Juana's grave
—Would scorn the folly. I applaud the knave!
He had the eye, could single from my brood
His proper fledgeling!"

                                        As I turned, there stood
In face of me, my wife stone-still stone-white.
Whether one bound had brought her,—at first sight
Of what she judged the encounter, sure to be
Next moment, of the venturous man and me,—
Brought her to clutch and keep me from my prey
Whether impelled because her death no day
Could come so absolutely opportune
As now at joy's height, like a year in June
Stayed at the fall of its first ripened rose;
Or whether hungry for my hate—who knows?—
Eager to end an irksome lie, and taste
Our tingling true relation, hate embraced
By hate one naked moment:—anyhow
There stone-still stone-white stood my wife, but now
The woman who made heaven within my house.
Ay, she who faced me was my very spouse
As well as love—you are to recollect!

"Stay!" she said. "Keep at least one soul unspecked
With crime, that's spotless hitherto—your own!
Kill me who court the blessing, who alone
Was, am, and shall be guilty, first to last!
The man lay helpless in the toils I cast
About him, helpless as the statue there
Against that strangling bell-flower's bondage: tear
Away and tread to dust the parasite,
But do the passive marble no despite!

I love him as I hate you. Kill me! Strike
At one blow both infinitudes alike
Out of existence—hate and love! Whence love?
That's safe inside my heart, nor will remove
For any searching of your steel, I think.
Whence hate? The secret lay on lip, at brink
Of speech, in one fierce tremble to escape,
At every form wherein your love took shape,
At each new provocation of your kiss.
Kill me!"

       We went in.

              Next day after this,
I felt as if the speech might come. I spoke—
Easily, after all.

              "The lifted cloak
Was screen sufficient: I concern myself
Hardly with laying hands on who for pelf—
Whate'er the ignoble kind—may prowl and **brave**
Cuffing and kicking proper to a knave
Detected by my household's vigilance.
Enough of such! As for my love-romance—
I, like our good Hidalgo, rub my eyes
And wake and wonder how the film could rise
Which changed for me a barber's basin straight
Into—Mambrino's helm? I hesitate
Nowise to say—God's sacramental cup!
Why should I blame the brass which, burnished **up**,
Will blaze, to all but me, as good as gold?
To me—a warning I was overbold
In judging metals. The Hidalgo waked
Only to die, if I remember,—staked
His life upon the basin's worth, and lost:
While I confess torpidity at most
In here and there a limb; but, lame and halt,
Still should I work on, still repair my fault
Ere I took rest in death,—no fear at all!
Now, work—no word before the curtain fall!"

The "curtain"? That of death on life, I meant:
My "word" permissible in death's event,
Would be—truth, soul to soul; for, otherwise,
Day by day, three years long, there had to rise
And, night by night, to fall upon our stage—

Ours, doomed to public play by heritage—
Another curtain, when the world, perforce
Our critical assembly, in due course
Came and went, witnessing, gave praise or blame
To art-mimetic. It had spoiled the game
If, suffered to set foot behind our scene,
The world had witnessed how stage-king and queen,
Gallant and lady, but a minute since
Enarming each the other, would evince
No sign of recognition as they took
His way and her way to whatever nook
Waited them in the darkness either side
Of that bright stage where lately groom and bride
Had fired the audience to a frenzy-fit
Of sympathetic rapture—every whit
Earned as the curtain fell on her and me,
—Actors. Three whole years, nothing was to see
But calm and concord: where a speech was due
There came the speech; when smiles were wanted too,
Smiles were as ready. In a place like mine,
Where foreign and domestic cares combine,
There's audience every day and all day long;
But finally the last of the whole throng
Who linger lets one see his back. For her—
Why, liberty and liking: I aver,
Liking and liberty! For me—I breathed,
Let my face rest from every wrinkle wreathed
Smile-like about the mouth, unlearned my task
Of personation till next day bade mask,
And quietly betook me from that world
To the real world, not pageant: there unfurled
In work, its wings, my soul, the fretted power.
Three years I worked, each minute of each hour
Not claimed by acting:—work I may dispense
With talk about, since work in evidence,
Perhaps in history; who knows or cares?

After three years, this way, all unawares,
Our acting ended. She and I, at close
Of a loud night-feast, led, between two rows
Of bending male and female loyalty,
Our lord the king down staircase, while, held high
At arm's length did the twisted tapers' flare
Herald his passage from our palace, where
Such visiting left glory evermore.
Again the ascent in public, till at door

As we two stood by the saloon—now blank
And disencumbered of its guests—there sank
A whisper in my ear, so low and yet
So unmistakable!

                "I half forget
The chamber you repair to, and I want
Occasion for one short word—if you grant
That grace—within a certain room you called
Our '*Study*,' for you wrote there while I scrawled
Some paper full of faces for my sport.
That room I can remember. Just one short
Word with you there, for the remembrance' sake!"

"Follow me thither!" I replied.

                        We break
The gloom a little, as with guiding lamp
I lead the way, leave warmth and cheer, by damp
Blind disused serpentining ways afar
From where the habitable chambers are,—
Ascend, descend stairs tunnelled through the stone,—
Always in silence,—till I reach the lone
Chamber sepulchred for my very own
Out of the palace-quarry. When a boy,
Here was my fortress, stronghold from annoy,
Proof-positive of ownership; in youth
I garnered up my gleanings here—uncouth
But precious relics of vain hopes, vain fears;
Finally, this became in after-years
My closet of intrenchment to withstand
Invasion of the foe on every hand—
The multifarious herd in bower and hall,
State-room,—rooms whatsoe'er the style, which call
On masters to be mindful that, before
Men, they must look like men and something more.
Here,—when our lord the king's bestowment ceased
To deck me on the day that, golden-fleeced,
I touched ambition's height,—'twas here, released
From glory (always symbolled by a chain!)
No sooner was I privileged to gain
My secret domicile than glad I flung
That last toy on the table—gazed where hung
On hook my father's gift, the arquebus—
And asked myself, "Shall I envisage thus
The new prize and the old prize, when I reach

Another year's experience?—own that each
Equalled advantage—sportsman's—statesman's tool?
That brought me down an eagle, this—a fool!"

Into which room on entry, I set down
The lamp, and turning saw whose rustled gown
Had told me my wife followed, pace for pace.
Each of us looked the other in the face;
She spoke. "Since I could die now" . . .

(To explain
Why that first struck me, know—not once again
Since the adventure at the porphyry's edge
Three years before, which sundered like a wedge
Her soul from mine,—though daily, smile to smile,
We stood before the public,—all the while
Not once had I distinguished, in that face
I paid observance to, the faintest trace
Of feature more than requisite for eyes
To do their duty by and recognize:
So did I force mine to obey my will
And pry no further. There exists such skill,—
Those know who need it. What physician shrinks
From needful contact with a corpse? He drinks
No plague so long as thirst for knowledge—not
An idler impulse—prompts inquiry. What,
And will you disbelieve in power to bid
Our spirit back to bounds, as though we chid
A child from scrutiny that's just and right
In manhood? Sense, not soul, accomplished sight,
Reported daily she it was—not how
Nor why a change had come to cheek and brow.)

"Since I could die now of the truth concealed,
Yet dare not, must not die,—so seems revealed
The Virgin's mind to me,—for death means peace,
Wherein no lawful part have I, whose lease
Of life and punishment the truth avowed
May haply lengthen,—let me push the shroud
Away, that steals to muffle ere is just
My penance-fire in snow! I dare—I must
Live, by avowal of the truth—this truth—
I loved you! Thanks for the fresh serpent's tooth
That, by a prompt new pang more exquisite
Than all preceding torture, proves me right!

I loved you yet I lost you! May I go
Burn to the ashes, now my shame you know?"

I think there never was such—how express?—
Horror coquetting with voluptuousness,
As in those arms of Eastern workmanship—
Yataghan, kandjar, things that rend and rip,
Gash rough, slash smooth, help hate so many ways,
Yet ever keep a beauty that betrays
Love still at work with the artificer
Throughout his quaint devising. Why prefer,
Except for love's sake, that a blade should writhe
And bicker like a flame?—now play the scythe
As if some broad neck tempted,—now contract
And needle off into a fineness lacked
For just that puncture which the heart demands?
Then, such adornment! Wherefore need our hands
Enclose not ivory alone, nor gold
Roughened for use, but jewels? Nay, behold!
Fancy my favorite—which I seem to grasp
While I describe the luxury. No asp
Is diapered more delicate round throat
Than this below the handle! These denote
—These mazy lines meandering, to end
Only in flesh they open—what intend
They else but water-purlings—pale contrast
With the life-crimson where they blend at last?
And mark the handle's dim pellucid green,
Carved, the hard jadestone, as you pinch a bean,
Into a sort of parrot-bird! He pecks
A grape-bunch; his two eyes are ruby-specks
Pure from the mine: seen this way,—glassy blank,
But turn them,—lo, the inmost fire, that shrank
From sparkling, sends a red dart right to aim!
Why did I choose such toys? Perhaps the game
Of peaceful men is warlike, just as men
War-wearied get amusement from that pen
And paper we grow sick of—statesfolk tired
Of merely (when such measures are required)
Dealing out doom to people by three words,
A signature and seal: we play with swords
Suggestive of quick process. That is how
I came to like the toys described you now,
Store of which glittered on the walls and strewed
The table, even, while my wife pursued
Her purpose to its ending. "Now you know

This shame, my three years' torture, let me go,
Burn to the very ashes! You—I lost,
Yet you—I loved!"

                              The thing I pity most
In men is—action prompted by surprise
Of anger: men? nay, bulls—whose onset lies
At instance of the firework and the goad!
Once the foe prostrate,—trampling once bestowed,—
Prompt follows placability, regret,
Atonement. Trust me, blood-warmth never yet
Betokened strong will! As no leap of pulse
Pricked me, that first time, so did none convulse
My veins at this occasion for resolve.
Had that devolved which did not then devolve
Upon me, I had done—what now to do
Was quietly apparent.

                              "Tell me who
The man was, crouching by the porphyry vase!"
"No, never! All was folly in his case,
All guilt in mine. I tempted, he complied."

"And yet you loved me?"

                              "Loved you. Double-dyed
In folly and in guilt, I thought you gave
Your heart and soul away from me to slave
At statecraft. Since my right in you seemed lost,
I stung myself to teach you, to your cost,
What you rejected could be prized beyond
Life, heaven, by the first fool I threw a fond
Look on, a fatal word to."

                              "And you still
Love me? Do I conjecture well or ill?"

"Conjecture—well or ill! I had three years
To spend in learning you."

                              "We both are peers
In knowledge, therefore: since three years are spent
Ere thus much of yourself *I* learn—who went
Back to the house, that day, and brought my mind

To bear upon your action, uncombined
Motive from motive, till the dross, deprived
Of every purer particle, survived
At last in native simple hideousness,
Utter contemptibility, nor less
Nor more. Contemptibility—exempt
How could I, from its proper due—contempt?
I have too much despised you to divert
My life from its set course by help or hurt
Of your all-despicable life—perturb
The calm I work in, by—men's mouths to curb,
Which at such news were clamorous enough—
Men's eyes to shut before my broidered stuff
With the huge hole there, my emblazoned wall
Blank where a scutcheon hung,—by, worse than all,
Each day's procession, my paraded life
Robbed and impoverished through the wanting wife
—Now that my life (which means—my work) was **grown**
Riches indeed! Once, just this worth alone
Seemed work to have, that profit gained thereby
Of good and praise would—how rewardingly!—
Fall at your feet,—a crown I hoped to cast
Before your love, my love should crown at last.
No love remaining to cast crown before,
My love stopped work now: but contempt the more
Impelled me task as ever head and hand,
Because the very fiends weave ropes of sand
Rather than taste pure hell in idleness.
Therefore I kept my memory down by stress
Of daily work I had no mind to stay
For the world's wonder at the wife away.
Oh, it was easy all of it, believe,
For I despised you! But your words retrieve
Importantly the past. No hate assumed
The mask of love at any time! There gloomed
A moment when love took hate's semblance, urged
By causes you declare; but love's self purged
Away a fancied wrong I did both loves
—Yours and my own: by no hate's help, it proves,
Purgation was attempted. Then, you rise
High by how many a grade! I did despise—
I do but hate you. Let hate's punishment
Replace contempt's! First step to which ascent—
Write down your own words I re-utter you!
'I loved my husband and I hated—who

He was, I took up as my first chance, mere
Mud-ball to fling and make love foul with!' Here
Lies paper!"

              "Would my blood for ink suffice!"

"It may: this minion from a land of spice,
Silk, feather—every bird of jewelled breast—
This poniard's beauty, ne'er so lightly prest
Above your heart there" . . .

                         "Thus?"

                              "It flows, I see.
Dip there the point and write!"

                              "Dictate to me!
Nay, I remember."

                    And she wrote the words.
I read them. Then—"Since love, in you, affords
License for hate, in me, to quench (I say)
Contempt—why, hate itself has passed away
In vengeance—foreign to contempt. Depart
Peacefully to that death which Eastern art
Imbued this weapon with, if tales be true!
Love will succeed to hate. I pardon you—
Dead in our chamber!"

                         True as truth the tale.
She died ere morning; then, I saw how pale
Her cheek was ere it wore day's paint-disguise,
And what a hollow darkened 'neath her eyes,
Now that I used my own. She sleeps, as erst
Beloved, in this your church: ay, yours!
                              Immersed
In thought so deeply, Father? Sad, perhaps?
For whose sake, hers or mine or his who wraps
—Still plain I seem to see!—about his head
The idle cloak,—about his heart (instead
Of cuirass) some fond hope he may elude
My vengeance in the cloister's solitude?
Hardly, I think! As little helped his brow
The cloak then, Father—as your grate helps now!

CENCIAJA

Ogni cencio vuol entrare in bucato.—ITALIAN PROVERB

MAY I print, Shelley, how it came to pass
That when your Beatrice seemed—by lapse
Of many a long month since her sentence fell—
Assured of pardon for the parricide,—
By intercession of stanch friends, or, say,
By certain pricks of conscience in the Pope
Conniver at Francesco Cenci's guilt,—
Suddenly all things changed and Clement grew
"Stern," as you state, "nor to be moved nor bent,
But said these three words coldly '*She must die;*'
Subjoining '*Pardon? Paolo Santa Croce
Murdered his mother also yestereve,
And he is fled: she shall not flee at least!*' "
—So, to the letter, sentence was fulfilled?
Shelley, may I condense verbosity
That lies before me, into some few words
Of English, and illustrate your superb
Achievement by a rescued anecdote,
No great things, only new and true beside?
As if some mere familiar of a house
Should venture to accost the group at gaze
Before its Titian, famed the wide world through,
And supplement such pictured masterpiece
By whisper, "Searching in the archives here,
I found the reason of the Lady's fate,
And how by accident it came to pass
She wears the halo and displays the palm:
Who, haply, else had never suffered—no,
Nor graced our gallery, by consequence."
Who loved the work would like the little news:
Who lauds your poem lends an ear to me
Relating how the penalty was paid
By one Marchese dell' Oriolo, called
Onofrio Santa Croce otherwise,
For his complicity in matricide
With Paolo his own brother,—he whose crime
And flight induced "those three words—She must die.'
Thus I unroll you then the manuscript.

   "God's justice"—(of the multiplicity
Of such communications extant still,

Recording, each, injustice done by God
In person of his Vicar-upon-earth,
Scarce one but leads off to the selfsame tune)—
"God's justice, tardy though it prove perchance,
Rests never on the track until it reach
Delinquency. In proof I cite the case
Of Paolo Santa Croce."

                 Many times
The youngster,—having been importunate
That Marchesine Costanza, who remained
His widowed mother, should supplant the heir
Her elder son, and substitute himself
In sole possession of her faculty,—
And meeting just as often with rebuff,—
Blinded by so exorbitant a lust
Of gold, the youngster straightway tasked his wits,
Casting about to kill the lady—thus.

He first, to cover his iniquity,
Writes to Onofrio Santa Croce, then
Authoritative lord, acquainting him
Their mother was contamination—wrought
Like hell-fire in the beauty of their House
By dissoluteness and abandonment
Of soul and body to impure delight.

Moreover, since she suffered from disease,
Those symptoms which her death made manifest
Hydroptic, he affirmed were fruits of sin
About to bring confusion and disgrace
Upon the ancient lineage and high fame
O' the family, when published. Duty bound,
He asked his brother—what a son should do?

Which when Marchese dell' Oriolo heard
By letter, being absent at his land
Oriolo, he made answer, this, no more:
"It must behove a son,—things haply so,—
To act as honor prompts a cavalier
And son, perform his duty to all three,
Mother and brothers"—here advice broke off.

By which advice informed and fortified
As he professed himself—since bound by birth
To hear God's voice in primogeniture—

Paolo, who kept his mother company
In her domain Subiaco, straightway dared
His whole enormity of enterprise,
And, falling on her, stabbed the lady dead;
Whose death demonstrated her innocence,
And happened,—by the way,—since Jesus Christ
Died to save man, just sixteen hundred years.
Costanza was of aspect beautiful
Exceedingly, and seemed, although in age
Sixty about, to far surpass her peers
The coëtaneous dames, in youth and grace.

   Done the misdeed, its author takes to flight,
Foiling thereby the justice of the world:
Not God's however,—God, be sure, knows well
The way to clutch a culprit. Witness here!
The present sinner, when he least expects,
Snug-cornered somewhere i' the Basilicate,
Stumbles upon his death by violence.
A man of blood assaults a man of blood
And slays him somehow. This was afterward:
Enough, he promptly met with his deserts,
And, ending thus, permits we end with him,
And push forthwith to this important point—
His matricide fell out, of all the days,
Precisely when the law-procedure closed
Respecting Count Francesco Cenci's death
Chargeable on his daughter, sons and wife.
"Thus patricide was matched with matricide,"
A poet not inelegantly rhymed:
Nay, fratricide—those Princes Massimi!—
Which so disturbed the spirit of the Pope
That all the likelihood Rome entertained
Of Beatrice's pardon vanished straight,
And she endured the piteous death.

                              Now see
The sequel—what effect commandment had
For strict inquiry into this last case,
When Cardinal Aldobrandini (great
His efficacy—nephew to the Pope!)
Was bidden crush—ay, though his very hand
Got soil i' the act—crime spawning everywhere!
Because, when all endeavor had been used
To catch the aforesaid Paolo, all in vain—
"Make perquisition," quoth our Eminence,

"Throughout his now deserted domicile!
Ransack the palace, roof and floor, to find
If haply any scrap of writing, hid
In nook or corner, may convict—who knows?—
Brother Onofrio of intelligence
With brother Paolo, as in brotherhood
Is but too likely: crime spawns everywhere."

And, every cranny searched accordingly,
There comes to light—O lynx-eyed Cardinal!—
Onofrio's unconsidered writing-scrap,
The letter in reply to Paolo's prayer,
The word of counsel that—things proving so,
Paolo should act the proper knightly part,
And do as was incumbent on a son,
A brother—and a man of birth, be sure!

Whereat immediately the officers
Proceeded to arrest Onofrio—found
At football, child's play, unaware of harm,
Safe with his friends, the Orsini, at their seat
Monte Giordano; as he left the house
He came upon the watch in wait for him
Set by the Barigel,—was caught and caged.

News of which capture being, that same hour,
Conveyed to Rome, forthwith our Eminence
Commands Taverna, Governor and Judge,
To have the process in especial care,
Be, first to last, not only president
In person, but inquisitor as well,
Nor trust the by-work to a substitute:
Bids him not, squeamish, keep the bench, but scrub
The floor of Justice, so to speak,—go try
His best in prison with the criminal:
Promising, as reward for by-work done
Fairly on all-fours, that, success obtained
And crime avowed, or such connivency
With crime as should procure a decent death—
Himself will humbly beg—which means, procure—
The Hat and Purple from his relative
The Pope, and so repay a diligence
Which, meritorious in the Cenci-case,
Mounts plainly here to Purple and the Hat.

Whereupon did my lord the Governor
So masterfully exercise the task

Enjoined him, that he, day by day, and week
By week, and month by month, from first to last
Toiled for the prize: now, punctual at his place,
Played Judge, and now, assiduous at his post,
Inquisitor—pressed cushion and scoured plank,
Early and late. Noon's fervor and night's chill,
Nought moved whom morn would, purpling, **make amends**
So that observers laughed as, many a day,
He left home, in July when day is flame,
Posted to Tordinona-prison, plunged
Into a vault were daylong night is ice,
There passed his eight hours on a stretch, **content**,
Examining Onofrio: all the stress
Of all examination steadily
Converging into one pin-point,—he pushed
Tentative now of head and now of heart.
As when the nut-hatch taps and tries the nut
This side and that side till the kernel sound,—
So did he press the sole and single point
—What was the very meaning of the phrase
'Do as beseems an honored cavalier'?

   Which one persistent question-torture,—plied
Day by day, week by week, and month by month,
Morn, noon and night,—fatigued away a mind
Grown imbecile by darkness, solitude,
And one vivacious memory gnawing there
As when a corpse is coffined with a snake:
—Fatigued Onofrio into what might seem
Admission that perchance his judgment groped
So blindly, feeling for an issue—aught
With semblance of an issue from the toils
Cast of a sudden round feet late so free,
He possibly might have envisaged, scarce
Recoiled from—even were the issue death
—Even her death whose life was death and worse!
Always provided that the charge of crime,
Each jot and tittle of the charge were true.
In such a sense, belike, he might advise
His brother to expurgate crime with . . . well,
With blood, if blood must follow on *'the course
Taken as might beseem a cavalier.'*

   Whereupon process ended, and report
Was made without a minute of delay
To Clement, who, because of those two **crimes**

O' the Massimi and Cenci flagrant late,
Must needs impatiently desire result.

Result obtained, he bade the Governor
Summon the Congregation and despatch.
Summons made, sentence passed accordingly
—Death by beheading. When his death-decree
Was intimated to Onofrio, all
Man could do—that did he to save himself.
'T was much, the having gained for his defence
The Advocate o' the Poor, with natural help
Of many noble friendly persons fain
To disengage a man of family,
So young too, from his grim entanglement:
But Cardinal Aldobrandini ruled
There must be no diversion of the law.
Justice is justice, and the magistrate
Bears not the sword in vain. Who sins must die.

So, the Marchese had his head cut off,
With Rome to see, a concourse infinite,
In Place Saint Angelo beside the Bridge:
Where, demonstrating magnanimity
Adequate to his birth and breed,—poor boy!—
He made the people the accustomed speech,
Exhorted them to true faith, honest works,
And special good behavior as regards
A parent of no matter what the sex,
Bidding each son take warning from himself.
Truly, it was considered in the boy
Stark staring lunacy, no less, to snap
So plain a bait, be hooked and hauled ashore
By such an angler as the Cardinal!
Why make confession of his privity
To Paolo's enterprise? Mere sealing lips—
Or, better, saying "When I counselled him
'To do as might beseem a cavalier,'
What could I mean but 'Hide our parent's shame
As Christian ought, by aid of Holy Church!
Bury it in a convent—ay, beneath
Enough dotation to prevent its ghost
From troubling earth!'" Mere saying thus,—'t is plain,
Not only were his life the recompense,
But he had manifestly proved himself
True Christian, and in lieu of punishment
Got praise of all men!—So the populace.

Anyhow, when the Pope made promise good
(That of Aldobrandini, near and dear)
And gave Taverna, who had toiled so much,
A Cardinal's equipment, some such word
As this from mouth to ear went saucily:
"Taverna's cap is dyed in what he drew
From Santa Croce's veins!" So joked the world.

I add: Onofrio left one child behind,
A daughter named Valeria, dowered with grace
Abundantly of soul and body, doomed
To life the shorter for her father's fate.
By death of her, the Marquisate returned
To that Orsini House from whence it came:
Oriolo having passed as donative
To Santa Croce from their ancestors.

And no word more? By all means! Would you know
The authoritative answer, when folks urged
"What made Aldobrandini, hound-like stanch,
Hunt out of life a harmless simpleton?"
The answer was—"Hatred implacable,
By reason they were rivals in their love."
The Cardinal's desire was to a dame
Whose favor was Onofrio's. Pricked with pride,
The simpleton must ostentatiously
Display a ring, the Cardinal's love-gift,
Given to Onofrio as the lady's gage;
Which ring on finger, as he put forth hand
To draw a tapestry, the Cardinal
Saw and knew, gift and owner, old and young;
Whereon a fury entered him—the fire
He quenched with what could quench fire only—blood.
Nay, more: "there want not who affirm to boot,
The unwise boy, a certain festal eve,
Feigned ignorance of who the wight might be
That pressed too closely on him with a crowd.
He struck the Cardinal a blow: and then,
To put a face upon the incident,
Dared next day, smug as ever, go pay court
I' the Cardinal's antechamber. Mark and mend,
Ye youth, by this example how may greed
Vainglorious operate in worldly souls!"

So ends the chronicler, beginning with
"God's justice, tardy though it prove perchance,

Rests never till it reach delinquency."
Ay, or how otherwise had come to pass
That Victor rules, this present year, in Rome?

FILIPPO BALDINUCCI ON THE PRIVILEGE OF BURIAL

A Reminiscence of A. D. 1676

I.

"No, BOY, we must not"—so began
  My Uncle (he's with God long since),
A-petting me, the good old man!
  "We must not"—and he seemed to wince,
And lost that laugh whereto had grown
  His chuckle at my piece of news,
How cleverly I aimed my stone—
  "I fear we must not pelt the Jews!

II.

"When I was young indeed,—ah, faith
  Was young and strong in Florence too!
We Christians never dreamed of scathe
  Because we cursed or kicked the crew.
But now—well, well! The olive-crops
  Weighed double then, and Arno's pranks
Would always spare religious shops
  Whenever he o'erflowed his banks!

III.

"I'll tell you"—and his eye regained
  Its twinkle—"tell you something choice!
Something may help you keep unstained
  Your honest zeal to stop the voice
Of unbelief with stone-throw—spite
  Of laws, which modern fools enact,
That we must suffer Jews in sight
  Go wholly unmolested! Fact!

IV.

"There was, then, in my youth, and yet
  Is, by our San Frediano, just
Below the Blessed Olivet,
  A wayside ground wherein they thrust

Their dead,—these Jews,—the more our shame!
  Except that, so they will but die,
Christians may perchance incur no blame
  In giving hogs a hoist to sty.

v.

"There, anyhow, Jews stow away
  Their dead; and—such their insolence—
Slink at odd times to sing and pray
  As Christians do—all make-pretence!—
Which wickedness they perpetrate
  Because they think no Christians see.
They reckoned here, at any rate,
  Without their host: ha, ha! he, he!

vi.

"For, what should join their plot of ground
  But a good Farmer's Christian field?
The Jews had hedged their corner round
  With bramble-bush to keep concealed
Their doings: for the public road
  Ran betwixt this their ground and that
The Farmer's, where he ploughed and sowed,
  Grew corn for barn and grapes for vat.

vii.

"So, properly to guard his store
  And gall the unbelievers too,
He builds a shrine and, what is more,
  Procures a painter whom I knew,
One Buti (he's with God), to paint
  A holy picture there—no less
Than Virgin Mary free from taint
  Borne to the sky by angels: yes!

viii.

"Which shrine he fixed,—who says him nay?—
  A-facing with its picture-side
Not, as you'd think, the public way,
  But just where sought these hounds to hide
Their carrion from that very truth
  Of Mary's triumph: not a hound
Could act his mummeries uncouth
  But Mary shamed the pack all round!

ix.

"Now, if it was amusing, judge!
  —To see the company arrive,

Each Jew intent to end his trudge
  And take his pleasure (though alive)
With all his Jewish kith and kin
  Below ground, have his venom out,
Sharpen his wits for next day's sin,
  Curse Christians, and so home, no doubt!

x.

"Whereas, each phiz upturned beholds
  Mary, I warrant, soaring brave!
And in a trice, beneath the folds
  Of filthy garb which gowns each knave,
Down drops it—there to hide grimace,
  Contortion of the mouth and nose
At finding Mary in the place
  They'd keep for Pilate, I suppose!

xi.

"At last, they will not brook—not they!—
  Longer such outrage on their tribe:
So, in some hole and corner, lay
  Their heads together—how to bribe
The meritorious Farmer's self
  To straight undo his work, restore
Their chance to meet and muse on pelf—
  Pretending sorrow, as before!

xii.

"Forthwith, a posse, if you please,
  Of Rabbi This and Rabbi That
Almost go down upon their knees
  To get him lay the picture flat.
The spokesman, eighty years of age,
  Gray as a badger, with a goat's
Not only beard but bleat, 'gins wage
  War with our Mary. Thus he dotes:—

xiii.

" *'Friends, grant a grace! How Hebrews toil*
  Through life in Florence—why relate
To those who lay the burden, spoil
  Our paths of peace? We bear our fate.
But when with life the long toil ends,
  Why must you—the expression craves
Pardon, but truth compels me, friends!—
  Why must you plague us in our graves?

XIV.

" '*Thoughtlessly plague, I would believe!*
For how can you—the lords of ease
By nurture, birthright—e'en conceive
Our luxury to lie with trees
And turf,—the cricket and the bird
Left for our last companionship:
No harsh deed, no unkindly word,
No frowning brow nor scornful lip!

XV.

" '*Death's luxury, we now rehearse*
While, living, through your streets we fare
And take your hatred: nothing worse
Have we, once dead and safe, to bear!
So we refresh our souls, fulfil
Our works, our daily tasks; and thus
Gather you grain—earth's harvest—still
The wheat for you, the straw for us.

XVI.

" ' 'What flouting in a face, what harm,
In just a lady borne aloft
By boys' heads, wings for leg and arm?'
You question. Friends, the harm is here—
That just when our last sigh is heaved,
And we would fain thank God and you
For labor done and peace achieved,
Back comes the Past in full review!

XVII.

" '*At sight of just that simple flag,*
Starts the foe-feeling serpent-like
From slumber. Leave it lulled, nor drag—
Though fangless—forth, what needs must strike
When stricken sore, though stroke be vain
Against the mailed oppressor! Give
Play to our fancy that we gain
Life's rights when once we cease to live!

XVIII.

" '*Thus much to courtesy, to kind,*
To conscience! Now to Florence folk!
There's core beneath this apple-rind,
Beneath this white-of-egg there's yolk!
Beneath this prayer to courtesy,
Kind, conscience—there's a sum to pouch!

How many ducats down will buy
Our shame's removal, sirs? Avouch!

XIX.

" 'Removal, not destruction, sirs!*
Just turn your picture! Let it front
The public path! Or memory errs,
Or that same public path is wont
To witness many a chance befall
Of lust, theft, bloodshed—sins enough,
Wherein our Hebrew part is small.
Convert yourselves!'—he cut up rough.

XX.

"Look you, how soon a service paid
Religion yields the servant fruit!
A prompt reply our Farmer made
So following: *'Sirs, to grant your suit*
Involves much danger! How? Transpose
Our Lady? Stop the chastisement,
All for your good, herself bestows?
What wonder if I grudge consent?

XXI.

" '*—Yet grant it: since, what cash I take*
Is so much saved from wicked use.
We know you! And, for Mary's sake,
A hundred ducats shall induce
Concession to your prayer. One day
Suffices: Master Buti's brush
Turns Mary round the other way,
And deluges your side with slush.

XXII.

" '*Down with the ducats therefore!*' Dump,
Dump, dump it falls, each counted piece,
Hard gold. Then out of door they stump,
These dogs, each brisk as with new lease
Of life, I warrant,—glad he'll die
Henceforward just as he may choose,
Be buried and in clover lie!
Well said Esaias—'*stiff-necked Jews!*'

XXIII.

"Off posts without a minute's loss
Our Farmer, once the cash in poke,

And summons Buti—ere its gloss
    Have time to fade from off the joke—
To chop and change his work, undo
    The done side, make the side, now blank,
Recipient of our Lady—who,
    Displaced thus, had these dogs to thank!

XXIV.

"Now, boy, you're hardly to instruct
    In technicalities of Art!
My nephew's childhood sure has sucked
    Along with mother's-milk some part
Of painter's-practice—learned, at least,
    How expeditiously is plied
A work in fresco—never ceased
    When once begun—a day, each side.

XXV.

"So, Buti—(he's with God)—begins:
    First covers up the shrine all round
With hoarding; then, as like as twins,
    Paints, t' other side the burial-ground,
New Mary, every point the same;
    Next, sluices over, as agreed,
The old; and last—but, spoil the game
    By telling you? Not I, indeed!

XXVI.

"Well, ere the week was half at end,
    Out came the object of this zeal,
This fine alacrity to spend
    Hard money for mere dead men's weal!
How think you? That old spokesman Jew
    Was High Priest, and he had a wife
As old, and she was dying too,
    And wished to end in peace her life!

XXVII.

"And he must humor dying whims,
    And soothe her with the idle hope
They'd say their prayers and sing their hymns
    As if her husband were the Pope!
And she did die—believing just
    This privilege was purchased! Dead

In comfort through her foolish trust!
   '*Stiff-necked ones*,' well Esaias said!

XXVIII.

"So, Sabbath morning, out of gate
   And on to way, what sees our arch
Good farmer? Why, they hoist their freight—
   The corpse—on shoulder, and so, march!
'*Now for it, Buti!*' In the nick
   Of time 't is pully-hauly, hence
With hoarding! O'er the wayside quick
   There's Mary plain in evidence!

XXIX.

"And here's the convoy halting: right!
   O they are bent on howling psalms
And growling prayers, when opposite!
   And yet they glance, for all their qualms,
Approve that promptitude of his,
   The Farmer's—duly at his post
To take due thanks from every phiz,
   Sour smirk—nay, surly smile almost!

XXX.

"Then earthward drops each brow again;
   The solemn task's resumed; they reach
Their holy field—the unholy train:
   Enter its precinct, all and each,
Wrapt somehow in their godless rites;
   Till, rites at end, up-waking, lo,
They lift their faces! What delights
   The mourners as they turn to go?

XXXI.

"Ha, ha! he, he! On just the side
   They drew their purse-strings to make quit
Of Mary,—Christ the Crucified
   Fronted them now—these biters bit!
Never was such a hiss and snort,
   Such screwing nose and shooting lip!
Their purchase—honey in report—
   Proved gall and verjuice at first sip!

XXXII.

"Out they break, on they bustle, where,
A-top of wall, the Farmer waits

With Buti: never fun so rare!
  The Farmer has the best: he rates
The rascal, as the old High Priest
  Takes on himself to sermonize—
Nay, sneer, *'We Jews supposed, at least,*
  Theft was a crime in Christian eyes!'

XXXIII.

" *'Theft?'* cries the Farmer. *'Eat your words!*
  Show me what constitutes a breach
Of faith in aught was said or heard!
  I promised you in plainest speech
I'd take the thing you count disgrace
  And put it here—and here 't is put!
Did you suppose I'd leave the place
  Blank therefore, just your rage to glut?

XXXIV.

" *'I guess you dared not stipulate*
  For such a damned impertinence!
So, quick, my graybeard, out of gate
  And in at Ghetto! Haste you hence!
As long as I have house and land,
  To spite you irreligious chaps,
Here shall the Crucifixion stand—
  Unless you down with cash, perhaps!'

XXXV.

"So snickered he and Buti both.
  The Jews said nothing, interchanged
A glance or two, renewed their oath
  To keep ears stopped and hearts estranged
From grace, for all our Church can do;
  Then off they scuttle: sullen jog
Homewards, against our Church to brew
  Fresh mischief in their synagogue.

XXXVI.

"But next day—see what happened, boy!
  See why I bid you have a care
How you pelt Jews! The knaves employ
  Such methods of revenge, forbear
No outrage on our faith, when free
  To wreak their malice! Here they took
So base a method—plague o' me
  If I record it in my Book!

XXXVII.

"For, next day, while the Farmer sat
  Laughing with Buti, in his shop,
At their successful joke,—rat-tat,—
  Door opens, and they're like to drop
Down to the floor as in there stalks
A six-feet-high herculean-built
Young he-Jew with a beard that balks
  Description. '*Help ere blood be spilt!*'

XXXVIII.

—"Screamed Buti: for he recognized
  Whom but the son, no less no more,
Of that High Priest his work surprised
  So pleasantly the day before!
Son of the mother, then, whereof
  The bier he lent a shoulder to,
And made the moans about, dared scoff
  At sober Christian grief—the Jew!

XXXIX.

" '*Sirs, I salute you! Never rise!*
  No apprehension!' (Buti, white
And trembling like a tub of size,
  Had tried to smuggle out of sight
The picture's self—the thing in oils,
  You know, from which a fresco's dashed
Which courage speeds while caution spoils.)
  '*Stay and be praised, sir, unabashed!*

XL.

" '*Praised,—ay, and paid too: for I come*
  To buy that very work of yours.
My poor abode, which boasts—well, some
  Few specimens of Art, secures,
Haply, a masterpiece indeed
  If I should find my humble means
Suffice the outlay. So, proceed!
Propose—ere prudence intervenes!'

XLI.

"On Buti, cowering like a child,
  These words descended from aloft,
In tone so ominously mild,
  With smile terrifically soft
To that degree—could Buti dare
  (Poor fellow) use his brains, think twice?

He asked, thus taken unaware,
  No more than just the proper price!

XLII.

" '*Done!*' cries the monster. '*I disburse*
  Forthwith your moderate demand.
Count on my custom—if no worse
  Your future work be, understand,
Than this I carry off! No aid!
  My arm, sir, lacks nor bone nor thews:
The burden's easy, and we're made,
  Easy or hard, to bear—we Jews!'

XLIII.

"Crossing himself at such escape,
  Buti by turns the money eyes
And, timidly, the stalwart shape
  Now moving doorwards; but, more wise,
The Farmer—who, though dumb, this while
  Had watched advantage—straight conceived
A reason for that tone and smile
  So mild and soft! The Jew—believed!

XLIV.

"Mary in triumph borne to deck
  A Hebrew household! Pictured where
No one was used to bend the neck
  In praise or bow the knee in prayer!
Borne to that domicile by whom?
  The son of the High Priest! Through what?
An insult done his mother's tomb!
  Saul changed to Paul—the case came pat!

XLV.

" '*Stay, dog-Jew . . . gentle sir, that is!*
  Resolve me! Can it be, she crowns,—
Mary, by miracle,—Oh bliss!—
  My present to your burial-ground?
Certain, a ray of light has burst
  Your veil of darkness! Had you else,
Only for Mary's sake, unpursed
  So much hard money? Tell—oh, tell's!'

XLVI.

"Round—like a serpent that we took
  For worm and trod on—turns his bulk

About the Jew. First dreadful look
 Sends Buti in a trice to skulk
Out of sight somewhere, safe—alack!
 But our good Farmer faith made bold:
And firm (with Florence at his back)
 He stood, while gruff the gutturals rolled—

XLVII.

" 'Ay, sir, a miracle was worked,
 By quite another power, I trow,
Than ever yet in canvas lurked,
 Or you would scarcely face me now!
A certain impulse did suggest
 A certain grasp with this right-hand,
Which probably had put to rest
 Our quarrel,—thus your throat once spanned!

XLVIII.

" 'But I remembered me, subdued
 That impulse, and you face me still!
And soon a philosophic mood
 Succeeding (hear it, if you will!)
Has altogether changed my views
 Concerning Art. Blind prejudice!
Well may you Christians tax us Jews
 With scrupulosity too nice!

XLIX.

" 'For, don't I see,—let's issue join!—
 Whenever I'm allowed pollute
(I—and my little bag of coin)
 Some Christian palace of repute,—
Don't I see stuck up everywhere
 Abundant proof that cultured taste
Has Beauty for its only care,
 And upon Truth no thought to waste?

L.

" ' 'Jew since it must be, take in pledge
 Of payment'—so a Cardinal
Has sighed to me as if a wedge
 Entered his heart—'this best of all
My treasures!' Leda, Ganymede
 Or Antiope: swan, eagle, ape,
(Or what's the beast of what's the breed,)
 And Jupiter in every shape!

LI.

" 'Whereat if I presume to ask
    'But, Eminence, though Titian's whisk
Of brush have well performed its task,
    How comes it these false godships frisk
In presence of—what yonder frame
    Pretends to image? Surely, odd
It seems, you let confront The Name
    Each beast the heathen called his god!'

LII.

" 'Benignant smiles me pity straight
    The Cardinal. ' 'Tis Truth, we prize!
Art's the sole question in debate!
    These subjects are so many lies.
We treat them with a proper scorn
    When we turn lies—called gods forsooth—
To lies' fit use, now Christ is born.
    Drawing and coloring are Truth.

LIII.

" ' 'Think you I honor lies so much
    As scruple to parade the charms
Of Leda—Titian, every touch—
    Because the thing within her arms
Means Jupiter who had the praise
    And prayer of a benighted world?
He would have mine too, if, in days
    Of light, I kept the canvas furled!'

LIV.

" 'So ending, with some easy gibe.
    What power has logic! I, at once,
Acknowledged error in our tribe
    So squeamish that, when friends ensconce
A pretty picture in its niche
    To do us honor, deck our graves,
We fret and fume and have an itch
    To strangle folk—ungrateful knaves!

LV.

" 'No, sir! Be sure that—what's its style,
    Your picture?—shall possess ungrudged
A place among my rank and file
    Of Ledas and what not—be judged

Just as a picture! and (because
I fear me much I scarce have bought
A Titian) Master Buti's flaws
Found there, will have the laugh flaws ought!'

LVI.

"So, with a scowl, it darkens door—
This bulk—no longer! Buti makes
Prompt glad re-entry; there's a score
Of oaths, as the good Farmer wakes
From what must needs have been a trance,
Or he had struck (he swears) to ground
The bold bad mouth that dared advance
Such doctrine the reverse of sound!

LVII.

"Was magic here? Most like! For, since,
Somehow our city's faith grows still
More and more lukewarm, and our Prince
Or loses heart or wants the will
To check increase of cold. 'T is *'Live*
And let live! Languidly repress
The Dissident! In short,—contrive
Christians must bear with Jews: no less!'

LVIII.

"The end seems, any Israelite
Wants any picture,—pishes, poohs,
Purchases, hangs it full in sight
In any chamber he may choose!
In Christ's crown, one more thorn we rue!
In Mary's bosom, one more sword!
No, boy, you must not pelt a Jew!
O Lord, how long? How long, O Lord?'

SONG FROM "PIPPA PASSES"

The year's at the spring
And day's at the morn;
Morning's at seven;
The hillside's dew-pearled;
The lark's on the wing;
The snail's on the thorn:
God's in his heaven—
All's right with the world!

EPILOGUE, "ASOLANDO"

AT MIDNIGHT in the silence of the sleep-time,
　　When you set your fancies free,
Will they pass to where—by death, fools think, imprisoned—
Low he lies who once so loved you, whom you loved so,
　　　　　　　　　　　　　　　　—Pity me?

Oh to love so, be so loved, yet so mistaken!
　　What had I on earth to do
With the slothful, with the mawkish, the unmanly?
Like the aimless, helpless, hopeless, did I drivel
　　　　　　　　　　　　　　　　—Being—who?

One who never turned his back but marched breast forward,
　　Never doubted clouds would break,
Never dreamed, tho' right were worsted, wrong would triumph,
Held we fall to rise, are baffled to fight better,
　　　　　　　　　　　　　　　Sleep to wake.

No, at noonday in the bustle of man's work-time
　　Greet the unseen with a cheer!
Bid him forward, breast and back as either should be,
"Strive and thrive!" cry "Speed,—fight on, fare ever
　　　　　　　　　　　　　　There as here!"